CHINA'S AMERICA

SUNY series in Chinese Philosophy and Culture

Roger T. Ames, editor

CHINA'S AMERICA

The Chinese View the United States,
1900–2000

JING LI

Published by State University of New York Press, Albany

© 2011 State University of New York

All rights reserved

Printed in the United States of America

No part of this book may be used or reproduced in any manner whatsoever without written permission. No part of this book may be stored in a retrieval system or transmitted in any form or by any means including electronic, electrostatic, magnetic tape, mechanical, photocopying, recording, or otherwise without the prior permission in writing of the publisher.

For information, contact State University of New York Press, Albany, NY
www.sunypress.edu

Production by Eileen Meehan
Marketing by Fran Keneston

Library of Congress Cataloging-in-Publication Data

Li, Jing.
    China's America : the Chinese view the United States, 1900–2000 / Jing Li.
        p. cm. — (SUNY series in Chinese philosophy and culture)
    Includes bibliographical references and index.
    ISBN 978-1-4384-3517-6 (hardcover : alk. paper)
    ISBN 978-1-4384-3516-9 (paperback : alk. paper)
    1. United States—Foreign public opinion, Chinese—History—20th century.
2. Public opinion—China—History—20th century.   I. Title.

    E183.8.C5L313 2011
    327.7305109'04—dc22   2010023368

10 9 8 7 6 5 4 3 2 1

Contents

List of Illustrations   vii
Acknowledgments   ix
Note on Romanization   xi
Illustration Credits   xiii

Introduction   1

1   Statesmen, Scholars, and the Men in the Street, 1900–1949   11

2   "Farewell, Leighton Stuart!": Anti-Americanism in the Early Fifties   51

3   Challenging a Taboo: China's Liberal Critics and America in 1957   71

4   Communist Crusade and Capitalist Stronghold: Mao's
Everlasting Revolution and the United States, 1957–1979   91

5   A Balancing Act: The *People's Daily*, 1979–1989   121

6   Chinese Review America: The *Dushu* Magazine, 1979–1989   145

7   Popular and Not-So-Popular America: The Chinese Masses
and the U.S.A. in the 1980s   169

8   Shall the Twain Ever Meet? Old Themes and New Trends
in the Last Decade of the Century   191

Conclusion   227
Historiographical Note   233
Notes   237
Bibliography   275
Index   291

Illustrations

Figure 1.1. Text from Xu Jiyu's *Brief Survey of the Maritime Circuits*   14

Figure 1.2. A Chinese cartoon that appeared at the end of the
nineteenth century   19

Figure 1.3. The Chinese Student Club at Teachers College,
Columbia University, 1916   35

Figure 1.4. Mao's meeting with Patrick J. Hurley   44

Figure 2.1. Mao, Zhou, and Stalin   65

Figure 4.1. Anti-American materials from the 1950s and 1960s   106

Figure 4.2. Premier Zhou Enlai and President Richard Nixon   115

Figure 5.1. Deng Xiaoping at a rodeo in Houston, Texas   126

Figure 6.1. The *Dushu* magazine   149

Figure 6.2. The Statue of Liberty at Tiananmen Square   163

Figure 7.1. Gregory Peck in Beijing   187

Figure 8.1. MacDonald's, Starbucks, and *China Can Say No*   223

Acknowledgments

Many people kindly helped me as I wrote this book. It is impossible to name them all or thank them enough. I would like to identify the following individuals and institutions and express my deep appreciation of their support.

I am tremendously grateful to Dr. Richard J. Smith at Rice University, who taught me, kindly befriended me, and provided guidance and encouragement over the years. I thank my other professors at Rice University, from whom I learned a great deal, and thank the university itself for its generous support. My gratitude also goes to Dr. Roger Ames of the University of Hawai'i at Manoa, who took notice of my study and encouraged me to turn it into a book. I greatly appreciate the support of Duquesne University, especially that of my colleagues in the History Department and McAnulty College of Liberal Arts. Dr. Jean Hunter, the former head of the history department, helped me in innumerable ways and read most chapters in my manuscript. I am also indebted to my former colleagues at St. Mary's College of Maryland, particularly those in the Division of History and Social Sciences and in the Asian studies program of the college, whose friendship and support I greatly appreciate.

In Beijing, at the Institute of Modern History, the Chinese Academy of Social Sciences, I learned a great deal from many scholars, among them Professors Ding Mingnan, Zhang Zhenkun, and Tao Wenzhao, who guided me when I first started my academic career there. In 2000–01, I returned to the Institute and spent one year there as a visiting scholar. I thank Professor Zhang Haipeng, Professor Wang Jianlang, and Ms. Sun Siyuan for making the visit possible. Also at the Institute, Professor Li Xuetong has been a good friend for many years and has helped me in research on various occasions.

I thank Professors Li Shiyue, Chen Guizong, and Zhao Shiyuan who advised me at Jilin University.

I did much of my research at the following establishments: the libraries of the Chinese Academy of Social Sciences; the National Library of China; the Harvard-Yenching Library; the Hoover Institution on War, Revolution and Peace; the East Asian Library and the Center for Chinese Studies Library at

UC Berkeley; the U.S. National Archives; and the U.S. Library of Congress. I greatly appreciate the service and assistance provided by the staff at these institutions.

Many friends helped me in my early years in the United States, among them Kenneth De Ville, then a fellow graduate student. A grant from the Kalternborn Foundation partly funded my research in the initial stage.

For their assistance in turning my manuscript into a book, I express my heartfelt thanks to editors at the SUNY Press, especially Nancy Ellegate, Senior Acquisition Editor, who lent me much support as I worked on the project.

I alone am responsible for whatever errors and weaknesses remain in my work.

Finally, I want to thank all members of my family. To my parents I dedicate this study; I know they are very happy to see its publication.

Note on Romanization

The *pinyin* system of romanization is generally used in this book, with a few exceptions. Older romanizations of names and terms are used where these traditional transcriptions are more familiar to Western readers—for example, "Chiang Kai-shek" instead of "Jiang Jieshi," or "Sun Yat-sen" instead of "Sun Zhongshan." In these cases, at the first appearance of an older romanization, its new form is provided in parentheses.

Illustration Credits

Photographs on the pages indicated were used by kind permission of the following:

The Gottesman Libraries, Teachers College, Columbia University, page 35
The U.S. National Archives (Photo no. 80-G-32500), page 44
· Mr. Du Xiuxian, page 115
Mr. Guo Zhanying, page 126
Toshio Sakai/AFP/Getty Images, page 163
Mr. Li Shengnan, page 187

Introduction

One day in March 1998, while meeting with a group of delegates to the Chinese National People's Congress, Jiang Zemin, general secretary of the Chinese Communist Party and president of the People's Republic of China, suddenly started talking about Hollywood movies. High-spirited and expansive, Jiang told his audience how he had enjoyed certain American films. Some Hollywood creations promote good morals and have considerable educational value, Jiang said. He continued:

> A new movie will soon be shown in our country. It's called *Titanic*. This film does a good job of depicting tension between love and money, the gap between the rich and the poor, and how people behave in different ways facing adversity. . . . In any event, we shouldn't simply assume that, in cultural exchanges, the capitalist world has nothing worthy to offer us.[1]

Jiang went on to reminiscence how, back in the 1940s, he, a college student in Shanghai, took great pleasure in watching American movies. Among those he remembered fondly—*Gone with the Wind*, *Singin' in the Rain*, and *Waterloo Bridge*. "I recently suggested that our comrades in the Politburo all go see *Titanic*," he said. "I don't mean to beautify capitalism, but I do believe that we should all be knowledgeable not only on our own country but on the rest of the world too so that we can enrich and improve ourselves. One thing is clear—do not just assume that we alone are capable of moral education."[2]

These comments, coming from the head of the Chinese Communist Party, were remarkable. In a country where ideology reigned supreme and politics was full of symbolism and cultural nuances, government officials—especially those in high positions—were extremely cautious about what they uttered in public. Tight-lipped, they would stay close to official scripts and spoke mostly in party jargon, especially on a sensitive subject such as the United States.

Why would General Secretary Jiang go out of his way to comment so freely and so publicly on Hollywood and American culture? To understand this, we should consider the context for the incident, with particular regard to the interplay among the Chinese government's U.S. policies, Chinese intellectuals' views on America, and the popular sentiments in China at the time.

Jiang Zemin came to the helm of the Chinese Communist Party in late 1989, shortly after the Chinese government's violent suppression of a large-scale pro-democracy movement, a crackdown that resulted in the death of numerous protesters in Beijing, to the horror and outrage of the world. Jiang's tenure as China's top leader thus began rather inauspiciously. However, in the years that followed, dramatic changes took place in both China's domestic affairs and its foreign relations. After an initial period of uncertainty and hesitation, the Chinese Communist Party decided to continue the liberal economic reform of the preceding decade. China's economy once again boomed, bringing prosperity to a large number of Chinese people.

The relationship with the United States remained icy for a few more years. Immediately after the 1989 Tiananmen Square crackdown, the United States imposed a wide range of sanctions against China. In the middle of the 1990s, tension between the two countries further heightened as Beijing and Washington wrestled each other over various issues. There was, for instance, the serious disagreement over the status of Taiwan, which China viewed as a renegade province, and which the United States supported in its de facto separation from the People's Republic of China. When, in 1995, Washington allowed independence-minded Taiwanese leader Lee Teng-hui (Li Denghui) to go on a trip in the U.S.—an unprecedented event since 1949—the Chinese government reacted strongly. The Chinese People's Liberation Army staged large-scale military exercises in South China and test-fired missiles off the coast of Taiwan. In response, Washington deployed a sizable naval battle group to the region. The relationship between the two countries fell to its lowest point since the Mao-Nixon *rapprochement* more than twenty years before.

Meanwhile, inside China, some significant changes were also taking place, especially with regard to China's educated elite. In the 1980s, Chinese intellectuals had largely viewed America with a liberal inclination, taking the United States as an inspiration for the economic and political development of China. That partiality for America became quite evident when, at the height of the 1989 pro-democracy movement in Beijing, demonstrators set up a replica of the Statue of Liberty at Tiananmen Square. Entering the 1990s, however, the mood of China's intellectual life changed notably, transforming the Chinese elite's outlook on America. The failure of the 1989 pro-democracy movement poured cold water on political activism as renewed economic growth in China shifted attention from politics to business. Now there was a sense that China could do reasonably well without mimicking the West. A younger generation of Chinese intellectuals was coming of age, whose memory of the troubles in the Mao Era was more remote and less personal. Keenly aware of the national differences between China and the West, the new generation of educated Chinese had its reservations about Western liberalism as a universal value. Not surprisingly, these Chinese did not have much patience for American criticism of China, which they believed to be tainted with inherent U.S. hostility toward their motherland.

The new trend in China's intellectual life in the 1990s revealed itself in the phenomenal success of a little book published in 1995—*China Can Say No*. In a radical departure from the liberal tradition of the 1980s, the young and angry authors of this little book squarely condemned U.S policies toward China as well as American culture itself. The book provides a long list of China's grievances against the United States, including, among others, the U.S. effort to defeat Beijing's bid to host the Olympic Games, the American objection to China's membership in the World Trade Organization, and Washington's support for Taiwanese and Tibetan separatist movements. The Chinese had long been naïve and foolish in their adoration of the United States, the book authors argued. It was now the time for the Chinese to wake up, face reality, and take a stand against American harassment and intimidation.[3] With their sweeping denunciation and urgent exhortation, the authors of *China Can Say No* quickly became national celebrities, and their book sold more than a million copies.

One might simply dismiss cases such as this as acts of young provocateurs. Events like this, however, were indicative of some larger changes that were taking place in Chinese society at the time. About twenty years into the free market–oriented economic reform that Deng Xiaoping initiated at the end of the 1970s, the average Chinese were facing a new situation. Even though they were still largely supportive of the reformist policies that had brought them prosperity, the people became increasingly concerned with some side-effects of the liberal changes. The ruthless drive for profitability generated widespread social dislocation. Urban workers no longer enjoyed job security; they made good money as long as their companies or factories did well but faced the prospect of losing their livelihood altogether when, somehow, things went wrong. Poor peasants, unhappy with the miniscule yields from their paltry land, roamed the country in search for work at a time when millions of city workers struggled. The gap between rich and poor Chinese widened spectacularly, and belief in stability and harmony—so essential to Chinese society for so many centuries—was evaporating rapidly. Crime, prostitution, environmental degradation, along with a host of other social ills, ailed the country, as ever more fabulous shopping plazas and skyscrapers rose above China's horizon. Individualism seemed to be running amok, making a mess of China's moral fiber. Angst like this inevitably raised doubts on the wisdom of Western liberalism, especially the famed American Way.

Thus, in China of the 1990s, anti-American sentiments were gaining strength at all levels of Chinese society—state, intelligentsia, and general populace—creating a delicately difficult situation for the Chinese Communist Party. True, China's political leaders frequently benefited from anti-American feelings in China and often fanned the fire for their own gains. At the same time, anti-Americanism also posed a threat to a government that derived its legitimacy from China's recent economic success, which in turn came out of an ongoing liberal reform. If anti-Americanism spun out of control, it could seriously damage the reform in China, thus preventing the Chinese Communist Party from achieving its long-term goals. To sustain economic growth, China had to work closely with the United States; sweeping condemnation of America, on the other hand, would raise questions about the morality of a government that actively cooperated with the United States. For its own interests, the Chinese government had to manage the presentation and assessment of the U.S.A. carefully.

Viewed in this context, General Secretary Jiang Zemin's pro-American talk in March 1998, as related at the beginning of the current discussion, does not appear so odd after all. In the wake of the crisis over the Taiwan Strait in the mid-nineties, both Beijing and Washington recognized the danger of a Sino-American confrontation, and they moved to mend their relationship with each other. As part of this effort, an exchange of presidential visits took place: Jiang Zemin visited the United States in October 1997; Bill Clinton reciprocated and traveled to China in June 1998. It was in between these two important visits, both of which Chinese media covered extensively and enthusiastically, that General Secretary Jiang spoke favorably of Hollywood and paid his tribute to the moral elements in American culture.

It was quite unfortunate for Jiang that not long after the exchange of the Jiang-Clinton visits in 1997–98, certain highly destructive events took place, severely wounding the recently repaired Sino-American relations, leaving Chinese leaders such as Jiang in an awkward and embarrassing situation. On March 8, 1999, bombs dropped from U.S. warplanes taking part in a NATO air-raid campaign in Yugoslavia struck and destroyed the Chinese embassy in Belgrade, killing three and injuring twenty other Chinese diplomats and journalists. Washington's explanation that the strike was an accident could not dispel the widespread Chinese suspicion that this was a deliberate attack aimed to intimidate and humiliate China. Furious college students staged heated protests outside the U.S. embassy in Beijing. Then, on April 1, 2001, a U.S. plane on a reconnaissance mission off China's southern coast collided with a Chinese fighter that was tailing it, causing the crash of the Chinese aircraft, the death of the Chinese pilot, and the emergency landing of the U.S. plane on Chinese territory. Beijing lodged strong protests against the United States. The expression of indignation notwithstanding, the Chinese government, eager to avoid a serious escalation, speedily returned the American crew and the damaged spy plane to the U.S. (China had to reject an insulting offer from Washington in the amount of $34,576 to cover the costs related to the event.)

These events, taking place within a relatively short period of time, enraged the Chinese already angry with U.S. policies toward China and embarrassed reform-minded Chinese leaders such as General Secretary Jiang Zemin, who had recently spoken so favorably of the United States.[4] After the bombing of the Chinese embassy in Belgrade, one Chinese college student noted:

> When I first watched American film *Saving Private Ryan*, I was deeply moved by it. What recently happened to the Chinese embassy in Belgrade, however, made me think about how the United States often bullies other countries. American lives are certainly precious; but, aren't soldiers of other countries human beings too?[5]

The circumstances surrounding Jiang Zemin's seemingly trivial remarks about Hollywood demonstrate how Chinese views of the U.S. are fashioned in a broad and dynamic process. Generally, one people's images and opinions of another are often fragmented, constantly evolving, and full of undertones and subtexts. This is especially true with Chinese views of the United States, given the nature of the nations involved in the particular case. China and the U.S, two of the world's largest countries, are drastically different in their cultural backgrounds and historical experiences. In the twentieth century, these two nations played significant roles in world affairs and actively inter-acted with each other. The potential for misunderstanding was enormous and consequences of such misunderstanding immense. Because of all this, the Chinese looked at the United States with diverse considerations and in widely divergent ways, which in turn led to images and interpretations that were highly complex and often self-conflicting. It is no easy task, therefore, to make sense of the multifaceted Chinese views of America. To reconcile the differences among the varied and contradictory perceptions and opinions, we need to move beyond the fractional and fluctuating particulars to reach what works behind the scenes—the dynamic processes that created the Chinese outlook and rhetoric on the United States in the first place. By investigating the ways in which larger historical forces shaped Chinese perceptions and attitudes, rather than simply presenting various views, we may be able to achieve a unified understanding of not only *what* the Chinese think of the United States but also *how* they view and interpret the important nation sitting on the other side of the Pacific.

II

While many larger historical forces contributed to the making of the Chinese images and interpretations of the United States, this current study focuses on the following questions. First, how has China's relationship with the United States interplayed with China's internal affairs? Second, in the domestic context, how have the Chinese people's cultural predispositions interacted with the political life of China? Third, how have the major groups in Chinese society, most notably the Chinese state, intelligentsia, and general populace—each with its own particular cultural concerns and political agenda—contended with one another over the proper interpretation and presentation of America? Fourth, how, over time, have the general forces noted above aligned and realigned among themselves, generating new dynamics that shaped and reshaped the Chinese outlook on the United States? In the contexts created by larger historical forces we can better examine and evaluate particular Chinese views of the United States at given places and times.

What do we mean by the "larger historical forces" noted above? Throughout the twentieth century, the United States figured prominently in China's national consciousness. To the Chinese, the United States was more than a foreign country; it stood for a way of life, which had significant implications to China struggling in the modern age. The United States and China were remarkably successful at different points in history, a fact that led each of the two nations, in their respective ways, to regard itself as the very epitome of human civilization. In premodern times, China largely dominated her part of the globe, and the Chinese people came to believe that their country, the Great Flowering Central Kingdom, was situated at the very center of the whole world, both geographically and culturally. Foreign conquests of China did take place, but on each of these occasions, despite China's military defeats, the Chinese managed to maintain their way of life, eventually converting the conquerors into followers of Chinese traditions.

Events in the nineteenth century, however, shattered this old historical pattern when Western powers, armed with modern technology and new ideas on sociopolitical organization, subjugated China. This time, the outsiders not only defeated China militarily but also dictated a new way of life that the Chinese had to accept. China tried to fight off the predators, but the ailing empire lost one war after another, falling to the very brink of total colonization. With their traditional values and institutions in shambles, the Chinese found themselves struggling in a completely different world, helpless and confused. Quite perceptively, Li Hongzhang, an enterprising but ultimately ill-fated Chinese statesman in the late nineteenth century, characterized the upheavals he and his contemporary compatriots lived through as changes that China had not seen in over two thousand years.

The challenge to the Chinese nation in the modern times has been, therefore, twofold. On the one hand, it was a struggle against the Western powers to save China from national annihilation. On the other hand, it was a drive to modernize China by adopting Western ways. Rather aptly, Chinese Communist leader Mao Zedong once described the situation as one in which China, a humble journeyman, tries to learn a trade from a powerful but abusive master, the West.

As the Chinese struggled with their dilemma, they could not help noticing the rise of the United States, which, within a relatively short period of time, fought successfully for her independence and grew to be the most affluent and powerful country in the world. The national experiences of the U.S. and China thus sharply contrasted each other, with one country succeeding splendidly and the other failing miserably. Even more significantly, what lay behind the American success, the American culture and institutions, seemed to be so antithetical to those of China—creativity versus conventions, individuality versus collective thinking, progress versus tradition, and so on and so forth. Quite naturally, the United States of America fascinated the Chinese and compelled the Chinese to examine many of their fundamental beliefs as they endeavored to reinvigorate their country and reinvent their national identity. In this way, America as a way of life became an integral part of the Chinese effort to reshape China in the modern times.

But the United States was not just a concept; it was also an actual nation-state, with its own interests, a power that actively participated in the Western encroachment on China. As such, the United States was deeply involved in Chinese affairs, a fact that aroused strong sentiments and reactions in China, which at times proved to be strongly hostile. Such Chinese resentments complicated the Chinese fascination with America as an ideal and gave rise to conflicts and fluctuations in Chinese attitudes toward the United States. There is, therefore, an intricate connection between China's domestic affairs and China's relationship with the United States.

Within China, politics and culture also interplayed with each other to fashion Chinese views on the United States of America. As noted earlier, in the late nineteenth century and early twentieth century, having suffered repeated defeats at the hand of the world's imperialist powers, the Chinese learned the hard way that for China to survive as a nation, the people must let go many of their deeply cherished traditions and embrace a new civilization. Most important of all, they had to forego the ancient Chinese emphasis on the group over the individual, so as to liberalize Chinese society to allow the free growth of a modern economy and democratic institutions. This was a fundamental cultural revolution for a country with one of the longest continuous histories in the world, where the influence of the past was the most pervasive and enduring. It soon became clear that it was one thing to recognize the necessity for this fundamental change and quite another to actually effect the transformation and live with it on a daily basis.

The arduous task to achieve a cultural revolution was made even more difficult by the political environment in which the changes in values had to take place. Given the severe national survival crisis that China experienced in modern times, the Chinese had to take immediate and concerted actions to save their country; otherwise, their whole cause would be lost, leaving no nation behind for them to modernize. The political imperative was therefore largely collectivist by nature, calling for the loyalty and devotion of the Chinese people above everything else. This impetus inevitably conflicted with the cultural imperative that insisted on the emancipation of the individual as the ultimate solution to China's problems in the modern times. The tension thus created led to a kind of cultural politics characterized by painful choices on both political and personal levels. It was with such paradoxes and divided commitment in terms of cultural-political interplay that the Chinese had to confront the United States of America as a power and as an ideal.[6]

Furthermore, Chinese groups of different social and political standings—the Chinese state, intelligentsia, and general populace—tended to have different emphases in their contemplations on the U.S.A. The Chinese state, for one, was obsessed with political stability and was thus predisposed to view American presence in China as politically subversive, an effect it strived to control. Chinese intellectuals, who for the most part favored the idea of progress, were more willing to experiment with new and challenging ideas, including those of American origin. The masses of China, for their part, were more interested in issues with direct and immediate bearing on their daily life, including matters such as morals, security, and material well-being. With such divergent preoccupations and inclinations, the Chinese state, intelligentsia, and general populace frequently found themselves at odds on what to make of America. The tension and contention among these groups thus constituted yet another major element in the dynamic formulation of Chinese views on the United States.

Finally, in terms of changes over the twentieth century, the dynamics that shaped Chinese views on the U.S.A. manifested themselves in several major stages: from 1900 to 1949, from 1949 to 1979, from 1979 to 1989, and from 1989 to 2000. General circumstances in these historical periods varied greatly to influence the making of Chinese views on America in diverse ways. At the same time, the larger historical forces outlined above were actively at play in all of the four phases, generating some enduring themes and persistent patterns that held up throughout the twentieth century.

III

The current study contains eight chapters. Chapter 1 surveys the years from the beginning of the twentieth century to the Communist victory in 1949, a period in which war and revolution were wreaking havoc in China, when central control was weak, resulting in a relatively open and free setting for the Chinese to explore America. Chapter 2 examines the situation in the early 1950s, when the newly established Chinese Communist government carried out comprehensive social and political reorganization as China rejected American influence against the backdrop of the Sino-American confrontation in Korea. Chapter 3 focuses on the dramatic events of 1957, when China's liberal intellectuals, eager to deal with new problems in China, challenged the Chinese government on the proper interpretation and presentation of America, prompting the Chinese state to strike back. Chapter 4 inspects the developments from the late 1950s to the early 1970s, a period that witnessed the reestablishment, radicalization, and eventual disintegration of Communist China's official America. Chapters 5, 6, and 7 cover the years from 1979 to 1989 and respectively focus on the experiences of the Chinese government, intelligentsia, and general populace as related to the U.S.A. in the context of the post-Mao liberal reform in China. Chapter 8 follows, which inspects some old trends and new issues in the making of Chinese views on the United States of America in the 1990s, when China emerged as an economic and political power in world affairs and conditions in China differed substantially from any of the preceding decades in the twentieth century.

In many ways, the current study is an overly ambitious project, setting the author's limited abilities against broad and complex subject matter. Designed to demonstrate the workings of larger historical forces during an extended period, the study is sketchy on many specific issues and leaves some important questions unanswered. As such, the work is not meant to exhaust all the investigative possibilities in the field of study. Instead, the author attempts to suggest a way of understanding that attends to both particular cases and general forces, with the meaning and significance of the former elucidated in the contexts created by the latter. With regard to the gaps and spottiness in the study, the author finds consolation in Jacques Barzun's observation that "the historian can only show, not prove, persuade, not convince; and the cultural historian more than any other occupies that characteristic position."[7] It is hoped that, by following what Barzun termed as the "middle course between total description . . . and circumscribed narrative,"[8] the author can shed some light on how the Chinese people, in a century of dramatic changes, contemplated the United States of America as they carried on their own discourse on the proper relationships between the West and the East, between modernity and tradition, and between the individual and society.

Statesmen, Scholars, and the
Men in the Street, 1900–1949

On New Year's Eve 1900, Liang Qichao—thirty years old and already a prominent Chinese scholar and political activist of his time—was aboard a ship sailing across the Pacific to North America. Too excited to sleep, Liang stayed up that night and composed a long, passionate poem to mark the historic moment that he was experiencing: "At the turn of the century / astride the East and West."[1]

Reflecting on the rise and fall of various civilizations around the world in the past, Liang hailed the dawn of a new epoch, the Pacific Century. The new era, as Liang saw it, was full of potential and grave danger for his motherland, China, which, as an ailing empire, was struggling for survival and renewal. Eagerly, Liang anticipated his upcoming visit of the United States, "a wondrous republic" as he put it, so that he could "study her learning, inspect her polity, and behold her dazzling brilliance."[2]

In his outburst of enthusiasm for the United States of America, Liang Qichao exemplified a keen interest shared by many Chinese at the time. Deeply troubled by a severe national survival crisis that China had experienced ever since the middle of the nineteenth century, these Chinese recognized the urgent need for changes. The Western Powers, armed with modern technology, had repeatedly defeated the once-proud Chinese empire and were poised to carve up the ancient land as their colonies. Anxiously the Chinese looked abroad for secrets of national success and, from early on in their quest, a young republic sitting on the other side of the Pacific Ocean drew their attention. The United States, so extraordinarily different from China, was thriving splendidly. Not surprisingly, therefore, Liang Qichao, a perceptive scholar and an idealistic statesman recently exiled from China for his reformist efforts, had high hopes for his upcoming tour of America.

Fifty years later, the Chinese admiration and enthusiasm for America so typical of Liang and his generation would have all but evaporated, replaced by scorn and hostility. By then, the Chinese Nationalist government led by Generalissimo Chiang Kai-shek (Jiang Jieshi), which the U.S. strongly supported, had just lost a war to Communist rebels. The People's Republic of China thus created would soon confront the United States in a war on the Korean peninsula. These larger historical events alone would have been sufficient to turn warm feelings into bitter antagonism. Still, evidence indicates that the seeds of hostility had been sown long before the sharp downturn in Sino-American relations in the late 1940s. During the half-century between Liang Qichao's first visit to the United States and Chinese Communist leader Mao Zedong's famous farewell to U.S. Ambassador Leighton Stuart, the Chinese nation had heatedly debated the proper understanding and assessment of the United States—what kind of a country it was, and what lessons China might or might not learn from it. This was far from a leisurely discussion, because the argument had everything to do with what the Chinese people wanted to make of their own country. The Chinese debate on America during this period thus gives us more than a hint of how the Chinese would contemplate the United States in the coming decades.

|

Liang Qichao did not actually reach North America on his 1900 voyage. As it happened, upon arrival in Hawaii, he received news that some of his fellow reformers back in China would stage an uprising against the ruling Qing Dynasty. Two years before this time, in 1898, Liang and some progressive Chinese had pushed a reform movement to modernize China. That earlier endeavor had the backing of the young emperor then, Guangxu, but it was hated by many of the old guard in the government, who were led by the emperor's ultra-conservative aunt, Cixi. The dominant Empress Dowager put up with the idealistic reformers for about three months before she decided to crack down. She put the young emperor under house arrest and executed six of Liang's colleagues. The Hundred-Day Reform ended abruptly. Liang himself managed to flee abroad and that was when he set out for America.

From Hawaii Liang hurried home, only to find out that the new plot against the Empress Dowager was yet another false start. No sooner had he returned to China than the news came that the Qing court had uncovered and thwarted the rebellious conspiracy. Again Liang had to go into exile. It was three years later, in 1903, that Liang finally paid his first visit to the United States. Clearly, the spirited Chinese came to America not only as an inquisitive scholar but also as a politician with a burning desire for fresh ideas and new strategies.

To be sure, Sino-American contacts go back beyond Liang's 1903 trip. The first direct voyage from the United States to China took place in 1784, when a ship from Boston, the *Empress of China*, sailed to Canton on China's southern coast. For much of the following century, however, the young American republic appeared obscure to the Chinese. It was toward the end of the nineteenth century that the United States started to register more prominently in the national consciousness of China. At this time, the United States gave the impression that the country was more benign and peaceful than most other Western powers—Britain or France, for example, which fought wars with China and forced China to sign humiliating treaties. True, the U.S. did obtain the special rights and privileges that the Qing Dynasty had to sign off to the other powers, and the U.S. thus also contributed to China's national-survival crisis. For the most part, however, the United States seemed to be interested in commercial opportunities and did not harbor territorial ambitions in China, a fact for which the beleaguered Chinese were rather thankful. The U.S. did, in 1900, join seven other powers in an allied expedition to China to suppress an antiforeign uprising raging in China then, the Boxer Rebellion. But it was also at this time that Washington put forward the famous Open Door Doctrine, calling upon the foreign powers to respect China's territorial, if not sovereign, integrity. Under this arrangement, China could continue to exist as one country while the Western nations would maintain and expand their privileges in the eastern land. This was far from ideal for the Chinese; but, given their lot at the time, many Chinese were relieved to see that, partly due to the U.S. intervention, their country would avert partition or total colonization, for the time being at least.

China's relatively positive view of the United States also arose from the fact that many Americans were actively involved in charitable causes in China, having established and worked at numerous religious, medical, and educational enterprises. Deeds such as these mitigated the ill effects of American offenses such as the unfair treatment of Chinese immigrants in the United States, which in 1904–05 gave rise to a widespread Chinese boycott of American goods in protest of the U.S. government's discriminative policies.[3] Overall, compared to the other haughty Western powers, the United States appeared to be gentle, even benevolent, with a sense of justice as well as compassion for the less fortunate. On both sides of the Pacific, therefore, there was a feeling that a "special relationship" existed between China and the United States, a relationship in which the U.S. was destined to guide and assist China in her march toward modernization.[4]

To some Chinese, the appeal of the United States came not only from its benign policies toward China but also from America's particular national experience. The Chinese, who at the time were engaged in a difficult struggle for national survival, could not fail to notice that the U.S. had fought successfully for her own independence. Equally fascinating to the Chinese was how swiftly, in just one hundred years or so, a small group of colonies rose to become a great power in the world. Quite naturally, the Chinese wanted to know the secret for America's remarkable success.[5]

It was against this backdrop that Liang Qichao went on his tour of the United States in 1903. A prodigy from a small town outside Canton, Liang had received solid traditional Confucian training and passed the provincial level of China's onerous Civil Examination at the tender age of sixteen. He rose quickly in academic and political circles, emerging as a prominent leader of the Hundred-Day Reform that took place in 1898. As a man who took pride

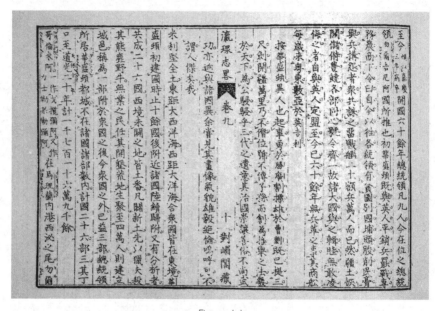

Figure 1.1

Text from *A Brief Survey of the Maritime Circuits*. Authored in the middle of the nineteenth century by Xu Jiyu, a Confucian scholar-official, the book was one of the earliest Chinese works that provided a reasonably detailed description of the world. Here, Xu tells the story of George Washington: "Washington is an extraordinary man. He was courageous as a rebel and more accomplished in taking control of territories than Cao and Liu [from the era of the Three Kingdoms in Chinese history]. Having conquered with his three-foot long sword and founded a state comprising vast land, he did not usurp the ruling position nor did he pass his power to his descendents. Instead, he created a system based on elections. This spirit approaches the high ideal of ancient Chinese sages—'The world belongs to all people.' Furthermore, in government, Washington respected good customs and did not rely on military strength only. This also differed significantly from the ways of other countries."

in constantly waging a war against his past self, Liang the scholar, politician, and popular journalist proved to be an astute observer of the American scene, who was particularly effective in relating his new experience to the situation back in China. After spending six months in North America, Liang published his observations and reflections in a book, *Notes on a Tour of the New Continent*, which became popular reading for a whole generation of Chinese eager to learn about a fascinating and yet mysterious land.

Liang traveled extensively in the United States. He toured the New England and Mid-Atlantic states; he went from Chicago on the Great Lakes to New Orleans at the mouth of the Mississippi; he journeyed across the great prairie, climbed over the Rocky Mountains, and arrived in the Golden State of California. Liang's status as a former statesman gave him wider access to American society than other Chinese in the U.S. at the time, who were mostly confined to a small and strangely mixed world of restaurants, laundries, and ivory towers of higher education. While in America, Liang not only mingled with his fellow-countrymen in Chinatowns but also met luminaries such as John Hay and Theodore Roosevelt.

America left strong impressions on Liang Qichao. At one point in his book, *Notes on a Tour of the New Continent*, Liang described what an extraordinary experience it was to travel and progress from the backwater countryside of China to the urban centers of America. Coming from interior China and arriving in Shanghai, the Chinese traveler marveled at the splendor of Shanghai and lamented the shabbiness of inland China. Leaving Shanghai behind and reaching Hong Kong, the traveler was struck by the magnificence of Hong Kong and now recognized the mediocrity of Shanghai. In similar fashion, with ever-growing awe, the traveler made his way through Japan and California, and finally arrived in New York—"the ultimate spectacle on the planet."[6]

What are the secrets of America's enormous accomplishment? In his search for an answer, Liang made a point of seeking out some prominent Americans for their opinions. In New York, for instance, he went to see J. P. Morgan, whom he described as "the Napoleon of the business world." The great banker's response to Liang's inquiry on the key to success was simple enough—"solid preparation"—a truism that Liang readily accepted, probably having the untimely death of the Hundred-Day Reform in mind.[7]

But surely there was more to America's triumph than good planning or effective execution? Upon much reflection, Liang settled on what he termed as "American Spirit." He discussed the issue with a friend and they agreed that this was what truly mattered. To understand why the American nation had done so well, they suggested, peopled could simply look at the operation or the upkeep of "an American school, an American platoon, an American drugstore, an American factory, an American family, or an American garden."[8] In all these establishments, present was a dynamic spirit of self-reliance and self-motivation. The vigor with which Americans went about their daily business indicated a kind of idealism, which Liang characterized as a mixture of aestheticism, heroism, and religious transcendentalism.[9]

With an understanding of America such as this, Liang faulted contemporary Chinese for their "lack of high ideals," which he considered a major flaw. Forget about lofty ideas such as national salvation, Liang said, "we Chinese do not even know how to walk." When a Westerner moves in the street, "he keeps his body straight and his head upright . . . and his steps are brisk, as if he is always on some important mission." In contrast, when a Chinese gets on the road, "his body bends, coils, twists, as if it cannot bear any weight at all"—"it is so maddening to see how the man saunters ever so slowly."[10] The lack of an enterprising spirit, Liang believed, was a major cause of stagnation and decay in China.

Admiring as he was of America, Liang did have his reservations. American politics, for instance, were far too plebeian and boisterous for Liang's taste. To this Confucian gentleman, the American political scene "resembles a rowdy market," where everybody tries to sell his wares—himself—for a good price.[11] Government officials in the United States, Liang thought, put too much effort into pleasing the electorate—to the point where they would sacrifice the long-term well-being of the people. So whereas bureaucrats in an autocracy serve their masters slavishly, politicians in a democracy kiss up to the public—"while differences do exist between these two situations, neither is ideal."[12]

Liang rationalized his reservations concerning American politics with what he had recently learned about scandals such as that surrounding Tammany Hall, which led him to conclude that politics in major American cities was the "dirtiest."[13] On the national level, Liang thought that the U.S. president's authority was overly circumscribed. In his view, this prevented the chief executive from accomplishing much. Partly due to this, "most U.S. presidents turned out to be of the average sort," with only five exceptions—Washington, Jefferson, Lincoln, Grant, and McKinley. The rest were just forgettable. "Only a few decades have passed since their times, but nowadays who in the world remembers Polk or Pierce?"[14]

It was not that Liang did not know about traditional American distrust of big government. He was aware that Americans valued autonomy and self-government; indeed, he spoke highly of the federal system of the United States. The success of the American republic, he stated, "does not arise from the union itself but from the states that form the whole, and, within a state, not from the state itself but from the municipalities and other localities that make up the state."[15] "Those who fail to understand this point have no right to discuss American politics."[16]

Here Liang seemed to be contradicting himself—he applauded the local and regional autonomy in the U.S. system, but he also felt that the central government did not possess enough power. This ambivalence reflects the distinction between Liang the scholar and Liang the politician, as well as the distinction between his understanding of America and his knowledge of China. Liang the scholar could well understand the rationale behind the American system, but Liang the politician could not see much hope that the American idea would work in China under contemporary conditions. At this time, Liang was still a constitutional monarchist rather than a republican; he remained loyal to Emperor Guangxu in Beijing, who was kept under house arrest by the dominant and reactionary Empress Dowager Cixi. Liang still hoped that before long the young emperor would reemerge to lead the reform in China.[17]

More broadly, Liang's misgivings about U.S. politics resulted from his distaste for what he deemed excessive freedom in American life as a whole. For instance, the ruthless economic competition under the capitalist system saddened him, especially the great disparity between the rich and the poor—"200,000 richest men claim seven-tenths of America's total wealth, with 79 million other Americans sharing the remainder."[18] The extraordinary power of business tycoons alarmed the Chinese observer, who, while in the United States, paid close attention to the ongoing antimonopoly movement. "The most critical concern of the American nation in the past decade has been the Trust," Liang reported. "Those who intend to understand America today, and those who intend to understand the world in our time, must be mindful of this issue."[19]

With this mindset, Liang demonstrated a keen interest in labor unrest in the U.S. "Having seen the slums of New York," he wrote, "I have to agree that a socialist revolution is indeed on its way!"[20] During Liang's stay in the United States, a number of American socialists tried to convert the Chinese dignitary to their cause. Liang praised the activists for their idealism and devotion but politely declined to join their movement. "Socialism is like a religion, and no one in this world is more powerful than dedicated men of faith. . . . It is for a good reason that socialism is sweeping across the world today."[21] Still, Liang felt that, for the time being at least, China needed liberty and free enterprise more than socialism. Progress comes in stages, Liang noted; the time for socialism in China "has not come yet."[22]

It is significant that Liang's objection to socialism in China was largely based on the ground of timing; he did not reject the soundness or the desirability of socialism as a fundamental principle. In this sense, Liang's commitment to liberalism was limited and shaky. This was particularly true when he thought about China's survival crisis. Freedom, creativity, entrepreneurship—these were among the values that made the United States a great country, Liang acknowledged. Differences between China and the U.S., however, seemed to be too large for Liang to believe that the American way would actually work in his home country. Whereas the Americans had a long history of self-government, the Chinese had lived under imperial rule and a patriarchal family system for centuries. The Chinese were strangers to notions such as individuality and independence, and to rush them into self-government was to call for trouble. Democracy was the rule of the majority; unfortunately, "the majority, the great majority, the absolute majority of Chinese at the present time are in such pitiful conditions" that nothing but disaster would ensue if they were given American-style liberty, Liang argued. Before attempting any substantial experiment with democracy, therefore, some wise leaders should first prepare the Chinese properly. "I wish, I pray, I beg," wrote Liang in yet another of his emotional outbursts, that a few "great men" would be born in China:

> Let them, like thunder and storm, with iron and fire, shape up the Chinese for twenty years, thirty years, why not fifty years; and then, only then, let the people read Rousseau and discuss the great enterprise of George Washington.[23]

That democracy should come with the guardianship of a few great men sounds odd, but for Chinese of Liang's generation, and indeed for Chinese of following generations, the idea was not altogether illogical. China was struggling to survive; just three years prior to Liang's visit to the United States, allied forces of eight foreign powers had invaded China to put down the Boxers' Rebellion, in which anti-Western and antimodern Chinese peasants tried, futilely, to expel all "foreign devils" from their country and restore the ancient glory of the Chinese Empire. To save their country, the Chinese had to adopt new ideas and generally modernize. At the same time, the people needed to band together and fight for a common cause; the failure to do so would have meant certain death for the Chinese nation. Famously, Liang used "a heap of loose sand" as a metaphor to criticize his fellow-countrymen for their inability to unite and take concerted action.[24] In a context such as this, the advocacy of liberty and individuality in China was politically unviable.

Thus, for both cultural and political reasons, Liang Qichao was ambivalent about American life. His case illustrates a predicament of the Chinese nation at the beginning of the twentieth century. In the years to come, this problem would grow more pronounced and continue to confound the Chinese as they tried to make sense of America and relate the American experience to their own country.

After Liang's visit to the United States in 1903, the situation in China changed quickly. Liang still preferred constitutional monarchy, but events in

Figure 1.2

A Chinese cartoon that appeared at the end of the nineteenth century. Entitled "The Current Situation," the cartoon illustrated China's national survival crisis unfolding then. In the image, imperialist powers dominate various parts of China and the United States, the eagle, is coming in to claim its share of the prey. Meanwhile, China's corrupt mandarin officials continue to indulge in money, opium, wine, and women.

China were overtaking him, as many Chinese felt that they could no longer put up with the ineptitude of the Qing Dynasty. In 1911, just three years after the death of the Empress Dowager Cixi, a revolution took place, which brought down China's last imperial dynasty and led to the establishment of the Republic of China. Championing the revolution and heading the newly created republic was Dr. Sun Yat-sen (Sun Zhongshan), a man who differed from Liang Qichao in many ways. While Liang was a reformed Confucian scholar-official, Sun's traditional training was far less consequential. As a teenager Sun had lived in Hawaii with his elder brother, a local businessman, and studied at an Anglican school there. In his preparation for the republican revolution, Sun maintained close contact with the United States, especially Chinese-American communities in the U.S., which generously supported his revolutionary career. Compared to Liang's brief encounter with the United States, Sun's knowledge of America was more substantial. Additionally, as a revolutionary, Sun could better relate to the American experience, which he considered a natural example for the unfolding Chinese revolution.[25] Once asked to define democracy, Sun responded: "The great U.S. President Lincoln put it the best: of the people, by the people, for the people."[26] After Lincoln, among other "American warriors for liberty and democracy,"[27] Sun admired George Washington the most, with whom he obviously identified personally.[28] When trying to boost the morale of his revolutionary followers, Sun frequently referred to the humble beginnings of the American Revolution and the hardships that American Founding Fathers had to endure before their eventual triumph.[29]

Unfortunately, it seemed that Sun's admiration for George Washington partly contributed to his decision, just weeks after the promulgation of the Republic of China in 1912, to resign from the presidential office so that Yuan Shikai, a former general of the Qing Dynasty, could take over. Sun did this out of his selfless desire to avoid a prolonged civil war in China and to demonstrate that new Chinese leaders, like George Washington, were democratic republicans, not imperial dynasty founders.

It turned out that Yuan Shikai was unworthy of Sun's trust. A man who thrived on court intrigues, with virtually no belief in republicanism, Yuan, having persuaded the Qing emperor to abdicate and having succeeded Sun to the Republican presidency, soon declared himself the emperor of a new dynasty, on the argument that the Chinese were not ready for democracy. Yuan died in 1916 amid nationwide protest against him, but his death only led to the deterioration of conditions in the country as numerous military strongmen across the land fought one another for private gains. China fell into chaos. Liang Qichao's worst fear seemed to have materialized.

Dr. Sun Yat-sen would not give up. He re-rallied his followers to fight for the troubled republic. Already, however, he had to reconcile his idealism with the reality in China. His naivete had cost him and his cause dearly. Now he strove to build a movement that was tightly disciplined, completely loyal to him. People would hear less and less from him about liberty or democracy. Instead, he would painstakingly lecture his followers on the need for devotion and sacrifice.[30] Speaking at a YMCA conference in Guangzhou in 1923, Sun urged his audience to be mindful of the differences between China and America. The YMCA had done great work in China, Sun said, but Chinese people should always remember that whereas personal self-improvement was admirable, it alone was not enough to save China. Gradual reform in America was possible and desirable "because over there the people already have a good government." Conditions in China were quite different, as the country suffered from rampant violence and utter chaos. Here, "we can only achieve national salvation through a collective effort."[31] To drive his point home, Sun invoked the metaphor that Liang Qichao once used to chide his fellow Chinese—"a heap of loose sand" would amount to nothing.[32]

At the core of Sun's revolutionary doctrine had been the "Three-People Doctrine": Nationalism, Democracy, and People's Livelihood. Although Sun occasionally likened his basic principle to Lincoln's government of the people, by the people, for the people,[33] the two ideas were actually rather different, especially with regard to "People's Livelihood," which was a mild form of socialism. Like Liang Qichao before him, Sun admired Western society for the freedom its citizens enjoyed. Also like Liang, however, Sun believed in the inevitability of a socialist revolution, which he expected to "take place first of all in the United States, because American capitalist tycoons have appropriated all economic means and privileges and virtually enslaved the farmers and urban workers."[34] The creators of the U.S. Constitution did not intend this to happen. If the U.S. Founding Fathers "saw the current situation in America, they would cry out in disbelief and regretfully admit their own errors" in setting up the American system.[35]

The mistake made by the American Founding Fathers, in Sun's view, was the failure to institute measures to prevent the excessive concentration of wealth. China, in her pursuit of liberty and democracy, should avoid the pitfall. Interestingly, Sun found his solution to the problem in some other Americans, this time populist economist Henry George and socialist activist Edward Bellamy. Specifically, Sun favored George's idea of a "single tax," a land tax that would prevent real estate speculation and provide revenue to be used for public good. This became an important component in Sun's doctrine on people's livelihood. As Sun envisioned it, the state would collect land taxes according to owners' valuation of their own properties; any subsequent increase in value would go to the state, which would then invest the money in public projects such as railroads, utilities, and other key industries considered too important to be left to the private sector.[36] With programs such as this, according to Sun, China would be able to industrialize and still avoid the evils that ailed Western society. Not coincidently, policies like this would also make the struggle for freedom in China a "moral" cause that appealed to the majority of the Chinese people.

Sun's critical view of the economic inequality in America was not the only factor that turned him away from the United States. There was also the very practical issue that the U.S. government, in spite of all its talk about liberty and democracy, had been reluctant to support Sun's revolution. After all, Sun was fighting not just for democracy but also for national independence, and the latter might very well put an end to Western privileges in China. Sun's repeated appeals for support thus generated little interest in Washington, which in fact continued to recognize the warlord-controlled government in Beijing as the legitimate representative of China. Frustrated, Sun eventually turned to Russian communists for guidance and aid. The Bolsheviks, who had recently risen to power and faced Western hostilities, were happy to have an ally such as Sun in China. Russian material and advisory aid came to China and Sun drifted farther away from America.

In 1923, Sun's revolutionary government, now based in Canton (Guangzhou), decided to reclaim control over China's maritime customs, which the Western powers had seized some decades ago. The foreign powers, the United States included, opposed Sun's move and reacted strongly—they sent gunboats to China's southern coast to put pressure on the revolutionaries. Sun issued an open letter addressed to the American people, in which he angrily denounced the recent actions of the U.S. government:

> When we first started our revolution . . . the United States was our model and inspiration. Now we wonder. . . . Has the nation of Washington and Lincoln abandoned the ideal of liberty and regressed from a liberator to an oppressor? We cannot bear the thought that this is true.[37]

Sun's complaints had little effect on the U.S. government. His revolutionary dream remained largely unfulfilled when he died in 1925.

Succeeding Sun as the leader of the Chinese Nationalist Party was Chiang Kai-shek, whose attitude toward the United States would soon reveal contradictions similar to those seen in Liang and Sun, only on a larger scale and with graver consequences. Unlike his mentor Sun, Chiang actually enjoyed American support from early on. Having led the Nationalist-Communist alliance left behind by Sun and defeated most of China's warlords in 1926–27, Chiang found his differences with the more radical Chinese Communists insufferable. When the tension between the two sides came to a head in 1927, Chiang conducted a bloody purge, killing and arresting some of the

Communists, driving the rest into political wilderness. The Western powers came to view Chiang as a moderate leader and decided to throw their support behind him. Also in 1927, Chiang strengthened his connection to the West, the United States in particular, in a very personal manner—he married one of the famed Soong (Song) Sisters. One of the richest families in China, the Soongs had a strong American background. The patriarch of the family, Charlie Soong, received Methodist missionary training in the United States; upon returning to China, Soong made his fortune first by selling the Bible and then through banking. All of Charlie Soong's four children were educated in the United States, and they established powerful business and political connections in the U.S. and China. The eldest child, Ai-ling (Ailing), married a Yale-trained Chinese banker who would later serve as Chiang's finance minister. Ch'ing-ling (Qingling), the second daughter, married Dr. Sun Yat-sen. The third sister, the Wellesley-educated Mei-ling (Meiling), became the wife of Chiang Kai-shek. The only boy in the family, T. V. Soong (Song Ziwen), was a Harvard graduate who also served in Chiang's government, first as finance minister and then as foreign minister. Of the Soong siblings, Madame Chiang proved to be especially effective in promoting her husband's cause in the United States, winning the staunch support of prominent Americans such as Henry Luce, the publisher of *Time* magazine, who was born to American missionary parents in China.

There were, therefore, many good reasons for Chiang to be close to the United States. In reality, however, beyond reaping the benefit of U.S. aid, Chiang was rather aloof toward America, both philosophically and politically. In some ways, Chiang was even more distant from America than his predecessor Sun Yat-sen. Very much of a revolutionary idealist, Sun developed a genuine intellectual interest in America early on in his life. In Chiang's case, the contact with the United States came rather late, far beyond his formative years. As a child, Chiang received a traditional Confucian education; he then went through military training in Japan, which constituted the main stock of the man's international experience. Culturally, therefore, Chiang was largely an old-fashioned Chinese, whose worldview featured a combination of diluted Confucianism, rigid military discipline, and some revolutionary catchphrases inherited from Sun Yat-sen. These fundamentals did not change much after his marriage with Mei-ling Soong, even though, as a condition for the union, the forty-year-old Chiang promised that he would start to study the Bible. In any event, the Soongs, so fabulously privileged, could hardly champion the cause of democracy in China.

Furthermore, whereas Sun Yat-sen was largely a rebel, Chiang came to lead a national government in the world's most populous country. In his position, Chiang had to deal with problems that Sun did not face. Indeed, in the years after 1927, Chiang met serious challenges on several fronts.

Some of China's warlords had pledged allegiance to Chiang only grudgingly; whenever they had their chances, they tried to expand their power at the expense of the central government. The Communists, having retreated into countryside, started a violent and resilient rural revolution that was to last more than twenty years. The Japanese militarists, taking advantage of China's weaknesses, sought further expansion on the continent, seizing Manchuria in 1931 and launching a full-scale war against China in 1937. Confronted with all these troubles, Chiang struggled to hold his shaky state together.

Therefore, both as a matter of personal inclination and out of political necessity, Chiang had little use for ideas such as individuality, liberty, or democracy. He needed, more than anything else, dedication and discipline on the part of his followers; these qualities, in his view, were essential to China's survival. Publicly, Chiang extolled the United States enthusiastically. For the most part, however, he did this to win American goodwill and support. Philosophically and politically, he had precious little to say about American values and system. When he did touch on any of these unwelcome subjects, it was usually to lecture his subordinates on the undesirability of fanciful Western ideas. He would repeatedly urge his people to honor their Confucian tradition with its emphasis on loyalty and self-control. He once squarely declared that "there is nothing in European and American political thought that surpasses" what is in Confucian classics such as "The Great Learning" and "The Doctrine of Mean."[38]

Whereas Sun Yat-sen likened his Three-People Doctrine to President Lincoln's definition of good government, Chiang stressed the connection between Sun's ideals and China's own "political, ethical, and philosophical legacy."[39] Speaking at a military academy, Chiang complained that nowadays "our schools have all but abandoned" the precious jewels of traditional Chinese culture. As result, "many students today appreciate only translated foreign works and dismiss Chinese teachings as useless."[40] In reality, "we needn't search overseas for ways to save our nation"; the ideas could be found right here in the country, in the heritage of China.[41]

Not surprisingly, while Chiang relied on the American-educated Soong crowd in the management of China's finances and foreign affairs, he turned to some other men for advice on ideological matters. One such close advisor was Dai Jitao, a devoted Buddhist, Confucianist, and Sinophile. For many years on end, Dai urged Chiang to strengthen the Nationalist cause by inculcating traditional values in the Chinese people. The austere Dai never did get along well with the Soong crowd, whom he considered corrupt and soft. In 1949, as the Nationalist government collapsed under Communist attacks, Dai committed suicide, as was expected of a virtuous Confucian councilor who had failed his emperor.

Another of Chiang's advisors, Tao Xisheng, is believed to be the ghost writer of *China's Destiny*, which was published in Chiang's name in the forties to provide spiritual guidance for the Nationalist cause. In the book, communism and liberalism in China were denounced and dismissed respectively as a Soviet Russian conspiracy and a mere echo of the West. China's unique cultural tradition, not half-baked foreign ideas, it was said, would ultimately ensure the Chinese nation's survival and resurrection.[42]

In other words, even though Chiang Kai-shek enjoyed strong U.S. support throughout his political career, in his heart he remained skeptical of American values and institutions. Fighting a long, arduous war against Japanese invaders, doing his utmost to control rebellious warlords and suppress Communist revolutionaries, Chiang found American ideas concerning liberty and democracy of little practical use in China. As an ally in war, the Generalissimo wanted U.S. cooperation as much as possible; as an old-fashioned Chinese and a Chinese politician, Chiang kept America at a distance.

In this regard, Chiang did not differ significantly from Liang Qichao and Sun Yat-sen before him. In fact, on this particular point, Chiang even bore a certain resemblance to his nemesis and eventual undoing, the Chinese Communists. Notwithstanding the political differences between Chiang and his Communist rivals, both sides, due to common Chinese background and shared political circumstances, proved to be wary and suspicious of American influence on their respective followers.

The Communists did not start out that way. Before converting to Marxism, many early Chinese Communists went through a brief liberal phase, characterized by positive views of the United States. Chen Duxiu, a founding member of the Chinese Communist Party and its first general secretary, played a leading role in the liberal New Culture Movement, in which he passionately advocated the emancipation of the individual and the enlightenment of the Chinese people. Chen's political career started with his participation in the Revolution of 1911 that overthrew the Qing Dynasty. He subsequently studied in Japan, and, upon his return to China, founded the famed magazine *Xin Qingnian* (*La Jeunesse* or *New Youth*), which quickly emerged as the flagship publication for the liberal cause in China. Writing in the debut issue of the journal in 1915, Chen urged Chinese youth to discard old ways and embrace a completely new culture—they should strive to be "independent rather than slavish," "progressive rather than conservative," "active rather than passive," "cosmopolitan rather than isolationist," "pragmatic rather than formalistic," and "scientific rather than delusive."[43]

In addition to Chen's inspiring call for the liberation of the individual, the first issue of *New Youth* also contained writings of American authors W. A. Marwick and W. F. Smith,[44] along with a biographical piece on an American industrialist and philanthropist—"Diligence and Success: The Story of Andrew Carnegie."[45] The second issue of the journal printed the national anthem of the United States, translated by Chen Duxiu himself.[46] Similar materials appeared in the following issues. There were, for example, excerpts from Benjamin Franklin's *Autobiography* and Edmund Burke's "Spirit of Liberty in the American Colonies."[47] *New Youth* also introduced to the public a young man by the name of Hu Shi, then a graduate student of philosophy at Columbia University, who would later become China's foremost liberal and pro-American intellectual, much to the chagrin of Chen the radical and his fellow Communists.

Chen's infatuation with the United States was short-lived. As time passed, Chen became impatient with the slow pace of the liberal cause in China, which had rather limited and superficial effect on Chinese society, barely denting the harsh reality that was warlordism in China. With his interest shifting from cultural affairs to the exercise of political power, Chen paid close attention to the success of the Russian Bolshevik Revolution in 1917, which converted him to Marxism. As this happened, Chen's view on Western democracy and his estimation of America turned negative.[48] Previously he had actively assisted Chinese students and scholars who studied in the United States—Dr. Hu Shi was one of them; now he revealed a vehement contempt and hostility toward their sort and toward pro-American feelings in general.[49] In 1924, some young Chinese in Manchuria, who were members of the local YMCA, protested against Japanese expansion in the region. Chen coldly questioned the motives of the activists. "The noblest thing to do here is to boycott the Japanese for the interests of China. Next to the best is to boycott the Japanese for the interests of Manchuria. The lowest of it all is to boycott the Japanese for the interests of the United States!"[50] On another occasion, some Chinese students admitted to American universities were stopped at the border by U.S. immigration officials due to a paperwork mixup. Chen gleefully expressed his "gratitude" to the U.S. government. Let those Chinese suffer, Chen wrote, because "it is public knowledge that almost every single American-trained [Chinese] student opposes revolution, worships money, and idolizes the U.S. The fewer such Chinese the better; none of them, the best for China!"[51]

Chen Duxiu himself never visited the United States. In fact, of the future top Chinese Communist leaders, only one or two spent any time in the U.S., and their experience was far from positive. Zhang Wentian, who in the 1930s headed the Chinese Communist Party, went to San Francisco in 1922. Unlike Chinese students generously supported with scholarships at elite universities, Zhang had to work—for a local Chinese newspaper—while taking some college courses. Writing home, Zhang, twenty-two years old, complained about working "like a machine": "I'm afraid that in America I will be a loner forever."[52] Later, Zhang wrote and published a novel based on his experience in the U.S. In the story, *The Journey*, a young Chinese travels to the United States with great hopes, determined to learn about modern democracy so that he can return home to clean up China. Reality in the U.S., however, soon leads to disillusion—there is no revolution, only loneliness. Eventually the young idealist winds up his sojourn, hurries back to China to join a rebellion, and dies heroically as the commander of a revolutionary army.[53] In real life, Zhang spent about one year in California before his return to China. Within months, a local warlord threw Zhang out of his hometown, charging him with "cultural radicalism."[54] The next stop for Zhang would be Moscow and the Chinese Communist Party.

About the same time that Zhang Wentian struggled in California, Zhou Enlai, the future premier of the People's Republic of China, discovered Marxism in Europe. Zhou had gone to France after World War I as one of China's work-study students seeking an affordable Western education. Before his trip to France, Zhou had taken part in the New Culture Movement. In France, however, young Chinese like him encountered a world devastated and demoralized by the Great War, unsure of its future. Zhou quickly became active in the emerging Chinese communist movement. Now, with disdain Zhou looked at the West, especially the United States, the lone Western nation that came out of the Great War better off. Writing in a communist journal for Chinese students in Europe, Zhou assailed the U.S. as an imperialist and monopoly capitalist power, hungry for material gains. Commenting on the U.S. presidential race of 1924, Zhou saw little difference among the major candidates. "Let's keep this in mind and fight against them all just the same."[55]

Meanwhile, back in China, Mao Zedong, son of a peasant, was agitating for revolution in his home province, Hunan. Like many other early Chinese Communists, Mao had been active in the liberal New Culture Movement. Around 1920, with the idea that "nothing is more urgent than spreading culture,"[56] young Mao and a few friends founded a book club to promote reading, a business they planned to expand across the province. Among their best-sellers were works by the American philosopher John Dewey, who had recently gone on a lecture tour in China, which made him a much revered man of thought among educated Chinese.[57] Mao himself obviously adopted a few liberal ideas from the materials he was selling. He had, for instance, high regard for the tradition of self-government in the United States, and advocated greater rights for his home province in its relationship to the central government of China. In this particular regard, he went so far as to call for "a Monroe Doctrine for Hunan."[58]

Mao, at this time, was experimenting with diverse ideas. Writing in the official publication of the Hunan Students' Association that he edited, Mao advocated "peaceful petition" and "bloodless revolution" as means of political and social transformation.[59] In the same issue of the journal, however, Mao seemed to be applauding terrorist bombings that had recently taken place in a number of U.S. cities, events that set off the Red Scare in America.[60]

Already, therefore, becoming evident were some philosophical and personal traits that would make Mao a Communist rebel. Unlike many ambitious young Chinese of his time, Mao did not go abroad to study; his first trip to a foreign country would not take place until 1949, after the founding of the

People's Republic of China, when he visited the Soviet Union. Mao thus had very limited international experience, and, as a revolutionary, he derived his ideas largely from what he learned about Marxism and from his knowledge of China. Having taken part in the creation of the Chinese Communist Party in 1921, Mao, now a ranking official in the Nationalist-Communist coalition led by Dr. Sun Yat-sen, operated as a sharp propagandist and successful peasant organizer in Chinese countryside. Under the overall title "The People's Movement," Mao edited a series of readings for the masses. Gone now were works by John Dewey and his like; added were tracts and pamphlets promoting an immediate popular revolution.[61]

After the Nationalist-Communist split in 1927, Mao took his fight to rural China. His lack of international exposure and connections now became a political asset rather than liability, as he was better prepared than any other Chinese Communist leaders to draw support from the largest social group in China, the peasants. As he fought against Chiang Kai-shek's Nationalist government, Mao came to recognize the great importance of maintaining class solidarity. He was still a man of ideas, but only ideas that served his political cause well. Whereas earlier Mao had revealed interest in the Monroe Doctrine and John Dewey, in the 1930s he was righteously writing about the need "to combat liberalism." Now, to Mao, liberalism meant nothing but an "extremely harmful tendency," which "disrupts unity, undermines solidarity, induces inactivity and creates dissension."[62] Mao's youthful flirtation with liberalism and America died hard.

Thus, in the first half of the twentieth century, China's major national leaders, their political differences notwithstanding, demonstrated a common inclination in their attitude toward the United States of America. In the beginning, they all recognized the need for China to liberalize in order to cope with the modern challenges; in this connection, they all found the example of the United States admirable and inspiring. Eventually, however, cultural preference and political necessity turned them away from America. The particulars in the cases of Liang Qichao, Sun Yat-sen, Chiang Kai-shek, and Mao Zedong varied greatly, but a common pattern was clearly there. These national leaders, initially fascinated by America, ultimately came to face true conditions in China, and, both as Chinese men and Chinese politicians, they started to voice their reservations on, even outright opposition to, ideas epitomized by the United States of America.

II

Compared to China's leading politicians, Chinese intellectuals in the early decades of the twentieth century were less inhibited in their exploration of

America. Free of the pressure to maintain the loyalty of a political following, Chinese men of thought could pursue their intellectual interests and examine China's problems in a more detached mood. It was, therefore, easier for these Chinese to acknowledge the merits of American ideas and institutions, which they readily referenced in their critique of their own country. Still, given the desperation of the whole Chinese nation at the time, even China's educated elite were not altogether free of the general anxiety over the country's survival crisis. In fact, many Chinese intellectuals in the early twentieth century, even if they received Western education, still cherished the long-standing Confucian idea that an educated man should concern himself with the fate of his country. Within this tradition, the very notion of education implied public service. So, out of a sense of duty and responding to pressing events, educated Chinese stepped up to meet the challenge. The consequent engagement led to animated discourse on what China should do in modern times, a debate that often took the form of reflections on the differences and commonality between Chinese and American ways of life.

In China before 1949, a large number of Chinese intellectuals were American-educated. During the first half of the twentieth century, approximately thirty thousand Chinese studied in the United States.[63] More Chinese studied in Japan, but the academic training in the U.S. was more rigorous. For example, even though more Chinese students spent time in Japan than in the U.S., about twenty times more Chinese received doctoral degrees from American universities than from Japanese institutions.[64] As result, American-educated Chinese scientists, scholars, and artists constituted the backbone of China's academic and intellectual elite in the years before 1949.

Additionally, American organizations and individuals played a key role in the establishment of a modern educational system in China. In the early decades of the century, all but one Christian missionary college in China had American affiliations.[65] By 1937, when the Sino-Japanese War broke out, about twenty American-supported institutions of higher education were operating in China.[66] Yenching (Yanjing) University, Peking (Beijing) Union Medical College, and Tsinghua (Qinghua) University (originally funded with the returned U.S. share of the Boxers' Indemnity) were among the top schools that contributed a great deal to the creation of a pro-American intelligentsia in China.

Among the most accomplished pro-American Chinese intellectuals in the years before 1949 was Dr. Hu Shi. More than any other Chinese of his time, Hu embodied the American liberal ideal, which he actively promoted as a solution to China's myriad problems. For this effort, Hu was warmly applauded by some Chinese and vehemently condemned by many others.

Hu went to the United States early in his life. In 1910, one year before the downfall of China's last imperial dynasty, Hu, eighteen years old, traveled to America to study, supported by a scholarship from the Boxers' Indemnity

Fund. Hu's father, a low-level government official, died when Hu Shi was small; his mother, following the Confucian tradition, put all her hope in her only child, sacrificing her own interests to bring up her son. Upon his arrival in the U.S., Hu first studied agriculture at Cornell but soon found his true calling in the humanities. He moved on to study for a doctoral degree in philosophy at Columbia University, where noted pragmatist philosopher John Dewey taught.[67] As a student Hu spent seven years in the United States; later in his life he would visit America frequently and also served, for four years during World War II, as the Chinese Ambassador to the U.S. Altogether, Hu spent about twenty-one years of his life time in the United States, which made him one of the Chinese intellectuals who knew America most comprehensively and most intimately.[68]

Hu highly valued his American experience. Once, while debating some radical colleagues, he suggested that those who believed in violent revolution should at least visit the U.S. once. That experience alone, Hu thought, would set them straight. Those who could observe America at a close range but refused to go, Hu said, were simply intellectually dishonest.[69] "Do not be taken in," Hu warned young Chinese who had been advised by their radical professors to avoid America, "do not use your ears for your eyes!"[70]

Hu himself seemed to have made good use of his time in the United States. He studied earnestly in school but also paid close attention to American society at large. "Wherever I live," Hu wrote, "I take local social and political affairs as if they were those of my hometown."[71] He enjoyed attending public events—fairs, assembly hearings, court trials—so that he could "investigate the strengths and shortcomings" of his host country.[72] With great interest he followed the presidential campaign of 1916 and eventually decided in favor of Woodrow Wilson, who he believed would be a "first-class" president."[73] That William Sulzer, governor of New York, was thrown out of office for misusing campaign funds also impressed the young Chinese. Events such as this made him even more angry at the lawlessness back home in China. He wrote in his diary: "I forfeit the right to pass judgment on politics in this land. I'm too busy grieving over the despotism and wickedness of officials in my own country!"[74]

As mentioned earlier, while studying in the U.S., Hu became involved in the New Culture Movement that was unfolding in China, starting with his contributions to the *New Youth* magazine edited by Chen Duxiu. It was at this time that Hu made the famous—and shocking to Chinese traditionalists—call for the abolition of the archaic classic Chinese, to be replaced with a vernacular style that could be easily understood by the Chinese masses. Hu believed that this would be a good starting point for gradual changes in China. John Dewey's pragmatist influence on Hu started to manifest itself.

Hu returned to China in 1917, where he quickly established himself as a prominent professor and liberal intellectual. He was now known for his advocacy of the so-called Wholesale Westernization, which he believed to be the only way for China to move forward.[75] He had little patience with those who suggested that China's problems in the modern times were merely technological or institutional. The real problem, Hu thought, was cultural by nature.[76] He rejected the notion that Western civilization was materialist and Chinese civilization spiritual; that the Westerners cared about power and the Chinese valued ethics; and that China needed only to borrow Western science and technology, nothing else. Those who held such views on the West knew little about the West, Hu declared. As evidence for the spiritual vitality in the West, Hu pointed to Christianity in premodern times, "Liberty, Equality, Fraternity" in the eighteenth and nineteenth centuries, and socialism in the twentieth century.[77] Hu urged his readers to compare lives of Chinese coolies and American carpenters or bricklayers who drive their automobiles to go to work—what was so "spiritual" about "this culture of rickshaw-pullers and sedan-bearers?"[78]

After a decade in China, Hu went on a trip to the United States in 1927. What he observed on this visit greatly boosted his confidence in the American Way.[79] The ongoing prosperity in the U.S. made him even more critical of the naysayers against the U.S., who argued that America's materialistic culture had run its course, an idea that was gaining popularity in China. Hu tried to convince his fellow-countrymen that works by authors such as Oswald Spengler on the decline of the West were "not worth reading."[80] "I can confidently declare," Hu wrote, "that no revolution will take place in the United States. It is so because the U.S. carries on a social revolution on a daily basis."[81]

Hu's idea about "revolution on a daily basis" was central to his understanding of America: continuous reform made violent revolution an unlikely scenario. "Revolution on a daily basis" was thus also his remedy for China's problems. The Chinese should not dream of reinventing their country overnight. Impulsive attempts at drastic changes would only worsen the existing situation and lead to more misery. The Chinese should, Hu thought, first carefully identify their particular problems, experiment methodically to determine the most effective solutions to each of these problems, and seek to improve their condition gradually but steadily. Hu urged his Chinese compatriots to focus on "issues" rather than "isms." Marxism in particular caused great concerns in Hu Shi, which, promising a total solution to all of China's problems, put many Chinese intellectuals under its spell. Among Chinese who converted to Marxism was Chen Duxiu, the former editor-in-chief of the *New Youth* magazine and a leading figure in the liberal New Culture Movement, who played a key role in the creation of the Chinese Communist Party.

Given his overall view on affairs in China, Hu frowned upon what he viewed as thoughtless political agitation. He was, for example, often critical of college students' political activism, which he once described as "heat that lasts no more than five minutes."[82] In late 1936, students demonstrating against the Chinese government's feebleness in dealing with Japanese aggression conflicted violently with the police. Hu castigated the young protesters for their impetuosity, contrasting their "lawlessness" to the peaceful marches that he had observed in the United States. Hu's criticism enraged some students, and one of them—who later would become a secretary to Communist leader Mao Zedong—wrote in a newspaper to ask Hu pointedly whether the city of Beijing under despotic rule could be reasonably compared to the "democratic New York." "Dr. Hu should be able to answer this question easily, whose good fortune it was to have studied in America."[83]

So, whereas Hu Shi believed the notion of Wholesale Westernization, he also thought that changes could only take place gradually, through step-by-step reform rather than revolution. There was, therefore, a contrast or incongruity between his radical goal (Wholesale Westernization) and his moderate approach (gradual reform). For Hu Shi, however, there was no contradiction at all; viewed in terms of his American experience, the combination of gradual changes and total Westernization made perfect sense.

The real test, however, was to what extent Hu Shi's American experience could be applied to conditions in China. Viewed in the American context, Hu's ideas seemed to be reasonable and progressive. Placed in China of the early twentieth century, a time and place of rampant chaos and violence, Hu's advocacy of Wholesale Westernization detached him from the actual political forces in the country whereas his insistence on peaceful transformation often appeared as acquiescence to the status quo.

The suspicion was not altogether groundless. By temperament, Hu was averse to confrontation and more inclined toward compromise, a tendency that was evident in both his public life and his personal affairs. Hu, for example, was known as China's foremost liberal intellectual for his earnest call for the liberation of the individual; in his own family life, however, he could not very well stand up against Confucian traditions and old customs. When Hu was still a teenager, his widowed mother chose a wife for him, a woman who was virtually illiterate and whom Hu hardly knew. Having no heart for the woman and trying to escape from the arranged marriage, Hu left to study in the United States without going home to bid goodbye to his mother. During the seven years he spent in the U.S., Hu thought much about annulling his engagement, but he could not bring himself to disappoint his loving mother and to reject the loyal woman who in Hu's absence had already served Hu's mother as a dutiful daughter-in-law. After years of agony, Hu gave in. Upon his return to China, he consummated his marriage. This was not a happy union; Hu would be involved in one or two extramarital affairs, but the husband and wife lived together to the end, as Hu's mother had wished.[84] Hu's defense of his decision: "It is my freedom to choose not to be free."[85]

While one should not simply equate personal matters with public life, Hu's behavior in family affairs does illustrate the difficulty of bridging the gap between Western ideas and Chinese reality. This may partly explain the curious relationship between Dr. Hu Shi and the Chinese Nationalist leader Chiang Kai-shek. The Generalissimo was far from a democrat. Yet, the supposedly liberal Hu Shi actively served Chiang, holding various offices in Chiang's government. This is probably one of the situations where an ideal is so lofty that it no longer has much of an effect on real life.

To better understand the issue, we can examine the experiences of two other Chinese intellectuals prominent in China before 1949. Of the two, Tao Xingzhi, like Hu, was a native of Anhui Province, and, also like Hu, studied at Columbia University. But, unlike Hu, who made his journey to the U.S. at the more impressionable age of eighteen, Tao traveled to America when he was twenty-three, having graduated from a Chinese university. Furthermore, whereas Hu stayed in America for seven years, working toward his doctoral degree, Tao spent short of three years in the United States and returned to China with a master's degree in education.[86]

Tao's stay in America did have a strong impact on his intellectual development and contributed a great deal to his rise as a leading educator in China. As was the case with Hu Shi, John Dewey's pragmatic philosophy influenced Tao, who for the rest of his life would consistently emphasize the importance of practicality. Many Chinese, Tao once wrote, enjoyed talking about "national salvation through education," but they should know that "not just any kind of education will achieve that goal—only experimental education can save our country."[87] In principle, therefore, Tao did not differ greatly from Hu Shi, especially in the beginning. His subsequent experience in China, however, would send him on a very different path.

Unlike Hu Shi, who came back to China to become a top professor at the prestigious Beijing University, where he also served as the dean of the humanities, provost, and eventually president, Tao, upon his return from the U.S., chose to base his career in rural China, where his father had made a modest living as an old-fashioned tutor. Starting in the early 1920s, Tao, along with a few similarly minded American-educated friends, initiated a program to promote folk education. In their statement launching the project, drafted by Tao, the group declared their ambition "to gather a million comrades, construct a million schools, and transform a million villages."[88] In 1927, Tao founded a school to educate teachers who could work with the masses of China. At his rather unconventional institute, known as Xiaozhuang School, Tao endeavored to implement Dewey's teachings on the "education of life," placing heavy emphasis on practical training to prepare students for rural life. Tao, for instance, introduced a program known as "Little Teachers," in which young pupils were instructed to teach the illiterate grownups in their own families how to read. Tao also made special efforts to reach the little pupils' mothers and sisters, who, by old custom, were expected to avoid contact with male strangers. Tao was highly proud of this particular program and used to hail his pupil-teachers the way Chinese traditionally honored their emperors: "Ten thousand years of life to the Little Teachers!"[89]

The combination of Dewey's pragmatic philosophy and conditions in China thus led Tao to Chinese villages and away from the part of China that was the most intimate with America. Tao remained a liberal, but his experience in the countryside also nurtured an egalitarian spirit in him. He continued to value freedom but believed that liberty should be something of which all Chinese, including those badly disadvantaged, could realistically partake. He summed up his philosophy with the expression "Equal Footing, Free Growth."[90]

Of course, it was difficult to find and maintain the balance between "Equal Footing" and "Free Growth," and Tao's sympathy for the poor and disadvantaged gradually set him apart from intellectuals such as Hu Shi, who insisted on the sanctity of liberty. In 1927, Hu Shi wrote an article defending the United States against charges that America was excessively materialistic and individualistic. There was nothing shameful about "Dollar Worship," Hu wrote. Acquisitiveness was not all negative; it contributed to progress and prosperity, as evidenced by the advanced state of affairs in the United States. Given the poverty and destitution in China, it was not for the Chinese to denounce the more successful Americans. Tao took personal offense at this writing by his old friend, which he viewed as appalling denigration of the Chinese people.[91]

Tao tried to stay faithful to his reformist philosophy, but his progressive activities in the countryside eventually led to friction with the government. At a time when the Chinese Communists were carrying on an armed struggle in rural China, which Chiang's Nationalist government could not very well suppress, Tao's efforts to educate and mobilize peasants smacked of radicalism. Pressure on him mounted. At one point, Dr. Jiang Menglin—himself a Columbia-educated scholar and at the time Chiang's minister of education—advised Tao to be mindful of his words and actions. Tao was defiant: "Don't try to sew up our mouths."[92] In 1930, the government arrested a dozen or so teachers and students at Tao's Xiaozhuang School for alleged Communist connections. Tao had to shut down his experimental institute, and went into exile for some time.[93]

Tao now reevaluated his Deweyan principles. From the philosopher's "education of life," he moved to "life as education."[94] In a symbolic gesture, he reversed the order of the two characters in his given name, from Zhixing to Xingzhi, that is, from "knowledge-action" to "action-knowledge."[95] Tao had clearly embraced the concept of finding solutions to China's problems from within Chinese culture and reality. As he struggled to educate China's vast and deprived rural population in a time of great upheaval, Tao discovered the limited usefulness of his American experience, which was predicated on the existence of a stable constitutional system and orderly socioeconomic life. To try to apply the educational strategy learned in the affluent nations of the world to poverty-ridden rural China, Tao suggested, was like making a peasant eat Chinese food with knife and fork—instead of filling his empty stomach, the man would only cut his tongue.[96]

Does the change in Tao constitute the abandoning of the liberal ideal and the betrayal of his American education? Tao did not think so. As he saw it, in stressing the importance of the Chinese context while developing his educational programs, he was simply carrying Deweyan ideas to their logical end.[97] Tao remained committed to democracy and continued to view the United States as a strong guardian of such high ideals. In 1937, while Tao was traveling in the U.S., Chiang Kai-shek's Nationalist government detained

Figure 1.3

The Chinese Student Club at Teachers College, Columbia University, 1916. Hu Shi is the first from left in the front row. Tao Xingzhi, fourth from right, third row. In the group is also Jiang Menglin, second from left, back row, who served as China's minister of education and the president of Beijing University in the Nationalist era.

several of Tao's associates in China's pro-democracy movement. Tao convinced Professor Dewey and other American notables to sign a petition for the release of his friends.[98] In the mid-1940s, as World War II came to its end and China once again had to choose a path into the future, Tao, endeavoring to come to terms with the changing world, put forward a concept of democracy for China that drew from diverse sources. To him, Lincoln's "government of the people, by the people, for the people" was a good definition of political democracy. Dr. Sun Yat-sen's "People's Livelihood" and Roosevelt's "Freedom from Want" pointed to economic democracy. Tao's own campaign for Commoners' Education and the legacy of China's New Culture Movement would provide cultural and social democracy. To complete the scheme, Tao recommended Woodrow Wilson's self-determination and Dr. Sun Yat-sen's nationalism as ways to achieve democracy among countries of the world. Not insignificantly, Tao believed that his contemporary, Chinese Communist leader Mao Zedong, also made many valid points in his most recent work, *On New Democracy*.[99]

In 1945, Tao fell seriously ill. A few months before his death, Tao sent Dewey a letter in which he criticized the United States for its continued support of Chiang Kai-shek in the looming civil war in China. He speculated that American military industrialists were manipulating U.S. policies toward China, and he called upon Americans such as Dewey to help foster democracy in China. Democratic politics could lead to the resolution of many of China's problems, and the United States, an advanced democracy, could lend China the greatest assistance in this regard. The realization of ideals espoused by Sun Yat-sen, Lincoln, and Roosevelt, Tao believed, would make China stable and prosperous and the world as a whole would benefit from such a development. The U.S. assistance for Chiang Kai-shek, Tao feared, would deny China such a prospect.[100]

Clearly, by the end of his life, Tao harbored mixed feelings about the United States. He continued to revere many ideals that America epitomized, but he was also deeply troubled by the tremendous difficulties in realizing these ideals in his own country—so much so that he started to have doubts about the United States itself. His friend Hu Shi remained firmly pro-American all his life, but this was not the case with Tao. In his attempt to utilize American ideas to transform China, Tao came to recognize the wide gap between America and China.

Tao, however, never actually turned his back on America. This sets him apart from the third Chinese intellectual to be examined here—Zou Taofen. Raised in a family of modest means in the southeastern province of Fujian, Zou grew to be a leading journalist, publisher, and political dissident in the 1930s and 1940s. For his college education Zou attended St. John's University in Shanghai, an American missionary school, where he, defying his family's desire for him to major in engineering, studied literature. Zou's time at St.

John's constituted his major exposure to American culture until his tour of the United States in 1935. Upon graduating from St. John's in 1921, Zou worked briefly for a stockbroker and taught English at a local YMCA. He found his true vocation in 1926 when he started editing a small weekly newsletter for those interested in adult education. Dedicated to his cause, Zou turned the humble weekly into an immensely popular publication, raising the circulation of the magazine to over a hundred thousand, no mean feat in China then.[101]

The secret of Zou's success, first with his adult education weekly and later with his other publications, was his ability to relate to his readers. These were modestly educated Chinese youth—an apprentice at a rice store, for example—who felt emotionally and spiritually neglected in a country where the gun spoke the loudest. Zou's capacity for empathy and understanding saw him rise quickly as an influential journalist and publisher. He and his colleagues founded a publishing house as well as a chain of bookstores, which they expanded to include fifty-five branch offices across the country.[102] As Zou gathered a loyal following, his progressive politics irked the Chinese government. In 1933, after the assassination of one of his close associates, Zou had to flee abroad. Zou first traveled in Europe and the Soviet Union and then, in 1935, he went on a trip through the United States. He spent two months in America, an experience he reported vividly to his readers back home.

Zou fully recognized the global importance of the United States, which he characterized as "a full-fledged and most advanced capitalist state, a major power in world politics . . . a nation whose merits China can emulate and whose mistakes China should avoid."[103] As it turned out, in the U.S., Zou found more mistakes than merits. His political conflict with Generalissimo Chiang Kai-shek—along with the American-educated Soong crowd—evidently predisposed Zou to unfavorable views of the United States. The resentment toward the establishment and the idealism that he and his youthful audience shared back in China also led Zou to disdain the materialist culture and self-complacency he found in America. Unlike Tao Xingzhi the educator, who utilized America as an instrument in his struggle for democracy in China, Zou viewed Chiang's government as a Chinese incarnation of American failings. It also mattered that Hu Shi and Tao Xingzhi came to know the U.S. earlier in the century, whereas Zou visited the U.S. in the 1930s, during the Great Depression. Furthermore, immediately before his trip to the U.S., Zou had gone on a tour of the Soviet Union, which left strong positive impressions on him. In fact, he came upon the idea of visiting the U.S. after running into a group of young Americans, members of the National Students' League, who were then touring the world's first socialist country.

Zou's American trip did not start too well either. While in London, as he arranged his transportation to New York, a U.S. immigration officer treated him rather rudely. The incident opened an old scar on the minds of many proud Chinese like him—the discrimination against Chinese immigrants in the U.S. Writing home, Zou made American racism the topic of his first dispatch on his U.S. tour.[104] American racial prejudices would remain a major concern throughout his stay in the U.S. In fact, he made a special trip through the Deep South just to see the situation there with his own eyes, an experience that certainly did not soothe him.[105] At one point, he reported that he did not know how to respond when, as he set out for the South, his white American friends advised him not to sit in the back of a bus while traveling there.[106]

It was thus that Zou started his U.S. tour with a critical mind. Given his short stay in the U.S.—two months, compared to Hu Shi's seven years and Tao Xingzhi's two years—there was little chance that the trip could fundamentally alter his negative view. It did not help either that Zou's first stop in the U.S. was New York, which, with all its monstrosity, shocked the Chinese visitor.[107] In his dispatch entitled "Dissecting the World's Richest City," Zou took his readers to the poor neighborhoods of the East Side and Harlem.[108] He wrote of Wall Street tycoons who played America like a toy.[109] Technological advances in America had not adequately improved the lives of working Americans, Zou observed. In fact, in Zou's view, the American capitalist system, with an inherent tendency toward economic anarchy, hindered further progress.[110] On cultural matters, Zou wrote about William Hearst, "Public Enemy No. 1," telling his readers about the magnate's reactionary politics, yellow journalism, and extravagant lifestyle.[111] Nor did Zou have any kind words for Father Coughlin, the highly political radio celebrity, who, in Zou's view, was trying to divert a revolutionary deluge destined to sweep capitalism off its foundation.[112]

So, in the United States of the 1930s, Zou saw signs of an imminent revolution. A political outcast in his own country, Zou naturally identified with the labor movement in the U.S. He interviewed many progressive political activists, and fondly remembered many such Americans he met at various grassroots meetings.[113] With sixteen million people out of work and thirty million of their family members starving, American capitalism could not pull through without making some fundamental changes, Zou thought.[114] For the future of the United States, Zou saw just three possibilities: jingoism, fascism, and socialism.[115] Whatever the outcome, one thing was certain to Zou—the so-called American Way was doomed. Zou warned his compatriots back home who still had illusions about America: "We should open our eyes, see the facts, and stop behaving like fools!"[116]

Zou sounded every bit the rebel. Was he? If so, what kind of a rebel? One of Zou's progressive American friends was the only son of a rich industrialist, with whom the young man constantly quarreled. Zou witnessed several such exchanges while staying with the family for a few days, and was quite startled by the way the young man confronted his parents. The Chinese guest counseled his American friend to be patient; regardless of the issues, one ought to treat one's parents with respect. He would give same advice to another American friend, this time a young woman, who had a similar problem.[117] The behavior was characteristic of Zou, who, as the head of his publishing concerns back home, had always emphasized that all employees should act as if they were members of a big family. The preference for harmony and order was quite evident, and if Zou was indeed a rebel, he was a rebel against disorder and excessive individualism, the kind of ills that the Great Depression exemplified on a very large scale.

Thus, on his tour of America in 1935, Zou showed relatively little appreciation of individual freedom. If anything, his experience in the U.S. reinforced his preexisting preference for communal life and solidarity among people. Zou's cravings for collective identity and security would eventually lead him away from liberalism and turn him into a communist. In 1944, nine years after his trip to the U.S. and in the wake of many more tussles with Chiang Kai-shek's government, which included a short stay in prison, Zou, now dying of cancer, left behind a will in which he asked that the Chinese Communist Party admit him as a member and that the party take care of his children.[118] (The Communist Party did honor both of Zou's requests. It made Zou a member posthumously and cared for Zou's children. Zou's eldest son was sent to study in the Soviet Union, who, decades later, served as a vice premier of the People's Republic of China.)

The cases of Hu Shi, Tao Xingzhi, and Zou Taofen, three Chinese men of letters prominent in China of the first half of the twentieth century, demonstrate the diverse outlooks of Chinese intellectuals on the United States during the period. Of the three, Hu Shi was the most dedicated to the American Way and did the most to preserve his American intellectual heritage. Tao Xingzhi, for his part, followed the experimentalist and democratic principles that he learned in America but tried harder in making the connection between these ideas and conditions in China; in doing so, Tao revised his original understanding of America. In the case of Zou Taofen, the last of the trio, American individualist influence was thin to begin with and was worn down rather quickly as Zou struggled with Chiang's Nationalist government, which left Zou a strong believer in collective thought and action. When, in 1949, the Chinese Communists defeated the U.S.-backed Chiang Kai-shek and conquered China, Zou Taofen was, posthumously, among the victors. Tao Xingzhi had passed away as a respectable liberal patriot. Dr. Hu Shi fled to the United States, never to return to mainland China again.

III

When the Chinese Communists took control of China in 1949, they did so with strong support from China's general populace, especially the peasants. The capacity for mass mobilization was among the greatest strengths of the

Chinese Communist Party. When the CCP was founded 1921, it was so small that it had to cooperate with Sun Yat-sen's Nationalist Party and play the role of a junior partner in the alliance. From early on, however, the Communists pushed for a comprehensive social and political revolution, which would pitch the working Chinese against China's feudal warlords and the Western powers that dominated China. Identifying the collaboration between Western imperialist powers and Chinese warlords as the major cause of misery in China, the Communists sought to convince the Chinese masses to rise and fight against the dual evil. The lyric of one popular revolutionary song clearly conveys the message:

> Down with the Foreign Powers!
> Down with the vicious warlords!
> We strive for the success of the National Revolution,
> So that we can sing and celebrate all together![119]

By the beginning of 1927, forces of the Nationalist-Communist alliance had succeeded in defeating most of the warlords and claimed much of China. It was also at this time that the differences between the radical and the moderate elements in the coalition became irreconcilable. The Communists grew ever more aggressive in their efforts to mobilize peasants and workers to engage in class warfare, which frightened Chinese from families of means. In foreign relations, the Communists' strong anti-Western stance also greatly alarmed Chiang Kai-shek, the new head of the Nationalist movement, who worried that the powers would intervene in China by force. The tension between the Nationalists and the Communists came to a head in April 1927, when Chiang ordered a purge of the Communists from his government and army, arresting and executing many radical activists. Shocked and infuriated, the Communists staged a number of urban uprisings, but failed in their attempts. Some of the Communists who survived the purge and the subsequent revolts, most notably Mao Zedong, retreated into some mountainous regions of China, where they started an armed struggle against Chiang's Nationalist government. From 1927 to 1937, as they fought the Chinese Nationalists, the Communists continued to mobilize the Chinese masses with programs such as land reform and the promise of a just and egalitarian society. The goal of their struggle, the Communists declared, was to overthrow "Three Big Mountains" that weighed so heavily on the back of the Chinese people, meaning the oppressive forces of imperialism, feudalism, and state capitalism. In easily understandable language, the Communists explained the hardship of the Chinese masses in broad historical and global contexts, rallying millions of poor Chinese to fight for a cause believed to be moral and destined to triumph.

All this took place far away from China's urban centers, where Western influence concentrated, where Chinese such as Dr. Hu Shi lived and taught. In actual terms, few participants in Mao's rural revolution had any direct contact with the West or Western presence in China. The revolutionary followers, however, with their rudimentary Marxist outlook, held some clear if simple notions about the larger world and their own place in history. Their life was now meaningful, no longer merely about subsistence. Mao's well-disciplined peasant-soldiers thus lived, fought, and died in a culture that emphasized devotion and sacrifice, a culture that differed dramatically from the American individualism promoted by Chinese intellectuals such as Dr. Hu Shi.

In the late 1930s, when a full-scale Sino-Japanese War broke out, the Chinese Communist Party found it necessary to modify what it had to say about the West to its followers. To fight against a common enemy, Japan, the Chinese Communists and Nationalists once again formed a nationwide coalition, and the United States would soon become a wartime ally of China. These events led to changes in how the Communists presented America to the masses. In a Communist booklet published in 1937, entitled *Zhongguo yü Meiguo* (*China and the United States*), the author discussed the dual nature of the United States from the Chinese revolutionary point of view. On the one hand, the author cited copiously from communist masters such as Marx, Engels, Lenin, and Stalin to make the point that, eventually, a communist revolution would destroy the U.S., a capitalist and imperialist power. On the other hand, the author pointed out that, under the current circumstances, the United States, as "an enemy of an enemy," was a friend of China.[120] Revolutionary Chinese should therefore cooperate with Americans for the time being, all the while keeping in mind that, ultimately, communism would sweep the capitalist and imperialist America off the historical stage.[121]

As China's wartime cooperation with the United States expanded, the rhetoric on America became less reserved and more positive. Even though Chinese Communists knew preciously little about America, they, as skillful propagandists, did remarkably well in spreading what they intended their followers to know, even in the remotest parts of the country. In the summer of 1944, a group of U.S. airmen on their way to bomb Japan had to bail out of their damaged plane and landed in Japanese-occupied North China. Peasants from nearby villages quickly took them under their care and protected them from Japanese troops that were just a few miles away. The villagers then contacted Communist guerrillas operating in the region and successfully transported the U.S. airmen to safety. Asked how they knew what to do, the peasants explained that they understood that the "Big Noses" were friends; Communist soldiers had been visiting their village, and, among other things, taught them some songs, one of which was about the opening of the Second

Front in Europe.[122] Similar events took place in East China, where the New Forth Army, another Communist-led fighting force, operated in the nominally Japanese-occupied territories. In August 1944, five U.S. airmen who survived a crash received warm treatment and protection from local villagers. These foreigners, an old woman in a village told others, "were from the American New Forth Army."[123]

Whereas Chinese Communists mostly focused on the U.S. contribution to the war with Japan in their teachings about America at this time, they also demonstrated a willingness to reevaluate American society itself. By this time, Chen Duxiu, the founder and the first general secretary of the Chinese Communist Party was no longer a member of the CCP, expelled for his failure to deal with the crisis in 1927. As we have seen, in his more radical years, Chen had fiercely attacked American-educated Chinese. Now living in the political wilderness, the liberal-turned-communist reevaluated the past and current events in China. One should acknowledge, Chen wrote, that "democracy and liberty still exist in Britain and America to a certain extent," a fact that "no one will deny but a Nazi, a Fifth Columnist."[124]

In Yanan, the Communist base in Northwest China, Colonel David Barrett, the head of the U.S. Army Observers Group stationed there, asked Communist leader Zhou Enlai: Which of the two, the United States or the Soviet Union, was more democratic? Zhou's response: We Chinese Communists consider the Soviet Union to be "the world's greatest democracy, but, recognizing that it may take a hundred years for us to attain that level of democracy, we'd be most pleased if, in the near future, we can enjoy the kind of democracy in the U.S. today."[125] Here Zhou was being his tactful self, but he was also telling some truth. For one thing, it was certainly true that in China at the time there was preciously little democracy; for another, in the U.S., the policies of President Franklin Roosevelt, especially the New Deal, gave the Chinese Communists the impression that progressive forces were quickly transforming capitalist America.[126] From this perspective, the wartime cooperation with the United States was not only militarily necessary but also morally correct, well in accordance with the Chinese masses' revolutionary struggle in China.

Indeed, Chinese Communists spoke highly of Roosevelt, whom they described as "a banner for democracy."[127] When Roosevelt won his fourth presidential election, Mao Zedong, based in the remote northwestern China, sent a congratulatory telegram.[128] Speaking about the election to a gathering at the CCP Central Cadre School, Mao attributed Roosevelt's victory to the strong support of the American working class.[129] At one point, frustrated by the lack of direct contact with the U.S. government, Mao Zedong and Zhou Enlai volunteered to travel to Washington to meet with Roosevelt. They were confident that the great president would give them, and the Chinese Revolution, a fair hearing. Upon Roosevelt's death, Chinese Communists eulogized him as "a democratic giant,"[130] memorializing him both for his leadership in the anti-Fascist war and for his domestic policies.[131] The Final Resolution of the Chinese Communist Party's Seventh National Congress, passed in April 1945, named Roosevelt, along with Dr. Sun Yat-sen, as a progressive forerunner whose just cause the Communists vowed to carry on.[132]

This is not to say that the Communists fully trusted the Americans; far from it. They never had an opportunity to deal directly with Roosevelt. They did meet and negotiate with Patrick Hurley, Roosevelt's special envoy and later U.S. ambassador to China, but this particular experience had a negative effect on the Chinese Communists. Hurley, arriving in China in mid-1944, faced a virtually impossible task: to reconcile the differences between Chiang Kai-shek and his Communist rivals. Without a clear understanding of the situation in China, Hurley hastily committed himself to certain terms suggested by the Communists, only to find out soon later that Chiang would not even consider such positions. Hurley then told the Communists that he could not honor what he had promised them. The Communists, who suspected Hurley's sincerity from the beginning, were furious. They thought they had seen Hurley's true colors—a slimy capitalist politician dead set against communist revolution, unworthy of their trust.

Additionally, Hurley's personal style, boisterous and loud, perturbed the Chinese Communists, who had little experience dealing with the Americans, especially a high-positioned one such as Hurley. What Hurley viewed as candor, they considered ignorance and arrogance. The special envoy arrived in Yanan, a small dusty town in northwestern China, without giving advance notice. Zhou Enlai, Mao's righthand man in charge of the Communist Party's external relations, had arrived at the airport to welcome some unspecified American guests. Upon finding out who was the main guest, Zhou rushed back to the headquarters to round up Mao and other dignitaries for an impromptu welcome ceremony. Stepping out of his airplane, Hurley startled everyone by making a loud Indian war-whoop. Riding into town with Mao in an automobile—one of the few motor vehicles available in the Communist region—Hurley yelled at a peasant whose mule, frightened, refused to leave the road: "Hit him on the other side, Charley!" Before setting out to meet the Communists, Hurley had bragged to the Americans around him how, in the past, a U.S. oil company paid him one million dollars to conduct an eventually successful negotiation with the government of Mexico. Such a mindset did not help his dealings with the Chinese Communists, who, doctrinal as they were, already held the conviction that American capitalists cared about nothing but money. Later, Mao would call Hurley "a clown."[133]

With Roosevelt's death and the end of World War II, Chinese Communists became increasingly anxious over American intentions in China. Only a few months before, Mao had expressed his great confidence in the continued

Figure 1.4

Chinese Communist leaders meet with President Franklin Roosevelt's personal representative to China, Patrick J. Hurley. Mao Zedong is the second from left. The first from
left is Zhu De, the commander-in-chief of the Chinese Communist forces. Hurley wears
a bowtie. The first from right, in full view, is Zhou Enlai, who served as the Premier of
China from 1949 to 1976. On Zhou's right hand is the Nationalist general who accompanied Hurley on the 1944 trip to the Communist base Yanan. Dismayed by Hurley's
pro-Nationalist stance, Mao later called Hurley "a clown."

cooperation between the United States and the Soviet Union. In his words,
this was "one hundred percent dependable, one thousand percent dependable."[134] Now, facing the gloomy prospect of a civil war in China in which
the U.S. would clearly back Chiang Kai-shek's Nationalist government, Mao
quickly changed direction. Following the U.S. atomic bombings of Hiroshima
and Nagasaki in Japan in August 1945, some Chinese Communist newspaper-
men, who evidently had not quite grasped the true significance of the events
under the new circumstances, wrote to celebrate the formidable power of the
U.S. their ally. Mao was livid. Speaking at a party gathering, Mao lashed out
at the thoughtless officials, stating that some so-called Communists were so
shortsighted that they could not even compare to a "bourgeois general," Lord

Mountbatten of Britain, who did not believe that atomic bombs alone could dictate the outcome of a war. Mao warned his confused comrades to wipe off "capitalist pollution" from their dirty faces.[135]

After Japan's surrender, as civil war in China became imminent and the U.S. support for Chiang Kai-shek's Nationalist government was virtually certain in the event of an open conflict, the Chinese Communist Party moved quickly to educate the masses of China about the unjust American interference with China's internal affairs. In June 1946, the CCP launched a nationwide movement to push for the early withdrawal of U.S. forces still stationed in China. In a circular to its regional leaders, the CCP headquarters instructed party officials to mobilize people against Chiang Kai-shek and his American backers.[136] In an editorial dated July 4, *Jiefang ribao* (*Liberation Daily*), the Party's official organ, commemorated the creation of the U.S. Declaration of Independence. With this "historic document," the editorial said, the United States started a great tradition that was later continued and expanded by eminent figures such as Washington, Jefferson, Lincoln, and Roosevelt; the current U.S. government, by choosing to support Chiang Kai-shek's corrupt and dictatorial regime, trampled on the great American heritage.[137]

In September, the Communists took note of an incident in the U.S. in which President Truman dismissed from office Henry Wallace, then U.S. Secretary of Commence, because the latter openly criticized the U.S. government's anti-Soviet foreign policy. In an editorial, the *Liberation Daily* in Yanan observed that behind the particular incident was the conflict between Wallace and U.S. Secretary of State James Byrnes, which, the paper pointed out, epitomized the rivalry between the petty bourgeoisie and the capitalist establishment in America—the former wanted to continue Roosevelt's progressive policies whereas the latter tried to advance the interests of monopoly capitalists and some emerging "warlords."[138] Another Communist publication, *Qunzhong* (*The Masses*), declared confidently that even though Henry Wallace was forced out of office, "a second Wallace, a third Wallace, innumerous other Wallaces will soon come forward."[139]

In spite of such denunciation of the reactionary American capitalists, the Communist campaign, "U.S. Forces Out of China!," did not generate as much popular response as the CCP expected.[140] The U.S. aid to China during WWII was still fresh in the Chinese memory, and the general American presence in China before the war had also left some positive impressions. As noted earlier, before the war with Japan, the United States played a key role in the establishment of China's higher education. American Christian missions had also been active in Chinese society at large. In the eight years from 1928 to 1936, the Protestant churches of the United States alone sent approximately forty-five million dollars to support various activities in China. In fact, back then, more than half of all Christian missionaries in China had their origins back in the United States.[141] In the 1920s, in the coastal province of Shandong, American Presbyterian, Baptist, and Methodist churches founded and maintained about seven hundred elementary and secondary schools.[142] Some of these schools were created through the cooperation between American missionaries and local communities.[143] In one such case, a Daoist priest converted to Christianity volunteered his temple and land to the American Methodist mission for the construction of a school—a transaction endorsed by the local gentry.[144]

Medicine was another area in which the United States exerted strong influence in China. The Rockefeller Foundation, for example, committed large funds to the development of modern medicine in the country. Among other things, these efforts led to the creation of Peking Union Medical College, along with a hospital, which became a crucial center for medical training and research, graduating numerous professionals who led medical establishments across China.[145] At the end of the 1930s, a total of 148 U.S.-supported hospitals were in operation in China.[146] In 1936, when American journalist Edgar Snow visited the Communist Red Army in northwestern China, he came across a number of Red soldiers who had previously worked with American medical professionals, and who, in an odd historical twist, took part in the Chinese revolution partly due to the influence of Christian idealism. One of these Chinese, a barber in the Red Army, was nicknamed by his fellow soldiers "House of Christian Worship" because he still prayed daily. According to the barber, his former boss, an American doctor in Shanxi Province, was "a good man, who healed the poor without charge and never oppressed people." The man asked Snow to tell the doctor—if the reporter ever saw him—that "as soon as the revolution was over he was coming back to take his old job in the pharmacy."[147]

For better or worse, Hollywood also contributed significantly to the spreading of American influence in China. According to some estimates, in the years before 1949, about 70 percent of all movies shown in China were American productions.[148] One unfailing attraction of China's YMCA and YWCA, for example, was their frequent movie showings.[149] Schools in Guangzhou even found a way to integrate this popular youth hobby into their curricula—students were required to watch some American movies and then write essays about what they had viewed.[150]

After the United States entered the war against Japan, great efforts were made, by both the U.S. and Chinese governments, to enhance the positive image of America in China. The U.S. Office of War Information (OWI) played an active role in this endeavor. The OWI mobile movie team based in the southwestern city Kunming, for instance, served a monthly audience of 250,000. The Americans brought to their eager audience newsreels such as "We Fly for China," which featured Chinese aviators trained in the U.S; "Town," which showcased American democracy working at the local level;

and "The Biography of the Jeep," the Jeep being the archetypal American icon in China at the time.[151] Before one of these movie screenings, a local man with a gong would go around in the chosen village for the night to announce the event. Then, as the "tooting vehicle" carrying the movie man "crept up the narrow street . . . the lone American uniform set off a chorus of Ding Hows—that thumbs-up salute of good will."[152]

As more U.S. military personnel arrived in China, however, friction started to emerge, causing anxiety over American presence in China. This was especially true toward the end of the war, a time of heightened political sensitivity. Two particular areas generated much of the Chinese resentment—traffic accidents and sexual offenses. China's old, narrow streets were ill suited for motorized vehicles and young American GIs were not the safest drivers. In Beijing, in the month of January 1946, eleven traffic accidents involving American GIs took place, leading to the death of one Chinese and injuries to twelve others.[153] During the same period, in the neighboring city Tianjin, seventeen wrecks involving American GIs killed three Chinese and injured fifteen others; this was out of a total of twenty-two traffic accidents in Tianjin during the month.[154]

While the number of the incidents and resultant casualties was relatively small, the psychological impact was not. At the time, motorized vehicles were still new to many Chinese. The power and speed of automobiles had a shocking effect on the Chinese who were accustomed to a much slower pace of life, and who walked about or rode in rickshaws. Even more irritating to the Chinese, of course, was the fact that some flashy young foreigners, healthier, better-fed, better-clothed, were recklessly tearing up local streets, showing no respect to the natives. Understandably, Chinese newspapers covered such incidents extensively, further fanning public fury over the matter.[155]

As bad as traffic accidents seemed to be, it was another issue that generated the greatest concern—association between American GIs and local women. One newly minted term in the Chinese language quickly became popular, *Jipu nülang* or Jeep Girl, referred to young Chinese females who befriended American military personnel. A bitter contemporary lyricist thus portrayed the young woman:

> What is she cruising in?
> She is cruising in a Jeep.
> What does she keep chewing?
> She is chewing a piece of gum.
> What religion has she got?
> Just worship of America.
> Who is the girl anyway?
> An American made in China![156]

That Chinese women's association with foreigners became an issue should surprise no one. The Chinese, with their strong Confucian tradition, had always watched the activities of their women closely. Even Chinese Communists, who were supposedly radicals, were not tolerant in this regard and actively promoted asceticism and puritanical morality in their rank and file (which, one hastens to add, did not prevent Mao from marrying young movie star Jiang Qing, who had recently arrived from capitalist Shanghai). In an incident that took place in the Communist base Yanan, a U.S. Army officer stationed there with an observation group made a pass at a young Chinese woman. The matter was quickly reported all the way to top Communist leadership. Zhou Enlai, Mao's righthand man, personally approached Colonel David Barrett, the head of the American team, "to register his disapproval."[157]

In the Nationalist-controlled regions, given the larger number of U.S. troops deployed there, association between American personnel and Chinese women proved to be more prevalent. General Claire Chennault, who led the American Volunteer Group in China (the Flying Tigers, later reorganized as the Fourteenth Air Force), had to deal with quite a few disciplinary cases. Chennault punished and discharged some of the offenders, but he also tended to dismiss the accusations, attributing the troubles to the bad influence of some mischievous natives. At this time, General Chennault was courting Chinese journalist Chen Xiangmei (Anna Chen), and the two married in 1947.[158] The U.S. military authorities in the city of Xian took the issue more seriously. U.S. commanders in Xian noted that even though only a small number of Americans were reportedly involved in such incidents, the impression they left on the Chinese populace was striking. "All over this area," they wrote, "girls of middle-school age are cautioned by their teachers in class that the Americans are a dangerous bunch."[159]

Back in Washington, the State Department was concerned enough to bring the matter up with offices of War, Navy, War Information, and Strategic Services. On April 27, 1945, the State Department instructed U.S. diplomatic posts around the world to report on the subject.[160] Responses received suggest that the problem was not confined to China. According to the consulate in Algiers, French residents in the region often complained that some Americans were unable to "distinguish between 'good' or 'bad' women" and this frequently resulted in frictions with the local community.[161] Officials in Jerusalem reported that Orthodox Jews were dismayed over Jewish girls going out with American soldiers.[162] From Brussels, word came that while on the whole American troops there conducted themselves in an exemplary way, sometimes their "free-and-easy manner" was "interpreted as rudeness, or even brutality" and "excesses committed by individual members . . . in [the] realm of wine and women, if not of the proverbial song, did not advance the cause of Belgian-American understanding."[163]

The U.S. government's efforts to deal with the reported issues came too late in China, where one particular incident exploded to become a major political event, severely damaging the image of the U.S. in China. As the year 1946 came to its end, news broke out in Peiping (Beijing) that on Christmas Eve, Corporal William Pierson of the U.S. Marines abducted and raped a nineteen-year-old Chinese student and was arrested at the scene. A U.S. military court later convicted Pearson of rape, but the U.S. Department of the Navy later set Pierson free on the grounds of insufficient evidence. The Chinese government tried to keep the incident quiet but failed in the effort. The event, once it became public, caused a great uproar. To many Chinese this was the last straw. The incident was highly visible—it took place in Beijing and the victim was a preparatory student at Beijing University and the granddaughter of a prominent general under the late Qing Dynasty. The case rubbed the raw nerves of a proud people whose country, after suffering years of war and chaos, stood on the verge of collapse. Anger and frustration blew up. On December 30, students in Beijing took it to the street and led mass demonstrations. Within days, an "Anti-American Violence" movement evolved and soon spread to other Chinese cities.[164]

The Chinese Communist Party quickly responded to the new situation and seized leadership in the protest. On December 31, 1946, one day after student demonstrations in Beijing had started, the CCP headquarters telegraphed directives to its branch offices across the country, including those in Communist-controlled areas and those underground in the Nationalist regions. The party should take immediate actions to lead the popular protest and demand for the end of U.S. interference in China's internal affairs.[165]

A few days later, on January 5, 1947, the Communist headquarters sent another telegram to its regional leaders, providing further instructions on the unfolding anti-American movement. Party officials should "recognize the great significance of the campaign," which, according to the party's central leadership, "marks the arrival of the high tide in the nationwide revolution."[166] The next day, sensing that some party cadres still hesitated to commit all their strength to the anti-American movement, especially in the Nationalist-controlled areas, the party headquarters sent yet another order, criticizing these officials for being overly cautious and "lagging behind the masses." The central leadership urged party operatives to be more forceful in a critical struggle against American Imperialists and Chiang Kai-shek who had failed to protect Chinese people.[167]

The Anti–American Violence Movement seriously wounded Chiang's Nationalist government at a critical point in its rivalry with the Communists. A new constitution for China, introduced by the Nationalist government, went into effect on January 1, 1947, which should have been an occasion to highlight the progress made under Nationalist leadership. Now, instead

of celebrating the dawning of a new era, the government found itself struggling to suppress protests across the country and defending itself against the
charges that it slavishly served its decadent American masters. Less than a
month later, Washington declared that it would withdraw all remaining U.S.
forces in China. The pullout had been planned for some time, but the rising
anti-American sentiments in China certainly made the early implementation
of the policy more desirable.

On January 31, in an inner party directive, Communist leader Mao
Zedong hailed the great progress achieved in "the nationwide struggle against
imperialism and feudalism." "The students' movement that began in Peiping
[Beijing] has spread to other big cities all over the country" and created
"the second front" in the war against Chiang Kai-shek.[168] This was a critical
moment in the struggle over China's fate, which, along with other events
in the country, indicated that "the development in China is entering a new
stage." Based on this assessment, Mao confidently predicted an early victory
for the Communists.[169]

Mao had good reason to be optimistic. The Anti–American Violence
Movement drastically transformed the atmosphere in China, firmly placing
Chiang Kai-shek's Nationalist government and the United States on trial for
moral deficiency. In a country where all politics was cultural politics, where
the concept of Heavenly Mandate reigned supreme in the making and undoing
of governments, it was virtually fatal to lose the claim for moral superiority.
Three years of war still lay ahead, but the Chinese Communists had won a
critical battle.

2

"Farewell, Leighton Stuart!"

Anti-Americanism in the Early 1950s

On October 1, 1949, standing atop the Gate of Heavenly Peace in Beijing, Chinese communist leader Mao Zedong proclaimed the founding of the People's Republic of China. A new era in Chinese history thus began, one that would see drastic changes in almost all aspects of life in China, including the Chinese outlook on the United States. The revolutionaries who conquered China in 1949 owed very little to the United States or the American Way; if anything, they had triumphed in spite of them. The Chinese Communists had fought hard against Chiang Kai-shek's Nationalist government, which the U.S. had strongly supported. In the eyes of the Chinese revolutionaries, the American backing of the ill-fated Chiang clearly revealed the reactionary nature of the United States.

Nor did the American Way hold any appeal to Mao Zedong and his comrades. The Communists, in their long, strenuous struggle for power, had derived strength from iron-like discipline, stringent indoctrination, and vigorous mass mobilization. Liberal individualism had never been part of their strategy. In both philosophy and temperament, therefore, the Chinese Communists were squarely at odds with the United States of America. True, during World War II, Mao and his comrades actively courted Americans, but that was largely out of pragmatic considerations, which was also justified with some wishful thinking that President Franklin Roosevelt, with his New Deal, was leading America to socialism. The illusion of a progressive America quickly vanished at the end of World War II, when civil war broke out in China and a global contention between the capitalist West and communist East unfolded. Not surprisingly, by the time the Chinese Communists defeated Chiang Kai-shek, they had come to view the United States as a vicious and deadly enemy. The outbreak of the Korean War in 1950, which led to a direct Sino-American conflict on the Korean peninsula, only further hardened the hostility. When, in the early 1950s, the new rulers of China, following their communist ideology, set out to reorganize Chinese society, they did so with the conviction that the U.S. constituted China's most serious external threat and that America epitomized the very evil that they sought to uproot in China.

|

For a short while in 1949, when the Chinese Communists were poised to take control of China, some observers of Sino-American relations, both in China and the United States, were hopeful that China's new government and Washington would be able to maintain a working relationship with each other. By this time, the U.S. had resigned itself to the loss of the Nationalist cause in China and would not intervene directly on behalf of Chiang Kai-shek, who, along with some of his remaining troops, eventually fled to the island of Taiwan. Initially, the Chinese Communists did not seem to rule out the possibility of dealing with Washington, if only to keep the U.S. neutral as they took full control of China. When Communist forces captured the Nationalist capital Nanjing in April 1949, John Leighton Stuart, U.S. Ambassador to China, chose to stay in the city rather than retreat along with the Nationalist government to South China. Having learned about Stuart's decision, the Communists sent a young diplomat, Huang Hua, to pay a personal visit to the ambassador. Some years before, when Huang had studied at Yenching University in Beijing, Stuart was the president of that American missionary school.[1]

Larger events in China and worldwide, however, did not favor the mutual accommodation of Communist China and the United States. On the American side, Washington was not prepared to recognize China's Communist government. The State Department told American diplomats who were still in mainland China that their mission was solely to protect American interests and that their continued presence there did not mean U.S. recognition of China's new regime.[2] On the Chinese side, from early on, Mao considered domestic affairs his top priority and would handle U.S. relations with that agenda in mind. Specifically, he wanted to have a free hand in China, without the complications that continued American presence in China would inevitably entail. Speaking at a CCP Politburo meeting in January 1949, Mao observed:

> American Imperialists follow a two-fold strategy. . . . On the one hand, they support the Nationalists' war with us. On the other, they encourage Chinese Rightists to organize a legal opposition against us, demanding the right to veto our policies. . . . In the future, American Imperialists may even recognize New China, so that they can send agents over to sabotage. We must be alert to this possibility.[3]

Accordingly, Mao decided that his government should "clean house first and invite guests over afterward."[4] In other words, the communist state would take care of domestic affairs first; initiatives in foreign relations, especially those with regard to the United States, would have to yield to this main concern.

Two sources from the period well illustrate how Chinese communists viewed and presented the United States in connection to the overall conditions in China immediately after their rise to power in 1949. First, there was an official guidebook prepared by some party theorists at the time, *Meiguo shouce* or *The United States Handbook*. Then there was a series of commentaries that Mao penned for the New China News Agency.

The United States Handbook was by far the most sophisticated work on the United States that the Communists produced in the years before 1949. The chief editor of the work was Ke Bainian. A Guangdong native, Ke was educated at missionary schools who later turned against Christianity, joined the Communist Party, and rose to be a top CCP foreign affairs official. Toward the end of World War II, Ke served as the Communists' liaison officer to the Dixie Mission, the U.S. military observation group stationed in the Communist base Yanan at that time. In 1947, a group of Communist scholars started to work with Ke on his guidebook to the United States. Their goal, according to Ke, was "to draw a realistic and complete picture of the United States."[5] At this time, when the war with Japan had just ended and the conflict with Chiang Kai-shek just begun, there was a strong interest in the United States, which was poised to play a key role in Chinese affairs. The authors of the official manual on the U.S. diligently gathered their materials and delivered a reasonably factual coverage. As Ke recalled, "Over the course of a year and a half, a dozen or so of us worked tirelessly on the project. We heatedly discussed various issues among ourselves and revised our text several times before we brought the work to completion."[6]

Compared to works on the U.S. that appeared in China in the following years, *The United States Handbook* stood out with its broad scope and rich details. To be sure, the work was not free from ideological partiality, with an unmistakably negative verdict on America. Still, the general tenor of the book shows that it was intended to inform rather than simply denounce. The hefty manual contains more than five hundred main entries divided into fourteen chapters, respectively on geography, history, economy, corporate economy, government structure, finance, national defense, political parties, Sino-American relations, labor, progressive organizations, reactionary organizations, social issues, and cultural matters.[7] The book opens with simple entries such as "Where is the United States located?"[8] "When was America discovered?"[9] and, "Who were Washington, Hamilton, and Jefferson?"[10] Some of the matters covered seem ordinary or trifling, but they were new and interesting to the average Chinese in the 1940s, who still knew relatively little about the U.S. The book, for example, offered answers to questions such as "Does the U.S. President wear a uniform?"[11] and "What was the origin of the nickname 'Uncle Sam'?"[12]

Comprehensive in coverage, the handbook was also candid on many issues. It freely acknowledged, for instance, the affluence and power of the United States. "The United States is the strongest of all capitalist nations"; "before the war, of the world's total productions in a single year, the U.S. turned out thirty percent of the coal, thirty-five percent of the steel, and sixty percent of the oil." It also noted that half of the world's grain output came from U.S. farmers and that U.S. automakers manufactured eighty percent of all the cars on the planet. "In the postwar years, the United States accounted for fifty percent of the world's total industrial capacity."[13]

Similar frankness is evident in the coverage of political issues. The authors of the handbook cited the Taft-Hartley Act of 1947, which restricted labor union activities in the United States, as evidence for the "further Fascistiza-tion of the U.S. government."[14] At the same time, the authors took care to note that many Americans disliked that particular legislation, so much so that "Truman successfully ran for re-election . . . based on his opposition to the Act."[15] The handbook also presented the Wagner Act, characterizing it as "the most important federal legislation that protects workers' right to union-ize," which "outlaws practices such as 'yellow dog contracts,' 'black lists,' and 'company unions.' "[16] At another point, while applauding the "heroic growth" of "progressive movements" in the United States,[17] the handbook admitted that most of America's progressive organizations were "still very small and instable," often established "to address specific issues, tending to have relatively short life-spans."[18]

The United States Handbook also provided an extensive review of America's news media. The report on this subject begins with the *Daily Worker* pub-lished by the Communist Party USA and goes on to list eleven other daily papers, all of which had circulation numbers much larger than the modest 22,500 of the *Daily Worker*. The *New York Times*, the handbook reported, "represents the viewpoint of conservative Democrats," but in the election of 1948 the newspaper "chose to support the Republican Party."[19] The *Chicago Tribune*, the third largest daily newspaper in the U.S, was "controlled by the McCormick system" and was "a notorious fascist publication."[20] The *Chris-tian Science Monitor*, on the other hand, "is moderately enlightened on both domestic and international affairs."[21]

The introduction to American magazines opens with the *Masses and Mainstream*, "the authoritative publication of the American Left."[22] Descriptions of twenty-five other periodicals follow. *Time*, *Life*, and *Fortune*, "all owned by Henry Luce," were "extremely reactionary."[23] *Reader's Digest* was another "widely circulated reactionary publication, strongly anti-Soviet, anti-communist, and anti-democratic." In fact, "the Nazis frequently cited articles published in the *Reader's Digest*."[24] In contrast, the *Nation*, "a liberal journal slightly to the right, supported policies of the deceased president Franklin Roosevelt." The *New Republic*, for its part, "expresses the liberal views of lower and middle bourgeois American intellectuals," although recently the journal "has turned against [Henry] Wallace," its former editor.[25]

In short, while *The United States Handbook* demonstrated a clear communist doctrinal bias, it did offer a considerable amount of information on America. With the intention "to provide knowledge on the adversary,"[26] the authors of *The United States Handbook* revealed a healthy respect for the enemy.

Levelheadedness such as this, however, was on its way out. By the time Ke Bainian and his colleagues published their handbook on the U.S. in July 1949, China's domestic conditions and China's relations with the U.S. had both changed markedly. The People's Liberation Army swept across mainland China, smashing Nationalist resistance wherever it still existed. A Communist victory was now just a matter of time. The United States, seeing the hopelessness of the situation, virtually accepted as inevitable the defeat of Chiang Kai-shek and chose not to intervene directly on his behalf. With China under their control, Chinese Communist leaders felt that they did not have to bargain with the Americans for the time being, so that they could have a free hand in China to pursue their socialist agendas and also to demonstrate their solidarity with the communist bloc headed by the Soviet Union in the unfolding worldwide cold war.

This was evidently what Mao Zedong had in mind. On June 30, 1949, two months after the People's Liberation Army had captured the Nationalist capital Nanjing, Mao wrote to respond to some liberal Chinese who criticized the Chinese Communist Party for staying too close to the Soviet Union and too far away from the United States. In his writing Mao stated emphatically that "leaning to one side," the side of the Soviet Union, was indeed his government's policy. "Sitting on the fence will not do, nor is there a third road," Mao declared. He added:

> Only if we draw a clear line between reactionaries and revolutionaries, expose the intrigues and plots of the reactionaries, arouse the vigilance and attention of the revolutionary ranks, heighten our will to fight and crush the enemy's arrogance, can we isolate the reactionaries, vanquish them or supersede them.[27]

To accomplish these goals in China, Mao would accentuate rather than play down the difference between the Soviet Union and the United States so that his people could make a clear choice—to follow the good example of the

Soviet Union in the reconstruction of China. Certainly Mao was not bashful about telling the Chinese people what he thought of the Soviet Union and the United States.

On August 14, 1949, Mao authored a commentary for the Communist Xinhua News Agency. Entitled "Cast Away Illusions, Prepare for Struggle," this was the first of five articles Mao wrote over the course of one month in which he dissected a policy paper on Sino-American relations that the U.S. government had recently released. In the U.S. document, a white paper called *United States Relations with China: With Special Reference to the Period 1944–1949*, the Truman administration reviewed and defended Washington's China policies. Mao wrote to refute various claims made in the U.S. policy paper, but from the start it was clear that the Communist leader wrote primarily for the audience inside China, especially those Chinese who still wished to see the continuation of a close relationship between China and the United States in spite of the Communist victory. In particular, Mao took issue with the role of the so-called "democratic individualism" in China. In the China White Paper, Dean Acheson, the U.S. Secretary of State, had expressed his confidence that, the recent Chinese Communist victory notwithstanding, democracy and freedom would eventually prevail in China: "[U]ltimately the profound civilization and the democratic individualism of China will reassert themselves and she will throw off the foreign yoke. I consider that we should encourage all developments in China which now and in the future work toward this end."[28]

Acheson was foolhardy, Mao declared. He pointed out that the great majority of "Chinese students, teachers, professors, technicians, engineers, doctors, scientists, writers, artists and government employees, were [already] revolting against or parting company with" Chiang Kai-shek.[29] Some Chinese intellectuals "still want to wait and see," Mao acknowledged. These Chinese were "unwilling to draw a distinction between the U.S. imperialists, who are in power, and the American people, who are not. They are easily duped by the honeyed words of the U.S. imperialists." There were, indeed, Chinese "supporters of what Acheson calls 'democratic individualism,' " but the "social base" for "the deceptive maneuvers of Acheson" was at best "flimsy."[30]

"Flimsy" as it might be, Mao would not ignore the issue. To enlighten the wayward "democratic individualists of China," Mao hammered away at the injustice Imperialist America had done to China in the past. In his commentary entitled " 'Friendship' or Aggression?" Mao characterized Sino-American relations from 1840 onward as a story of American expansion at the expense of China, which, he said, "should be written into a concise textbook for the education of Chinese youth."[31] In another commentary of his, "Farewell, Leighton Stuart!" Mao downplayed the importance of the United States as an advanced and progressive nation. He admitted that the U.S. possessed impressive science and technology but argued that the know-how and material power only served the interests of American capitalists, who utilized them to "exploit and oppress the people at home and to perpetrate aggression and to slaughter people abroad."[32] As for American democracy, how could it be authentic if Washington chose to support "Chiang Kai-shek reactionaries, who are rotten to the core"?[33]

In "Why It Is Necessary to Discuss the *White Paper*," Mao took on the issue of "informed and critical public opinion," which, according to Acheson, "totalitarian governments, whether Rightist or Communist, cannot endure and do not tolerate."[34] Acheson's "informed and critical public opinion," Mao stated, was nothing but the propaganda of American capitalist media, "which are controlled by the two reactionary parties in the United States . . . and which specialize in the manufacture of lies and in threats against the people."[35] For the time being the U.S. government still wanted to hide behind "a veil of democracy," Mao pointed out; as class struggle intensified, the veil would be "cut down to a tiny patch." In any event, the so-called American democracy was no longer "what it used to be in the days of Washington, Jefferson and Lincoln."[36]

In his last commentary on the *China White Paper*, Mao warned his fellow countrymen not to be deceived by American capitalists; Acheson's appeal to Chinese "democratic individualists" revealed American Imperialists' attempt to "organize a U.S. fifth column" to overthrow the new revolutionary government of China. This effort, Mao was happy to declare, only "alerted the Chinese, especially those tinged with liberalism, who are promising each other not to be taken in by the Americans."[37]

Just in case the voluntary "promising" not to be deceived by the Americans did not provide enough guarantee, the Chinese Communist Party launched a major publicity campaign to eliminate remaining American influence in China. In Shanghai, General Chen Yi, the Communist leader for East China, spoke on the subject at a "study conference" for academics and intellectuals. "It is naïve to think that the 'democratic individualists' Acheson referred to no longer exist in New China," Chen warned. He urged his audience to "cleanse ourselves, organizationally as well as ideologically, so as to prevent the invasion of imperialist viruses."[38]

An agenda was set, one meant to uproot American influence in China, which, in the form of "democratic individualism," constituted a major obstacle in the path of China's socialist revolution. Both in terms of ideology and in terms of practical politics, the Chinese Communists believed that New China would fare much better without the complications that would inevitably come from continued American presence in their country. The Chinese revolution was to continue, and this demanded that the reactionary America get out of the way. A line was thus drawn, which would soon harden with the outbreak of the Korean War in June 1950, a conflict in which China and the United States came to confront each other.

II

The so-called democratic individualists,[39] who, in Mao's view, personified American influence in China and constituted a threat to his revolution, actually behaved rather meekly after the Communist victory in 1949. In some cases, this was due to the pressure from the new government. In some other cases, Chinese intellectuals willingly cooperated with the new authority in the country. Whatever one might say about communism, the Communist victory in 1949 ended a long period of civil war and foreign aggression, a development that was warmly welcomed by many Chinese. In contrast, Chinese liberals' effort to reform China in earlier years had amounted to virtually nothing. This made some of the progressive Chinese intellectuals feel an inner guilt, a sense of inadequacy, which prompted them to reexamine themselves and to try to immerse themselves in the prevailing revolution in the country. To do otherwise would be selfish and unpatriotic, especially now that China was fighting against U.S. forces on the Korean peninsula.

For decades before 1949, members of China's educated elite, many of them trained in the West, had actively advocated liberal changes in China, only to see their country, especially the Chinese masses, sink ever deeper into chaos and misery. Then there came the rescuers—simple, sturdy peasant-soldiers led by the Communist Party, who, dedicated and strictly disciplined, fought courageously and successfully for goals larger than individual fulfillment. Upstaged and overshadowed by this development, many Chinese intellectuals actively sought to reinvent themselves in New China. One way to achieve redemption was to sever the link to the self-centered, decadent America.

Some of these Chinese intellectuals made their conversion to the communist revolution well before 1949, in struggles against Japanese invaders and Chiang's Nationalist government. In 1936, when American journalist Edgar Snow traveled to northwestern China and interviewed Communist guerrilla fighters there, accompanying him was a young Chinese by the name of Huang Hua. Huang studied at Yenching University, an American missionary school in Beijing; after joining the CCP in the thirties, Huang rose to be a leading Communist diplomat. As noted earlier, in 1949, it was Huang who paid a personal visit to John Leighton Stuart, the former president of Yenching University who, as the U.S. Ambassador to China, had chosen to stay in Nanjing after the Communists' capture of the Nationalist capital.[40]

Sharing a similar experience was Yang Gang, another Yenching graduate and a sharp-minded young woman who, in the 1930s and 1940s, worked as a noted reporter for *Dagong Bao* (*Ta Kung Pao* or *Dagong Daily*), a prominent liberal newspaper. From 1944 to 1948, Yang lived in the United States, studying at Radcliffe College while writing as a columnist for her newspaper back home.[41] In her reports during these years, Yang relentlessly denounced the U.S. government. By supporting Chiang Kai-shek, Yang felt, the Untied States was putting money ahead of humanity, turning away from the great legacy of Franklin Roosevelt, and drifting into an antidemocratic and anti-Soviet hysteria.[42]

In 1948, as the Chinese Communists took control of China, Yang left for home. The Communist Party warmly welcomed her, applauding her for her dispatches from the U.S.[43] When Mao declared the founding of the People's Republic of China on October 1, 1949, Yang was on hand to witness the event, which she reported with great excitement: "Our thousand-year-old great hope, our thousand-year-old quest for a state of independence, democracy, peace, unity and prosperity, will no longer be just a dream. . . . It is becoming reality." In the coming years Yang held important positions in the Chinese government—at the foreign ministry and the Premier's office.[44]

Yang's enthusiasm for New China accorded well with her negative views of America. In 1951, when her writings about the U.S. were published as a book, Yang reasserted her opinion that the United States was all about money. In America there was "a raider's mentality," Yang wrote, which made people "fend for themselves and care little about others," which "exalts extreme freedom with no regard for the fellowmen and society at large."[45] In the previous year Yang had written about F. O. Matthiessen, a leftist professor whom she had come to know while taking courses at Harvard University and who had recently committed suicide. Yang remembered Matthiessen as a warm, progressive intellectual, and expressed her "shock and anger" at his sudden death, which she believed to have taken place as result of political persecution. The case of Matthiessen, an "honest man with a conscience," made it clear that "the American bourgeois democratic tradition" was contending with "American imperialism and militarism," but the former, "frail and vulnerable," was losing the fight."[46]

While some educated Chinese turned against the United States—"achieving enlightenment" as Yang Gang put it[47]—prior to 1949, many other Chinese intellectuals, especially the older and more established ones, came to the moment of reckoning after the Communist conquest. Painstakingly, these intellectuals reviewed their past and tried to come to terms with new reality. In a way, this was not just about communism; self-examination and self-cultivation had been an important part of China's long Confucian tradition. Many intellectuals, eager to repudiate their "bourgeois" and "individualist" mindset, carefully scrutinized their life and found no small number of failings in character and conduct. This happened to Cao Juren, a Western-educated essayist. When, immediately after the Communist conquest, some Chinese urbanites sneered at the hillbilly ways of the newly arrived Communist peasant-soldiers, Cao came to the troops' defense:

> Having muddled along in metropolises for over two decades, I now understand how [Oswald] Spengler once felt. We live in a "civilized, modern world": a 1950 car, sweet and charming social-ites, air-conditioned skyscrapers, dazzling neon lights, dance and songs, so on and so forth. With all this, what did we achieve? Inner void and despair. . . . This metropolitan existence is nothing more than an imitation of Hollywood.[48]

The longing for authenticity in life surged forward in the context of post-1949 events, when drastic social and political changes took place in China. The Communists, in a sharp contrast to the helplessness and timidity of China's liberal reformers in the preceding decades, moved resolutely to deal with some major problems that had ailed their country for a long time. The new government, for instance, quickly carried out a nationwide land reform, confiscating fields of large landowners and distributing them among hundreds of millions of poor peasants, thereby eradicating a root cause of instability in China. In the social domain, the Communists speedily eliminated widespread vices such as prostitution and opium smoking, accomplishing feats that few Chinese thought possible just a few years before.

To be sure, the changes came at a high cost, as the Communists utilized many heavy-handed measures in the name of social progress. Still, to a people who had experienced so many failures and seen so much despondency in the past, the results were stunning and impressive. Before 1949, Xu Zhucheng served as the chief editor of a foremost liberal newspaper in China. In the late 1950s, Xu would run afoul of the Chinese government and was denounced as a Rightist opposed to the revolution. Prior to these events, however, Xu, along with many Chinese like him, had been impressed by how much the Communists accomplished within just a few years after 1949. Decades later, while reviewing the diary he kept in the early 1950s, Xu, elderly and much weathered, still marveled at the idealism and "democratic atmosphere" that he witnessed back then.[49]

Not surprisingly, American-educated Chinese intellectuals had the most soul-searching to do, whose U.S. connection was clearly at odds with New China. Dr. Zhou Peiyuan, a renowned physicist trained at Caltech, was the provost of Qinghua University in Beijing when the Communists came to power. Inspecting his past life, Zhou faulted himself for "selfishly seeking personal glory and hardly caring about anybody or anything else."[50] Zhou related how his college education at Qinghua University, which started as a preparatory school for Chinese students who wanted to study in the United States, set his mind on "becoming a scientist of international fame."[51] With such single-mindedness, once he arrived in the U.S. in the 1920s, he saw "only skyscrapers and automobiles . . . but little of working people's misery."[52] Upon his return to China, Zhou continued to believe that "expertise trumps everything else" and stayed aloof to the rising revolution in his country.[53] After 1949, however, even his own children rebelled against him. His teenage daughter, in defiance of her father's arrangement for her to finish high school and attend college, joined a corps of Communist cadres selected to work in newly liberated South China. When the father tried to sabotage his daughter's plan by checking her into a hospital, the girl walked out and set out on her revolutionary journey.[54]

Dr. Zhou Jinhuang at the Peking Union Medical College also reflected on the way he handled the conflict between personal aspiration and public service. Founded with funds from the Rockefeller Foundation, the PUMC had been built as "China's Johns Hopkins," with a mission to engage in advanced medical research and educate leaders for China's medical profession. This plan, said Zhou Jinhuang, led to elitism and disregard for the well-being of the vast Chinese masses. In 1949, when Zhou had a choice of either continuing to work in the city of Wuhan in Central China or relocating to Beijing, Zhou opted for the better research facilities and higher living standards in Beijing. This was in spite of local officials' appeal to him to stay in Wuhan, which had a greater need for Zhou's expertise.[55] The particular decision, Zhou now reflected, could be easily justified with his "liberal-individualist" education at the Union Medical College; from the new revolutionary point of view, however, the action was morally lacking.[56] This liberal-individualist way of thinking, Zhou noted, also explained why, up till now, "no Union men have ever worked for extended periods of time" in the Chinese countryside.[57] For the same reason, Zhou thought, his colleagues at the Union College had been notoriously slow in developing medical treatments that were accessible and affordable to the peasants of China.[58]

In Shanghai, Zheng Junli, a celebrated film director, probed deep into his background to account for "bourgeois individualism that had long infected" him. The son of a struggling grocer, Zheng grew up an ambitious young man determined to rise above the debts and humiliation that had ruined his father's life. This early experience made him susceptible to American individualist influence, Zhheng thought. To succeed in the movie industry, Zheng "whole-heartedly embraced American cinematic commercialism," and, in doing so, he turned his back on the progressive theater movement in which he had been briefly involved.[59] (One of Zheng's acquaintances during his progressive phase was Lan Ping, later known as Jiang Qing, the actress who in 1937 left Shanghai for Yanan, the small dusty town in Northwest China, where she married the Communist leader Mao Zedong.)

Educated Chinese of lesser status, eager to demonstrate their own political consciousness and gain recognition in the prevailing revolution, also searched dark corners of their inner being for slightest indication of American individualist influence. One such aspirant was Chen Jieying, an architecture student at Jiaotong University in Beijing. When Chen was small, her father, an American-educated engineer, frequently talked to her about the wonderland that was the United States. Growing up, Chen Jieying fashioned herself "in the images of American movie stars," indulging in expensive dresses and playing "romantic games" with her boyfriends.[60] Shortly before the Communist takeover, Chen's father sent her to America to attend college. The young woman, however, was unhappy. Chen recalled how once she hosted a rowdy party that lasted for three days, and how, at the end of the event, she felt even more depressed.[61] Chen soon gave up her life in the U.S. and returned to China, where the new Communist government sent her and some other progressive-minded college students to rural areas where they were to organize peasants for the revolution. Living a new, rustic life in the countryside, Chen continued to search for her moral deficiencies. She was troubled, for example, by the fact that she still enjoyed American jazz, more so than Chinese folk music. She was also worried that, having become accustomed to milk and bread, she could not very well accept sorghum porridge, nor could she very well resist the urge to dine out at restaurants."[62]

Some other Chinese, however, did not let their inner guilt to break them down, and refused to go along with the revolution. Among these was Shi Qili. Having spent some years in the United States, Shi returned to China after 1949. Initially, Shi, like many other young Chinese captivated and inspired by the revolution, eagerly sought opportunities to serve the great cause. After spending so many years in the U.S., however, Shi found it hard to accept certain policies and practices of the Communist government. For example, rationally he recognized the need for land reform in China, but the violence and brutality that accompanied the reform, which he witnessed in his home village, made him worry about the loss of individuals' rights, which he still cherished.[63] He also objected to the ideological control that was being established in China. He lamented what happened to local libraries, where politically unacceptable books were removed from shelves. In America, said Shi, "one can find both socialist and capitalist materials. . . . Here, one does not smell one bit of capitalism."[64] Shi attended the Revolution University, a cadre training camp set up to reeducate Chinese intellectuals like himself. He found the stringent lifestyle insufferable—some trainees were denounced as "degenerates" simply because they would gather at a local teahouse to sip tea. Before long, Shi left China again.[65]

Whereas Shi could choose to leave China, most Chinese did not have such an option. In any event, the resistance on the part of people such as Shi did not escape the attention of the Chinese government, which kept up its effort to reform Chinese intellectuals. In 1954, for example, the campaign against "democratic individualists" took the form of a drive to criticize Dr. Hu Shi, China's leading pro-American intellectual, who had left the country to reside in the United States when the Communists came to power in 1949. Critics condemned Hu as a reactionary opposed to the Chinese revolution and a traitor who chose America over China.[66] By this time, the euphoria surrounding the Communist victory in 1949 had cooled down significantly and many Chinese intellectuals started to wonder anew about the merits and weaknesses of the systems in China and America. In due time, such quiet contemplations would erupt into a heated public debate.

III

In the meantime, revolutionary changes in the country were transforming the way the Chinese masses viewed the United States of America. The Chinese Communists, in their rise to power, had been extremely successful in mobilizing average Chinese to support their political cause. After taking control of China, as they moved to consolidate their position in the country, the Communists continued to emphasize the importance of educating the general populace to create a proper and unified worldview. The onset of the Sino-American conflict in Korea in 1950 only made the particular task even more urgent. After all, not too long before, the Americans had fought alongside the Chinese against Japanese aggression, and in China the United States had been widely celebrated as the world's mightiest democracy. The Communist victory in China, which took place despite American support for Chiang Kai-shek, together with the U.S. entry into the Korean War, demanded that the Chinese masses view the United States correctly, that is, as the most vicious and dangerous enemy of revolutionary China.

In November 1950, one month after Chinese forces entered the war in Korea, the CCP central leadership issued guidelines for a nationwide anti-American campaign. In a document entitled *How to View the United States*, the party instructed its operatives to take action to dispel certain widespread misconceptions about the U.S. Among the erroneous ideas targeted: "China depends on the U.S."; "The U.S. is a civilized democracy from which China should learn"; and "The U.S. is immensely powerful, the ill-will of which no country should risk."[67] According to the official document, there were three key elements in a proper attitude toward the United States. "First, hate the U.S.—the U.S. is a deadly enemy of the Chinese people." "Secondly, despise the U.S.—the U.S. is a corrupt imperialist state, headquarters of worldwide

decadent reactionary forces." "Thirdly, stand up to the U.S.—the U.S. is nothing but a paper tiger, definitely defeatable."[68]

The message was simple and clear. The real challenge was how to convey
the message to hundreds of millions of average Chinese. Confronting the task,
the Communist Party organized meticulously at the grassroots level and also
took care to integrate their larger ideas with the everyday concerns of the
Chinese people. In this regard, Northeast China, which borders Korea, set
an example for the rest of the country. The particular region (aka Manchuria) had been a Japanese colony when the Communists took control in the
late 1940s. Finding the area "politically backward," the Communists moved
quickly to deal with the problem. As part of this effort, in the spring of 1950,
an extensive propaganda network—*xuanchuan wang*—was created, staffed
with local activists whose duty was to explain to their neighbors, in easily
understood language, what was happening in the country and in their own
life. By the end of 1950, the said network in the Northeast had enlisted the
service of 117,238 folk activists.[69]

After China entered the Korean War in October 1950, the Communist
Party, anxiously searching for ways to rally popular support for the war effort,
took note of the initiative in Northeast China. On January 1, 1951, the CCP
Central Committee sent out a directive ordering party officials across the
country to follow the example of the Northeast and institute a nationwide
propaganda network.[70] In the directive, the Party Center criticized insufficient
attention to ideological work, noting that "rumors and reactionary misinforma-
tion have been circulating among the masses, virtually unchecked." This had to
stop. To guide officials in the new initiative, the Party Center provided a series
of themes on which the new propaganda network should focus its attention.
Among the talking points were simple ideas such as "China has emerged as
a major political and military power in the world" and "Chinese and Korean
peoples have won great victories in their resistance to the U.S. aggression."[71]

The Party Center's instruction led to immediate actions across China. The
Party Committee of East China passed a resolution demanding the establishment of a regional propaganda network within six months; leading officials
at all levels would be held personally responsible for failures in the particular
task.[72] In the Northeast, where the idea for a folk publicity network had first
appeared, the praise from the Party Center as well as the region's proxim-
ity to Korea provided additional incentives for local officials to move fast.
Activists in the region strove to explain to people around them why China
had to fight Americans in Korea and why China would definitely win the
war. "The American devils mean to follow Japan's example, using Korea as
a springboard to invade China." "If American devils come here, we won't be
able to continue the good life we enjoy now." "We must assist Korea; it is like
helping a neighbor to put out a fire in his house." "Winning a war depends

on men, on morale, not on weapons." "We have five million soldiers. The Americans have more airplanes, but they cannot hold ground with planes. Nor can battleships sail on dry land." "We also have a big brother, the Soviet Union, to help us, so victory is surely ours."[73]

The folk publicists, just like their audience, were ordinary men and women with relatively little education. This, however, proved to be an advantage rather than handicap since what mattered in the particular situation was not so much intellectual acumen but trustworthiness. At the First Machinery Factory in Shenyang, of the twenty-two activists enlisted for publicity work, one had a college education; three were high school graduates; seventeen others studied in elementary schools; the remaining one was described as "roughly literate."[74] These men and women spoke the language of their coworkers and were intimately familiar with what these people thought. Meng Tai, a "model worker" at Anshan Steel Plant, thus explained to his fellow workers the weakness of the United States: "It is like a beast with its hind legs in Europe, its body over America, and its front limbs stretched all the way out to Asia. How long do you think the creature can hold up like this?"[75] Zhao Guoyou, a worker at the Third Machinery Factory in Shenyang, referred to recent changes in

Figure 2.1

Zhou Enlai, the Chinese premier and foreign minister, signs the Sino-Soviet Treaty of Friendship, Alliance, and Mutual Assistance, with Mao and Stalin witnessing. This took place in February 1950, four months after the founding of the People's Republic of China.

his own life to reinforce the message he was promoting. Given how he had benefited from the revolution, said Zhao, he, for one, would hate to see the Americans bring back Chiang Kai-shek's Nationalist rule. When Chinese forces in Korea suffered setbacks and some of his coworkers panicked, Zhao brought his quilts to the factory and lived at the workshop to shore up his friends' confidence.[76]

The effects of rudimentary measures such as these must be understood in the overall context of China in the early fifties, when contacts with the United States, direct or indirect, came to end. Take, for example, the case of American Christian schools in China. As noted earlier, prior to 1949, these American-supported institutions figured prominently in China's modern educational system, with at least seventeen colleges, more than two hundred high schools, and some fifteen hundred primary schools.[77] After 1949, links between these schools and America weakened; after the outbreak of the Korean War, such connections stopped to exist, when the Chinese government issued new guidelines to regulate "American-sponsored cultural, educational, charitable, and religious organizations."[78] Furthermore, as part of the socialist revolution in China, teachers and students at the schools historically linked to the United States were urged to cleanse themselves of any lingering American influence. At Huanan Women's College in the southern city Fuzhou, a school that used to be affiliated with the Methodist Episcopal Church, students rose to denounce the way "American vanity" had reigned on their campus, where girls "were obsessed with nice dresses, good looks, money, and English proficiency, which would help them achieve social respectability." The motto at the school back then had been "All by American Standards," so much so that students "hardly remembered that they were actually Chinese."[79]

In Beijing, at Huiwen High School, another American missionary institution, students condemned American publications and movies with sexual and violent themes as a major source of wicked influence. One student recalled how he would skip class to go to theaters to watch American movies, sometimes two or three of them a day:

> My life was empty then. I did not know what I was living for. I thought I was happy as long as I had American films to watch, chocolate to chew, and American clothes to put on. I drank and smoked, trying to imitate heroes in the movies.[80]

His life hung by such a thin thread, the boy said, that when theaters stopped showing American films after the Liberation, he attempted suicide. Students and teachers at the school gathered several hundred pieces of the offending materials—American books, periodicals, phonograph records, pictures—and burned them in a bonfire.[81]

The cultural void thus created did not remain unfilled. New, proper materials soon became available. In 1950, the year after the founding of the People's Republic, of the roughly 1,750 translated books in the humanities and social sciences published in China, more than three-fourths were of the Russian origin.[82] Most of the few dozen works about the United States were authored by Soviet authors too. Three publishing houses brought out their own editions of Maxim Gorky's scathing account of the United States, *In America*. A book by R. Parker, *Conspiracy against Peace*, was published in four different versions, as was A. Bucar's *Truth of American Diplomats*. In contrast, a complete list of American literary works published in China in that year does not go far beyond Jack London's *White Fang* and *Call of the Wild*, Mark Twain's *Life on the Mississippi*, and Howard Fast's *Freedom Road*.[83]

The following year, 1951, witnessed an explosion in the number of publications on the United States—about two hundred of them came out in the first three months.[84] This, of course, took place in reaction to the outbreak of the Korean War. Predictably, the publications applauded China's war with the U.S. on the Korean peninsula and condemned the U.S. as an imperialist aggressor. Some of these works were simple and plain, clearly meant for Chinese with little education. There were, for example, picture books such as *The American Life Style* (*Meiguo shenghuo fangshi*), which featured two dozen or so photographs, evidently reproduced from American publications. Captions for the images in the booklet included "Unemployment drives people to search for food in garbage cans"; "According to statistics, one-third of the U.S. population live in shanties like this"; "Due to Fascist agitation and racial discrimination, blacks can be whipped or even killed on account of some frivolous charges, and all this is tolerated by U.S. law"; "Alcoholism is one way for many Americans to escape from their misery"; and "Poverty, unemployment, and persecution turn these people into psychopaths; . . . patients like these numbered two hundred thousand a year."[85]

In the East China Military Region, soldiers of the People's Liberation Army received readers such as *The True Face of American "Civilization."* Among subjects covered in the tract were "The United States—A World Full of Secret Agents"; "A Man Who Sells His Blood"; "Suicide, Robbery, and Striking It Rich"; and "Heaven for Dogs, Hell for Men."[86]

Theatergoers now watched plays featuring similar themes. In *Transformation* (*Zhuanbian*), a play situated in the late 1940s, the last days of American presence in China, members of a family in Beijing argue over what to make of the United States. The eldest son and his sister are diehard admirers of the U.S., until their American "friends" swindle and betray them.[87] In *The Bright Sky* (*Minglong de tian*), an American-trained scientist awakens to the futility and injustice of his individualist ways, rejects his American past, and devotes himself to serving the working people of China.[88] In the drama *This*

Is the American Way of Life (*Zhe jiu shi Meiguo de shenghuo fangshi*), a wide range of American characters make their appearance. A U.S. Senator scams everyone around him but always does so within legal bounds. A former FBI agent now edits a McCarthyist journal, *Red Channels*, which he uses to blackmail progressive Americans. An aerospace industrialist meets with General McArthur in Tokyo, from whom he secures his contracts. Members of a local citizens' committee harass a school teacher, questioning her loyalty to the United States. A black woman strives to help her son who faces false criminal charges. The real hero in the play, a labor activist who happens to be the nephew of the corrupt senator, supports a dock porters' strike, and for this he is shot and wounded.[89]

On the big screen, changes were probably the most noticeable. As mentioned earlier, Hollywood movies had been highly popular in China. Before World War II, as many as 350 American films were screened in the country every year. In the years between the end of World War II and the Communist victory in 1949, Chinese audience saw even more American movies.[90] After 1949, for about a year Hollywood productions continued to show in Chinese theaters. For instance, in Shanghai, in the month of May 1950, a total of seventy-five American movies were screened, drawing in a half-million viewers.[91] The run came to its end when China entered the Korean War in 1950, as the Chinese government proscribed all American movies.[92] Fans of Hollywood were now urged to think about the ill effects of Hollywood,[93] to reflect on how American movies induced people to live in "a world of fantasies," making them "detest hard, honest work."[94] In the coming years, virtually no U.S. movies would be publicly shown in China, with rare exceptions such as *Salt of the Earth*, which is scripted by Michael Wilson and tells the story of a miners' strike in New Mexico.[95]

Some Chinese became quite serious about the drive against American influence. In the city of Jinan, an elementary school teacher wrote to an educational journal and complained about the portrayal of the United States in an instructor's handbook on geography. In his view, there was too much emphasis on the economic strength of the U.S. For example, the textbook stated that China's coal reserve averaged five hundred tons per capita, compared to the eleven thousand tons for the United States; also presented in the handbook was that the United States accounted for 77 percent of all the automobiles produced in the world. "All these statistics and comparisons," the teacher wrote, "obscures the fact that Imperialist America is suffering from severe crisis."[96]

In a village in Henan province, a first grade teacher tinkered with an old fairy tale to instruct his pupils on the fight against American Imperialism. In the original story, a hardworking grandpa grows such a huge turnip that he himself cannot dislodge it from the soil and has to get the help of grandma and the dog and cat in the family. In the new version of the tale, the big turnip is the United States and the other characters in the story are the peoples around the world who unite to uproot the evil that is American Imperialism. Eventually the eager young teacher had to give up his new class plan; his colleagues pointed out to him that he could not very well explain why the turnip—American Imperialism—had grown so strong in the first place.[97]

All this may sound a little eccentric or frivolous, but China in the 1950s was largely a country of peasants who were experiencing a revolutionary euphoria and facing a war against their country. To these people, the issues at hand were quite real and critical. China was engaged in a violent war in Korea, confronting the world's mightiest power, the United States. Just as importantly, inside China, a sweeping political, economic, and social revolution was taking place that, in essence, was a movement toward collectivization, which called for the sacrifice of personal interests for public good. In this sense, radical as it was, Mao's communist revolution also reaffirmed certain traditional Chinese values that focused on loyalty and dedication. In this overall context, American culture, with its emphasis on individual freedom, appeared as an antithesis to the Chinese revolution. Given this, many Chinese in the 1950s found it quite logical to conclude that commitment to the Chinese revolution meant the rejection of America, and vice versa.

Of course, all revolutions, albeit originally meant to effect change, have a tendency to create their own set patterns. Fresh ideas turn into ideology, and inflexibility becomes the norm. In China of the 1950s, after a few years of drastic changes early in the decade, the revolution that had excited and inspired so many Chinese started to demand conformity. Becoming concerned with the new trend, some Chinese would take a fresh look at the situation and raise new questions on how China should view the United States of America. That turned out to be a momentous move with serious consequences.

3

Challenging a Taboo

China's Liberal Critics and America in 1957

For Chinese intellectuals, 1957 was a year of high-flying hope and heart-wrenching sorrow. In one powerful outburst known as the Hundred Flowers Movement, China's liberal critics spoke out against the Chinese government. Voicing their discontent on a wide range of issues, venting anger that had been building up since 1949, the Chinese intellectuals called for the ruling Communist Party to mend its authoritarian ways. Just as swiftly, the Chinese government struck back. A political warm spring quickly relapsed into a bitter icy winter.[1]

Strangely enough, it was Mao Zedong, Chairman of the Chinese Communist Party, who initiated the liberal thawing of 1957. Eight years after the founding of the People's Republic of China, the Communists had successfully consolidated their position in the country and made impressive economic progress. The accomplishments, however, came at a very high cost. To assume full control over the country, the Communist Party had resorted to many heavy-handed measures, including the silencing of the slightest political dissent. Consequently, dictated policies preempted public debate, which in turn led to bureaucratic arrogance, the lack of self-initiative, and a slew of problems typical of a state with unconstrained power.

Mao, ambitious to turn China into a great power quickly, recognized the flaws of the system that he headed. The nation was not progressing fast enough and state dominance led to disgruntlement among the people. When, in 1956, popular protests shook communist rule in East Europe, Mao became alarmed. A strong believer in offense as defense, Mao decided to confront his problems head-on. Starting in the middle of 1956, he called for the "opening-up" of China's political and cultural life, encouraging people to speak out about the shortcomings of the government. As Mao famously put it, "Let a hundred flowers bloom and a hundred schools of thought contend."

Even on a highly sensitive issue such as the proper assessment of America, Mao gestured the loosening of control. On May 2, 1956, while making a speech to top officials, Mao made positive remarks about the United States

repeatedly. Discussing the rigid relationship between China's central government and provinces, Mao attributed the problem partly to the fact that the
People's Republic of China had copied the constitution of the Soviet Union.
When this was done, he had his doubts and reservations, Mao said. "The
United States has something different," Mao now observed. "The states in
the U.S. have their own right to legislate, and some of their state legislations
even conflict with the federal constitution."[2] For a long time, Mao added,
grain production in the Soviet Union could not match the best years back
in the Tsarist era. "If this is true, it is a serious problem. . . . How can you
then argue for the superiority of socialist system?" In contrast,

> The United States is a developed country. It developed in just over
> a hundred years. This deserves our attention. We hate American
> Imperialism, which is truly bad, but there must be some good
> reasons that the U.S. has grown to be such a developed country.
> Its political system should be studied.[3]

Mao went on to suggest that the central government of China should allow
Chinese provinces and localities greater freedom in decision making. Such
ideas, coming from Mao, may seem strange at first glance. In reality, they were
not altogether uncharacteristic of Mao. In Mao's thinking there had always
been a strain that favored self-initiative and resisted bureaucratic control. In
his youth, before his conversion to Marxism, Mao had strongly advocated
regional autonomy in China, going so far as to call for a "Monroe Doctrine
for Hunan," Hunan being his home province.[4]

   In late 1956 and early 1957, Mao continued to promote a free exchange
of opinions between Chinese people and their government. On February 27,
1957, in a keynote speech to the Supreme State Council, Mao declared that
"contradictions among the people" were not confrontational and could be
properly resolved through well-intentioned criticism and self-criticism. With
Mao urging them along, officials in the party and the government moved
to create a more relaxed political environment, inviting Chinese citizens
to come forward and speak their mind. After some initial hesitation and
skepticism, some Chinese, especially Chinese intellectuals, responded to the
call and started to comment on various aspects of the government's work.
What came to be known as the Hundred Flowers Movement thus began and
quickly spread across China.

   Events then took an unexpected turn. In deciding to launch the Hundred Flowers Movement, Mao had underestimated the scope and intensity
of discontent then existing in Chinese society. Overconfident of the Communist Party's accomplishments since 1949, Mao had expected that citizens'
criticism of his government would be mild and limited, delivered along with

lavish praise and abundant affirmation of loyalty to the socialist cause. To his surprise and dismay, voluminous and pungent disapproval poured forward, with numerous critics denouncing the government on a whole range of issues, and, in some cases, questioning the very legitimacy of the one-party rule by the Communists. As this happened, serious concerns arose within the Communist Party that the government might lose control of the situation. Humiliated and infuriated, Mao changed direction. Rescinding his previous guarantee of free speech, Mao ordered a major counterattack to strike down the heedless critics. Identified as ill-intentioned Rightists, hundreds of thousands of Chinese were condemned and reprimanded for their hostility to the Communist Party and socialism.

The Hundred Flowers Movement ended abruptly. As long as it lasted, however, many Chinese found opportunities to comment on some critical issues in their country. Among them was the proper evaluation of the United States and the ideas that America embodied. The events of 1957 thus afford a rare glimpse into the way Chinese intellectuals made sense of America in the overall context of Mao's China at the time.

|

Prominent among China's liberal critics of 1957 were many American-educated Chinese scholars and scientists. In the decades before the Communist victory in 1949, more than thirty thousand Chinese had studied in the United States. In the fifties, these American-educated Chinese made up a big part of the top echelon in China's intellectual establishment.[5] More Chinese had studied in Japan during the same period, but their academic training there was not as rigorous—about twenty times more Chinese received doctoral degrees in the U.S. than in Japan.[6] Additionally, many Chinese attended American missionary colleges in China, which accounted for all but one of the foreign-supported Christian institutions of higher education in China.[7] In 1937, the year the full-scale Sino-Japanese War broke out, nineteen American-sponsored colleges and universities were operating in China.[8] Not surprisingly, American-educated Chinese held many prestigious positions in China's academia and constituted a major force in China's intellectual circles.

After 1949, given the drastically transformed circumstances, American-educated Chinese scholars, scientists, and artists experienced great difficulties in adjusting to life under communist rule. Their American education and connections were reasons for distrust; their values and lifestyle were at odds with the new reality in the country. This was true even with Chinese who had chosen to return to China from the U.S. after 1949 so that they could serve New China. Zhang Quan, a celebrated musician, did just this to work as a vocalist at the Central Troupe of Experimental Opera in Beijing. Her independent ways, however, soon earned her the nickname "the American Lady," a label that was deadly, given what was happening in China at the time. Officials and colleagues at the opera house came to view her as unfit for roles in revolutionary shows. Her career at the theater languished. "I shouldn't have studied in the U.S. I should have gone to the Soviet Union," said the disheartened singer.[9]

Qian Xuesen, a rocket scientist trained at Caltech who eventually became the father of China's aerospace programs, found himself in a similarly difficult situation after his much celebrated return from the U.S. to China in 1955. He went on a trip to the Soviet Union to consult Russian experts, only to find that, even in academia, the Soviet system was rigid to the point of being "suffocating." Back home in China, the situation was no better, where traditional Chinese emphasis on seniority reinforced Soviet-style bureaucratic control to stifle creativity and self-initiative. Because his work was critically important to the state, Qian was able to take his problems to China's top leaders. He turned to Premier Zhou Enlai for help, who personally intervened on Qian's behalf to create a favorable working environment for the famed scientist.[10]

But not everyone was a rocket scientist. Many other Chinese could not solve their problems so easily, especially when it came to political matters. Luo Longji makes one notable case. Having received his doctoral degree in political science at Columbia University in 1928, Luo returned to China where he emerged as an eminent liberal political activist, a strong critic of the authoritarian government led by Chiang Kai-shek.[11] During these years, Luo maintained a close connection to the U.S., so when in 1947 the Nationalist government arrested him for his political activities, John Leighton Stuart, U.S. Ambassador to China, came forward to secure his releas.[12] Later, in 1949, as the Chinese Communists were about to take control of China, Luo tried to act as a broker between Ambassador Stuart and the triumphant Chinese revolutionaries, but he was unsuccessful in this endeavor.[13]

After 1949, in view of his struggle against Chiang Kai-shek and his status as a top leader of the Democratic Alliance (one of the "bourgeois" parties from the pre-1949 era that the Communists allowed to survive), Luo hoped for a key appointment in the new regime. The Communist Party did give Luo a position in the government, but, instead of the Minister of Foreign Affairs that Luo had anticipated, they made him the Minister of Timber Industry. Grudgingly Luo accepted the appointment, complaining to his associates: "They do not trust me. They put me in charge of the woods."[14] Actually, Luo should have known better; there was no chance the Communists would entrust him with an important office such as the foreign ministry (for much of the fifties Premier Zhou Enlai personally held that post, which was later turned over to Marshal Chen Yi from the People's Liberation Army). In fact, even as the

Minister of Timber Industry, Luo had limited influence. His own secretary wisely declined membership in Luo's Democratic Alliance and secretly applied to join the Communist Party.[15]

When the Hundred Flowers Campaign began, Luo leapt into action. He traveled across the country to collect evidence on the government's mistreatment of intellectuals, eventually compiling a report that was a half-million words long.[16] Based on the account, Luo suggested that the National People's Congress should create a multiparty commission to review wrongdoings in past political campaigns to address grievances.[17] In his capacity as a vice-chairman of the Democratic Alliance, Luo set up task forces on a number of other issues, including the role of noncommunists in the government, the Communist Party's dominant presence on university campuses, and the lack of academic and intellectual freedom.[18] For these activities, Luo was later denounced as a leading antisocialist Rightist—Mao personally identified him as one of the two "generals" who directed the Rightist attack on the Communist Party.[19]

Luo did not actually have a tightly organized following, but he did have extensive connections among China's liberal intellectuals, especially those who shared with him the common background of an American education. As one of his detractors later pointed out, Luo's "political capital" mainly consisted of Chinese scholars and scientists who had either studied in the United States or been educated at American-supported schools in China.[20] Among Luo's close and active associates during the Hundred Flowers Campaign, for instance, were Zeng Zhaolun, Qian Weichang, and Huang Wanli. All three had studied in the United States. All of them, like Luo, had graduated from Tsinghua University (Qinghua University) in Beijing, which was originally created with the U.S. share of the Boxer Rebellion Indemnity to prepare Chinese students to study in America. Zeng Zhaolun did his postgraduate work in chemistry at the Massachusetts Institute of Technology, and, upon his return to China, emerged as a leading scientist who presided over China's Chemistry Society for more than twenty years. In 1957, when the Hundred Flowers Movement began, Zeng was a deputy minister in charge of China's higher education. Sharing Luo's critical views on many issues, especially those related to education, science, and culture, Zeng closely cooperated with Luo to solicit criticism of the Communist Party.[21] He, for instance, led the effort to draft a liberal platform on culture and education, which later came under heavy fire from the Communist Party.[22]

As for Qian Weichang, when the Hundred Flowers Movement began, he was a vice president at Qinghua University in charge of academic affairs. An engineer trained at Qinghua and then the University of Toronto, Qian had the ambition to build Qinghua into "China's Caltech."[23] Playing an active role in the task force on science and education that Luo Longji had created, Qian drew up a plan by which the Soviet-style, state-sponsored research-only institutes would be turned over to universities, where scientists and scholars would combine research with teaching.[24] At his own university, among the many reform measures he promoted in 1957, he argued for a greater role for the faculty in the governance of Qinghua.[25] Additionally, Qian questioned the reorganization of Chinese universities and colleges that the government carried out after 1949, as part of which Qinghua lost its programs in the humanities and social sciences and became a pure natural science and engineering school. Qian encouraged students to initiate a petition to reverse these changes.[26] Inevitably, Qian came into conflict with the Communist Party and became a target when the government launched its counterattack on the liberal critics.[27]

The third of Luo's old classmates at Qinghua University, Huang Wanli, was a meteorologist educated at the University of Illinois. Before the Hundred Flowers Movement, Huang had famously fought against a plan by the Chinese government to build a major reservoir on the Yellow River. In this effort, Huang clashed with Chinese officials with their arbitrary ways and their blind faith in Russian advisors. When the Hundred Flowers Campaign began, Huang wrote a sarcastic story for a newspaper, denouncing irresponsible officials for mismanaging public works projects. In Huang's view, the so-called "corrupt politics in Imperialist America" was not so bad when compared to what he observed in China:

> Over there, if administrative errors of this sort are committed, tax-payers will rise up to protest. Executives and engineers will lose their jobs, and the mayor of the city will face a tough election next time around! Over here, however, we Chinese are so nice and so easy to handle.[28]

Later, when the Chinese government cracked down on the liberal critics in the Anti-Rightist Movement, Chairman Mao, in one of his speeches, made a specific reference to Professor Huang. To Rightists such as Huang, Mao said, "even the Moon is so much rounder and brighter in America than in China."[29]

In addition to Qinghua University, other institutions with a significant American past also figured prominently in the Hundred Flowers Movement. Peking Union Medical College, founded in 1921 by the Rockefeller Foundation as "a Johns Hopkins for China,"[30] had graduated many students who became leaders in China's medical profession.[31] After 1949, the Communist government seized control of P.U.M.C. and placed it under military management. Such a drastic change did not rest well with the professionals at the college, who in 1957 expressed their discontent and demanded a return to the old ways—what they termed "Union Standard."[32] In the Anti-Rightist Movement that followed, P.U.M.C. was denounced as a stronghold of "American imperialist cultural aggression."[33] Similarly, at Beijing University, which had annexed the American missionary school Yenching University, students were highly outspoken in their criticism of the Chinese government. They put up posters on campus that faulted the government on a wide range of issues, including the official presentation of the United States. One particularly bold student openly called official propagandists liars. The government, said the student, should stop repeating its own lies; if officials were confident in what they were saying, they should invite over some Americans—U.S. Secretary of State John Foster Dulles, for example—to openly debate on various issues and make that part of the Hundred Flowers Movement.[34]

Outside the national capital there were sympathizers for critics such as Luo, Zeng, and Qian. In Sichuan Province, a key associate of Luo's was Pan Dakui, another Qinghua alumnus and America-returned scholar, whose activities partly account for the exceptionally intense student unrest in the region during the free-speech movement.[35] Pan's detractors attributed his behavior to his thirteen years of American education.[36] In Gansu Province, a leading liberal critic was Chen Shiwei, an American-educated scientist who, at the time, was a vice president at Lanzhou University.[37] Like Qian Weichang at Qinghua University, Chen pushed for active faculty involvement in university governance. During the government's anti-Rightist counterattack, Chen was condemned for "adulating the U.S. and opposing the Chinese people."[38]

In Shanghai, one of the leading liberal critics was Sun Dayu, a Yale-trained professor of literature at Fudan University. When the Hundred Flowers Movement started, Sun spoke out against the Communist Party on various issues, including ideological control on campus and the persecution of intellectuals. When the political tide turned and the Anti-Rightist Campaign began, Sun was denounced for his attacks. Feeling unfairly accused, the professor declared his intention to fight the false charges in court. No such proceedings took place, however. Instead, a large crowd of "revolutionary masses" stormed his residence, demanding a debate right there in his bedroom. Sun remained defiant, but decided to stay silent from then on.[39]

Also in Shanghai, there was Wang Zaoshi, a lawyer who had studied political science at the University of Wisconsin. Before 1949, Wang had contended with Chiang Kai-shek's Nationalist government and had gone to jail for his political activism (he was one of the political prisoners for whose release the liberal educator Tao Xingzhi had appealed to John Dewey). During the Hundred Flowers Movement, Wang urged the Communist Party to be more democratic. At a meeting of the National Political Consultative Conference, he delivered a speech entitled "Our Democratic Life Will Flourish by the Day."[40] Additionally, speaking as a lawyer and a former political prisoner, Wang criticized the Communists for showing no respect to the rule of law. He contrasted the situation in China to that in the United States, declaring that "the rule of law in the United States is rather rigorous, from which we can learn a great deal."[41] Given Wang's anti-Nationalist and pro-Communist stance in the years before 1949, his criticism of the Chinese government in 1957 proved to be particularly embarrassing to the authorities. Wang did not go to jail this time but was duly marked as a reactionary Rightist.

Thus, eight years after the founding of the People's Republic of China, many American-educated Chinese who had harbored great hopes for the new era found themselves disillusioned and disappointed by conditions in their country. Their American background made them the odd men out in an environment that placed loyalty above everything else. When they had an opportunity, they became the most prominent and vocal critics of the Chinese government and spearheaded the movement of liberal criticism in 1957.

II

Of the many issues raised by China's American-educated intellectuals in 1957, particularly exasperating was the Chinese government's relentless "Learn from the Soviet Union" campaign. Given the common ideology shared by the Soviet Union and the People's Republic of China and given the lack of contact between China and the West after 1949, the Chinese Communists' emphasis on Sino-Soviet cooperation was quite understandable—after all, the Soviet Union was the only developed country in the world at that time from which New China could hope to obtain aid and advice. Additionally, the "Learn from the Soviet Union" campaign had a political dimension in the domestic context. By promoting the Soviet Union as an advanced country, the Chinese government could boost its people's confidence in socialism and thus counter the lingering American influence in China. In any event, ideological fervor and the rural origin of Mao's revolution—most of its followers were "country bumpkins" who suddenly found themselves in urban centers and in charge of a large country—combined to generate considerable dogmatism and widespread excesses in the drive to learn from the Soviet Big Brother.

The issue at hand was twofold. For one thing, it concerned what kinds of relations China should maintain with the Soviet Union and the United States respectively. For another, it addressed the question what to make of the Soviet Union as a developmental model for China. On the former subject, as noted earlier, as soon as the Chinese Communists came to power, Mao squarely rejected the suggestion that China should follow a middle path in between the United States and the Soviet Union; New China's policy on this particular issue, Mao said, was "Lean to One Side," the side of the Soviet Union. Mao's idea turned into reality when, in February 1950, the newly created People's Republic of China and the Soviet Union signed a treaty of friendship and alliance. The outbreak of the Korean War and the subsequent deployment of

U.S. naval forces to the Taiwan Strait further solidified Sino-Soviet cooperation and hardened Sino-American hostility.[42]

Those Chinese who had hoped for at least a working relationship between
China and the United States followed unfolding events with intense interest and mounting disappointment. From early on, for instance, Luo Longji,
Minister of Timber Industry and Vice Chairman of the Democratic Alliance,
questioned the wisdom of Mao's "Lean to One Side" policy and considered
approaching Mao personally to convey his concern. Luo and his close associates
also recognized that North Korea, not South Korea, had started the military
conflict on the Korean peninsula, dragging China into a regrettable war.[43] A
few years later, during the 1956 Suez crisis, Luo commended the policy of the
U.S. government under President Eisenhower, suggesting that the pressure from
the U.S. prevented the escalation of the Middle Eastern conflict.[44] In the same
year, after Khrushchev initiated de-Stalinization at the Twentieth Congress of
the Soviet Communist Party, Luo concluded that global communism was on
the wane. It would be wise, Luo thought, for China to keep its distance from
the Soviet Union now, and Chinese liberals like himself should prepare to
play a more active role in Chinese politics and in China's foreign relations.[45]

In the Hundred Flowers Campaign, hitherto hidden dissatisfactions with
the Chinese government's fervent promotion of the Soviet Union and its total
rejection of the United States came out into the open. Long Yun, a turncoat
general who had served Chiang Kai-shek in the years before 1949 and later
cooperated with the Communists, voiced his strong disapproval of China's
involvement in the Korean War, reminding his audience that during World
War II the U.S. generously supported China whereas in the recent Korean
conflict the Soviet Union had done little for the Chinese nation.[46] Many
Chinese also resented the continued Soviet military presence in Northeast
China (Manchuria) in the post-1949 years, which they viewed as a violation
of China's sovereignty. Among notable figures who openly expressed this
objection were Wang Yunsheng, a renowned journalist and expert on foreign
affairs; Tian Tiwu, a former Nationalist official; and Wang Zizhi, another
former Nationalist.[47]

Equally controversial was how Chinese officials zealously pushed the
modeling of China after communist Russia. Partly, the Chinese state engaged
in this endeavor to disperse remaining American influences in China. Mao
himself once explained that China "needed Soviet experience and experts
to demolish China's old bourgeois authority," an authority that was largely
American by origin.[48] The following statistics illustrate the scope and intensity
of the "Learn from the Soviet Union" campaign. In the four years from 1952
to 1956, a total of 1,393 Soviet textbooks were published and used in China's
college classrooms.[49] During the period from 1949 to 1957, more than six
hundred Soviet professors taught at Chinese universities and colleges, where

they trained more than eight thousand Chinese graduate students and young instructors.[50] The Russian language now replaced English as the country's first foreign language, taught in colleges as well as secondary schools. The government set up five colleges devoted exclusively to the study of the Russian language and literature, the largest of which—the Beijing Institute of the Russian Language—enrolled five thousand students.[51] Between 1949 and 1956, Chinese presses published 2,683 translated Russian and Soviet literary works, with a total of 67 million copies in print.[52] All this took place at a time when there was virtually no information on the U.S. except stern condemnation.

In 1957, as the Hundred Flowers Campaign went on, many Chinese intellectuals took the government to task for its arbitrary imposition of Soviet ways and its unqualified dismissal of Western culture. Scientists objected to the designation of Russian as the only required foreign language for college students, pointing out that most references in sciences were still in English or German.[53] Professors of Western literature complained about discrimination they suffered due to their field of study and their use of English.[54] Students at the Beijing School of Law and Politics questioned the wisdom of using mostly Soviet textbooks in their education; after all, upon graduation they would serve in China, not the Soviet Union.[55] At the Beijing Institute of the Russian Language, which, as noted above, had an enrollment of five thousand, students became furious when they found out that many of them would be unemployed upon graduation since the country simply did not need so many Russian language specialists. Angry students marched to the State Council to protest against the officials who had actively recruited them in the first place.[56]

The publishing industry also reexamined its editorial policies and prepared to publish more inclusively. For several years, the foreign literary books published by the People's Press, China's leading publisher, were almost exclusively from the Soviet Union. Now, encouraged by the new atmosphere, editors at the press drew up plans to bring out more Western works, including those by American writers such as Walt Whitman, O. Henry, and Edgar Allen Poe.[57]

Even Chairman Mao himself became aware of the excesses in the "Learn from the Soviet Union" campaign and the related total rejection of anything American. As noted earlier, about this time, Mao openly praised the United States for its accomplishments in various fields, including economic development and decentralized constitutional structure. Expressing concerns over the rigidity of the Soviet system, which China had largely transplanted after 1949, Mao encouraged the investigation of American culture and institutions to see in what ways China could benefit from the experience.[58]

Before long, however, the political showdown between the Chinese government and its liberal critics would sweep away the willingness to conduct a rational and cool-headed study of the Soviet Union and the United States. As the Anti-Rightist Campaign put a sudden end to the Hundred Flowers

Movement, the Communist Party denounced Chinese intellectuals who had disparaged the government's policies on the Soviet Union, suggesting that these bourgeois detractors were merely trying "to lure Chinese people back to the United States and enslave them to the American imperialist masters."[59] One official wrote: "Mr. Rightist insists that we compare the Soviet Union and the United States," but the Chinese people had done precisely that in the past decades and had decided to embrace communist Russia. The official continued:

> The American system and lifestyle suit no one but capitalists and their subservient men of letters, the kind of people loathed by the great masses in this country and by the even greater population of the world. Regarding an imperialist country such as the United States, the collective will of our people is very clear: they are determined to stay away from it and shall never model their own country after it."[60]

III

Many Chinese scholars, especially those in various fields of the humanities and social sciences, would beg to differ from the official view on the Soviet Union and the United States presented above. Ever since 1949, these academicians had been listless and restless. Frequent political campaigns left many of them exhausted and frustrated, unable to engage in scholarly pursuits. This was particularly true in disciplines such as sociology and economics, the applicative nature of which made them politically sensitive. To be effective, scholars in these areas had to confront contemporary life in China and their conclusions might not agree with official positions. Additionally, these social sciences were relatively new in China, and, more than traditional disciplines such as historical or literary studies, they bore greater Western influence as they developed in China.

"Chinese sociology was 'single-handedly' created by some Chinese educated abroad (mostly in the United States) and at American missionary schools in Old China," one critic of the Rightist academics in sociology thus observed in late 1957.[61] The disparaging tone aside, the statement was largely true.[62] Sociology was nonexistent in China at the beginning of the twentieth century and its establishment was largely due to the efforts of fifty or so Chinese scholars who received their doctoral training in sociology in the United States during the years before 1949.[63] For example, teaching on the sociology faculty of Qinghua University in the 1930s and 1940s were Chen Da, PhD, Columbia University, 1923; Wu Jingchao, PhD, University of Chicago, 1928; Wu Wenzao, PhD, Columbia University, 1928; and Pan Guangdan, who was educated at

Dartmouth and Columbia. There was also Fei Xiaotong, who graduated from Yenching University (the American missionary school in Beijing), obtained his master's degree at Qinghua University, and completed his doctoral program at the London School of Economics; from 1943 to 1944 Fei was a visiting scholar sponsored by the U.S. Department of State and conducted research at the University of Chicago and Harvard University.[64] Upon his return to China, Fei taught at Qinghua University and soon emerged as a leading scholar in sociology and anthropology.

Over at Yenching University, the American missionary school in Beijing and Fei Xiaotong's alma mater, the situation was similar. One critic later noted: "Prior to the Anti-Japanese War, courses offered at the Yenching Department of Sociology and Social Services could all trace their origins back to the University of Chicago. The professors of the department were trained in the United States, and American and British bourgeois scholars such as [Robert Ezra] Park and [A. R. Radcliffe-] Brown visited and lectured frequently."[65] In 1952, when the new Chinese government reorganized China's higher education system, it dissolved all sociology departments, and sociology as a distinct discipline ceased to exist in the country. Homeless sociologists were assigned to tasks deemed less troubling—for instance, teaching statistics or researching the cultures of ethnic groups in remote regions.[66] Fei Xiaotong later described the bleak situation thus:

> British and American books take up space on our shelves? Sell them as waste paper. It is too late to learn Russian? Buy a few translated booklets. When teaching and writing, quote [Marxist] classics and choose a few British and American scholars to denounce. . . . All this can be done easily, very much in the way of a little kid watching one of those Chinese operas staged in the countryside: he cannot very well figure out what is happening up there, so he bases his judgment on the actors' make-up; when a guy with white paint on his face is beaten up, he applauds.[67]

When the Hundred Flowers Campaign started, Chinese sociologists voiced their protests. In January 1957, Professor Wu Jingchao opened the discussion with an article in the *People's Daily*, "Is Sociology Useless in New China?"[68] Fei Xiaotong followed up with an opinion piece entitled "Speak out on Behalf of Sociology."[69] At a high-level conference on cultural and academic affairs convened by the Communist Party in March 1957, Fei made a formal appeal for the resurrection of sociology in China.[70] Other scholars soon joined the drive. Li Jinghan complained that the Communist Party talked about "catching up with the world in advanced sciences" but had wrong ideas on how to accomplish the goal—hence the government's obsession with the Soviet Union.[71]

Under the new, more relaxed political atmosphere, some American-trained sociologists resumed scholarly work. In the May 1957 issue of *Teaching and Research* (*Jiaoxue yu yanjiu*), for instance, Chen Da of Qinghua University published an article on the living standards of Shanghai workers in the pre-1949 years, with comparisons to conditions in foreign countries, including those in the United States.[72] This was exactly the kind of research that had made the Chinese state uncomfortable, which partly contributed to its decision to abolish sociology a few years before.

The scholars, nostalgic for the heyday of sociology at Qinghua and Yenching, attempted institutional restoration. They petitioned the National Political Consultative Conference to take up the issue.[73] They formed a task force under the auspices of the Chinese Academy of Sciences and did preparatory work to revive China's Association of Sociological Studies.[74] Additionally, they drew up plans to establish a number of teaching and research centers in Beijing and across the country.[75]

Similar events took place with economic studies. Like sociology, economics as a discipline had suffered severely since 1949. In this field, as in sociology, many leading scholars were American-educated. In the new era, these scholars found themselves distrusted and excluded from decision-making processes. They had no access to official data, which was no small impediment to economic research. Although not abolished outright, as was the case with sociology, economic studies in China struggled to survive.

During the Hundred Flowers Campaign, Chinese economists came forward to present their grievances. One leading advocate was Chen Zhenhan, a Harvard-trained economist now teaching at Beijing University. In the spring of 1957, Chen gathered a small group of leading economists to put together a platform on how to improve economic research and teaching in China. Of the four scholars who cooperated with Chen, two had been Chen's schoolmates at Harvard. Together the scholars drafted "Our Opinions on the Current State of Economic Studies," which they circulated among economists for comment, with the intention to submit it for the consideration of the Communist Party.[76] In the document, the economists criticized the Chinese government's total rejection of the so-called "Old Economics," the kind of learning Chen and his American-educated colleagues knew and cherished. They charged that the disregard for some basic economic principles had led to ignorance and poor judgment in the government's decision making. The scholars observed that the connection between deficit spending and inflation should be common knowledge, but it was only recently that some Chinese officials in charge of China's economy conceded the obvious.[77] Such absurdities, said the scholars, resulted from "the failure to recognize objective economic law" and "our overdependence on Soviet experience and practices."[78] The group suggested that economists should be included in decision making and should be free in pursuing their research, including the investigation of "capitalist ideas." "Capitalist economics have advanced notably in recent years," and "certain elements in the methodology of bourgeois economics" might well serve China's economic development.[79]

Other economists echoed the views expressed by Professor Chen and his study group. At a symposium held by the *People's Daily* in April 1957, Professor Lei Haizong (PhD, Chicago, 1927) reminded his audience that China had little firsthand experience with capitalism and that Marxism had not kept up with new developments in the capitalist world. Instead of simply reiterating basic Marxist doctrines, Chinese economists should carefully examine the reality of modern capitalism, Lei suggested.[80]

In particular, Chinese economists advocated a careful consideration of Keynesian economics, which they viewed as a key to the understanding of Western economies, especially the U.S. economy, in the years after the Great Depression and World War II. Articles on the subject appeared in academic journals, universities offered related courses, and publishers brought out translations of Keynesian works.[81] Scholars suggested that Keynesian economics, which had contributed enormously to the economic recovery and growth in the West, could help manage China's socialist economy. Professor Chen Zhenhan and his study group, for instance, proposed the use of Keynesian concepts such as the "multiplier effect" to analyze and guide investment policies in China.[82]

Keynesian economics drew the particular attention of Chinese scholars not just because of its technical merits; a more important issue involved was of great political significance, namely, the proper explanation of the economic conditions of the West in the postwar era. As strong believers in classical Marxism, Chinese Communists had paid close attention to notions such as the periodic crises in the capitalist system, which, according to Marx, would inevitably lead to the demise of capitalism and the triumph of communism. Unfortunately, the postwar performance of Western economies, especially the U.S. economy, seemed to have defied Marx's forecast and put an end to the capitalist decline marked by the Great Depression in the 1920s and 1930s. One article in the *Guangming Daily* presented the troublesome issue thus: "Before World War II, crises of over-production in the capitalist world recurred at certain intervals of time (for example, every eight or twelve years). After the war, however, the situation in the United States became abnormal. Although production fell by about ten percent in 1948–1949 and again in 1953–1954, neither of the two drops led to a perilous crisis."[83]

Qian Jiaju, an economist and editor-in-chief of *Zhengming* (*Contention*), a newly created journal of the Democratic Alliance, felt that Chinese economists had been timid on the issue of capitalist periodic crises. He decided to break the silence.[84] In February 1957, Qian's journal published a lead article entitled "On the Question of a Postwar Economic Crisis in the United States." In the piece, Hu Dunyuan, an economist educated at Columbia University, made the point that the 1948–49 downturn in the U.S. economy was by no means an "economic crisis" but simply a recession.[85] In May, Qian took the liberty of publishing in the *Contention* a recent resolution by the American Communist Party, in which the party admitted errors of expecting imminent economic crisis and basing the party's strategy on such unrealistic expectations.[86] Chinese officials had intended to keep this a secret to avoid ideological confusion in China, so Qian's publication of the document annoyed them. For this, and for his other activities during the Hundred Flowers Movement, Qian was later denounced as a Rightist.[87]

In the meantime, even China's official theorists could not very well ignore the issues raised. The *People's Daily*, the Communist Party's official organ, published an analysis that acknowledged the decent performance of the U.S. economy in recent years.[88] In another article that appeared in the same paper, entitled "The Current State of Studies on the U.S. Economy," Wu Dakun, professor of economics at Beijing University, drew attention to the lack of serious scholarship on a critically important subject, a problem that he attributed largely to prevailing dogmatism. Wu advised a more realistic view on conditions in the U.S.: "If we stubbornly search for an immediate crisis on the scale of the 1929 Great Depression, we will only set ourselves up for a major disappointment."[89]

Others voiced similar opinions. The Institute of International Relations based in Beijing, for instance, organized five forums on conditions of the U.S. economy. Participants of the events stressed the need for serious research on the subject. Working together, they drafted an agenda for the study of certain topics that, in their view, demanded immediate attention.[90]

In addition to matters related to cycles of the U.S. economy, another hotly debated subject was the living conditions of American workers. At the core of this particular issue was a Marxist concept first popularized by Soviet theorists, namely "absolute poverty," which suggests that workers in a capitalist society not only suffer from relative deprivation (the widening gap between the rich and the poor) but also continuously drift toward absolute poverty (outright decline in their living standards). Postwar conditions in the United States seemed to belie this prediction and created a difficult theoretical and political problem for China's official economists. In the Hundred Flowers Campaign, China's liberal critics counseled realism. Chen Zhenhan and his study group pointed out that Marxist forefathers were not all-knowing gods, whose "works were published over a hundred years ago," long before the Western development after World War II in the twentieth century. The scholars suggested dropping concepts such as "absolute poverty."[91] In June 1957, *Dushu Yuebao* (*Reader's Monthly*) published an article about the ongoing debate over this particular subject within the international communist community.[92] In Shanghai, Professor Yang Sizheng took the issue to his students. Rejecting both the idea of absolute poverty and the idea of relative deprivation, Yang pointed out that, in postwar America, "the income of the American working class accounts for a larger, not a smaller, percentage of the national income of the U.S."[93] Another economist in Shanghai, Wu Chengxi, declared that absolute deprivation in the U.S. in the postwar era was fictional; in fact, he said, during the period the United States had performed much better economically than both the Soviet Union and China.[94]

Suggestions like this can well explain why the Chinese government had been uneasy with "old-school" social sciences. If capitalism is so wonderful, how does one justify communist revolution? Clearly such challenges were not just academic but also political and the Chinese Communist Party felt compelled to respond strongly. When the Anti-Rightist Movement began, liberal academicians came under fire, condemned for their bourgeois ideas and pro-American stance. Professor Chen Zhenhan at Beijing University, for instance, became the focus of six "struggle meetings." Critics accused him of attempting to turn the economics department at Beijing University into "a Harvard-style, reactionary training-camp for bourgeois economists,"[95] and they denounced the platform on economic studies that Chen and his associates drafted as a "political conspiracy" against socialism.[96]

IV

While drawing up their plan for the revival of economic studies in China, Professor Chen Zhenhan and his colleagues had stressed the scientific nature and technical merits of certain economic concepts and measures—the Keynesian idea of "multiplier effect," for example. Such concepts or measures, they said, would function equally well in free-market or planned economies.[97] This emphasis on the "objectiveness" of certain ideas and methods reflected a desire to separate scholarship from ideology to avoid, as much as possible, political controversies. Maneuvers such as this did not always work, as evidenced by what happened to the liberal economists and sociologists in the Anti-Rightist Campaign that followed the Hundred Flowers Movement.

In fact, within the overall atmosphere in China during the 1950s, even disciplines less politically sensitive than economics or sociology could not escape from the long arm of ideological dispute, especially where lingering American influence seemed to be an issue. One case in point, admittedly a rather extreme one, is the Morganist-Lysenkoist dispute in Chinese biological and genetic studies, which became another focal point of contention during the Hundred Flowers Campaign and the subsequent Anti-Rightist Movement.

In the years leading up to 1957, as a part of the "Learn from the Soviet Union" campaign, the Chinese government had actively promoted Russian biologist Trofim D. Lysenko as a model scientist. Lysenkoism emphasized the impact of environment on the evolution of species and rejected modern genetic studies developed in the West, which it equated with "gene-determinism." Lysenkoism was believed to exemplify well the Marxist materialist worldview; as such, it had enjoyed Stalin's personal support and dominated Soviet biological research for some years. In China, the promotion of Lysenkoism raised a particularly acute personnel and institutional issue, namely, leading Chinese biologists were mostly trained in the United States and in genetic studies they were strongly influenced by the research spearheaded by American scientists such as Thomas Morgan.

The extent to which the American connection shaped modern biological studies in China can be seen in the career of Dr. Tan Jiazhen, China's leading geneticist. Tan received his bachelor's degree in biology in 1929 from Soochow University, an American Methodist school located in East China. For his Master's degree, Tan attended Yenching University in Beijing, yet another American missionary school, where he studied with Professor Li Ruqi, a Columbia PhD who had worked under the guidance of Thomas Morgan. With Dr. Li's recommendation, Tan went on to pursue his doctoral degree at Caltech, to which Morgan had migrated from Columbia University. Having completed his doctoral program and conducted research at Caltech, Tan accepted an invitation to serve as the dean of sciences at Zhejiang University, which was an American Presbyterian institution located in Hangzhou, China. This appointment came from Dr. Zhu Kezhen, a Harvard-educated meteorologist who presided over Zhejiang University at the time. In due course, Dr. Tan sent several students of his own to study in the U.S., who returned to China to hold key positions in biological sciences.[98] In this particular case, therefore, three generations of Chinese scientists shared a common American educational background. Scientists like them formed the backbone of biological research in China before 1949.

Not surprisingly, when the new government of China promoted Soviet influence in general and Lysenkoism in particular, the Morganist dominance of China's biological studies came to be challenged. Educational officials mandated the reading of Lysenkoist writings in all biology departments and agriculture schools in China.[99] During the Thought Reform Movement of 1952, the elimination of Morganist influence became a priority in the circles of biological research. An article published in the *People's Daily* in June 1952 declared that "the current state of affairs in our biological sciences is simply intolerable," and called for speedy rectification.[100] In the fall of 1952, biology courses bearing Morganist influence were dropped from college curricula and research in the Morganist tradition was arbitrarily terminated.[101] Dr. Tan

Jiazhen, now at Fudan University in Shanghai, tried to teach, but no student would register for his classes.[102] When he refused to acknowledge the "reactionary bourgeois nature" of Morganist biology, he was reassigned, losing the right to teach any kind of genetics.[103]

When Stalin died in 1953, Lysenkoist dominance over biological research in the Soviet Union began to falter. In China, some Chinese biologists rose to voice their dissatisfaction. In a book published in 1955, botanist Hu Xiansu (PhD, Harvard, 1925) openly criticized Lysenko. Although only a small part of Hu's book deals with the Lysenko affair, it was notable enough that Soviet advisers working at China's Ministry of Higher Education lodged protests with the Chinese government. Hu had long maintained a strong stance against Lysenko, which cost him membership in the Chinese Academy of Sciences. The Chinese government, responding to the Russian protest against Hu, organized a rally in Beijing to denounce the troublemaking Chinese scientist.[104] Shortly afterward, however, there came the news about Khrushchev's secret speech at the Twentieth Congress of the Soviet Communist Party in which the new Soviet leader condemned Stalin for his purges and autocratic ways. Clearly embarrassed by its recent public defense of the now disgraced Lysenko, the Central Propaganda Department of the Chinese Communist Party tried to repair its relationship with Dr. Hu Xiansu. At a meeting of the CCP Politburo held in April 1956, China's top leaders discussed Hu's case. Lu Dingyi, head of the Central Propaganda Department, admitted treating Hu too harshly. Mao indicated that it was not right to deny Hu membership in the Chinese Academy of Sciences for simply disagreeing with Lysenko.[105]

The Central Propaganda Department then took the unusual step of sponsoring a national conference on the particular issue of genetic studies. The meeting took place in August 1956, which drew a large number of scientists and philosophers from around the country and provided a forum for China's Morganist scientists to express their opinions. Of the fifty-six scientists who spoke formally at the conference, about one-third were American-educated.[106] The participants criticized the government's single-minded support for Lysenko and warned against the consequences of such arbitrary policies. They, for example, pointed to the dramatic increase in grain production in the United States in recent decades, in contrast to the lackluster performance of the Soviet Union in the same field, a difference they partly attributed to inadequate seed breeding in Russia.[107] The scientists called for the revival of genetic studies in China and demanded to reinstall Morganist genetics as part of college curricula. The conference participants also urged the government to expand China's scientific exchanges with the outside world and even suggested, at a time when virtually no direct contact between China and the U.S. existed, that American scientists, such as H. J. Muller at Caltech, be invited to visit China.[108]

This Morganist uprising against the Lysenkoist hold on China's genetic studies had wide ramifications; it became a key event in the launching of the

Hundred Flowers Campaign. Mao Zedong himself followed the events closely. After the national conference on genetic studies in August 1956, Mao met with Dr. Tan Jiazhen and a few other prominent scientists to hear them out. Mao admitted that the government had committed errors; he encouraged the scientists to carry on their research as they saw fit.[109] In April 1957, Mao again expressed his support for free debate in biological research. As he followed the related events, he took particular interest in an article in the *Guangming Daily*. In this article, Li Ruqi, the Columbia-educated biologist who had taught Dr. Tan Jianzhen at Yenching University, criticized the Lysenkoist suppression of Morganism in China and argued for free debate as the only way to expand man's knowledge. Mao instructed the *People's Daily*, the Communist Party's official daily newspaper, to republish Li's article, together with an editor's commentary that Mao himself authored. Mao declared that "we support this article" and that "we welcome thorough criticism of our mistakes, along with constructive ideas."[110]

Gestures like this encouraged Chinese scientists. At the Chinese Academy of Sciences, Dai Songen, a Cornell-educated scientist, denounced officials who were so fixated on ideology that they turned blind eyes to hard reality. Some of these officials ignored the fact that corn production in the United States had increased by sixty-five percent in recent years, and they continued to condemn American scientists for having "wrong theories."[111] At Beijing Agricultural University, Morganist professors, previously silenced and sidelined, now reclaimed their positions in research. Li Jingxiong (Cornell) was once again directing graduate students and headed a new laboratory; Bao Wenkui (Caltech) offered courses that drew a large number of students on campus as well as scientists from outside Beijing.[112] In fact, the relative fortunes of Lysenkoism and Morganism at this particular institution changed so much and so quickly that a few young scientists who had recently returned from the Soviet Union now worried about reverse discrimination.[113] Over at Beijing University, Dr. Li Ruqi, whose article in the *Guangming Daily* Mao had endorsed, was now writing a column on biological issues for *Shengwuxue Tongbao* (Biology Gazette) to popularize Morganist theory.[114]

All this excitement, along with the Hundred Flowers Movement as a whole, came to a sudden stop in June 1957. By this time, popular criticism of the Chinese government had become a national phenomenon, with some radical critics calling for an end of the Communist Party's monopoly on political power. Many Communist leaders now feared that they would lose control over the situation. Mao, humiliated and infuriated by the extent and intensity of the criticism voiced, decided to reverse course and strike back. As Mao saw it, the recent actions of the liberal critics, especially those with close ties to America, proved that these Chinese were a deadly threat to socialism and could not be trusted. The party launched a major counterattack, denouncing liberal critics as "Rightists"—malicious reactionaries and public enemies. The outspoken Rightists would suffer various punishments in the coming years, including demotion and banishment. Among the best-known targets of this anti-Rightist movement were Luo Longji, Minister of Timber Industry and vice chairman of the Democratic Alliance; Qian Weichang, vice president of Qinghua University; Qian Jiaju, editor of the journal *Contention*; Fei Xiaotong, professor of sociology at Qinghua University; Chen Zhenhan, professor of economics at Beijing University; and Hu Xiansu, biologist at the Chinese Academy of Sciences.[115]

The struggle over America in the Hundred Flowers Movement well illustrates the dynamic and complex relationships between China's domestic affairs and foreign relations, between culture and politics, and between Chinese intellectuals and the Chinese state. The events of 1957 make it clear that, eight years into the Mao Era, many Chinese, especially Chinese intellectuals, still held strong positive views of the United States. These Chinese liberals maintained a keen interest in America not so much out of a simple or romantic admiration for the foreign country across the Pacific but due to their genuine concern over the numerous problems afflicting their motherland and their desire to address these serious deficiencies. In this sense, the Chinese intellectuals' debate with the Chinese state over the proper treatment of American teachings constituted an integral part of the Chinese nation's continuous effort to reinvent itself in modern times. The liberal criticism of 1957 was forcefully silenced, but many of the themes it highlighted would live on to shape events in China during the coming decades.

4

Communist Crusade and Capitalist Stronghold

Mao's Everlasting Revolution and the United States, 1957–1979

The fiasco that was the Hundred Flowers Movement of 1957 taught the Chinese government an unforgettable lesson: never take public opinion lightly. Its confidence shaken and its prestige damaged, the state grew ever more vigilant in its efforts to shape public outlook on the world. Guidance must be constant and heretical ideas must be dispelled swiftly. The government was now convinced, more than ever, that for China to be strong and productive, her people must unify in one common worldview and share the same aspirations.

With convictions such as this, the Communist Party gave the Chinese people some daunting tasks in the years that followed. In the Great Leap Forward from 1958 to 1960, Mao tried to speed up the industrialization of China through total mass mobilization. Chinese peasants were compelled to surrender land ownership to newly created communes; Chinese from all lines of work were called upon to take part in an all-out drive to expand China's industries—in particular, to double China's steel production almost instantly. The improbable campaign, featuring the so-called Backyard Furnaces set up all across the country, turned out to be a disaster. Instead of fostering economic growth, it led to the negligence of crops in the fields. Widespread famine followed.

This terrible blunder, however, only reinforced Mao's desire to prove himself as effective a leader in peace as he had been in wartimes, leading him to even more radical measures to build China into a classless, well-ordered, powerful communist state that could stand up against the West. When some of his comrades questioned his judgment and challenged his decisions, Mao fought back. At the Lushan Conference in July 1959, Mao removed from office his defense minister Marshal Peng Dehuai, who had boldly spoken out against the Great Leap Forward. A few years later, in 1966, Mao launched an even wilder campaign, the Great Cultural Revolution, starting a political maelstrom that would last a whole decade. Mao urged his revolutionary followers to rise up and strike down the so-called "capitalist roaders," especially those officials at various levels who, in Mao's view, had abandoned communism and would settle for a capitalist way of life. Mao's devout followers, especially the young, ardently responded to the Great Helmsman's call, embarking on a fervent crusade against anyone who showed any individualist inclinations. As Mao's Red Guards attacked those who were suspected of disloyalty to the Everlasting Revolution, China was plunged into a great turmoil that would not end until Mao's death in 1976.

Many factors contributed to the unremitting radicalization of Chinese politics from the late 1950s to the mid-1970s. On the personal level, Mao's great hunger for power and his utopian vision for an egalitarian society played a major role. In terms of general domestic affairs, China's centrally controlled economy dictated an emphasis on devotion and collectivist thinking. With regard to foreign relations, during much of the period under examination, the United States was fiercely hostile to China and pursued policies aimed to isolate and undermine the communist state. In particular, Washington continued its support for Taiwan, which riled the Chinese to no end. When in the late 1950s the Soviet Union decided to soften its stance against the United States and sought "peaceful coexistence" with the Americans, Mao broke ranks with the Russian leaders, whom he denounced as "revisionists." This ideological debate and division within the international communist movement further radicalized Chinese politics.[1]

Given the circumstances, not surprisingly America faired very poorly in China during the period in question. The sporadic expressions of warm sentiment toward the Untied States in 1957 were now a matter of the past. The official verdict on America as a decadent and yet deadly enemy of the Chinese revolution was firmly reestablished. At the height of the Great Cultural Revolution, the United States, along with Russian revisionists who had surrendered to the vicious Americans, appeared as the root of the very evil that the Chinese revolutionaries sought to eradicate from their country and from the whole world once and for all.

The virtually complete isolation of China from the Western world from the 1950s to the 1970s made feasible the reduction of America to sheer evil. A whole generation of Chinese grew up with no exposure to the United States other than the official presentation of the U.S. as the last stronghold of wicked capitalism and imperialism. Defined as such, America became the target and an integral part of Mao's Everlasting Revolution.

In due time, however, the starkly all-negative view of the United States would become a political liability for the Chinese state. In the early 1970s, when Mao, for various reasons, decided to seek *rapprochement* with Washington, Chinese leaders found it an arduous and awkward task to explain to the Chinese people why Communist China was now cooperating with the irredeemably evil American Imperialists. The government tackled the problem as best as it could; still, its credibility suffered severe damage. The government's ironclad control over the presentation and interpretation of America would soon begin to disintegrate.

|

When, in May 1957, the Chinese Communist Party decided to crack down on the liberal critics who had spoken out in the Hundred Flowers Movement, it wasted no time in reclaiming its authority on the proper assessment of the United States. This was done by various means. The state launched a well-orchestrated press campaign to shape public opinion. Mandarin theorists moved to combat unorthodox ideas in academic circles that had surfaced during the Hundred Flowers Movement. The Communist Party also reestablished the Soviet Union as a shining model for China, for a short period of time anyway, so as to counter any remaining infatuation with America.

Given how actively they had urged the Chinese people to speak their minds in the Hundred Flowers Movement, Mao and his fellow leaders in May 1957 found it difficult, not to mention embarrassing, to swallow their pride and clamp down on their liberal critics. Ever resourceful, the government did find ways to make the radical turn. Starting on May 24, major Chinese newspapers reported extensively on a recent homicide case in Taiwan, in which a U.S. Army officer was acquitted even though he had shot and killed a local resident.[2] The intensity of the coverage on the particular story signaled a significant change in policy, making the point that those liberal critics who had spoken positively about the United States were not only erroneous but also unpatriotic. "Slaves Lead Hard Lives," the *Liberation Daily* in Shanghai headlined one of its reports on the murder case, suggesting that Taiwan under Chiang Kai-shek's Nationalist rule was no more than a colony of the abusive American imperialists.[3]

Just as conspicuously, Chinese media reported on another event occurring at the time, this one in the U.S.—the Civil Rights March on Washington. A commentator for the Beijing-based *Guangming Daily* wrote:

> Today we are publishing an extended report on a march of American blacks in Washington. Our readers can see that, in the very heart of a nation where the ruling class boasts of democracy and

liberty, sixteen million blacks are suffering endless humiliation. In that so-called civilized country, numerous cases of medieval lynching are still taking place.[4]

A few Chinese scientists who had recently returned from America also came forward to urge their compatriots to be realistic about life in the United States. Some of these Chinese had planned to leave the U.S. for China immediately after the Communist victory in 1949, but the U.S. government, reluctant to see the departure of these American-trained talents, took various measures to prevent them from returning to China. One Chinese student, who had studied chemistry at Purdue University, related how he was committed to a mental hospital because of his political views.[5] Others told tales about McCarthyist persecution, the "fraud that is called the freedom of speech," as well as social decadence in America.[6] The *People's Daily*, in an eye-catching headline, quoted Dr. Qian Xuesen, the Caltech-educated expert in missile technology, as saying: "After Muddling along for 20 Years in the U.S., I Choose Socialism."[7]

Having fired such warning shots, the Chinese government launched what came to be known as the Anti-Rightist Movement, in which the liberal critics who had questioned China's socialist system and spoken of the West positively were denounced and reprimanded. As part of this effort, the government kept up the effort to expose the dark side of American life. In a series called "The True Face of Cultural Freedom in the U.S.," the *Guangming Daily* in Beijing carried excerpts from *Freedom Is As Freedom Does: Civil Liberties Today*, a work that condemned McCarthyism.[8] In Hubei Province, *Changjiang Ribao* (*Yangzi River Daily*) started a Q & A column entitled "Are There Democracy, Liberty, and Prosperity in the U.S.?" The forum featured questions such as: "In the U.S., even workers own automobiles. Doesn't this indicate that Americans live a nice life?" In response to the particular question, the columnist explained that an automobile was not a luxury but an everyday necessity for American workers who otherwise could not go to work, so car ownership did not necessarily suggest an easy life and definitely not happiness itself.[9]

A wide range of other issues also appeared in the Q&A column in the *Yangzi River Daily*. Among them, the terror tactics of America's "secret police" (the FBI "keeps the fingerprints of 131 million Americans");[10] the myth that is free speech in the U.S. ("five financial groups control most newspapers" in America and novelist Albert Maltz fled to Mexico to escape persecution);[11] inequality in education (40 percent of American high school students drop out to make a living);[12] racial discrimination (the governor of Virginia closes down public schools to avoid desegregation);[13] the oppressive nature of the U.S. legal system (Julius and Ethel Rosenberg were executed);[14] and the dominant role of money in U.S. politics (contributions to the Republican Party in 1956: "Du Pont, $88,300; Mellon, $99,150; Rockefeller, $100,500.").[15]

As Chinese media endeavored to reeducate China's general populace about America, in academia official theorists set out to discredit certain ideas put forward during the Hundred Flowers Movement. In economics, a major issue was how to evaluate the performance of the U.S. economy in the postwar era. As noted earlier, the quick recovery and robust growth of the Western economy after World War II had confounded China's official economists who took seriously the Marxian theory on capitalist periodic crises and who had vainly anticipated an early repeat of the Great Depression. During the Hundred Flowers Movement, some Chinese scholars had suggested that significant changes had taken place in the Western economy, especially the U.S. economy, creating a situation different from the days of Marx and the years before the Great Depression. These scholars had called for a more sensible appraisal of modern capitalism. It so happened that as the Hundred Flowers Movement came to its sudden end and the new Anti-Rightist Movement started, the U.S. economy began to show signs of a recession. Feeling vindicated, defenders of classical Marxist theories went on counterattacks. In early May 1957, economist Chu Yukun had written to the monthly journal *Shijie zhishi* (*World Knowledge*) to protest what he viewed as overly positive assessment of the U.S. economy. At that time, Chu's view was out of sync with the general trend in the Hundred Flowers Movement.[16] Now, as the Anti-Rightist Campaign swept across China, Chu published an article in the same journal to declare that recent troubles in the U.S. economy proved that Marx was right after all.[17]

The 1957 recession in the U.S. economy also drew the attention of Zhang Wentian. Zhang was the Communist leader who, as a young man, had spent some time in California. In the 1930s, Zhang served as the general secretary of the Chinese Communist Party but later lost an intraparty power struggle to Mao. Now, as a deputy foreign minister of China, Zhang was a party specialist on international affairs. As the year 1958 began, Zhang brought out a major article on the state of the U.S. economy, which appeared in the debut issue of *Hongqi* (*Red Flag*), a journal recently created as an official organ of the Chinese Communist Party. Two previous downturns in the U.S. economy in the postwar era, first in 1948–49 and then in 1953–54, did not display strong symptoms of overproduction crises, and this had caused confusion among some Chinese, Zhang noted. Now these comrades could put their doubts aside because the most recent economic difficulties in the U.S. clearly arose from overproduction, which in turn resulted from the anarchic nature of capitalism.[18] "Now, bourgeois economists are no longer arguing whether there will be a crisis (they call it 'recession'), but only how severe it will be and how long it will last."[19] History would demonstrate that American capitalism was no exception to the universal law discovered by Karl Marx. "Capitalist spokesmen and the various breeds of revisionists" could try their best to defend capitalism, but "American Imperialism is clearly the most reactionary, most decadent, and most decrepit capitalism, with no future whatsoever."[20]

Under the new circumstances, some Chinese economists who had previously spoken positively of the U. S. economy conducted self-criticism. During the Hundred Flowers Movement, Professor Wu Dakun at the People's University in Beijing had argued that, given the U.S. government's counteractive measures, a crisis on the scale of the Great Depression was unlikely to take place in postwar America. Now, Wu tried to defend himself by explaining that he never meant that there would be no broad economic crisis in the U.S. ever again—he was merely pointing out that, in contrast to the tightening of credit in the earlier crises, inflation had now become a major problem for the United States.[21]

Wu's students and colleagues at the People's University would not let him off so easily. They criticized him for overemphasizing the financial sector and for implying that some simple budgetary or monetary measures could eliminate the fundamental contradictions of capitalism. Wu's view was still "revisionist" and unacceptable, his critics said.[22]

China's official economists refused to consider any kind of financial or monetary explanations for the performance of the U.S. economy in the postwar era because of their strong dislike of Keynesian economics, which they viewed as the last resort of the defenders of the capitalist system. During the Hundred Flowers Movement, some Chinese economists had shown strong interest in the Keynesian concept of the Multiplier, which they viewed as a key in understanding the relative stability in the U.S. economy after World War II; now, at the height of the Anti-Rightist Movement, the particular concept was singled out and denounced as false and deceptive. Writing in *Jingji yanjiu* (*Economic Studies*), Ding Gu rejected the notion that Keynesian economics could somehow save capitalism. Keynes, Ding wrote, could not acknowledge the root cause of capitalist economic crisis, which is simply the deprivation of the working-class people, who have no money to spend to keep up the necessary consumption. This was an unpleasant truth, Ding wrote, that could not be explained away with some fickle "psychological" factors.[23] The Multiplier could not save capitalism, which was bankrupt and hopeless, with or without Keynes.[24]

It turned out that the 1957–58 recession did not last long; the U.S. economy climbed out of it relatively easily and moved on. China's official theorists had to look farther down the road for signs of a severe decline in the U.S. economy. In early 1959, *Red Flag* published an article by Meng Yongqian to explain the uncooperative recent events. Certain anticrisis measures of the U.S. government did produce some effects and contributed to an early economic recovery, Meng conceded. However, fundamental contradictions within the American capitalist system still existed; the combined impact of erratic investment expansion, the unreliability of artificially created demand (mainly military), and a persistently high unemployment rate portended future woes. The 1957–58 economic troubles did not turn into a full-scale crisis, "but they made clear the fact that the postwar U.S. economy has been in constant fluctuation. Judging by current conditions in the U.S. and in the capitalist world as a whole, we are confident that the U.S. industry is headed to yet another decline."[25]

In addition to frontal assaults such as these, the Chinese state also engaged in some flank movements against the United states, including the revival of the Soviet Union as a counterinfluence. As we have seen earlier, Mao himself had serious concerns over the rigidity of the Soviet economic and political system, which had partly motivated him to launch the ultimately ill-fated Hundred Flowers Movement. In fact, in just a couple of years, Mao would return to these old themes and once again voice his reservations on the Soviet Union. The priority in late 1957, however, was to rein in remaining American influence in China, a task that called for the glorification of the Soviet Union the Big Brother. In November 1957, to celebrate the fortieth anniversary of the Russian October Revolution, the Chinese government orchestrated broadly based celebrations and an intense press campaign to highlight Soviet accomplishments. This effort involved government offices and mass organizations at all levels. The national headquarters of China's labor unions, for instance, sent a directive to its regional branches one month in advance, instructing them to utilize all means of publicity—Sino-Soviet friendship museums and exhibits, mobile performing teams, billboards, lectures, concerts, storytelling, poetry readings—to underscore what could be accomplished under a socialist system.[26]

Chinese newspapers did their part and brought to their readers a great amount of good news to demonstrate how the Soviet Union had outperformed the United States. For several days on end, the Beijing Daily carried full pages of pictures and statistics to make a convincing case.[27] On October 24, for example, the paper compared industrial growths in the Soviet Union and the U.S. According to the news report, the Soviet industrial output in 1957 was 330 times that of Tsarist Russia in 1913; in contrast, during the same period, U.S. industries expanded just 4.1 times.[28] Other newspapers were as diligent. The People's Daily, in one of its own reports, compared the Russian people's hefty bank deposits to the $18.8 billion that U.S. farmers had incurred in debt.

When the Soviet Union successfully launched the first manmade satellite, Sputnik, on October 4, 1957, the event gave a timely boost to Beijing's celebration of socialist superiority over capitalist America. For weeks, Chinese newspapers covered the event in vivid details and published lengthy reports on space science. One article in the People's Daily, entitled "Soviet Satellite Shatters the Myth of American Technological Supremacy," drew its readers' attention to the fact that with the rocket technology used in launching Sputnik, the

Soviet Union could propel nuclear weapons to the world's remotest corners, rendering U.S. military bases around the globe useless. The *People's Daily* liked the article so much that it published three different versions of it.[29]

The launching of the second Soviet satellite in November 1957 kept Chinese enthusiasm high, and Chinese media took care to report on the U.S. government's reaction to the Soviet breakthrough—disbelief and dismay.[30] When, in December 1957, the U.S. botched an effort to launch a satellite of its own, Chinese media reacted with gleeful ridicule and sarcasm. There, for example, came a boisterous stage play, called "Alas! America's Little Moon!" which features caricatured American characters starting with President Eisenhower. The *Guangming Daily* commented: "Let the U.S. ruling class tremble in anguish. Their satellite won't fly, and their capitalist system is crumbling down fast."[31] The *People's Daily* drew the larger lesson to learn: "Under socialism, an economically and culturally backward country can, within a short period of time, overtake the most advanced capitalist nation. . . . In the Soviet Union, this possibility has turned into reality."[32]

In November 1957, Mao, who rarely traveled abroad, journeyed to Moscow to celebrate the fortieth anniversary of the October Revolution. In his speech to the Supreme Soviet, Mao declared China's determination to stay loyal to the legacy of the Bolshevik Revolution. He reiterated his confidence in the eventual triumph of communism:

> Socialism will displace capitalism. This is an objective law that no human force can alter. American imperialists have tried and are still trying to sabotage the liberation of the Chinese people, but they will never succeed in their attempts to stop the six hundred million Chinese in their march down the socialist thoroughfare.[33]

II

Through the Anti-Right Movement of late 1957 the Chinese government managed to reclaim full control over ideological matters that had gone loose in the Hundred Flowers Movement. Events of 1957, however, left behind some long-term effects. In spite of all the explanation and justification, the fact remained that Mao had invited criticism of his government and then mercilessly struck down those who had taken him up on his offer. Having thus rudely spurned its critics, the Chinese Communist Party was under heavy pressure, more so than ever, to prove its own worthiness and demonstrate to Chinese people the party's ability to lead China to national success. This was particularly true in the field of economic development. After all, at the very heart of Marxism lies the idea that technology and economy drives the progress of human society—from feudalism to capitalism and on to communism. China must achieve industrialization quickly; otherwise, the claim for socialist superiority would become questionable. Extolling the Soviet Union and belittling the United States would buy Chinese leaders some time; ultimately, however, the Chinese Communist Party had to produce real results in China to maintain the confidence of its people.

These considerations, among others, contributed to Mao's decision to launch the Great Leap Forward of 1958–1960, a campaign aimed to speed up China's economic development through mass mobilization and participation. In a way, the Great Leap Forward continued an old strand in Mao's thinking, that is, in spite of his open and highly public praise for the Soviet Union, Mao had serious doubts on the Soviet model of development, which in his review was too bureaucratic and rigid to meet his expectation for the rapid industrialization of China. Notwithstanding the massive press campaign to glorify the Soviet Union in the wake of the Hundred Flowers Movement, Mao privately and not so privately scorned excessive adoration for the Russian Big Brother. Speaking at a party conference in March 1958, the Chairman chastised his comrades for their slavish attitude toward the Soviet Union. (In this speech, Mao even complained that when Chinese artists painted Stalin and himself standing together, they always made the Russian leader look taller. Having met Stalin in person, Mao said, he knew that it should be the other way around.)[34] Mao believed in communism, but his was a kind of communism with a populist twist. Before 1949, he defeated the initially superior forces of Chiang Kai-shek by rallying the support of Chinese peasants; now he wanted to put the same revolutionary spirit to work for China's socialist construction.

Confident with soaring ambitions, Mao pushed the Chinese nation into the Great Leap Forward. Amid a great euphoria, wildly unrealistic goals were set—especially for steel production, which led to the erection of the so-called backyard furnace all across China. The government issued a resounding slogan for the massive drive—*chao Ying gan Mei*—"To overtake Britain and catch up with the U.S." It was declared that, given what China was to accomplish through the Great Leap Forward, the country could surpass Great Britain in economic strength within fifteen years and should be able to close the gap with the United States not too long thereafter. This turned the vague idea of economic growth into a race that greatly animated the Chinese people.

The challenge was put to the whole nation, and good news soon poured in. In July 1958 the *People's Daily* reported with great fanfare that China's wheat harvest exceeded that of the United States.[35] *Red Flag* published an article to commemorate the success, attributing the feat to the superiority of socialism and, curiously, to the failure of the American capitalist system to "solve the problem of overproduction."[36]

Curious or not, "Overtake Britain and Catch up with the U.S." thus had a strong effect on the imagination of the Chinese in the Great Leap Forward. Mao himself, speaking to a party gathering in December 1958, explained why he was stepping down as the president of the People's Republic but would stay on as the chairman of the Chinese Communist Party: "I still want to work for a few more years. Ideally, until we have overtaken the United States. Then I will happily depart to meet up with Marx."[37]

The fixation on "catching up" with the United States indicated something that Mao and his fellow leaders could not very well face, which was the disparity between China and the United States, especially in terms of military strength. Nowhere else was this more evident than in the continued Sino-American contention over Taiwan. After the Korean War, Washington signed a treaty with Chiang Kai-shek's Nationalist government, committing the U.S. to the defense of Taiwan. With the U.S. Seventh Fleet patrolling the Taiwan Strait, it became virtually impossible for the People's Republic of China to take control of the outlying island, unless it chose to go to war with the United States. This immensely frustrated Mao, who, deep in his heart, was as much a nationalist as he was a communist, hungry for the complete reunification of China.

After three years of fruitless U.S.-China ambassadorial talks in Geneva, Mao grew increasingly impatient with the stalemate over Taiwan. To demonstrate his determination and test American resolve, in August 1958 Mao ordered the bombardment of Jinmen (Quemoy), a Nationalist-controlled small island just off the mainland. Mao had no intention to wage war against the U.S.; indeed, he specifically cautioned his front commanders to avoid U.S. targets in the shelling. The attack created a crisis in the Taiwan Strait, with Washington urging Chiang Kai-shek to show restraint. In the end, the limited offensive achieved little for China. Leaders in Beijing were understandably aggravated, ruing the fact that they were not strong enough to confront the evil Americans.

Prior to the August 1958 offensive, General Liu Yalou, Commander in Chief of China's Air Force, had declared in an article that appeared in the *Liberation Army Daily* that "American Imperialists are no big deal. They just have a few more tons of steel—for the time being."[38] After the Jinmen crisis, *Red Flag* commented:

> American aggressors bully us because we have too little steel. This compels us to develop our steel industry as fast as possible. . . . American aggressors still view us as the China of old, believing that we Chinese are just a pile of loose sand, easy to trample on. This demands that we get further organized . . . to demonstrate that the six hundred million of us are of one single mind.[39]

The United States thus weighed heavily on the minds of Chinese leaders as they strove to industrialize China through the Great Leap Forward. Mao himself showed some genuine interest in the U.S.; he called upon his party leaders to study the U.S.—not just for the narrow purpose of conducting diplomacy, but to understand some larger issues. Speaking to some party leaders in December 1958, Mao even complimented the U.S. Secretary of State John Foster Dulles as a "worthy enemy." Most U.S. officials, unlike their crafty British counterparts, did not care much about strategy; Dulles was a notable exception, said Mao. In a few recent speeches, Mao observed, Dulles addressed hefty issues such as nationalism, atomic energy, outer space rivalry, and international communism. "This is a man who thinks. Read his speeches, word by word. Use an English dictionary," Mao urged.[40]

Given Chinese leaders' obsession with the relative strengths of China and the United States, it was quite unfortunate for them, not to mention for the Chinese people, that the Great Leap Forward imploded. The effort failed to speed up economic growth; instead, unrealistic goals and mismanagement in the frenzied campaign brought China's economy to the brink of collapse, as a widespread famine descended upon the country. The drive to surpass Britain and catch up with the U.S. ended in a great setback.

Mao had to assume some responsibility for the fiasco. He stayed on as the chairman of the Chinese Communist Party, but allowed some moderate leaders, led by President of State Liu Shaoqi and CCP General Secretary Deng Xiaoping, to implement some rehabilitative policies so that the country could rest and recover. Peasants gained greater freedom in farming and received material incentives for their work. The production of consumer goods, neglected by the government in the previous years, revived and expanded.

There were even signs of a new willingness to be less dogmatic on ideological matters. In early 1962, at a national conference on cultural affairs held in Guangzhou, some top party leaders called for a more tolerant attitude toward China's scientists, scholars and artists, including those educated in the United States. Chen Yi was one of those who espoused the new line. Back in the 1920s Chen spent some time in France as a work-study student, and, after 1949, became one of the ten marshals in the People's Liberation Army and China's foreign minister. In his youth, Chen also tried his hand as an aspiring writer. Now, speaking at the Guangzhou conference, Chen declared that "we should not make our America-returned students to give up what they learned in the U.S. and to conform to the Soviet way. . . . Soviet and American stuff can coexist; let them compete in real life."[41]

This new trend toward moderation, however, displeased Mao. Sitting in the back seat, the Chairman grew increasingly restless with the "front-line" officials who, since the failure of the Great Leap Forward, had their hands on the daily business of the country. The Chairman could not stand the permissive policies of his colleagues, which he considered tantamount to the betrayal of the communist revolution, not to mention that, as a personal matter, his hunger for power meant that he simply could not stay idle for very long.

Mao reflected on some large issues as he justified a counterattack. In 1961 and 1962, while reading some Soviet works on political economy, Mao pondered questions of peace, war, and revolution, writing down lengthy notes. Had the possibility of war with the capitalist world been eliminated? Mao did not think so. Insofar as social classes continue to exist, there would always be the possibility for war.[42] Communism and capitalism were bound to contend with each other, and, as Mao saw it, communism was winning the battle; there was no justification for pessimism and retreat. World War II had ruined some imperialist powers and considerably weakened the others; the victor out of the war, the United States, was now in serious trouble, Mao thought. "Economic crises in the capitalist world after WWII differ from those in Marx's time. Generally, prior to the war, there was one [economic crisis] every seven, eight or ten years; in the fourteen years from the end of WWII to 1959, however, three crises have already taken place."[43] Capitalism was clearly in decline. All true communist revolutionaries should recognize this historical trend. "Too bad there is only one United States," Mao said at a party meeting about this time. "If there were ten more, we could handle them all."[44]

Mao's fighting spirit frightened Russian leaders in Moscow, who had no intention of provoking a showdown with the Americans, with whom they were pursuing a policy of "peaceful coexistence." Mao now loathed the Russians for what he viewed as their cowardice in the face of the U.S. power. He started to warn against the danger of "revisionism" both in China and in the worldwide communist movement.

In fact, even prior to the open split between Beijing and Moscow, Mao's ideologues had been busily condemning Yugoslavian leader Tito, who, his communist background notwithstanding, maintained a close tie with the United States and who, in Mao's view, was one of the revisionists that he warned people about. Those who freely fraternized with Americans could not be true revolutionaries; they were traitors to the communist cause. Writing for the *People's Daily* in June 1958, Kang Sheng, Mao's righthand man in charge of ideology, accused Tito of betraying communism. Kang recounted the words and deeds of Yugoslavian leaders in their dealings with the Americans, which "exposed the ugly face of Yugoslavian revisionists."[45] Tito considered himself independent and creative, Kang noted; for a self-proclaimed communist revolutionary to "sing praise" for the United States, "the number-one enemy of peoples around the world," this "must be some kind of ingenuity."[46]

Chen Boda, Mao's long-time secretary and another of China's leading ideologues, also accused Tito of selling out to the Americans: "Judas was paid a meager amount of thirty gold coins; American Imperialists today are paying Tito a million times more."[47] Because of Tito's betrayal, capitalism had returned to Yugoslavia, the Chinese charged. Thus, the once proudly independent Yugoslavian nation had come to depend on U.S. aid, which arrived with decadent American culture.[48] "Turn a few pages of Yugoslavian publications and you'll see what famed and popular Western authors are spewing out and what kind of American lifestyle Western movies propagate."[49] In this environment, so-called artistic freedom was nothing more than "the freedom for the corrupt and reactionary American imperialist culture to overflow."[50]

First the Yugoslavs and now the Russians capitulated under American pressure. In China, there were the permissive policies implemented after the Great Leap Forward. Mao did not want to wait for China's Khrushchev to come forward to denounce him, China's own Stalin; Mao meant to take his stance and fight. He made public his differences with Moscow and started an ideological war with the Soviet Union. In a series of "open letters" written in the name of the CCP Central Committee and addressed to Soviet leaders, Mao chastised the Kremlin for selling out to the United States. "It is the biggest hoax in the whole world," the Chinese proclaimed, for the Russians to portray the U.S., "the leading enemy of world peace," "as a loving guardian angel of harmony."[51]

The Soviet Union was making a fatal mistake, the Chinese warned. The United States was bent on world domination; it was self-deceiving for anyone to assume otherwise.[52] "It is quite evident that imperialism remains the main cause of armed conflicts in the world today, and American Imperialism is the chief culprit of aggression and war."[53]

The open letters to Moscow were widely publicized in China, an indication that they were intended as much for audiences abroad as for Chinese people. Mao wanted to warn the Chinese about the menace of revisionism and stir them up for combat. Against this background, the election of Democratic presidents in the United States—first John F. Kennedy and then Lyndon Johnson—only further heightened Chinese leaders' anxiety. In their view, American Democrats could feign "progressive" and "peace-loving" more convincingly than the Republicans and seemed to be more adroit at beguiling the fainthearted and weak-kneed revisionists in the communist ranks.

JFK's penchant for taking the moral high ground, for instance, was particularly irritating to the Chinese. As soon as Kennedy was elected to the presidential office, Chinese media moved to point out that little difference existed between Kennedy and his Republican predecessor. If one had to find a distinction, it was simply that Kennedy was more deceptive.[54] "Kennedy enjoys talking about history, but he seems to know very little of it," wrote Guo Jizhou in Red Flag. After occupying the presidential office for six months,

Kennedy had yet to do anything new, Guo noted. Like his Republican pre-decessor, Kennedy was unable to recognize the prevailing trend of history, which would soon "sweep him away."[55]

Another commentator, Chen Yuan, observed that Kennedy, in his 1962 State of the Union speech, used the word *freedom* more than twenty times. Yet, as Kennedy spoke, the U.S. Supreme Court was preparing to put American communists on trial and the U.S. State Department was revoking the pass-ports of these communist activists. "In the 1930s Hitler staged a Fascist 'trial' of communists; now Kennedy has foolhardily stepped on the same path."[56]

Chinese critics were no less severe with Lyndon Johnson. As with Kennedy, they characterized Johnson as an agent of American monopoly capitalists. Writing in *Red Flag* shortly after Johnson's election, Guo Jizhou stated that, given the dominant role of money in the United States, it made little differ-ence who was the president: "Republican Eisenhower, Democrats Truman and Kennedy—they are brothers in the same family, representatives of monopoly capital; Johnson is no exception."[57] Another Chinese commentator noted that Johnson "owns tens of thousand acres of land as well as a TV station with exclusive rights."[58] Yet another Chinese columnist pointed out Johnson's poor congressional record and called Johnson a hypocrite for claiming to be an advocate of civil rights.[59]

By this time, Chinese observers of American affairs had taken notice of the expanding civil rights movement in the United States. Following Mao's class-analysis approach, Chinese theoreticians presented the struggle for racial equality in the U.S. as a particular manifestation of the fundamental conflict between American capitalists and American working class. "Living at the very bottom of the American system of exploitation, American blacks are merely a source of surplus value for American monopoly capitalists," observed one critic. Racial inequality and oppression would continue insofar as the American capitalist system itself existed and no piecemeal legislations could solve the problem.[60]

This was how Mao himself presented the issue. "Of white Americans in the United States," pronounced Mao in 1963, "it is only the reactionary ruling circles that oppress the black people," and these reactionaries "do not repre-sent the great majority of white workers, farmers, revolutionary intellectuals, and other enlightened elements."[61] After the assassination of Martin Luther King Jr., Mao again voiced his support for the civil rights movement in the U.S., reiterating his view that the African Americans' struggle for equality was part of a larger war against capitalism. "The conflict between America's black masses and the American ruling clique is a class conflict," Mao declared. This struggle "will eventually converge with the American labor movement to terminate the evil reign of American monopoly capitalists."[62]

Mao's characterization of the civil rights movement as a class conflict rather than a racial struggle was consistent with his vision of a worldwide revolution against the American imperialist establishment. In doing so Mao was evidently drawing from his experience in the Chinese revolution before 1949, when his party successfully mobilized millions of poor Chinese to topple the U.S.-supported Nationalist government. For the Chinese people who knew this history, Mao's prediction of the inevitable failure of American imperialism was quite believable, and Mao's call for a noble struggle against American imperialism quite inspiring:

> The people in the socialist camp should unite, the people of the countries of Asia, Africa, and Latin-America should unite, the people of every continent should unite, all peace-loving countries should unite, all countries subjected to US aggression, control, intervention, or bullying should unite, and [all should] form the broadest united front to oppose the US imperialist policies of aggression and war and to defend world peace.
>
> The struggle of the people of the world against the US imperialism is bound to triumph!
>
> US imperialism, the common enemy of the people of the world, is bound to fail![63]

By continuously denouncing American imperialism and condemning Russian revisionists who allegedly capitulated to the evil Americans, Mao drew a clear line between capitalism and communism and kept the fire of revolution burning in China, especially in the mind of younger Chinese. The fervor, thus roused, would contribute significantly to the Great Cultural Revolution—"a revolution within a revolution"— that Mao was soon to launch to eliminate all "capitalist roaders" from Chinese society.

III

Zhang Xianliang was one of the unlucky Chinese who, in 1957, was identified as an antirevolutionary Rightist. For his criticism of the government in the Hundred Flowers Movement, the young man was exiled to China's desolate west, where he would spend the next twenty years. When the Mao Era ended in the 1970s, Zhang would reemerge as a novelist to write about his sad but fascinating past. In one of his stories, Zhang recalls life in a hamlet in China's remote northwest. The folks in the village, all members of the local commune, believed that a certain woman had traded sex for favors from officials of their Productive Team. As result, the woman and her family had enough to eat year-round, which was no small feat back then. Tellingly, the villagers dubbed the free spirit's home *Meiguo fandian*—"American Hotel"—bountiful but immoral.[64]

By the middle of the 1960s, many years had passed since China had her last direct contact with the United States. During those years China's official portrayal of America permeated the public mind, meeting little resistance, with the notable exception of the Hundred Flowers Movement. Now few Chinese actually knew much about America and a whole generation grew up in an environment where the United States was a mere concept, the very embodiment of evil and the main obstacle to overcome in the glorious march toward an ideal human society. Thus, when in the mid-1960s Chairman Mao called on his followers to take part in the Great Cultural Revolution to battle revisionist traitors in China and American imperialists abroad, a great many Chinese, especially the young, responded readily and earnestly.

Figure 4.1

Anti-American materials from the 1950s and 1960s. One poster caption reads: "People of the World, Unite and Defeat the U.S. Aggressors and All Their Lackeys!" Among songs listed in a music book: "The Great Anti-American Demonstration of the Chinese People" and "American Imperialist, You Scoundrel!"

The Great Cultural Revolution from 1966 to 1976 was Mao's final drive for communism in China. Politically, Mao intended to remove Chinese leaders who, according to him, had lost their revolutionary spirit. To achieve his goal, Mao did not simply seek personnel or organizational changes; instead, the Chairman resorted to the strategy and technique that he knew the best, mass movement. This approach would not only ensure victory over his powerful political rivals such as President of State Liu Shaoqi and General Secretary Deng Xiaoping, but also, Mao thought, fundamentally transform Chinese society as a whole. The goal was nothing less than "an explosive revolution from the very depth of the human soul," as a common saying put it back then. This "revolution within a revolution" appealed to the young Chinese who, as they grew up, had heard so much about the heroic deeds of their parents' generation and yet had done so very little of the kind in their own mundane life. Passionate and romantic, they dreamed of a great cause in which they would thoroughly rebuild China, and, for that matter, the whole world. When in May 1966 some ardent youngsters at the Affiliated High School of Qinghua University organized themselves as "Red Guards"—the first of fervent vanguards in the unfolding political crusade—they vowed to combat "any and all reactionary forces" and boldly declared their "unalterable moral commitment to the liberation of the whole mankind."[65] In a manifesto they issued, entitled "Long Live the Rebellious Spirit of the Proletarian Revolution!" the pioneering Red Guards challenged their audience:

> Today, have all old thought, old culture, old customs, and old habits been eliminated? No!
> Have all evil policies and evil forces been destroyed? No!
> Even if we sweep away all evil policies and evil forces now, can we be sure that they will not return in the future? No!
> Have all imperialists, modern revisionists, and other reactionaries been exterminated? No! No! No!
> Then, shouldn't the proletariat continue to revolt? May the rebellious spirit of the proletarian revolution soar ever higher!

Such passion pleased Mao, who personally corresponded with that particular group of Red Guards, applauding their "revolutionary uprising."[66] A few days later Mao issued a fiery proclamation of his own: "Bombard the Headquarters: My Big-Character Poster," in which he effectively declared war on the so-called capitalist roaders hiding in his own party and government.[67] In the three months that followed, Mao would repeatedly receive and review young Red Guards who made their pilgrimage to Beijing—more than ten million of them, all ecstatic to behold the Great Helmsman for but a second.[68]

Thus roused and mesmerized, the Red Guards set out to cleanse China. Anything that was not up to their standard of a pure communist world, anything that appeared to be "feudal" or "capitalist," had to go. The United States, the "last stronghold of capitalism," was naturally a target. Anything associated with America, however remotely, had to be destroyed. Red Guards in Beijing stormed Quanjude Restaurant, which was best known for Beijing Roast Duck and had many foreign visitors among its patrons. The young rebels smashed the old-fashioned decorations of the restaurant and set up banners and billboards that bore Mao's quotations, such as "Unite, the people of the world, defeat American aggressors and all their running dogs!"[69] In streets across China, the so-called "cowboy style" clothing became a taboo; young men and women caught wearing such garments ran the risk of having their pants shortened or ripped open by scissors-waving Red Guards. Similarly, women who had their hair artificially curled must straighten it out quickly or suffer inevitable humiliation. To avoid waste, Red Guards helpfully suggested that owners of so-called rocket shoes to cut off the offending pointed fronts and turn their Western-looking fancy footwear into sandals.[70]

Matters like these are no trifles, it was declared, because they signified self-centeredness, which was bourgeois and had no place in a communist society. People "should never underestimate the effects of such social ills; they can very well lead to capitalist restoration."[71]

Given this, even names of streets and institutions that did not sound right should be changed. In Beijing, at a rally attended by hundreds of thousands of Red Guards and amid thundering slogans such as "Down with American Imperialism!" a street in the city's embassy district was renamed "Anti-Imperialist Avenue." The street where the Vietnamese Embassy was located was now called "Support-Vietnam Road." Students at the Affiliated High School of Qinghua University, the birthplace of the Red Guards, resented their school's historical connection to the United States—Qinghua University had been founded in the early twentieth century as a preparatory school for Chinese students who were to study in America. Discarding the name Qinghua, the young rebels now declared their school to be "School of Fighting Red Guards."[72] Another notable American legacy in China—the Peking Union Hospital, founded by the Rockefeller Foundation decades before—was now known as "Anti-Imperialist Hospital."[73]

Above-mentioned activities of the Red Guards indicate that, in spite of all the anti-American fury, by the middle of the 1960s, very little American presence remained in China. Still, as the very embodiment of evil, America cast a long shadow on the minds of the Chinese people. In the wild political storm that was the Great Cultural Revolution, therefore, one easy way to ruin someone was to link the person to the United States. Once such a connection, however flimsy or contrived, was established, innocent matters suddenly appeared sinister. This happened not only with ordinary Chinese but also with those who held high office, including Liu Shaoqi, Mao's chosen heir and president of the People's Republic of China. Back in 1949, when the Communists first took control of China, Liu, the number two leader in the Party, trying to avoid a drastic economic decline, had made efforts to assure the business community of China that they had nothing to fear from the Communist Party. Speaking to a gathering of merchants and industrialists in the recently liberated city Tianjin, Liu told his audience that the new government had no intention of destroying private businesses. "The exploitative capitalist system plays an important historical role, a fact that we Communists readily recognize."[74] At the same time, Liu gently prodded the business owners to treat their employees well: "I heard that, at factories in the U.S., one cannot easily tell a manager or an engineer apart from a floor worker by just looking at them. That's the spirit of bourgeois democracy."[75]

What Liu said made good sense in 1949, but in the heated environment of the Great Cultural Revolution in the late 1960s, he was denounced for speaking of America approvingly and for giving credit to the exploitive capitalist system:

> If we go with this theory, American Imperialism must be the most meritorious system in the whole world today and deserves the greatest thanks because it exploits not only the working people of its own country but also the masses of Asia, Africa, Latin America as well as those of Europe, Australia and the rest of North America. In reality, of course, American Imperialists are the most monstrous oppressors, the most aggressive robber barons of the present time. Evidently, these are the heroes that Liu Shaoqi worships the most.[76]

Another weakness of Liu Shaoqi was his young wife, Wang Guangmei, which provided Liu's attackers a logical explanation for the alleged pro-American stance of Liu. At the end of World War II, Wang, the daughter of well-to-do parents and a graduate of a missionary college in Beijing, worked briefly as an interpreter for the U.S. forces in China. This was raised as an issue in the Cultural Revolution and led to the accusation that Wang was a U.S. spy—"an agent of strategic intelligence for the United States," carefully installed next to Liu to influence the long-term policies of China. Condemned as a "traitor, spy, and scab," Liu would die in captivity, and his wife would spend a dozen years in jail until the end of the Great Cultural Revolution.[77]

It was thus that association with America became a kind of vile disease, to be avoided by all means. In the late 1940s, Gao Yuqian worked as a typist for U.S. troops in China. Since then she had grown to be a star performer in traditional Chinese opera. In the 1960s, she was cast for a role in a stage play, the production of which Mao's wife Jiang Qing personally supervised. Some colleagues, however, objected to Gao's participation, believing that her questionable past made her unfit to play the role of a revolutionary heroine. It was only with the direct intervention of Premier Zhou Enlai that Gao's stage career was saved.[78]

Playwright Huang Zongjiang did not get away so easily for his alleged pro-American sentiment. Before 1949 Huang studied English at Yenching University, the Beijing-based American missionary school. After the Liberation, Huang joined the August First Studio, the moviemaking branch of the People's Liberation Army. In 1964 Huang went on a tour in Vietnam to make a documentary about the war and revolution there. While in Vietnam, Huang penned a play, *South, My Dear South*, which pays tribute to the Vietnamese resistance to the U.S. intervention. Portrayed in the play are members of an American family who hold conflicting views on the Vietnam War, some supporting, some opposing. In the Cultural Revolution, radical rebels denounced Huang as a "bourgeois humanist" who idealized America. Labeled "an agent of American cultural imperialism," Huang had to conduct public "self-criticism" and confess his crimes at numerous rallies and attack meetings.[79]

As Huang's case indicates, by this time, America in China had definitely become synonymic with wickedness, with no redeeming value, which people readily used to make a counterpoint. This was even the case with Chinese who did not like the Great Cultural Revolution so much. Some generals of the People's Liberation Army, who deplored the disorder caused by the Great Cultural Revolution, cited the threat of the ill-intentioned U.S. as a major reason for maintaining stability in China. In November 1966, the top leadership of the People's Liberation Army held a public rally attended by one hundred thousand military personnel, including radical soldiers and officers who considered themselves Red Guards and who had recently stormed various military headquarters and installations. At the meeting, senior commanders of the PLA warned their young audience that turmoil in China might render the country vulnerable to U.S. attacks. Marshal Ye Jianying, vice chairman of the Communist Party's Central Military Commission, reminded the young rebels that the Americans "are escalating the war in Vietnam; they're expanding their deployment in Vietnam to three or four hundred thousand, also mobilizing some servile countries to assist them, with Soviet Revisionists lending them a helping hand." Given all this, Marshal Ye stressed, the People's Liberation Army must maintain good order and strict discipline.[80]

Marshal Chen Yi, whose military career dates back to the 1920s when Mao first created the Red Army, also spoke to emphasize that no one should stir up trouble in the Chinese military if only to maintain vigilance against external threat. "Our army must be ready for war at any given moment. Will American Imperialists attack us through Vietnam? If they choose to fight and attack us, our troops should be able to react instantly and rush to the front to take on U.S. forces."[81]

While arguments like this won some breathing room for moderate Chinese leaders in the frenzy of the Great Cultural Revolution, more broadly their warnings about the evil intentions of the United States became part of the anti-American fervor raging then. China's young rebels, longing for a sweeping world revolution, were already highly agitated. In Beijing, with no immediate American targets in sight, Red Guards stormed and burned down the office of the British chargé d'affaires.[82] In South China, small bands of Red Guards, acting in violation of China's own law, secretly entered Vietnam to take part in the war against the U.S. and spread Mao's Everlasting Revolution. This latter activity created a problem for the Chinese and North Vietnamese governments, neither of which wanted to see the free crossing of their border, which would only further complicate their delicate relations. In the end, the Chinese government managed to persuade most of the uninvited Red Guards in Vietnam to return to China. A small number of the Red Guards were allowed to stay on, probably for symbolic reasons.[83]

The same revolutionary romanticism also led hundreds of young Chinese to enter Burma, where they joined local communist guerrillas fighting against the Burmese government. In a letter to friends back home, one teenager who had gone on this adventure thus explained his action:

> China's future is in our hands! The world's future is in our hands! We must bear in mind that two-thirds of all mankind still live in excruciating misery, struggling in overflowing torrent and scorching fire. We must remember that it is our historic mission to achieve the victory of the worldwide revolution. The cause of the Red Guards must go on. Growing ever stronger, the revolution will sweep away all the filth and refuse hidden in every single corner of the world. A new era will dawn soon, one with no exploitation, no oppression—it will be a thoroughly new world of *Internationale*![84]

As the Red Guards saw it, the ultimate battle in this global communist crusade would be the one with the United States, which was the last citadel of worldwide capitalism. A long poem, authored by an anonymous Red Guard and widely hand copied by the young rebels of the Great Cultural Revolution, conjures up just such a scenario. Entitled "Ode to Warriors of World War Three," the elegy begins with scenes of celebrations and festivities in America, immediately after communist forces have conquered the land. In the joyous crowd is a Chinese soldier who has fought his way through Asia, Africa, and Europe, and who now remembers a fallen comrade. He recalls how he and his friend have pledged to carry the struggle all the way to the United States, with the understanding that "Whether one's heart is truly red / will be shown in the final battle for America." The friend dies just as the communist revolution climaxes—"busts of Robber Barons of the Dollar Empire are smashed to pieces / and blood-soaked red banners triumphantly fly atop skyscrapers."[85]

> Lilies of North America
> Will bloom and wither again,
> You, my dear friend,
> Will sleep here, year after year.
> Tomorrow, at dawn,
> We'll return to our motherland,
> But you, my dear friend,
> Will remain here, forever,
> On this Atlantic coast.[86]

With the revolutionary romanticism of the Red Guards reaching such lofty heights and the gap between utopian fantasies and dreary reality widening to such improbable extent, a correction was bound to happen. In due time, a retrenchment would mercilessly destroy the hope and ambition that had inspired so many young Chinese, resulting in sudden and severe disillusion.

IV

In April 1969, the Chinese Communist Party convened its Ninth National Congress in Beijing. The meeting took place behind the closed doors, announced to the public only after the conference had concluded. The secrecy surrounding the meeting reflects the ongoing political strife and uncertainty in China at the time, three years after the beginning of the Great Cultural Revolution.

It was for a good reason, therefore, that the core message that came out of the party's Ninth National Congress was unity, as Mao personally exhorted Chinese people to "Unite to achieve greater victories." In the first three years of the Great Cultural Revolution, Mao succeeded in ousting his political rivals Liao Shaoqi and Deng Xiaoping, along with many of their followers. This took place, however, at a prohibitive cost for the Chinese nation. Now Mao wanted to stabilize the situation in the country. Partly to show that he had no intention to hang on to power forever, the Chairman hand-picked Marshal Lin Biao, a military man who had been Mao's comrade-in-arms and protégé for decades, as the new heir apparent. With Lin Biao at his side and the influence of the Chinese military greatly expanded, Mao sought to reestablish order in China.

Some radical leaders who risen during the Great Cultural Revolution moved into high offices, among them Mao's wife Jiang Qing. The great majority of the Red Guards, however, fared poorly. The Chinese economy, neglected amid all the political upheavals, now languished and could not provide enough jobs for China's baby-boom generation. Now that the government wanted to reestablish order in the country, it had to find a way to deal with the suddenly idle youth of China. Conveniently, Mao launched a campaign called "Go up the Mountains and down into Countryside," in which former Red Guards were encouraged—later required—to relocate themselves to rural China, where they would work in the agricultural communes, be "re-educated" by peasants, and supposedly become better revolutionaries. Within a few years, millions of urban youngsters, mostly middle and high school graduates, left their homes in cities and towns to settle in faraway villages to contribute to "the construction of new socialist countryside."

As this happened, it gradually dawned on many Chinese that, after years of revolution, conditions in their country had not improved; if anything, the quality of life in many areas had deteriorated considerably. People started to have second thoughts about their revolution, and melancholy set in. The urban youths who now lived in the remote countryside—in some cases borderlands such as Inner Mongolia and Manchuria—experienced the greatest shock and disappointment. Driven by the euphoria in the Great Cultural Revolution, they had thought that a great enterprise was awaiting them in rural China; reality, however, was dismal and disheartening. Scratching a living out of soil was nothing exciting, and local peasants frowned upon the city kids who crowded the already scarce cultivated fields, who, knowing nothing about farming, had to be carried along by the native villagers. The once proud and haughty Red Guards suddenly found themselves struggling at the bottom of Chinese society, doing little more than subsisting.

Miserable and terribly homesick, many young Chinese tried to make sense of what was happening. Not too long before, these young men and women had sung "Ode to Warriors of World War Three," vowing to save all humankind once for all. Now they were thinking very different thoughts. A poem by an anonymous author, which was part of an emerging underground literature among the despondent former Red Guards, conveys the mood:

> Little, preciously little,
> We know about tomorrow.
> There will be another sunrise, that much we know.
> By then, however, our prolonged sleep
> May have become
> Interminable.[87]

An event in the fall of 1971 awoke many Chinese. Marshal Lin Biao, the officially designated successor to Mao, could no longer bear all the pressure from the Chairman. Friction between the two grew, to the point where Lin felt that he would be eliminated just as some other leaders before him. Lin and his family tried to flee to the Soviet Union, where Lin had stayed during World War II, but their airplane crashed in Mongolia as it attempted an emergency landing, killing all those on board.

In a highly public manner, the Lin Biao affair revealed the failure of the Great Cultural Revolution, demoralizing many Chinese who had put their faith in the Great Helmsman. Mao himself knew this very well. With the Great Cultural Revolution going nowhere, Mao's health deteriorating quickly, and China having troubles with both of the world's superpowers, the United States and the Soviet Union, the situation was becoming untenable. Reality brought Mao back to his senses. Once again pragmatic rather than simply doctrinal, Mao initiated a retrenchment. Domestically he rehabilitated and reinstalled some veteran leaders ousted during the Cultural Revolution, among them Deng Xiaoping, the number two "capitalist roader." In foreign relations, Mao decided to make deals with Washington so that China could better defend against the Soviet Union, which Mao now viewed as a greater threat. One additional benefit of improved Sino-American relations would be the weakening of the U.S. support for Taiwan, which remained under Chinese Nationalists' control and which Mao longed to reintegrate into China.

In Washington, President Nixon favored the idea of establishing direct contact with Communist China. A move such as this would strengthen the position of the United States in the global struggle with the Soviet Union; it would also help the Nixon administration disengage from the quagmire that was the Vietnam War. After some behind-the-scene negotiations, including a secret flight to Beijing by Nixon's national security advisor Henry Kissinger, Mao invited the U.S. president for a visit. In February 1972, Nixon made his historic trip to China.

The reopening of Sino-American relations, taking place at a time when many Chinese were already skeptical of the Great Cultural Revolution, created a difficult problem for the Chinese government. In some ways, the Chinese state at this time resembled a theocracy, whose claim for political legitimacy rested on some sacred revolutionary precepts. The dealings with Nixon clearly violated some of these cardinal principles, a move that, if not properly explained and justified, could easily lead to a political backlash. The Chinese government had to move quickly to present its new policies to its people in ways that would facilitate Sino-American reconciliation and still maintain revolutionary morale among the Chinese people.

The task was daunting, which was further complicated by an ongoing power struggle within the Chinese Communist Party. After the death of Marshal Lin

Figure 4.2

Premier Zhou Enlai greets President Richard Nixon at the Beijing Capital Airport. Nixon's trip to Beijing and his meeting with Mao in February 1972 took place at a time when China was still going through the Great Cultural Revolution. The Sino-American *rapprochement* surprised many Chinese, prompting them to reevaluate the United States after more than twenty years of isolation and intense hostility.

Biao in 1971, radical elements in the party rallied around Jiang Qing, Mao's wife, who rose to prominence in the Cultural Revolution and harbored the ambition to succeed Mao. The moderate leaders, for their part, gravitated to Premier Zhou Enlai and, later, the rehabilitated Deng Xiaoping. Zhou was now fighting off a bad case of cancer and Deng was poised to succeed him. The moderate leaders supported and actively implemented Mao's policy for the Sino-American *rapprochement*, which they hoped would also have some effects on China's domestic affairs. The radicals, who had benefited from the Great Cultural Revolution, felt uneasy about Sino-American reconciliation, which they feared, with good reason, would undermine the revolution in China. Unable to challenge Mao's decision directly, the radicals watched, with eagles' eyes, for any moral lapse on the part of the moderate officials.

Mao himself knew very well about the sensitivity of the issue at hand. He did his best to balance conflicting considerations. Under his guidance, the Chinese government moved cautiously to introduce the idea of Sino-American reconciliation to Chinese public. On May 20, 1970, Mao issued yet another of his hotly worded anti-American declarations, in which he again denounced

American imperialism and called on people around the world to resist the aggression of the United States.[88] Privately, however, the government was exploring ways to start a dialogue with Washington. Later that year, Mao spoke with American journalist Edgar Snow, who, back in the 1930s, with his book *Red Star over China*, brought Mao and his Red Army to the attention of the Western world for the first time. To Snow, Mao expressed his opinion that "existing problems between China and the United States should be solved with Nixon" and that he would not mind playing host to Nixon in Beijing.[89]

Methodically, Chinese officials prepared their people for what was to happen. On April 27, 1971, the *People's Daily*, in an editorial, offered "A Salute to the Heroic American People." Starting with praises for the antiwar movement in the U.S., the *People's Daily* went on to celebrate the "great revolutionary tradition of the American people." "American workers make a great revolutionary force"; they are the "grave-diggers for American monopoly capitalism," by no means the "silent majority that Nixon believes them to be." It is these working-class Americans, the *People's Daily* declared, who will ultimately determine the destiny of the United States.[90]

A message such as this appeared impeccable from either the ideological or the pragmatic perspective in China's political environment. It carried on the traditional condemnation of American capitalism. At the same, it pointed to some revolutionary potential in the United States, thus hinting at the possibility, indeed the desirability, of reestablishing contact with the U.S.

Behind closed doors, the party was more candid on what was taking place. In November 1971, a few days after the government officially announced an upcoming visit by President Nixon, Premier Zhou Enlai personally briefed high-level officials at a conference. Zhou made only cursory remarks about the Soviet threat to China as a factor in Mao's decision to cooperate with the United States. Instead, the premier stressed the revolutionary nature of Beijing's new policy: "An American imperialist chieftain's visit of China is a victory for peoples around the world and indicates the failure of the U.S. government's past China policies." Nixon had no choice but to make such a move, said Zhou; the fear of the Soviet Union, the pressure of the upcoming presidential election, and the rising tide of revolution both inside and outside the U.S., compelled Nixon to "suit up and come to knock on our door."[91]

As for "why we assent to Nixon's request to visit," Zhou cited the need to "work on the American people directly." "The revolutionary force in the U.S. is gaining strength steadily, a fact of which we should take notice." Still, in the short term, it would be with the conservative leaders of the U.S. that China would seek to solve problems in Sino-American relations—"not just the left wing, or the middle, or even mere average conservatives," but diehard anticommunist conservatives such as Nixon.[92]

Given the circumstances, Zhou did his best to present and justify China's new policy toward the United States. He tried to be forthright and provided some practical explanations for the changes being made. At the same time, he took great care in maintaining his revolutionary posture, so as not to create too drastic a break from past rhetoric and policies of the government—and, as importantly, not to render himself vulnerable to attacks by the radical leaders in the Communist Party.

Understandably, therefore, Zhou was supersensitive on the political and ideological correctness of China's new policy toward the U.S. He chastised those who considered the unfolding Sino-American reconciliation a "betrayal of principles, a betrayal of revolution, and a betrayal of Vietnam."[93] Such charges were all "nonsense," Zhou said. He likened the upcoming Nixon visit to Mao's negotiation with Chiang Kai-shek at the end of World War II, and to Lenin's China policy after the Bolshevik Revolution in 1917, when Communist Russia recognized the warlord-controlled Chinese government and at the same time aided Chinese revolutionaries fighting against the warlords. Since great leaders such as Lenin and Mao could not be wrong, China's new policy toward the United States was beyond reproach. Chinese people should have confidence that, with improved relations with the U.S., China could better advance the revolutionary cause in America and around the world.[94]

After Nixon's trip to China in February 1972, which went smoothly and drew a great deal of attention both in and outside China, Zhou Enlai once again briefed China's high-level officials. This time, with the success of the Nixon trip in hand, Zhou was more confident and more candid. "Combat both of the two superpowers" was just a slogan; the Soviet Union was China's real concern. Zhou now downplayed the theme of revolution in the new Sino-American relations, suggesting that China should avoid "adventuristic moves" in its efforts to promote world revolution. China's priority should be growing its own economy, partly through "learning from the developed nations of the world."[95]

Still, Zhou would not let go of the revolutionary theme altogether. China "would continue to condemn the United States" because "there is still the Pentagon, which is a den of warmongers and is backed by military industrialists." Furthermore, for Zhou, there was still domestic politics to consider. Mao himself was quite blunt on this particular issue. At one point during a meeting with Henry Kissinger, Mao told his American guest that in order to rally domestic support, it was advisable for both China and the United States to denounce each other now and then. "It would not do to do otherwise," Mao said.[96]

Meticulously the Chinese government utilized various channels to convey its carefully crafted message to China's general populace. Shortly after Nixon's visit to Beijing, the headquarters of the People's Liberation Army ordered a new round of *xingshi jiaoyu* (briefings on contemporary affairs), with an emphasis on world politics and Sino-American relations in particular. The army responded quickly and dutifully. Commissars of the Kunming Military

Region in Southwest China, for instance, first tested their approaches and techniques on small groups of troops, developing in the process a set of educational materials (labeled "Secret") which they then distributed to party functionaries in military units to use in their instruction of soldiers.[97]

Following the example of Premier Zhou Enlai, the Kunming Military Region presented the reopening of Sino-American relations as a victory for the Chinese revolution, "a great success of Chairman Mao's revolutionary foreign policy." The Kunming educators noted that there had been "misunderstandings" and "slanders" on the issue, to the effect that China was "colluding with" American imperialists. Such accusations were groundless, the Kunming educators insisted.[98] "When Chairman Mao invited Nixon over, he had his eye on the American people." The talk with Nixon opened America up and created a great opportunity for the progressive forces in the world to advance the revolutionary cause in the U.S., and made possible "the fusion of Marxism, Leninism, and Mao Zedong Thought with the indigenous conditions of America."[99]

The military, which at the time was more closely allied with China's moderate leaders, pointed fingers at the so-called misunderstandings and slanders for good reason. The radical elements in the party and government, led by Jiang Qing, did not intend to sit by idly while their political rivals undermined the legacy of the Great Cultural Revolution. Two months after Nixon's China trip, the monthly journal *Red Flag*, the official organ that the radical ideologues tightly controlled, published a major article on a seemingly esoteric subject, the study of history. Authored by Shi Jun ("Warriors of History," a pen name for a group of official theorists), the article was so long that it had to appear in three installments, which respectively addressed the need to study "the history of the world," "the history of the modern world," and "the history of the modern world in the imperialist age." The authors of the article never directly discussed Nixon's visit; instead, in oblique terms, even for that age of innuendo and doubletalk, the radical propagandists lectured their readers on long-term historical trends. Human civilization would inevitably progress as Karl Marx had predicted; this forward movement, however, would not follow a straight line; rather, it would go through numerous zigzags, even reversals. For example, in the nineteenth century, peoples of Latin America liberated themselves from Spanish and Portuguese colonialism. What has happened since then? American imperialists, "in the name of 'Pan-Americanism,' waving both 'sticks' and 'dollars,' have harnessed many Latin-American nations under the yoke of neocolonialism."[100]

In view of such historical experience, Chinese people should be both confident of the inevitable triumph of their revolutionary cause and be aware of possible setbacks. Only thus prepared could the people see through all the intrigues of treasonous revisionists and be steadfast in their commitment to communism. As for the United States, the *Red Flag* writers went on to say, Great Leader Chairman Mao had long accurately characterized it as a "paper tiger," a prediction that recent events such as the Vietnam War had borne out perfectly.[101] American imperialists, however, would not step off the historical stage without a fight; to avoid defeat, they resorted to a wide range of tactics, including the manipulation of "opportunists in the labor movement." The pro-American traitors hiding in the ranks of the working class would try to "beautify imperialism, spread capitalist ideas, disarm the worldwide revolutionary people, and achieve what the imperialists themselves cannot accomplish directly."[102] Revolutionary Chinese must stay alert to this grave danger.[10]

Such charges and warnings made Zhou Enlai and his moderate associates nervous. Officially, the Great Cultural Revolution was still going on; the loss of the ideological battle could easily result in political ruin. Precisely for this reason, the radicals would not relent in their assaults and would pounce on any missteps on the part of the moderates. In 1973, for instance, there occurred the so-called "Snail Incident." As part of the Sino-American trade that had recently started, the Fourth Machinery Ministry of China dispatched a delegation to the United States to negotiate the importation of certain machinery. At the end of the delegation's visit, its American host presented the Chinese group with some souvenirs, among them handicraft snails. Having heard about this, the hypersensitive radical ideologues drew the conclusion that, by presenting the visiting Chinese with snails, the devious Americans intentionally insulted China, insinuating that the pace of China's industrial development was like snail-crawling. They charged that the foolish Chinese officials, in their eagerness to do business with the Americans, had let down their guard and brought shame upon China.

Jiang Qing took a personal interest in the incident. She went on an inspection tour of the Fourth Machinery Ministry, where she angrily denounced the offending Chinese officials and the wicked Americans. With the snails, Jiang said, "the Americans ridiculed us, humiliated us." She would, Jiang said, place the snails on public exhibition to show just how "slavish" some Chinese had become. She also instructed the ministry to cancel the planned purchase of American equipment. On this last point, however, Jiang Qing did not have the support of the majority in the Politburo, which concluded that Jiang Qing had made too much of a fuss over a minor incident.[104]

The radical leaders refused to give up. They saw clearly that closer relations with the United States would lead to the rehabilitation of America in China and would thus undermine the ideology of the Great Cultural Revolution, which was based on the concept of a "continuous revolution" against capitalism. Jiang Qing, who was now engaged in a fierce struggle with the reform-minded Deng Xiaoping for the right to lead China after Mao, could not tolerate an ideological retreat at a time when Mao could die at any moment.

Speaking to a gathering of government officials in 1975, Jiang Qing earnestly presented herself as a true revolutionary who stood firm against American imperialism. The prevailing trend in the world, Jiang said, was still the uprisings in the Third World "for independence, liberation, and revolution." The United States was in rapid decline, which heralded the "total collapse of both old and new colonialism." China must grasp this historic opportunity and mobilize peoples around the world "to achieve global socialist revolution."[105] She assailed those who overlooked or chose to ignore this prevailing trend. Instead of promoting revolution, the traitors of the communist cause were busily "making backroom deals" with characters such as Henry Kissinger.[106] "Like all reactionary agents," said Jiang, "Kissinger is at once a gambler and a pessimist."[107] Let the revisionist allies of Kissinger and his like keep their "white friends, big friends, and rich friends"; we revolutionary Chinese, Jiang declared, would stand by our "black friends, little friends, and poor friends."[108]

In effect, Jiang was trying to follow the strategy that Mao had utilized in his conquest of China—broad mass mobilization through the active agitation of class struggle, only this time it would be done in the context of the worldwide revolution. Jiang Qing, however, utterly lacked the pragmatic streak found in Mao, without which ideas remain doctrines on paper. Even more important, times had changed. True, for much of the Mao Era, Evil America had been an effective instrument in the Communist Party's effort to rally popular support for the Chinese people's revolution. Entering the 1970s, however, many Chinese, having struggled in Mao's "Everlasting Revolution" for more than twenty years with a dwindling sense of accomplishment, appeared exhausted and dispirited. Now the people longed for concrete improvement in their life, not mere revolutionary slogans. In any event, in terms of what to do, Jiang Qing did not have much of a choice. She had risen to prominence during the Great Cultural Revolution, and she had to carry on, if only to avert the very likely retribution of her political enemies. (Among so many others who had suffered during the Great Cultural Revolution, Wang Guangmei, the wife of President Liu Shaoqi, who had been accused of espionage for the U.S., publicly humiliated, and jailed for many years, would not forgive so easily.) Given this, Jiang had to go against the overall trend in the country and fight a desperate battle. When Mao passed away in September 1976, the inevitable came and Jiang Qing herself went to prison. Broad changes would soon follow, dramatically transforming China and Chinese views of the United States.

5

A Balancing Act

The *People's Daily*, 1979–1989

In 1973, while meeting with Henry Kissinger, Mao Zedong had told his American visitor that, notwithstanding the newly forged strategic cooperation between China and the United States, the Chinese government had to continue its denunciation of American imperialism. In doing so, Mao was being candid. For a very long time the notion that U.S. was the greatest evil in the world had been thoroughly integrated into the collective mind of the Chinese nation, so much that any hasty tinkering with the idea would have serious political repercussions. This could be extremely dangerous at a time when Mao's health was rapidly deteriorating and affairs in China were becoming more delicate and precarious by the day.

As it happened, within weeks of Mao's death on September 9, 1976, an intraparty power struggle broke out. In the subsequent showdown, some moderate leaders in Beijing defeated their radical rivals led by Mao's widow Jiang Qing. A year later, Deng Xiaoping reemerged from political disgrace and became the most powerful man in China. Deng, the short, tough-minded Long March veteran, had been condemned as a leading "capitalist-roader" in the Great Cultural Revolution; now he was determined to reform and reenergize the dilapidated communist state that Mao had left behind. The Mao Era came to its end and the Reform Age in China thus began.

Deng's reforms, which centered around the injection of market mechanism into China's state-controlled economy, did not come easily. Even though many Chinese were unhappy with conditions in their country, they had long become accustomed to the egalitarianism in Mao's China. Now, Deng's government promoted ideas such as competition in the market, and they began to feel nervous. Private businesses mushroomed, systems of accountability were established, and bankruptcy laws passed. Yes, as a slogan then popular put it, "To get rich is glorious!" But what if you did not get rich and was actually left behind, or, even worse, left jobless? Gradually, however, tangible benefits of the new policies converted many of these skeptics. The reforms in China picked up speed, and people grew more tolerant of change. Measures once considered heretical and outrageous came to be accepted as necessary and commonplace. Individual peasant families acquired their "responsibility field," which they could cultivate in whatever ways they liked, a policy that soon led to the demise of Mao's communes. Chinese citizens could now set up their own businesses and be their own bosses. Ambitious and talented individuals took control of many state-owned or collectively owned enterprises and turned the previously money-losing businesses around for profitability. The new entrepreneurs accomplished their goals by implementing many policies unheard of back in the Mao Era, including the firing of unneeded workers and declaring bankruptcy. By the end of the 1980s, even stock markets made their appearance in the so-called Communist China, drawing millions of *gu min*—"stocks people"—to the terrifying and yet thrilling game of money grabbing in China's evolving free-market economy.

Changes such as these significantly transformed the ways in which the Chinese of various sociopolitical standings—the Chinese state, intelligentsia, and general populace—viewed the United States. The Chinese government, in particular, encountered new challenges. On the one hand, to promote reform in China and openness to the world, the Communist Party had to forego its old verdict on America as nothing but a decaying empire destined for the historical dustbin. On the other hand, the Chinese state had to be careful not to give the West too much credit; otherwise Chinese citizens might very well question the legitimacy of their own political system, which the Chinese leaders did not intend to change any time soon. Throughout the 1980s, therefore, the Chinese state struggled between two conflicting imperatives in its presentation of America to the Chinese people. As conditions of China and Sino-American relations evolved and fluctuated, the Chinese government had to shift focus on America frequently to meet the particular political challenge at a given time.

The dramatic expansion of China's contact with the outside world in the 1980s further complicated the government's task of presenting America properly. Back in the Mao Era, when China was isolated from foreign countries, the Chinese state had the advantage of shaping America for Chinese consumption in a virtual vacuum, where contesting official views was not only politically forbidden but also practically impossible due to the lack of information. In the Reform Age, however, as economic and cultural exchanges forced the door of China ever wider open to the outside world, it became increasingly difficult for the government to control the flow of information in and out of China. America ceased to be a simple theoretical construct that the state could arbitrarily manipulate; now what the government propagated had to stand up under public scrutiny. This new situation, along with the Communist Party's self-contradictory desire to grow China's economy quickly and still keep intact its rigid political system, compelled Chinese leaders to play a delicate game of balance on the proper presentation of America. To grow China's economy, the government had to adopt and promote new ideas from abroad. To maintain political stability, the state needed to keep foreign influence, especially American influence, within certain bounds. The balance was hard to find and harder to maintain, and, throughout the 1980s, the Chinese government grappled with the troublesome task of properly presenting the United States of America.

The experience of China's top newspaper *Renmin ribao* (*People's Daily*) in the 1980s well illustrates the conundrum outlined above. The *People's Daily* was then among the most widely circulated publications in China, which, as the official publication of the Chinese Communist Party, played dual roles. Like any newspaper, the *People's Daily* brought news to its readers, however dull or limited its coverage might be. At the same time, the paper served as a mouthpiece for the government, providing official guidance on all aspects of life in China. The *People's Daily* thus wielded tremendous influence and shouldered massive responsibilities. Everything the paper published was supposed to be truthful, right, and authoritative, directly reflecting the integrity and wisdom of the Chinese Communist Party. Because of this, the *People's Daily* was not supposed to err, ever.

In reality, of course, it was impossible to avoid missteps altogether. Given the rapid changes that took place in China during the 1980s, and given the delicate and complex nature of the America issue, it was especially difficult for the *People's Daily* to be consistent, however hard it tried. The struggle of the *People's Daily* in the eighties thus makes clear the challenge facing the Chinese state that tried to rationalize and present a high-impact polity and culture drastically different from itself, all in a rapidly changing environment.

|

In 1978 Deng Xiaoping was preparing for a visit of the United States, a historic event scheduled to take place in January 1979. Officially a vice premier in China's State Council, Deng had emerged to exercise real power in the country. Deng's upcoming visit to the U.S. was significant both in substance and as a symbol. During his visit, Deng would discuss global and regional issues with U.S. officials and meet with American business leaders to promote Sino-American economic cooperation. China and the U.S. would also take the opportunity to normalize their diplomatic relationship. Equally important was the general message that the Chinese government would convey to its own people—China was serious about opening up to the world and engaging in meaningful cooperation with the international community.

To accomplish these goals, the Chinese government first had to break away, as gracefully as possible, from its own past. In the two years after Mao's death in 1976, the Chinese state had more or less carried on the old practice, fashioned in Mao's last years, in which the government separated strategic cooperation with the U.S. from the vexing issue of the fundamental difference between communist China and capitalist America. According to the official line then, America was still evil, its only redeeming value being its usefulness in China's effort to fend off the threat posed by the Soviet Union. Now that Deng was initiating more comprehensive Sino-American cooperation, not only in geopolitics but also in areas such as economy and education, the Chinese state's old rhetoric on the United States became problematic. If not anything else, Deng did not want to be cast in a politically unpleasant light—if America was all evil, why would he want to befriend the Americans?

Clearly, once again the government needed to prepare its people for a major change in its policy. In the middle of 1978, the government set out to do what was necessary. The *People's Daily* first published a series of news stories about certain "old friends" of China—American officers and soldiers who had fought alongside Chinese Communist guerrillas during World War II. This made a good icebreaker for the Chinese government since the Chinese Communist Party had always recognized the U.S. contribution to China's resistance to Japanese aggression in the 1930s and 1940s.

When veterans of the Dixie Mission—the wartime U.S. Army observation group stationed in the Communist base Yanan—visited Beijing in May 1978, the event became a fitting occasion to celebrate old friendship and comradeship, an event that the *People's Daily* covered extensively and proudly. Marshal Ye Jianying, chief of staff for the Communist forces in the 1940s who now headed China's National People's Congress, was shown warmly reminiscing with the American visitors. Deng Yingchao, wife of the deceased Premier Zhou Enlai, brought "roses of friendship" to the American group. The flowers, it was reported, came from a bush presented to her and her late husband a few years before by the widow of an American pilot who had fought in China in World War II and whose life had been saved by Chinese Communist fighters.[1]

Just as warmly and conspicuously, the *People's Daily* told the story of William Hinton. In the 1940s, Hinton, an idealistic young man from Pennsylvania, worked as an agricultural technician in North China. While there, the young American became fascinated by the Chinese Communists' rural reforms, which seemed to be helping the poor peasants long neglected by China's elites. Hinton later wrote about his experience during the Chinese revolution, and, in the 1970s, after a long interlude, he returned to China, eager to lend a hand to China's drive for agricultural modernization. Hinton's Chinese hosts highly appreciated this American friend's efforts; Premier Zhou Enlai met with Hinton five times. The *People's Daily* lauded Hinton as a noble American who worked tirelessly to help Chinese people. The paper even broke away from the customary laudatory tone of the time and reported on Hinton's gentle criticism of China's sluggish socialist system. In the U.S., Hinton reportedly said, inefficient farmers had to face bankruptcy; in China, with no such danger, many people were not working particularly hard to increase their productivity.[2]

The rehabilitation of America's reputation in China thus began softly with the celebration of Americans who had associated with the Chinese revolution affirmatively in one way or another. By doing so, the Chinese government started to speak of America positively without rejecting its own revolutionary past, so as to accomplish a difficult but necessary transition as smoothly as possible.

In the months that followed, the Chinese government dispatched to the U.S. several groups of journalists and artists, whose reports and performances would further warm up the atmosphere for the upcoming Deng visit. For the first time after a long period of isolation, Chinese from the People's Republic of China traveled extensively in the United States, and the journalists and artists sent home largely positive observations of American life. The reporters told about their encounters with many Americans who were friendly to China and interested in Chinese culture, as indicated by the great excitement surrounding Chinese artists' performances in Washington, New York, Minneapolis, and Los Angeles. Many aspects of American life, down to its smallest details, fascinated the Chinese observers. The reporters, for example, marveled how thick American newspapers were, especially the Sunday editions, which was a wonder to the Chinese who were accustomed to the daily fare of four to eight pages from their own newspapers.[3]

One member of the journalists' delegation, Wang Ruoshui, was especially candid and thoughtful in his writings. Wang, who some years later would emerge as a leading liberal dissident in China, was then a key editor at the *People's Daily*. On his U.S. tour in 1978, Wang reported on many aspects of American life unknown to Chinese back home. Among other matters, Wang noted that, contrary to the typical Chinese impression of the U.S. as a place of rampant self-indulgence and decadence, many Americans were serious and hardworking. True, "some Americans do say that they live in a 'consumers' society,'" Wang wrote, "but, as we know, there has to be some production to make consumption possible."[4]

Wang also observed that, notwithstanding the counterculture of the 1960s, religion continued to play a large role in American life—another point that was not very well understood in China. Wang noted that in his hotel rooms there was always a copy of the Bible, and one too on the desk of the U.S. president in the White House. At a Tennessee motel, a young man "with long hair and a big beard" approached Wang's group for a discussion on Asian philosophies.[5] The idea that some Americans actually worked and thought may sound commonplace, but this was something that had long been absent from Chinese images of the United States. The depiction of some Americans as ordinary, even serious, thus infused a little humanity into what used to be a lifeless abstraction.

As the date scheduled for Deng's visit drew near, the *People's Daily* became more proactive in its positive portrayal of the United States. On December 18, the paper published an article on the Declaration of Independence, which, the paper noted, "is the most important document in U.S. history" and "the pride of the American people." With this historic document, the U.S. Founding Fathers proclaimed the fundamental principles that man possesses unalienable rights and that the supreme authority in a state rests with the people. "These progressive ideas eventually spread beyond U.S. borders, heartily embraced by the Europeans and peoples around the world." Both Karl Marx and Lenin, the *People's Daily* pointed out, paid their tributes to this valuable American heritage.[6]

Figure 5.1

Deng Xiaoping attends a rodeo in Texas and receives a cowboy hat as a present. This photograph appeared in China's leading newspaper, the *People's Daily*, which was an extraordinary event at the time. Episodes like this on Deng's 1979 trip to the U.S. probably did more than his official dealings in Washington to rehabilitate America in the mind of Chinese people. Soon this would become part of the momentous reform that Deng launched in China.

In its effort to rehabilitate America, the *People's Daily* invoked the good names of Marx and Lenin as well as Chairman Mao himself. On January 29, 1979, the day Deng Xiaoping started his visit to the United States, the *People's Daily* published an article by Wu Liangping, who, during World War II, served as Mao's English interpreter. Wu told about Mao's long-standing goodwill toward the American people, as evidenced in a letter to an American lady who had written the Chinese Communists to express her support for their fight against Japanese invaders. Mao instructed Wu: "Please tell American brothers and sisters that we stand shoulder to shoulder with them." A photograph of Mao's handwritten note appeared along with Wu's recollection in the *People's Daily*.[7]

Deng's visit to the United States took place in late January and early February 1979, and the *People's Daily* covered the event extensively and enthusiastically. Reports were numerous and their tone celebrative. Deng's visit opened "A New Chapter in Sino-American Relations";[8] an evening spent at the Kennedy Center in Washington was "Touching and Exhilarating";[9] when Deng and President Carter spoke to reporters outside the White House, "Spring Arrives at Rose Garden";[10] when Deng traveled to Atlanta and Houston, the *Daily* felt the "Warmth of the Sun Belt"[11] and joyfully celebrated, "Hurray to the Cowboy Spirit!"[12] After Deng had wound up his visit, the *Daily* lost no time in characterizing the trip as "A Historic Visit with Far-reaching Impact."[13] "The friendship between the American and Chinese people is very strong," the *Daily* declared. Many differences existed between China and the United States, but these differences "will not stop the powerful growth of mutual goodwill."[14]

The flowery language aside, Deng's trip to the U.S. did much to accelerate the normalization of Sino-American relations and to transform Chinese perceptions of the United States. The event certainly shattered a long-standing taboo and made the exploration of America a permissible and even desirable endeavor. In China, a market-oriented economic reform was unfolding nationwide, and the Chinese government, eager to promote the reorganization of China's economic system, was arguing that China needed to learn from the advanced countries around the world. Agriculture, for instance, was always a major concern for a country such as China, and the *People's Daily* made serious efforts to introduce its readers to the advanced farming in the United States. In September 1978, when the *Daily* reported on William Hinton's return to China, it pointed out that Hinton the Pennsylvanian farmer cultivated 1,700 acres of land and could produce 1.5 million *jin* (half a kilogram) of grain every year.[15] To average Chinese peasants, these figures were almost astronomical.

After Deng's trip to the U.S. in 1979, the *People's Daily* organized a series of articles about farming in the U.S., focusing on the particular subject of mechanization—which, erroneously or not, the Chinese government at that time believed to be the solution to China's agricultural problem. One article in the *Daily* series was adapted from a *Time* magazine story, which describes the daily routine of an American farmer. Benny's farm is so large that he drives to get to his fields; his family owns 1,900 acres of land and leases 1,600 acres more. Benny uses a computer to process statistics of his business; in his possession are four large trucks, three pickups, and three tractors, along with some other machinery; Benny even has a small telecommunication system of his own, by which he keeps in touch with his wife while he is out in the field.[16] To Chinese peasants who were still scratching out their living with bare hands, this sounded more like science fiction than real life.

In addition to advanced farming, the *People's Daily* also brought to its readers the new concept of the "Tertiary Sector" or "Service Industry." In Mao's China, manufacturing and farming were considered real and valuable "production"; trade and services were viewed as superfluous at best, capitalistically exploitive at worst. In the United States, the *Daily* reported now, the service sector of the economy employed more than 60 percent of American workers and accounted for one-half of the country's gross domestic product.[17] To Chinese, this was eye-opening news. It so happened that at this time Chinese cities were overflowing with Chinese youth who had recently returned from countryside, where Chairman Mao had sent them during the Great Cultural Revolution. Unemployment was thus a serious problem for China and a bad headache for the Chinese government. In this context, the idea of "service industry" was not only novel but also downright useful. All of sudden, presented under the shining new concept of "service industry," setting up a tea stand in the street or operating a diner around street-corner no longer sounded as desperate or depressing as they would have been otherwise; after all, even in the advanced America, the Tertiary Sector was the future.

Indeed, the China press was not shy about portraying the United States as the archetype of modernity. Shortly after Deng's visit, an official delegation of China's leading economic experts toured the United States to examine the training of business leaders, and the *People's Daily* followed the group and reported its findings. While in the U.S., the Chinese investigators visited business schools at Stanford, Harvard, the University of Indiana, and the University of Pennsylvania, which impressed the Chinese visitors with their professionalism in the education of America's business managers.[18] To the Chinese, this was an important discovery because, under the system established in the Mao Era, there were no professional business executives, only officials appointed not so much for their expertise but for their political consciousness, their loyalty to the Communist Party. Clearly there was a larger issue, one that transcended mere business training. At the time, such an issue could not very well be explored in China, but the importance of expertise in decision making certainly drew the attention of the *People's Daily*. For the same reasons, the *People's Daily* took an interest in how various "think tanks" and advisory bodies were involved in decision making by the U.S. government. Reporters of the *People's Daily*, for example, wrote about the roles played by President's Council of Advisors on Science and Technology, the Rand Corporation, the Brookings Institution, and the Council on Foreign Relations.[19]

From the celebration of old friendship to the introduction of new economic concepts and on to the examination of the institutional aspect of decision making, the thematic coverage of the U.S. in the *People's Daily* steadily broadened. Geographically, the paper's report on the U.S. expanded too. In March 1980, the *Daily*'s U.S. correspondents went on a lengthy tour of America, going from coast to coast. They followed up with another tour, this one through the South, in April 1981. While in San Francisco, the reporters observed Dianne Feinstein campaigning for mayoral office. Echoing Liang Qichao, the Chinese scholar and statesman who first visited the U.S. at the beginning of the twentieth century, the reporters marveled at the boisterous and highly confrontational electoral process.[20] In Los Angeles, the Chinese journalists had a difficult time finding the "city" they expected to see—what they beheld was one endless sprawl.[21] As for Hollywood, the reporters decided that, indeed, money overshadowed art.[22] In Atlanta, Georgia, scenes in daily life led the Chinese to conclude that the civil rights movement had produced positive changes: formal segregation in public places had disappeared; half of the city's councilmen were African American; in the offices of banks and insurance companies there were many black employees.[23] In Mississippi, the *Daily* reporters took note of the sharp contrast between magnificent mansions and rundown shacks.[24] In Dallas and Houston, what impressed the Chinese most were the changing skylines of these rapidly growing cities.[25]

Back in China, a young American woman also made news in the *People's Daily*, revealing a different side of American culture to the Chinese. Carma Hinton, daughter of China's "old friend" William Hinton, came to visit some places in Shanxi Province, a remote and poor region of China where her father had worked as an agricultural technician thirty years before. Local officials, eager to welcome their guest, one of the relatively few Americans who came to China at this time, prepared a lavish banquet in her honor and generally went out of their way, not to mention beyond their means, to make her stay comfortable. Much to their dismay, at the sight of the dinner set up for her, Carma protested against the extravagance and refused to sit at the table. The *People's Daily* reported the incident under the title "American Youth Carma Boycotts Banquet." The paper reproached the responsible officials, who, nominally communist, proved to be lacking in virtue when compared to a simple young American.[26]

Thus, in the first few years in China's Reform Age, the *People's Daily* made a generally smooth transition from the fierce denunciation of America dating back to the Mao era to a far more positive presentation of the United States. To be sure, China's official media continued to cover the less than rosy aspects of American life; for example, the Miami riot in May 1980, the attempted assassination of President Reagan, and the serial murders of black children in Atlanta all appeared in the pages of the *People's Daily*.[27] Still, the overall change from unreserved condemnation to a more temperate depiction was conspicuous and unmistakable.

II

Deng's market-oriented reform had its detractors. From the beginning, many Mao loyalists felt uneasy about the new policies, which they feared would eventually destroy socialism in China. More specifically, some of these conservatives objected to the emergence of an individualist culture, which they equated with despicable selfishness. To a great extent, the critics attributed the particular trend to the corrosive influence of the West, which they in turn blamed on Chinese media's overly positive coverage of Western world, especially the United States. As Deng's reforms broadened, the hardliners became increasingly concerned. They called for an ideological rectification, which, in late 1983, led to the launching of a national campaign against what was termed as "Spiritual Pollution."

Facing such a challenge, China's reformist leaders had to react carefully. After all, they still considered themselves communists and they could not afford to concede the moral high ground to their detractors. The problem was not a new one. Back in early 1981, in response to mounting conservative complaints, the CCP Central Committee passed a special resolution on journalistic practices, in which the party admonished reporters for excessive liberal views.[28] A few months later, while meeting with U.S. Secretary of the Treasury Donald Regan, Deng Xiaoping personally reiterated his commitment to a revolutionary ideology. The Chinese Communist Party, Deng said, would keep alive the Yanan Spirit and stay loyal to Mao's legacy. Deng's pledge, witnessed by an American, appeared prominently in the *People's Daily*.[29]

Hu Yaobang, a Deng protégé who at the time served as the general secretary of the Communist Party, also took actions to appease the hardliners. Speaking at a party conference in April 1982, Hu cautioned officials and journalists not to go too far in their positive presentation of America. "When it comes to news reports, the first important thing is not to publish materials that encourage the adoration of foreign countries." The coverage of the capitalist world, said Hu, should be handled most cautiously. China's media should keep the Chinese people informed on progress made abroad, Hu acknowledged, but "we should not beautify, nor should we attempt to practice the so-called 'objective journalism.' "[30] In short, mass media were an instrument of the Communist Party and they should be sensitive to the government's needs at any given time.

These efforts, however, did not satisfy the conservatives, who felt that the reformers were feigning commitment and paying lip service to communist principles. They continued their push for more rigorous ideological control. In mid-1982, Hu Qiaomu, who for decades had served as Mao's secretary, asserted his authority as the party's leading ideologue and spoke out on behalf of the hardliners. In a major article published in *Red Flag*, entitled "On Bourgeois Liberalization and Related Matters," Hu cautioned against the indulgence of Western liberalism, which in his view would inevitably lead to mindless adulation of the West and eventual rejection of socialism.[31]

To illustrate the danger of so-called bourgeois liberalization, Hu pointed to a movie recently made in China. Called *Kulian* or *Bitter Love*, the film, based on a script by the well-known writer Bai Hua, tells about the misfortunes of a Chinese artist. The hero of the movie was an idealistic young patriot who lived in the United States at the time of the Chinese communist victory in 1949. Eager to embrace the liberation and to serve his beloved motherland, the young man returned to China. In the years that followed, however, the artist, with liberal ideals and Western connections, suffered endlessly in political whirlpools and eventually died of persecution in the Great Cultural Revolution. Hu Qiaomu, in his article, denounced the creators of the film for drawing such a contrast between America and China to make it appear that "in China there is no sunshine, no freedom; Chinese intellectuals are destined to be persecuted and humiliated; sunshine and freedom can only be found in the U.S., in the capitalist world."[32] The Communist Party should not tolerate such falsehoods, Hu insisted.

Another incident that took place in 1982 also provided ammunition for the hardliners' attack on "bourgeois liberalization." Hu Na, a teenage female tennis player, sought political asylum while attending a tournament in the United States. Infuriated by the scandal, the Chinese government reacted strongly, accusing intelligence officers from Taiwan and some malignant American individuals of inducing the young Chinese to defect.[33] In the eyes of the Communist hardliners, Hu Na's betrayal exemplified the ill effects of Chinese media's rosy portrayal of the West, which led many Chinese, especially the young, to see the West as a carefree paradise.

The reformers once again found themselves on the defensive. On March 14, 1983, the Communist Party held a high-profile rally to mark the centennial anniversary of Karl Marx's death. General Secretary Hu Yaobang delivered a speech in which he reiterated the reformers' dedication to Marxist principles.[34] The performance, like his earlier efforts, failed to placate the conservatives, who launched a concerted assault on the reformist leaders at a meeting of the CCP Central Committee held a few months later. Heading the charge was veteran leader Chen Yun, who had been a top economic planner under Mao and whose status in the party rivaled that of Deng Xiaoping. Physically feeble due to advanced age but still sharp-tongued, Chen lashed out at Chinese officials who, in his view, had lost their revolutionary spirit. "Some of our people," Chen scolded, "having taken a few glimpses of the skyscrapers and freeways abroad," jumped to the conclusion "that China is inferior to foreign countries, that socialism is no match for capitalism, and that Marxism is no longer valid." These party members, Chen declared, should be "re-educated," especially those in charge of the party's ideological work. Those who would not repent should be removed from offices. At the end of his speech, an evidently agitated Chen called out: "Long live socialism! Long live communism!"[35]

Deng Xiaoping himself, the leading architect of the economic reform, had to face Chen's accusation. Hadn't he gotten his "glimpses of the skyscrapers and freeways" when he traveled to the United States in 1979? It was he, too, who, just ten days before the current Central Committee meeting, sent an inscription to a high school in Beijing, in which he declared that "[o]ur education should face modernization, face the world, and face the future."[36] Powerful as he was, Deng lacked the sort of absolute authority that Mao used to possess, so he had to carefully balance between his desire to push the economic reforms and the need to maintain political stability, first of all within the party itself.

Deng had to make some concessions. He gave the green light to the drive against so-called Spiritual Pollution, much of which, the conservatives believed, came from the West.[37] The hardliners, having thus secured Deng's approval, leapt into action. Fiery editorials calling for an ideological rectification appeared in newspapers and on the airwaves; the party headquarters issued directives on particular actions to combat individualism and liberalism; prominent conservative leaders spoke out one after another against Western influence. A nationwide campaign was now under way.

The *People's Daily*, which the Party Center controlled directly, was obliged to reexamine its coverage of the West and revise its editorial policy to take into consideration the hardliners' position. Changes in the pages of the newspaper soon became evident. Increasingly, its stories about the United States were in the nature of cautionary tales, intended to warn its readers that life in the United States was not as rosy as many of them assumed. In early 1982, shortly after Deng had reaffirmed his commitment to communism in his meeting with Donald Regan, the *Daily* published a series of personal accounts of hardship in America. A middle-aged school teacher, who had recently visited his relatives in the U.S., explained that life in the so-called land of opportunity was not all that easy. His two brothers were both university professors, yet they were busy with their work all the time. His sister had a doctoral degree too, but, after giving birth to a baby and after numerous futile attempts to find a suitable job, she had started to work in a secretarial position.[38]

A Chinese visitor to Disney World observed how workers dressed up as lovely cartoon characters had to work long hours, suffered from hard working conditions, and earned low wages. Next to the news story, the *People's Daily* carried a cartoon captioned "Tears in Heaven." The drawing shows a forlorn-looking, skinny fellow taking off a heavy Mickey Mouse costume, splashing sweat all around. Drops of his perspiration roll on the ground and turn into dollar coins, which a fat cat capitalist happily picks up and put in his over-crammed pockets.[39]

In similar fashion, the *People's Daily* reported on some other horrible events in the United States. The People's Temple, the religious cult, led mass suicides and murders at Jonestown.[40] More than 150,000 children went missing every year, of whom 80 percent would not be recovered.[41] More than eleven million Americans could not find jobs, with unemployment rate staying at a high level.[42] Urban decay in cities such as Detroit consistently worsened.[43] More Americans lived in poverty than before,[44] and homeless people died in the streets right outside the White House.[45]

With stories like these, the *People's Daily* tried to strike home the point that bourgeois liberalization would not bring everyone freedom and prosperity; injustice and misery were the likely outcome. Ru Xin, a vice president at the Chinese Academy of Social Sciences, made this same point in a more scholarly presentation, a long article that appeared in the *People's Daily* in January 1984. In the three-installment article, Ru Xin stated that, in a socialist society, public ownership ensures a natural bond among all people; in contrast, "in the capitalist world, social relations are poisoned by bitterness, selfishness, deception, and greed, with human beings debased to behave like mere animals."[46]

Ru Xin's experience makes an interesting case, one that illustrates the fast pace of political changes in China in the early 1980s and the great pressure that China's mandarin theorists had to bear during the period. Back in 1980, Ru Xin had published an article in the *People's Daily* in which he expounded the humanist, rather than the revolutionary, element in Marxian thought.[47] At the time, the humanization of Marxism was quite fashionable in China, which tended to shift the focus in Marxist theory from class struggle to the alienation of man in the modern industrial age. This made popular the idea that humanity transcends national borders and political divides. As esoteric as this theoretical exercise may be, in China during the early eighties it provided much needed ideological justification for Deng's economic reform and openness to the West.

That was 1980. Now, three years later, as hard-line Chinese communists moved to rein in what they deemed as excesses of the reform and of liberal thought in general, Ru Xin returned to the *People's Daily* to qualify his earlier assertions. It was never his intention, Ru Xin wrote, to obliterate the fundamental difference between capitalism and communism.

Ironically, not long after Ru Xin did his backpedaling in the *People's Daily*, the political tide in China turned yet again. In fact, on the very day that the last of the three installments of Ru Xin's article appeared in the *People's Daily*—January 11, 1984—Zhao Ziyang, the Premier of China, arrived in Washington for a three-week-long visit of the United States. This event, like Deng Xiaoping's trip to the U.S. five years earlier, had a strong impact on how the Chinese state presented the United States to Chinese people.

III

By the beginning of 1984, the ferocity of the conservative assaults on Deng's reform programs had greatly alarmed China's reformist leaders. When Deng Xiaoping originally gave the green light to the campaign against "Spiritual Pollution," he acted both out of some concerns that he shared with the hard-line critics and out of political expediency. Deng wanted to promote economic growth without abandoning political control. Reform should move forward in an orderly fashion, carefully led and managed by the Communist Party. Additionally, by keeping his reforms moderate and within the field of economy, Deng felt that he could avoid unnecessary arguments with the hardliners over ideological matters. So, when the conservatives in the party demanded a crackdown to clean up China's cultural scene, Deng gave his approval. He hoped that such an effort would help, rather than damage, his economic reform.

However, once the campaign against "Spiritual Pollution" was in motion, it displayed a tendency to go far beyond the limits that Deng had in mind. The hardliners came out strong. They did not simply denounce what they viewed as cultural decadence but also started to fault policies of reform and openness as causes of such social problems—rising crime rates, prostitution, etc. In a way, the conservatives were quite logical in their reasoning as indeed a link existed between the overall changes in the country and the particular social ills that they deplored. The question was, therefore, whether one would accept the said problems as an inevitable cost of economic growth in China. Deng had suffered personally during the Great Cultural Revolution; one of his sons was paralyzed in a suicide attempt while facing Red Guards' persecution. As a young man Deng had also spent some time in Europe. These experiences, along with decades of inside knowledge of Communist politics, made Deng convinced that not only the Chinese nation but the Chinese Communist Party needed the reforms for long-term survival. Deng, therefore, could not abide to see the conservatives question the political correctness of his policies. Seeing that the campaign against "Spiritual Pollution" put his reform in jeopardy, Deng moved to rein in the hardliners. He spoke out boldly in favor of the reform and warned his critics not to go too far with their effort for ideological rectification. As the year 1984 began, Deng went on an extended tour of China's southern coast, where he inspected the Special Economic Zones he had established a few years before to experiment with Western economic practices. This was a gesture on his part to indicate his commitment to reform (he later would resort to the practice again). The conservatives, with only complaints but no constructive plans of their own, had to defer to Deng.

It was at this time that Premier Zhao Ziyang set out for his visit to the United States. Zhao, like the party's General Secretary Hu Yaobao, was a Deng protégé, well known for his boldness in pursuing reformist policies. In the late 1970s, while serving as the governor of China's most populous province, Sichuan, Zhao implemented family-based agricultural policies that were later applied to the whole country. Now, as the premier of the People's Republic and a top leader in the reform camp, Zhao naturally did not want to set out for the U.S. in an environment in which the West, especially America, was condemned as a major source of decadence and problems in China.

Zhao, therefore, had good reason for calling on the conservatives to ease their attack on the United States as he prepared for his visit. He had his way. What had previously happened with Deng's 1979 U.S. trip repeated itself. As Zhao visited the U.S., China's official media covered the event highly positively, with festive language and symbolism befitting such an occasion. At Andrews Air Force Base, where Zhao arrived, Chinese and U.S. national flags "flew high and proud," the *People's Daily* reported.[48] A large front-page photo pictured Premier Zhao and President Reagan standing at attention while anthems of the two countries were played.[49]

In Williamsburg, Virginia, Zhao was shown riding down the main street in a horse-drawn carriage.[50] After watching a demonstration of printers attired as early colonials, Zhao, the *People's Daily* reported, inquired whether that was the way "The Declaration of Independence" was printed.[51] Children at a local kindergarten sent Zhao a letter to tell him that they were making a dragon for a parade and that they liked pandas.[52] Speaking on behalf of the premier, China's foreign minister congratulated the United States for her "glorious past," especially the American people's memorable fight for national independence.[53] The *Daily's* coverage of Zhao's other activities in the U.S. was equally high-spirited, featuring reports that proclaimed the "Tremendous Potential" for Sino-American economic cooperation[54] and the "Great Prospect" for Chinese-U.S relations in general.[55] All in all, it was said, Zhao's trip was "A Remarkably Successful Visit," which showcased the "Heart-Warming Friendship"[56] between China and the United States and would help "make the Pacific Ocean truly pacific."[57]

When Deng finished his Southern Tour and Zhao returned from the United States, the conservative drive against "Spiritual Pollution" all but collapsed. The hardliners found it impossible to pick up from where they had left off. Back in Beijing, Deng Xiaoping summoned Zhao and a few other top party leaders for an important meeting. Deng decreed that the reform in China should continue and should, in fact, move forward at a faster pace.[58] Later, the Communist Party would quietly disuse the term "Spiritual Pollution," on the basis that it was not a "scientific" concept.[59]

In April 1984, the Chinese government received U.S. President Ronald Reagan on a reciprocal visit. In the spirit of openness, the Chinese arranged for Reagan to speak to a large audience in the Great People's Hall in Beijing, where Reagan chose to preach Free Enterprise. The *People's Daily* carried the speech, in a slightly abridged version.[60] In an even bolder gesture, the government let Reagan speak to students at Fudan University in Shanghai.[61] The coverage of the Reagan visit remained prominent in the *Daily* even on May 1, the International Workers' Day, when traditionally China celebrated the solidarity of worldwide labor movement.[62]

Gone were the concerted reports on the dark side of American life that had crowded the pages of the *People's Daily* at the height of the campaign against "Spiritual Pollution." In fact, the *Daily* engaged in a minor rectification of its own and reflected on the ill-fated ideological crusade. In an article entitled "What Is the So-called Capitalist Lifestyle Anyway?" a commentator sought to clarify the all important issue. A materially abundant life is not necessarily corrupt, said the *Daily* commentator; "while frugality is a virtue, this does not mean that we should resign ourselves to poverty."[63] Another commentator wrote to reproach those who considered advanced science and technology "wicked" and viewed foreign culture as "immoral" and "subversive"; the writer called for rational analysis of the outside world so that China could wisely borrow from the developed countries.[64]

In this spirit, the *People's Daily*, after Zhao's visit to the United States, made efforts to publicize the concept of "New Technological Revolution." On March 4, 1984, the newspaper published an article entitled "The Rise of New Technology Industries in the United States." "A new technological revolution is sweeping across America, rapidly transforming human life."[65] The *Daily* urged Chinese people to pay close attention to the new development. From May 18 to May 25, the *People's Daily* published an eight-part series on Silicon Valley in California. "The triumphs and setbacks, the joy and heartbreaks of the Silicon Valley tell us a great deal about how the most advanced capitalist nation is moving into the Information Age."[66]

Before long, in the pages of the *People's Daily*, America's new respect-ability expanded beyond science and technology. On June 24, 1985, under the headline "U.S. Banker Believes Reform Will Speed up China's Economic Progress," the *Daily* reported on how Thomas Johnson, CEO of Chemical Bank, evaluated the prospect of China's economy.[67] Lin Xi, writing about meritocracy in American society, told the story of an American acquaintance who had worked as a janitor before he rose to be the personnel manager of a company.[68] Zhang Hongyi, for his part, was quite impressed by the works of idealistic volunteers that he witnessed in the U.S.—from those who helped out at the Los Angeles Olympic Games to those who assisted patients in local hospitals. Explaining the phenomenon, Zhang pointed to religious influence and America's immigrant origin. "American volunteers make me realize that even in a money-driven society like the U.S., virtues are present."[69]

Gradually, therefore, America, as presented in the *People's Daily*, lost some of its exoticism and wicked reputation and began to look somewhat familiar and sensible. Illustrative of this change is a column in the *People's Daily*, penned by Yu Lihua, a Chinese American educator and writer. The column first appeared in the *Daily* in 1985, under the overall title "Letters from America." Written specifically for a young audience and focused on daily life in the U.S., the series dealt with issues such as dating rituals, the generation gap, food, and fashion. In spite of the legendary American permissiveness, Yu wrote in one installment, most American youngsters grow up to be well-behaved citizens.[70] The reason for this lies in the fact that American children are taught not only to be free but also to assume responsibility. A nine-year-old American boy that she knew, for instance, would get up early every morning to deliver newspapers, which is something that few Chinese parents would even consider for their children.[71] Cases like this, Yu observed, make clear the American emphasis on self-reliance.[72]

Writings such as this may not be extraordinary in themselves. Significant, however, is the fact that such writings appeared in the *People's Daily*, which was the official publication of the Chinese Communist Party, directly managed by the party's Central Department of Propaganda. Actions like this indicate an official effort to present the U.S. in a way that was conducive to the reformist cause in China.

In fact, by the end of 1986, reform in China had reached a critical point. China's economic success up to that time had benefited many Chinese; it also gave rise to even higher expectations, leading some Chinese to believe that they would achieve far more if only they could move faster forward with the reorganization of China. Growing impatient with the pace of the reform, these Chinese blamed the rigidity of China's political system for the lack of greater accomplishments. In the meantime, economic inequality started to emerge, as some Chinese fared better than others in the new free market economy. Increasingly there came forward grumblings about favoritism and corruption.

Toward the end of 1986, idealistic college students took their demands to the street, where they called for faster and more comprehensive reforms, including political changes. The Chinese government managed to suppress the protests. Two and a half years later, an even larger pro-democracy movement broke out. Raging across the country, the protests culminated in open confrontations with the Chinese government and ended in a bloody crackdown at Tiananmen Square in Beijing in June 1989. China's mounting political crisis in the late 1980s would, once again, alter the way in which the Chinese state presented the United States to the Chinese people.

IV

As China entered the latter half of the 1980s, the economic reforms in the country had made considerable headway and also created a slew of new problems. On the one hand, the experiment with the free market revitalized Chinese economy and led to notable improvement in Chinese people's living standards. In both rural and urban areas, citizens were assuming greater responsibility for their own lives and were freer in their social life. On the other hand, new troubles reared their ugly heads. One of the most serious and scandalous problems was corruption, which, to a large extent, arose from the fact that now in China a free market economy coexisted with what remained of the old command economy. These two parts of China's economy functioned by very different rules, and profiteers abounded to take advantage of the situation. Officials strategically positioned could, for instance, easily sell much needed and state-controlled raw materials or energy to favored owners of private businesses for kickbacks or bribes.

Such problems, China's liberal reformers suggested, came from the incompleteness of the reform and could be solved only through further reforms. China must now take the next logical step and reorganize politically. The conservatives, however, took a different view. As they saw it, the so-called reformers had caused severe damage to socialism in China and allowed greed to run rampant. To eliminate corruption, the hardliners argued, the state must tighten control and crack down.

At a national party conference in September 1985, the conservatives, who never quite got over the failure of the drive against "Spiritual Pollution," renewed their denunciation of perceived excesses in the reform. Senior statesman Chen Yun once again spoke out, this time warning the party against "despotism," which evidently was a veiled attack on Deng Xiaoping himself.[73] Peng Zhen, another senior conservative leader and the chairman of China's National People's Congress, asked his fellow party leaders to answer one simple question: "Which of the two systems is superior? Socialist democracy or bourgeois democracy?" To him, the answer was so obvious. Yet, "some people, yearning for bourgeois democracy, seem to see a rounder moon in the capitalist world."[74]

The reformers tried to counter the assault. In August 1986, Teng Teng, a reform-minded official who headed the Communist Party's Central Propaganda Department, spoke to editors of the country's major newspapers. He encouraged his subordinates to be more courageous in covering the outside world. It had been a long-standing practice in our newspapers, said Teng, that international news never makes the lead story. "Why does it have to be so?"[75]

Then, on August 26, the *People's Daily* published an article by an American political scientist who argued that the reform in China was multifaceted—not only economical and social but also political.[76] This was a rather subtle way to open discussion on a subject that was still taboo in China at the time. On November 15, Deng Xiaoping gave the reform cause another boost when he personally met with a delegation from the New York Stock Exchange, at a time when Chinese reformers were preparing to do what the hardliners considered unthinkable—set up China's own stock markets.[77]

Toward the end of 1986, therefore, the rift between the reformers and the hardliners in the Communist Party was quickly deepening and widening. The division within the CCP's top leadership encouraged the Chinese who were already dissatisfied with conditions in their country. College students staged large demonstrations in several major cities, calling for political changes. Extremely rare in China, such open protests shocked Chinese leaders. The hardliners in the party blamed the serious trouble on the lenient policies of the reformers, who, they charged, gravely endangered Communist rule in China. Hard pressed by the conservatives, Deng Xiaoping had to give ground. Hu Yaobang, the reform-minded CCP general secretary, was removed from office.

With Hu out of office and students returning to campuses, the hardliners greatly expanded their influence in the Communist Party. Some personnel changes took place at the *People's Daily* and the paper yet again adopted an editorial line designed to discourage infatuation with the West. To speak with authority, the *Daily* enlisted the help of Zhou Gucheng, a senior history professor at Fudan University in Shanghai. Zhou was a personal friend of Mao Zedong when the two were young; in the decades that followed, while Mao fought his revolutionary wars, Zhou established himself as an academic with a progressive and liberal reputation. Now, under the title "Western Democracy Is Not All Rosy," Zhou wrote to caution Chinese college students on the danger of falling in love blindly with Western ideas. Young Chinese, Zhou wrote, should recognize that the Western system is not perfect and cannot solve all of China's problems. "In the West, everyday, a whole legion of sociologists, political scientists, and philosophers scratch their heads over the deficiencies of their own society."[78]

In addition to Zhou, the *People's Daily* brought forward some other academic dignitaries to share their thoughts on the West with restless students. In an article published on January 3, 1987, Lu Yizhong, a Taiwanese who had studied in the United States and then taught in mainland China, reproved Chinese students for romanticizing the West. Money drives the political machine in the West, over which the common people have relatively little control,[79] Lu testified. Qin Deqian, a Chinese American writing from the United States, offered some blunt advice for Chinese students: "Quit fooling around with the so-called democracy and liberty!" Having visited the U.S. since the early 1950s and resided there since 1977, Qin was confident that he knew more about America than the young students back home, especially the darker side of the United States: "billions of dollars in deficit," "street crimes that amount to a new, never-ending civil war," "distrust toward strangers and even among friends," "sexual diseases," and "the overflowing of illegal drugs." Qin also blasted Professor Fang Lizhi, a physicist and China's leading political dissident, for misleading young Chinese based on "the tidbits he picked up during his three-month stay" in the United States.[80]

In addition to enlisting the service of people such as the ones mentioned above, the *People's Daily* also did some of its work in the effort to admonish young Chinese naïve enough to be fascinated with the West. On December 31, 1986, just as the government tried to persuade protesting students to get off streets, the *Daily* published a report in which it informed its readers on the "Eighteen Types of Free Speech That the U.S. Constitution Does Not Protect."[81] In another article, the paper invited its readers to take a look at the "True Face of Capitalist Democracy: America's Ruling Elite." As early as 1972, the paper noted, it took $150,000 to run for a seat in the U.S. House of Representatives and anywhere from half a million to one million dollars to campaign for a Senate seat. The article went on to cite statistics from a book authored by G. William Domhoff, *Who Rules America?*, to show that a relatively small group of affluent Americans dominated the United States. As further evidence for its argument, the *Daily* pointed to the backgrounds of the recent U.S presidents: "All of the eight pairs of presidents and vice presidents after WWII were members of certain monopoly financial groups, or were backed by such groups," the *Daily* stated. Most cabinet members in the Reagan administration were top CEOs of big corporations, and "even Reagan himself, before becoming president, had not been the impoverished actor that many took him to be"—he was a millionaire too.[82]

The *Daily's* frantic effort to move young Chinese away from the fatal attraction of the West revealed the great anxiety of the Chinese government at the time. In fact, for a short while, it appeared that the hardliners in the Communist Party would completely overrun the reformers. However, as with the campaign against "Spiritual Pollution" in 1982–83, Deng Xiaoping was unwilling to abandon his reform programs. Once again, China's paramount leader managed to control the damage. In place of Hu Yaobang, whom the hardliners had brought down for alleged indulgence of liberalism and for the failure to rein in the students, Deng installed Premier Zhao Ziyang, a pragmatic but similarly staunch reformer, to serve as the Communist Party's general secretary.

Once in his new office, Zhao tried to carry on the reforms without unnecessarily antagonizing the hardliners. He tried to be realistic and endeavored to convince impatient reformers that overzealousness was counterproductive to their cause. At the same time, he fought haughty conservative leaders to prevent them from destroying the reform.

On January 12, 1987, Chen Junsheng, who served as the chief of staff for Zhao Ziyang, published a lengthy article in the *People's Daily*. In an unusually candid discussion, Chen eschewed doctrinal jargon and tried to explain, in easily understood common terms, why China could not simply adopt the Western system of democracy. Those Chinese who were impatient with the pace of the reform often compared China with the United States, but this was not a fair comparison, Chen wrote. Among other things, the United States possessed enormous natural resources, and, over the past two hundred years, had generally enjoyed peaceful development. Even among the world's developed capitalist nations, the United States was an exceptional case. More than one hundred countries in the world were capitalist, Chen wrote, but most of these nations are backward and chaotic. China, therefore, should not simply attempt to follow the American Way. Chinese people should continue to experiment with socialism—the reformed version, of course.[83]

In effect, Chen was suggesting a new line of argument for the Chinese government on what to make of the West, the United States in particular. In this way of thinking, one should not simply place China and the United States next to each other and force people to choose between the two as they stand at the present time. Instead, one should first investigate what has happened in each of the two cases over time. In other words, differences indeed exist between China and America, but this does not mean that the two sides are simply antithetical to each other; instead, the gap can be more plausibly explained in a historical perspective, as differences between stages of development. There is, therefore, no need to deny the merits of the United States, as Chinese conservatives are inclined to do, nor is there the need to be completely despairing of China's own system, as the radicals are often are. Given time, China will not only catch up with the United States but also surpass it because China has the advantage of making decisions based on the experience of both America and China.

Zhao Fusan, in a major article that appeared in the *People's Daily* in March 1987, further expanded the argument that Chen Junsheng had laid out.

Another heavyweight reformist theorist, Zhao Fusan, like Ru Xin mentioned earlier, was a vice president at the Chinese Academy of Social Sciences. His article, "Reflections on Modern Western Culture," took up two full pages of the *People's Daily*'s regular eight. Zhao opened his discussion with a question posed by American cultural historian Jacques Barzun, whether democratic theory is for export. Zhao then went on to present the Western discourse on the subject, starting with John Locke, Benjamin Franklin, and Alexis de Tocqueville. He explicated Barzun's idea that democracy is an abstract concept, the application of which in real life very much depends on specific historical and cultural contexts.[84] Affirming the desirability of democracy, Zhao suggested that no democratic system can be readily transplanted. China can benefit from the Western experience, but the country can only do so through careful "selective absorption."[85]

This new, middle-road outlook on the relationship between China and the West soon came to be reflected in the Chinese government's official line. Delivering the keynote speech at the CCP Thirteenth National Congress, held in November 1987, General Secretary Zhao Ziyang emphasized that China at present was in "the initial stage of the socialist development"—the country was socialist, but much was to be done before China could claim the true success of socialism and the triumph over capitalism.[86] With this new concept, Zhao was able at once to validate socialism (dear to the conservatives) and to acknowledge that in many ways the West was more advanced than China (as emphasized by the reformers). Evidently, Zhao and his reformist associates hoped that, with a compromise like this, they could calm China's political waters and concentrate on the particulars of their reform program.

The new approach produced some desired results. Student protests subsided; conservative attacks abated. The *People's Daily* quietly discontinued its nervous drive to warn young Chinese against the allure of the West and resumed diverse coverage of the United States. The paper dutifully brought out "bad news"—the crash of the U.S. stock market in October 1987, for instance—but it did so in generally rational and measured ways, with analysis, refraining from sweeping ideological condemnation.[87] In a moderate tone, the paper also offered upbeat tales of American life, such as successes achieved by some Chinese American families,[88] along with various seemingly insignificant human-interest stories—baby Jessica rescued from a well, or, Nashville as America's country music capital.[89] In one photograph, George H. W. Bush and his wife Barbara pose happily with their bicycles at Tiananmen Square. On the same page, one could find a story about pop music with the headline "Madonna Rocks Europe."[90]

It seemed, therefore, that the *People's Daily*'s U.S. coverage had reached a state of mundane normalcy and inconsequentiality. The appearance was deceptive. In China of the late 1980s, the acceptance of American life as normal or ordinary was in itself part of the "bourgeois liberalization." More than anybody else, the hardliners in the Communist Party knew that China was gradually but unmistakably drifting away from the revolutionary past that they cherished so much.

But the struggle was far from over. In retrospect, the political troubles in 1986–87 were just a small tremor preceding a big shake. The Communist Party's swift actions in the earlier unrests prevented the full release of pent-up energy, which would continue to accumulate quietly. Many Chinese were still unhappy with conditions in the country, but for different reasons. Some of them, especially younger ones such as college students, longed for greater freedom in their life and loathed the political and social constraints. Some other Chinese, among them workers who had been recently laid off from privatized state-owned enterprises, resented their own suffering at a time the rest of the society, especially the greedy and the well-connected, were making big bucks. There were, therefore, different sources of discontent, but the ire was all directed against the Chinese Communist Party and the Chinese government.

In early 1989, the tension within the Chinese state and society erupted violently. Popular demonstrations broke out across the country, leading to a political crisis far larger than the troubles in 1986. For weeks, college students from all over the country, along with local residents, occupied Tiananmen Square in the heart of Beijing, insisting on immediate political reforms. General Secretary Zhao Ziyang urged moderation. He intimated to the demonstrators that he favored further reform, but the hardliners and Deng Xiaoping himself prevented him from moving forward. He appealed to the protestors to be patient and to give him some time. Zhao's plea could not placate the protesters; it only alienated Deng and conservative party leaders. As the occupation of Tiananmen Square and indeed the siege of Beijing continued, the danger of a total collapse loomed. Deng decided to send in military forces. In the early hours of June 4, units of the People's Liberation Army broke though blockades of the protesters and took control of Tiananmen Square, causing the death of numerous demonstrators. Blamed for the failure to control the protesters, General Secretary Zhao Ziyang, like Hu Yaobang back in 1987, fell from office.

Throughout the 1980s, the Chinese Communist Party struggled with the proper presentation of the United States. Torn by desires to reform China and still maintain political stability, the government swung back and forth wildly between rendering the United States as an advanced country from which China could surely learn and condemning America as an atrocious influence that brought about serious social and political problems in China. The dilemma troubled the Chinese state throughout the decade and contributed to the outbreak of political upheavals at the end of the 1980s. The government had to carry on its arduous search for a balance between conflicting considerations, all the while adjusting to the evolving general circumstances in the country and in Sino-American relations.

6

Chinese Review America

The *Dushu* Magazine, 1979–1989

Dushu, or *Reading*, a book review monthly based in Beijing, came into being in 1979, when the wave of reform started to sweep across China. Riding the tide of the dramatic changes that followed, the journal soon achieved respectability and popularity among educated Chinese. The circulation numbers were never truly large, ranging from forty to one hundred thousand monthly copies. The relatively small circulation, however, does not tell the full story because among readers of *Dushu* were the best minds of China.

In part, *Dushu* derived its success from a particular persona—it was scholarly but not overly academic. This special trait had an interesting effect on the journal's fate. Generally, authorities in China kept a vigilant watch over standard academic publications because these journals enjoyed official or semiofficial status. The state was equally alert in regulating popular magazines in view of their large circulations and their massive following. In the 1980s, *Dushu* was one of the few periodicals that fell somewhere in between the two categories of periodicals mentioned above. More than most Chinese publications in the 1980s, therefore, *Dushu* could speak its own mind.

The greater freedom enjoyed by *Dushu* also came about as a matter of tradition. The journal was a publication of Beijing-based Sanlian Shudian (Joint Publishing House), the origin of which can be traced back to Zou Taofen, the pro-Communist journalist and publisher active in the 1930s and 1940s. Because of Zou's progressive and revolutionary past, after the communist victory in 1949, the Chinese government allowed his publishing house to continue its operation, in a consolidated form. The press came to specialize in translated works and books on world affairs. This gave the Sanlian Press a special status and unique identity, which partly accounts for *Dushu*'s critical mind and its sense of independence. In some ways, one can compare *Dushu* to *The New York Review of Books* in the United States—it is respectable, liberal, and politically engaged.

While *Dushu* covered books of all kinds, it was particularly strong in the introduction of Western works, which was much needed with the end of the Mao Era in China. Not surprisingly, works by American authors and books about America took up considerable space in the journal. *Dushu* thus served as a lively and important forum for Chinese intellectuals who were actively involved in a continuous discourse on the United States, an enterprise intricately linked to the intellectual life and other larger events of China during the 1980s.

I

Dushu made its first appearance in April 1979, three months after Deng Xiaoping's historic trip to the United States. Officially, a new era had dawned in China. In many ways, however, the Chinese continued to live in the long shadow of the Great Cultural Revolution. This was particularly true with regard to the United States, which for decades had been China's archenemy, condemned as the very embodiment of evil. Yet, the impulse for change was strong, and so was Chinese intellectuals' desire to learn about the mysterious land on the other side of the Pacific. As soon as it came into being, *Dushu* boldly took on what was formerly a taboo subject and set out to open a new vista upon America.

Dushu made its mission clear with the very first article in its debut issue. In an essay entitled "There Should Be No Prohibition in Reading," Li Honglin, a liberal party theorist who later would rise high in the reformist camp, blasted censorship and book burnings during the Great Cultural Revolution. Back then, Li wrote, of hundreds of thousand books, only a thousand or so were "kindly cleared and approved" by authorities as fit for public eyes. Decrying such horrors, Li called for "an emancipation of books, regardless of their origins—Chinese or foreign, ancient or modern."[1]

Li's article kindled a heated debate. "Just reading the title of the article makes me sick," one reader thus began his tirade. Shouldn't reactionary works be banned? Should pornography be allowed to flood the country? "With no prohibition whatsoever, our world would be a total mess!"[2] No less furiously, another reader warned people about the importation of "spiritual opium"—particularly the Western variety, which was supposedly the most harmful.[3] Yet another reader wrote in to express his surprise that the matter had even become an issue: "What of the capitalist world is worth our envy anyway?"[4]

Furious as they were, the outcries against the freedom to read went against the prevailing trend in China at the time. Having recently emerged from the horrors of the Great Cultural Revolution, relatively few Chinese—especially within intellectual circles—were in the mood to argue for tightening state control. The defenders of censorship were fighting a hopeless battle, at least in the pages of *Dushu*.

The theoretical establishment of the right to read freely, however, does not mean that the Chinese could actually do so, if only for the simple reason that for the time being there was precious little for them to read, especially on a traditionally taboo subject such as America. As it happened, in *Dushu*, the first American work that drew notable attention was Margaret Mitchell's *Gone with the Wind*.

In the Chinese context, the prominence accorded to Mitchell's particular novel was not so odd as it may appear to some people. Translated into Chinese soon after its original publication, *Gone with the Wind* had achieved great popularity in China prior to 1949. When the Chinese Communists came to power, they determined that Mitchell's epic novel was reactionary and poisonous, a "yellow book" harmful to the public. After the onset of the Reform Age, *Gone with the Wind* reappeared in China. Apparently, the notoriety it achieved in the Mao Era had turned it into a forbidden fruit, which many Chinese, especially the young, eagerly picked and devoured, the book's decades-old shabby translation notwithstanding. This was such a notable cultural phenomenon that, in early 1981, *Dushu* decided to organize a forum devoted to the subject.

Participants in the discussion were sharply divided in their assessment of Mitchell's work. Regardless of whether they liked it or hated it, however, they all viewed the subject in the tradition of Marxist literary realism. A critic fond of Mitchell's epic tale spoke of its "educational value." In his view, Mitchell truthfully presented life in the American South in the old days, including slavery, the plantation system, the Civil War, and the Reconstruction, making her work a great fictional recreation of "a revolutionary era in American history."[5]

Those who disapproved Mitchell faulted her for grossly distorting U.S. history. "As we all know," Huang Songkang wrote, "slavery is the most brutally exploitive system in human history"; yet, in Mitchell's novel, African American slaves seem to lead a leisurely, almost joyous, life. To make his point, Huang contrasted *Gone with the Wind* with *Jubilee*, a recent work of fiction by African American writer Margaret Walker, which tells the story of an irreconcilable relationship between a young black slave and her white father, a plantation master.[6]

The intense interest in *Gone with the Wind*, both among general readers and among Chinese scholars, well illustrates the limitedness of Chinese knowledge on American culture at the time. The people were still in the process of working out some old issues dating back to the Mao Era, and Chinese intellectuals, hard as they tried to embrace the new age, still looked at the world through eyes that were accustomed to signposts such as Marxist economic determinism and class analysis.

Slowly but steadily, changes came about. In the April 1980 issue of *Dushu* there appeared an article on another American novel, *The White Slave*, by

Richard Hildreth. In this review, Huang Shaoxiang, a specialist in U.S. history, denounced Hildreth as a reactionary. In Hildreth's book, Huang noted, the main character, a white slave, eventually secures his freedom by fighting for British forces in the War of 1812, which, as Karl Marx clearly pointed out, was an unjust war of aggression. In contrast, another character in the novel, an African American who chooses to confront slavery, suffers from his foolish decision. No wonder, Huang said, when American communist leader William Foster wrote his *Negro People in American History*, he did not bother to discuss Hildreth and his work.[7]

Soon after the appearance of Huang's article in *Dushu*, her own book, *Meiguo tongshi jianbian* (*An Outline History of the United States*) came under scrutiny in the journal. The reviewer, Deng Shusheng, was one of the liberal Rightists condemned by the Chinese government in 1957, and he now took issue with Huang's history of the United States. In particular, Deng thought that Huang did not give proper treatment to prominent figures in American history. In his view, Huang tried too hard to write a "people's history" of the United States; as result, leading Americans such as Washington, Jefferson, and Lincoln are virtually absent from Huang's main text, to be found mostly in footnotes. In places of these Americans, Huang prominently installs figures such as John Brown and Eugene Debs. Deng found this unacceptable. Can we Chinese, Deng asked, write a legitimate history of the Chinese Revolution of 1911 with only a passing reference to Dr. Sun Yat-sen?[8] Deng attributed the weaknesses in Huang's work to the undesirable influence of the Great Cultural Revolution. To demonstrate his point, Deng compared the work under consideration to another history of the U.S. that Huang wrote before the Great Cultural Revolution. In the earlier work, Deng noted, the U.S. Founding Fathers and similar historical figures feature conspicuously. Deng urged Chinese scholars to free themselves from the ill effects of the past and be less dogmatic in presenting America.[9]

In a similar fashion, Deng examined Liu Zuochang's *History of the U.S. Civil War*, another of the few works on America recently published in China. Professor Liu had started writing his particular work in the 1950s. The political troubles in the intervening years, however, prevented him from completing his study until the end of the Mao Era. This difficult birth left its marks on Liu's book. Deng took issue in particular with what he viewed as the excessive criticism of President Lincoln. In his book, Liu emphasizes that when Lincoln issued the Emancipation Proclamation, he had "doubtful motives and was largely pressed into action by circumstances."[10] Deng thought that Liu was too harsh on a historical figure who acted heroically at a time of tremendous challenges.[11]

Yet another incident indicates that, at the beginning of China's Reform Age, Chinese intellectuals were still viewing America in an old-fashioned, moralistic way formulated in the Mao Era. This particular debate concerns

Walt Whitman, whom the Chinese had always revered as a poet who represented the voice of working Americans. When an article in *Dushu* hinted
that Whitman was probably less than puritanical in his personal life, some
Chinese refused to accept the horrifying idea. Writing in the June 1979 issue
of *Dushu*, Huang Wu categorically rejected such allegations, defending Whitman as a highly ethical man who was incapable of uttering a single word that
would embarrass a grandmother.[12]

Figure 6.1

The journal *Dushu* (*Reading*) played a prominent role in China's intellectual life in the
Reform Era. In particular, the monthly book-reviewing publication served as an open
forum for the Chinese discourse on American ideas and institutions, an intellectual undertaking that became inextricably intertwined with the overall development in China.
Among authors heatedly discussed in *Dushu* were Margaret Mitchell, Thomas Kuhn,
Milton Friedman, Richard Hofstadter, Samuel Huntington, Reinhold Niebuhr, and Edward Said.

New ideas, however, were streaming into China. With enthusiasm and vigor, some Chinese writers experimented with new ways of thinking and new ways of looking at the world. This began with literary works. Some Chinese critics, for instance, endeavored to decode Modernism in American literature. Traditionally, in Communist China, Modernism was condemned as a sign of cultural decadence. Now the attitude was changing. In the September 1980 issue of *Dushu*, Qiu Xiaolong took on "A Rose for Emily," the short story by William Faulkner of which two different Chinese translations had been published in the preceding year. Explaining to his readers the odd tale of a woman who for decades sleeps next to her lover's skeleton, Qiu sought to enlighten the Chinese on the intricacies of post-Freudian literature.[13] Shi Xianrong, for his part, dealt with neo-surrealism in American poetry. His effort, however, did not seem to be very successful; at the end of his essay he readily acknowledged that he could not very well tell the difference between neo-surrealism and old-fashioned surrealism.[14] Such difficulties notwithstanding, many critics plodded on. In Terry Stokes's strange poem *Boning the Dreamer*, for instance, Cheng Bukui detects rebellion against capitalist oppression of man.[15]

In the field of traditional realist fiction, Chinese critics were more sure-footed. Here, *Dushu* reviewers focused on contemporary works, not only because the Chinese were already familiar with American writers of older generations such as Mark Twain, Upton Sinclair, or Theodore Dreiser, but also because Chinese readers were more interested in contemporary American life. Among authors covered in *Dushu* were Irwin Shaw, Isaac Bashevis Singer, James Michener, Joyce Carol Oates, and Herman Wouk. In these early years of *Dushu*, it was not uncommon that *Dushu* would review works that were not yet published in China. In these cases, *Dushu* was literally ahead of its time.

Before long, however, American works covered in *Dushu* did become available to Chinese readers, with some of them emerging as best-sellers. Among the most popular were works that "realistically" portrayed life in the United States. One particularly well-liked novelist at the time was Arthur Hailey. Technically a Canadian, Hailey gathered a large Chinese following with his detailed depictions of American scenes: *Airport*, *Hotel*, *Wheels*, and *The Moneychangers*. One *Dushu* reviewer wrote:

> You have never been in the Golden State California? Never had a glimpse of the Motor City Detroit? Then you must read Arthur Hailey. . . . If Dreiser's America was suffering from a high fever, Hailey's America is shivering in a cold that penetrates the very soul of America and is freezing its light out.[16]

Similarly, writing in the May 1982 issue of *Dushu*, Zhu Shida commented on the *Time* magazine's 1981 Books of the Year list. According Zhu, those works that showed up on the list well illustrated America's troubled "spiritual world."[17] John Irving's *Hotel New Hampshire*, John Updike's *Rabbit Is Rich*, Philippe Aries's *Hour of Our Death*, Diana Trilling's *Mrs. Harris: The Death of the Scarsdale Diet Doctor*—all these works, Zhu observed, convey "a sense of excruciating confusion, desolation and helplessness."[18] *Dushu* had crusaded for the right to read freely. It appeared, however, that once its critics actually had a chance to do so, they had relatively little to say other than the old verdict from the Mao Era—that America was decadent and in rapid decline.

This does not mean that nothing new was happening in *Dushu*. Their old way of thinking notwithstanding, many Chinese intellectuals were confronting materials of thought that had not been available to them previously. Furthermore, conditions in China were rapidly changing, which stimulated and inspired Chinese intellectuals in no small ways, urging them to expand their cultural horizons.

II

As we have seen, *Dushu*'s initial encounter with America centered around literature and its interpretation. This happened for good reasons. Of all elements in a given culture, literature is probably the most accessible to foreign observers. Furthermore, more than any other discipline of the humanities or social sciences, literature focuses on the darker side of human life—the agony, the struggle. In the context of China at the beginning of the 1980s, America in misery made a subject that the Chinese could easily understood. In this sense, what happened in *Dushu*'s coverage of America at this time was a logical transition, a link between the old and the new.

In the meantime, developments in China as a whole led the country's intellectual life in a new direction. With Deng at the helm of the Chinese Communist Party, industrialization and modernization became a common aspiration for Chinese people. In this connection, there emerged a strong interest in science and technology, which were believed to be the key to China's national success—with political reform not even a legitimate issue at this time and economic reform just beginning to unfold, the emphasis on science and technology was quite natural. This inevitably affected the thinking of Chinese intellectuals.

In October 1981, *Dushu* published an article to celebrate the launching of the Chinese edition of *Scientific American*. The origin of this particular project, it was pointed out, dated back to a conversation between Chairman Mao and Chinese-American physicist and Nobel laureate Dr. Yang Zhenning that took place in 1972. After close to ten years, Dr. Yang's suggestion to publish the Chinese translation of the particular U.S. journal in China had finally come to fruition. The *Dushu* article that marked the event was entitled "Science Has No National Boundaries."[19]

Apparently, given the political atmosphere in China at the time, Mao's endorsement still did wonders and provided good political cover, especially on a sensitive issue such as America. To fend off frequent conservative assaults, *Dushu* would resort to this tactic again. In February 1984, moving against the mighty waves of the conservative drive against the so-called "Spiritual Pollution," *Dushu*, in an editor's note, told a story about Lenin. On the eve of the October Revolution, the story goes, Lenin came across a book on agriculture in the United States, authored by someone called Haywood. The advanced farming in America described in the book left a strong impression on the Russian communist leader. After the Bolshevik victory, as the Russian communists struggled with reconstruction, Lenin remembered the Haywood book and had it republished; he would hand out copies of the book to Soviet officials who visited him. Later, when Lenin fell seriously ill and was lying in his bed dying, he thought about that book again and ordered officials to collect more materials on the subject from abroad. The bureaucrat charged with the mission, however, was a man who "rarely read and had never heard of the book," and he let Lenin down. The moral of the story: Lenin, a far-sighted revolutionary, was genuinely interested in progress and ardently searched for knowledge around the world, including the capitalist America.[20]

Soon *Dushu* discovered its own Haywoods for China. Figuring prominently in *Dushu* at this time were two best-selling authors of the United States, Alvin Toffler and John Naisbitt, whose respective works, *The Third Wave* and *Megatrends*, came to China in 1980 and 1982. What fascinated the Chinese the most was the American authors' futuristic visions of a human society fundamentally transformed through a new technological revolution. There was a feeling that if only China could harness the great power of the fantastic new technologies, the nation might be able to skip the dirty and messy Industrial Revolution and ride "the third wave" and "the megatrends" directly into the postindustrial age—like leaping off an oxcart and landing in a jet plane.

Dushu led the way in the introduction of Toffler and Naisbitt to China. In November 1981, one year after the original publication of *The Third Wave* in the U.S., *Dushu* took notice of it and started to carry excerpts from the book.[21] In the same issue of the journal there was a collection of articles devoted to the confluence of social and natural sciences.[22] In October 1983, one year after the U.S. publication of *Megatrends* and at the height of the Chinese conservative assault on the so-called Spiritual Pollution, *Dushu* published excerpts from the Naisbitt bestseller.[23]

Other pieces on the subject soon followed, including a two-part article by Yang Mu that appeared in *Dushu* in February and March 1984. In his writing, Yang evaluated the Toffler-Naisbitt thesis in the Chinese context. While carefully toeing the official line by noting the difference between the future envisioned by Toffler and Naisbitt and the future foreseen by Karl Marx, Yang nevertheless urged his fellow countrymen to listen carefully to what Toffler and Naisbitt had to say. If China ignores the New Technological Revolution, Yang warns, the nation may be doomed to lag behind the West forever. "On the other hand, if we heed the new trend and adjust our technological strategy accordingly, we can greatly reduce the time needed for us to catch up with the developed nations."[24]

Given the great benefits promised, there seemed to be very little reason not to like Toffler and Naisbitt. One unlikely convert to the teachings of Toffler and Naisbitt was Xia Yan, a veteran member of the Communist Party, an accomplished writer, and once upon a time a high-level official in charge of China's cultural affairs. Now in his eighties and physically fragile, Xia developed a strong interest in science and technology. As Xia himself reported in a *Dushu* article, he kept a copy of *The Third Wave* on his desk and would happily discuss with his visitors subjects such as "the fifth-generation computer" or "genetic engineering."[25]

Dushu itself was euphoric. In the editorial note for its January 1984 issue, the journal described its role in terms of the emerging Information Society—"a mere conveyer of information."[26] In another issue, the journal explained why it had paid so much attention to Toffler and Naisbitt: "The rapid progress of human society and the unprecedented expansion of knowledge have enabled us to do more than fantasizing about what is ahead of us: now we can foresee the future. We should make good use of the opportunity and better prepare ourselves for what is surely to come."[27]

Given this mindset, it is not surprising that, in addition to Toffler and Naisbitt, *Dushu* also showed strong interest in American science historian Thomas S. Kuhn, whose ideas on the structure of scientific revolutions enthralled the Chinese. In the two years from 1982 to 1984, *Dushu* brought out a dozen articles on Kuhn.[28] One exponent of Kuhn's ideas, Yang Yang, compared Kuhn's book *The Structure of Scientific Revolutions* and a treatise by Liang Qichao, the famed Chinese scholar and statesman active in the late nineteenth and early twentieth century. In his *Qingdai xueshu gailun* or *An General Introduction to Scholarship in the Qing Dynasty*, Liang traced the rise and fall of various Chinese scholarly traditions, primarily Confucian, from the seventeenth century through the nineteenth century. In Liang's delineation of China's academic evolution Yang saw Kuhn's paradigms. In identifying similar general patterns in intellectual and scientific growth, Yang said, Liang and Kuhn corroborated each other. "This is probably what is known as the consensus among the wise."[29]

Evidently, the Chinese interpreted Kuhn liberally and broadly, believing that what Kuhn had to say about sciences applied to the development of human society at large. Writing in *Dushu*, Ji Shuli stated: "It is when Kuhn superimposes his depiction of scientific progress onto broader social history that his work blossoms in full splendor."[30] To the Chinese, therefore, the Kuhnian "structure of scientific revolutions" not only sheds light on the dynamics of scientific communities but also explained the functioning of larger economic, social, and political institutions.[31] They believed that in Kuhn they had found an answer to a major question that had baffled many Chinese: Why did China, historically more advanced than Europe, fail to achieve indigenous scientific and industrial revolution? The Chinese did not fail for the lack of intelligence or diligence; they failed because they did not have proper "structures"—social, economic, and political. Kuhnian ideas, thus interpreted, became an instrument of social criticism for the Chinese.

To be sure, the Chinese were not the first to turn Kuhn into a social critic, but their eagerness in this undertaking is notable. The same spirit can be seen in the Chinese interest in the American biologist Edward O. Wilson. When Wilson first published his *Sociobiology: the New Synthesis* in 1975, his ideas on the biological basis of social behavior generated a controversy in the United States. Many scientists denounced Wilson for advocating racist gene-determinism and the news made it to the cover of the *Time* magazine.[32] In China of the mid-1980s, when Chinese reviewers introduced Wilson to their readers, they seemed to be oblivious to the original controversy. In fact, they were hardly interested in the issues that had generated the original debate; what inspired them was the great potential of fusing natural and social sciences, which they deemed as Wilson's "great accomplishment."[33] Writing about Wilson in *Dushu*, Li Kunfeng lamented what he viewed as the sorry state of Chinese social sciences—"mediocre, banal, timid, and despondent."[34] Social sciences in China are inadequate, Li suggested, because they lack the scientific spirit. Li wrote:

> Today, science has yet to enter many fields of human life, from which it has been arbitrarily excluded. . . . Unfortunately, wherever science is absent, theology thrives. Modern theology, often disguised as science, reduces human society to ignorance, backwardness, and regression.[35]

In China of the 1980s, "modern theology . . . disguised as science" was an easily recognizable codename for Marxism, which the Chinese government still stringently upheld. Edward Wilson, in this particular case, was effectively drafted to serve as a spokesman for the Chinese unhappy with the predominance of China's official ideology. The Chinese intellectual discourse was now moving beyond science and technology and onto some important structural changes that China was contemplating, first economic and then political.

III

In an editorial note in its August 1984 issue, *Dushu* declared that from then on it would devote greater attention to the economic reform that was quickly unfolding in China and that it intended to do so by "comparing China . . . to the outside world."[36] This conscious shift of interest reflected the changing conditions in China. By the middle of the 1980s, the economic reform in China had made significant progress and reached a critical point. When Deng Xiaoping first initiated the reform at the end of the 1970s, he made the introduction of the free market mechanism the core of his program, aimed to reenergize China's sluggish economic system. In years that followed, the policy produced impressive results. Privately owned businesses mushroomed across the country while state-owned and collectively owned enterprises became more productive and efficient. Up until the mid-1980s, however, all this had been taking place on a makeshift basis, in an ideological gray area, because officially China was still a communist country. Deng Xiaoping, known for his pragmatism, preferred action over theorization. To him, the best approach to the reform was "finding underwater stepping stones one by one as you wade across the river." Deng knew fully well that his reform program, if held up closely to the Marxist ideology that he and his party still subscribed to, would reveal innumerable embarrassing inconsistencies. Understandably, the Chinese leader would rather not talk about the ideological basis for his reform.

Many Chinese, however, found Deng's one-step-at-a-time approach unbearable. Such a makeshift approach, they felt, entailed too much uncertainty, which in the long run would harm the reform. As events in China unfolded, they observed a widening gap between what was actually taking place, the emergence of a free-market economy, and what remained on paper as the official ideology for the country, Marxism. Their logical mind expected the incongruity between practice and theory to be addressed early in the process so that China's reform could go forward healthy and proud. These Chinese intellectuals, therefore, refused to heed the government's cue that everyone should do but not talk; instead, they called for open discussions on the merits and flaws of various economic systems.

Interestingly enough, liberal Chinese critics at this time did not seek to emphasize the divide between socialism and capitalism. If anything, they tried to minimize the difference. This may seem strange at first glance but made sense under contemporary circumstances. At a time when the hardliners in the Communist Party were openly calling for the heads of the reformers, it took courage as well as tact to promote a free market economy. In the May 1985 issue of *Dushu*, Wang Yizhou reviewed a book by American economists Egon Neuberger and William Duffy, *Comparative Economic Systems: A Decision-Making Approach*, the Chinese translation of which had recently been published. In their study, Neuberger and Williams paid relatively little attention to ideological divisions among capitalism, socialism and communism, Wang observed. The authors instead focused on certain factors universal to all economic systems—Decision Making, Information, and Motivation (DIM). Given how ferociously the Chinese had fought highly destructive ideological battles in the past, this issue-specific approach, Wang said, was refreshingly sensible. Wang entitled his article "From Ism to DIM."[37]

In China of the 1980s, placing capitalism on an equal footing with socialism, reducing their difference to a mere technical one, was in effect legitimizing the capitalist system. Once the fundamental divide between the two sides was bridged, free exploration over the whole landscape became possible. Before long, critics in *Dushu* began to discuss a wide range of Western economists, including John Maynard Keynes, Joseph Schumpeter, and Milton Friedman.

Keynes was no stranger to the Chinese. As noted previously, back in 1957, some liberal Chinese scholars argued for the validity of certain Keynesian idea, an action for which they suffered political retribution. Ever since then, the British economist had been a target of continuous condemnation in China, even though it was not clear what exactly Keynes's crime was. The official line was that Keynes, a wrong-headed bourgeois economist, attempted futilely to save the doomed capitalist system. The real reason behind the Chinese hostility, however, seemed to be the belief that Keynesian economics had worked to certain extent and was thus responsible for the postwar economic prosperity in the West, especially the United States.

In the 1980s, as China went through economic reform, the fortunes of Keynesian economics in China started to improve. Some Chinese scholars now looked at Keynes in a very different light. To them, Keynes was a master economist who successfully combined capitalist free market with socialist state intervention, a measure that saved the West and the United States in particular from the destructive forces seen in the Great Depression. The Keynesian approach, it was believed, could be very useful for China as the nation tried to inject the market mechanism into its socialist system. In this regard, the only difference between China and America was that while the United States moved a short distance away from the free market to embrace limited state intervention, China was moving a short distance away from socialism to experiment with the free market—the end result was similar. Writing in the March 1985 issue of *Dushu*, Liang Xiaoming underscored this point, calling for "a reappraisal of the Keynesian Revolution." In terms of macroeconomic management, Liang wrote, "Keynesian ideas and Keynesian measures adopted in many capitalist nations offer us valuable lessons."[38] Thus, Keynes, the leftist economist of the West, was made to speak for the free-market–oriented reform in China during the 1980s. For the liberal Chinese at this time, the greatest value of Keynes was his argument for the feasibility of a hybrid economy.

In the same spirit the Chinese read Joseph Schumpeter. As was the case with Keynes, the socialist element in Schumpeter made him "relevant" to China in the 1980s. There is more to Schumpeter than socialism, of course, and this combination appealed to the Chinese. In 1987, when two young Chinese scholars, Zhang Weiping and Wu Xiaoying, reviewed in *Dushu* Schumpeter's *Capitalism, Socialism, and Democracy*, they did not pay much attention to the economist's socialist tendencies and instead emphasized his ideas on business innovation, especially the concept of "creative destruction." "Schumpeter's prediction of the inevitable emergence of socialism aside . . . his 'innovation theory' deserves our greatest attention," Zhang and Wu suggested.[39] In fact, the two critics were so appreciative of Schumpeter's stress on the critical role of entrepreneurs in economic development that they confidently declared that the time had arrived for China to produce her own Fords and Rockefellers.[40]

Not surprisingly, those who passively accepted socialism and actively promoted the free market found it relatively easy to connect to economists such as Milton Friedman, whose works *Free to Choose* and *Capitalism and Freedom* appeared in China in 1982 and 1986 respectively. Friedman was a very different kind of economists than Keynes or Schumpeter, so the Chinese approached his theories very cautiously. When, in April 1984, Nan Shizhong reviewed Friedman's *Free to Choose* for *Dushu*, he entitled his article "Not So Free to Choose." In his writing, Nan, insisting that the so-called invisible hand could no longer effectively manage modern capitalist economy, criticized Friedman for trying to explain away the Great Depression.[41] At the same time, however, Nan expressed his enthusiasm for many other ideas Friedman presented, in particular Friedman's assault on welfare state. Friedman, Nan wrote, demonstrates convincingly that "whichever field of people's lives the government moves in—be it social security, education, or health care—inefficiency, high cost, corruption, negligence, and lethargy inevitably follow."[42]

Making observations such as this, Nan obviously had in mind China's own problematic economic system, which, the ongoing reform notwithstanding, was still largely controlled by the Chinese government. Two years later, in 1986, when two other Chinese economists wrote about Friedman's *Capitalism and Freedom*, they were more candid in their criticism of state dominance in China. Zhang Weiping and Wu Xiaoying, who had previously praised Schumpeter for his ideas on "creative destruction," found much to like in Friedman. Reading Friedman's criticism of public housing in America, they deplored China's own housing system:

> For over thirty years now we have been singing to the tune of "to each according to his labor," but our way of providing shelter, which is fundamental for human existence . . . has never reflected that principle. As result, we have had some dismal results. This

testifies to Friedman's credo: you cannot force equality to grow; if you try to do so, you would only sacrifice efficiency and freedom.[43]

As a solution to the problem, Wu and Zhang suggested Friedman's concept of "customer sovereignty." Their slogan, "Long live the customer!" shows how far China had come since the days when everywhere in China one could hear "Long live Chairman Mao!" and "Long Live the Chinese Communist Party!"[44]

Wu and Zhang went on to write a few other articles for *Dushu*, under the overall title "Dialogues on Economic Liberalism." In the series, Wu and Zhang covered a number of neoconservative American authors. They, for instance, showed much appreciation of George Gilder's *Wealth and Poverty*, generally agreeing to the Reaganomics view that persistent poverty exists only in a stagnant society and that ultimately only economic growth can defeat poverty.[45] Another American economist considered by Wu and Zhang was James Buchanan, whose idea on "economic man" and "public choice" drew the attention of the Chinese critics. Because public ownership dominated in China, Wu and Zhang wrote, the "economic man"—the individual with clearly defined economic interests and rights—did not exist in Chinese society, a fact that had grave consequences.[46] The absence of the "economic man" not only led to economic inefficiency, it also stifled Chinese people's ability to evaluate their government as an economic entity, that is, its cost-effectiveness. As result, the people could not make a true, rational "public choice." In truth, Wu and Zhang wrote, "the state exists simply because traders seek to reduce the cost of their transactions, but we Chinese top the world in our tendency to mystify and deify the state"[47]—hence China's woes.

What to do? Based on their reading of Buchanan, Wu and Zhang felt that the solution would be, no more and no less, the dismantling of the Chinese system of public ownership so as to create the badly needed "economic man." As a rational being conscious of his own interests and rights, the Chinese "economic man" could then make an enlightened decision to create a responsive government. This, of course, was no longer a proposition for economic change but a call for political revolution.

IV

Wu and Zhang's exposition of James Buchanan appeared in *Dushu* in January 1987, immediately after the political unrest at the end of 1986, in which Chinese students staged demonstrations in major cities of China, demanding political reform. The protests shocked the Chinese government and led to the downfall of the CCP General Secretary Hu Yaobang, whom conservative leaders blamed for failing to maintain control. It was no coincidence, therefore, that liberal intellectuals such as Wu and Zhang looked beyond economics to ponder on political issues.

There had been heightened anxiety over the political situation in China in the two years leading up to the student unrest at the end of 1986. After half a decade of Deng's reforms, China's economy continued to surge forward, but discontent in the country was on the rise too. Issues such as corruption and inequitable distribution of wealth created no small amount of bitterness in Chinese society and prompted calls for political changes. Many liberal Chinese intellectuals believed that the reform in China had arrived at a point where continued progress would not be possible without political reorganization.

In September 1986, Su Shaozhi, a political scientist based at the Chinese Academy of Social Sciences, wrote in *Dushu* to make just such an argument. Since the beginning of the Reform Age, China had made the so-called Four Modernizations—bringing up to date China's agriculture, industry, national defense, and science and technology—as the goal for the whole country. The concept was flawed, Su now suggested. In his article, which was entitled "A Preliminary Proposal for Political Reform," Su argued for a fifth "modernization," the modernization of China's political system, without which the four other modernizations would not succeed.[48]

Su's call for political changes was direct and bold, but he was not the only one who contemplated the all-important issue in *Dushu*. Another scholar who wrote on the subject, though not as directly, was Zhao Yifan, who had recently studied American literature at Harvard University and returned to work at the Chinese Academy of Social Sciences in Beijing. Zhao's first contribution to *Dushu* appeared in December 1986, at the very height of the students' demonstrations then ongoing. In this piece, Zhao chose to discuss the evolution of party politics in the United States, as presented in Richard Hofstadter's *Idea of a Party System*. In contrast to widely held Chinese assumptions, Zhao wrote, party politics has not always been an accepted and integral part of American life; in fact, quite a few of the revered U.S. Founding Fathers vehemently denounced partisan politics, which they believed would ruin the young American republic. In other words, the party politics now so central to American democracy is not a given; it has its own difficult past and has evolved into its current state by fits and starts. Some of the best minds in the early history of the United States were strongly opposed to the idea. It was under a rather modest and average president, Van Buren, that the principle of "legitimate opposition" finally came to be recognized and established.[49] Were the Chinese students currently protesting in the street starting China's own tradition of "legitimate opposition"? Were Chinese Communist hardliners trying to stop an inevitable trend? Zhao left these questions for his readers to ponder.

While Hofstadter spoke from the ivory tower, another American author represented a more plebeian voice in *Dushu*—Hendrik Willem Van Loon, whose works such as *The Story of Mankind* were popular reading in the United States during the early twentieth century. In 1985, the Joint Publishing House in Beijing, which is *Dushu*'s parent publisher, issued a new edition of Van Loon's *Tolerance*, a history of the struggle against religious persecution and political oppression from ancient Greece to the time of Thomas Paine. *Dushu* carried excerpts from the book. In an editor's note, *Dushu* recounted the history of the particular Van Loon book in China. Initially published in China in the early twentieth century, *Tolerance* became unavailable in the country after the Communist victory in 1949. "Now someone has dug him [Van Loon] out and has, from his numerous works, chosen *Tolerance* to republish. The choice may just be fortuitous. In any event it will serve some good purpose."[50]

Given conditions in China at the time, the decision to republish Van Loon's *Tolerance* could not have been just a chance happening. In fact, after its appearance, *Tolerance* quickly became a best-seller and a much-discussed subject, especially among young Chinese.

As the country pondered on the need for political reform, top leaders of the Chinese Communist Party engaged in debates on the very issue among themselves. The high-level arguments soon spilled into the open. In April 1986, Zhu Houze, who at the time headed the CCP Central Department of Propaganda, delivered a notable speech at a national conference on ideological work. Zhu, a liberal-minded and outspoken reformist official, emphasized the importance of maintaining a politically tolerant environment in China. Coming at a critical point in the ongoing intraparty struggle, the speech was obviously designed to gather public support. *Dushu*, which rarely published official pronouncements, carried Zhu's speech, next to a long article on Van Loon's *Tolerance*. In their piece on Van Loon, Chen Kuide and Chen Jiade explained the significance of the particular American author in contemporary China:

> It is quite understandable that [Van Loon's] book should arouse strong emotions among Chinese people today. After all, it was only recently that the Chinese emerged from the "Ten Years of Turmoil." So, people's feelings on such matters are extremely intense, mixed with indescribable fear. It is remarkable that a book from the past can produces such enormous effects now, which we can rightfully characterize as "old words with new meanings."[51]

Still worrying that its readers might not get the point, *Dushu*, in an editor's note, explicitly linked Van Loon's *Tolerance* to Zhu's speech, which appeared in the same issue of the journal:

> Van Loon observed that incidents of intolerance have taken place in the past, are taking place today, and we can only hope they will never take place again in the future. How is the situation in

China today? What is in waiting for us Chinese in the years to come? To help our readers to reflect on these issues, we present Comrade Zhu Houze's speech.[52]

Dushu was being bold in thrusting itself into contemporary politics. Some of its readers, however, felt that more could have been said. One reader, in a letter to the editor that appeared in the October 1986 issue of *Dushu*, directly attacked Communist hardliners who were resisting political changes:

> Those high-positioned, majestic senior officials have locked themselves up in the past. . . . They refuse to consider new lifestyles, new ways of thinking, new ideas that spring out of the ever-changing historical circumstances. They implacably expect future generations to live by the rules that they have set up. . . . Their behavior clearly stifles free thinking and is doubtlessly intolerant.[53]

This might be just one young Chinese venting his anger at the older generation except for the fact that many others in the country shared the sentiment expressed here. Two months later, in December 1986, widespread discontent erupted. In a country where demonstrations against the government were virtually forbidden, thousands of college students in several major cities swamped into the streets, demanding democratic reforms. Greatly shocked, the Chinese government moved quickly to pacify angry protesters. Demonstrations ended peacefully, but a number of top reformist leaders fell from grace, including the CCP general secretary Hu Yaobang. Gone with him was Zhu Houze, the official in charge of the party's ideological work, whom *Dushu* had praised for his tolerant attitude just two months before.

The result of the clash between China's reformist and conservative forces in 1986 was indecisive and led to a standoff. Reform advocates staged a strong show of force, making clear their intention to push for further changes in the country. The conservatives flexed their muscles too, taking the opportunity to warn the troublemakers to stay away from "bourgeois liberalization." Top leaders of the Communist Party worked out a compromise among themselves. Succeeding Hu Yaobang to serve as the CCP general secretary was Zhao Ziyang, who, as the Premier in the State Council, had implemented reformist policies but was generally perceived to be more cautious and pragmatic. Now Zhao had to keep the decision making within the party, staying clear of dissidents in China at large, so that he could carry on the reform without antagonizing the party's hardliners.

Outside the Communist Party, China's liberal intellectuals also reviewed the events of 1986. The popular protests, impressive as they were, did not accomplish a great deal in the advancement of reform. If anything, they had weakened the position of the reformist leaders in the Communist Party.

Under the circumstances, the mood of *Dushu* became more pensive and reflective. In March 1987, three months after the failed student demonstrations, Zhao Yifan, who had previously written about "legitimate opposition" in American history, returned to the pages of *Dushu*. This time Zhao commented on the reform tradition in the United States, once again as presented by historian Richard Hofstadter. Throughout U.S. history, Zhao wrote, three dichotomies or conflicts exerted great influence—radicalism versus conservatism, anti-intellectualism versus science, and morality versus reason.[54] Hofstadter demonstrates that whereas it was passionate radicals, anti-intellectuals, and moralists who initiated major reform movements in American history, often it was the moderates who eventually brought these political campaigns to actual fruition. It was so because the moderates could more effectively broker between the past and the future. In other words, ultimately it was Americans such as Theodore Roosevelt, Woodrow Wilson, and Franklin Roosevelt, rather than William Jennings Bryan or Huey Long, who held in their hands the destiny of the United States.[55]

Zhao Yifan's argument accorded well with a trend that was quickly gaining strength in China's political life. Summing up the new idea was *jingying zhengzhi* or "elite politics." The concept implied that popular democracy was not the solution to China's complex problems, and that only the exercise of power by an enlightened authority could lead to genuine and orderly changes in China. Not surprisingly, among the keen advocates of this new line of thinking were some young and ambitious scholars who were close to the new Party General Secretary Zhao Ziyang. Confident that political changes guided from above could better serve the reformist cause than popular drives in the streets, these proponents of "elite politics" were eager to try their hands at an "insiders' revolution."

Dushu seemed to have an ambivalent attitude toward the idea of elite politics. Reacting to a suggestion that *Dushu* could rightfully claim a prominent position in China's "elite culture," the journal hastened to decline the honor. The journal would be quite satisfied if it could serve as a bridge leading up to the "elite."[56]

Dushu's reluctance to identify itself with the so-called "elite culture" was quite understandable. If nothing else, for a publication to distance itself from a larger audience would be bad business. Still, *Dushu* did seem to have a certain amount of elitism in itself and was not altogether averse to the new emphasis on "elite politics" in China. Zhao Yifan, who had written about party politics in the United States as presented by Hofstadter, now drew *Dushu* readers' attention to writings such as *The Visible Hand: The Managerial Revolution in American Business* (Alfred Chandler Jr.), *The Future of Intellectuals and the Rise of the New Class* (Alvin Gouldner), and *White Collar: The American Middle Class* (C. Wright Mills).[57] These works, of course, highlight how the well-to-do and middle-class Americans transformed their society in an orderly fashion. In the wake of the failed student protests of 1986, it was these rational and respectable Americans, rather than banner-waving, street-fighting populist rebels, who appealed to the Chinese eagerly looking for progress but not chaos in their country. To these Chinese, the idea that an enlightened middle class serving as an agent of sociopolitical transformation was a very comforting thought.

To further support the idea of controlled and managed progress, Chinese proponents of "elite politics" turned to another American author, the political scientist Samuel Huntington, who figured prominently in *Dushu* about this time. As the Chinese understood it, Huntington, in his works such as *Political Order in Changing Societies*, placed political stability above democratization. In this view, an authoritarian government capable of fostering economic growth is far preferable to one that clumsily experiments with democracy and only generates a great deal of confusion and turmoil.

Figure 6.2

At the height of the 1989 pro-democracy movement in Beijing, Chinese students protesting against their government erected a replica of the Statue of Liberty at Tiananmen Square, which crystallized the desire of the young Chinese for a freer China. The event, at the same time, raised questions on difficult issues such as national identity and the applicability of the American experience to Chinese reality. Photograph credit: Toshio Sakai/AFP/Getty Images.

There is one simple lesson that China can learn from Huntington, wrote one Chinese critic: "Forget Utopia." For far too long, Yang Bofei argued, China had suffered from a utopian craze. Mesmerized by their fantastic vision of popular democracy, Chinese people had engaged in a long hopeless struggle, wasting much of their precious energy in the process. The recent political disturbances only further illustrated this tendency.[58] This assessment was shared by another critic, who, in his own writing on Hungtington, argued that what China needed now was not popular democracy but "a strong state."[59]

Events in China, however, soon disappointed the advocates of "elite politics." Ten years of reform in China had aroused among Chinese people great hopes and aspirations. When these high expectations went unmet, they turned into deep resentment and bitterness. The student unrest at the end of 1986 already signified this unhappiness; its swift suppression by the government only further heightened the sense of frustration. The pent-up anger finally exploded in 1989, when massive demonstrations shook major cities in China, especially Beijing. Zhao Ziyang and his followers, who had hoped for a top-down approach to political reform, did their best to persuade the protesters to get off streets so as not to further antagonize hardliners in the Communist Party; Zhao even made a personal appearance at Tiananmen Square, which demonstrators had occupied for weeks. The popular movement, however, was far beyond the control of Zhao and associates. General Secretary Zhao, after his controversial appearance at Tiananmen Square, was soon removed from his position. Deng Xiaoping, hard pressed by the hardliners and fearful of a total collapse, finally decided to send in armed troops to clear out the protestors, a move that resulted in numerous deaths, probably several hundred.[60]

The great violence and bloodshed that put an end to the Tiananmen Square protests shocked even self-proclaimed realist Chinese. The talk about "elite politics" and about political reform in general ended in a great disaster, which left conservatives, popular democrats, and elite-politics proponents all in dismay. Despair loomed large. Writing in the June 1989 issue of *Dushu*, Gu Xi thus concluded his discussion on "democracy and authority": "I put down my pen and turned another page. It is going to be a long night."[61]

V

The melancholy of Chinese intellectuals in the late 1980s did not arise from political frustration alone; there had been many vexing social and cultural issues too. The economic reform during the eighties created not only political tension but also social dislocation and a sense of spiritual uncertainty. The introduction of free market mechanism delivered a heavy blow to China's communist ideology. As individuals actively pursued their own economic interests, as the gap between the rich and the poor continued to widen, and as crime rates went up, Chinese people had to do some soul-searching. How could they maintain social stability and harmony in a time of free competition and rapid changes? What made the Reform moral and good? Given all its side effects, was the Reform worthwhile in the final analysis?

Dushu, ever sensitive to new social trends, probed this newly emerged doubt and uneasiness. When, back in the early 1980s, a *Dushu* writer reviewed Terry Stokes's "neo-surrealist" poems, he lightheartedly joined Stokes in deriding the banal bourgeois values of the *Reader's Digest*.[62] Now, a few years later, some Chinese critics came to find cultural conservatism rather comforting and took hold of it like a man struggling in treacherous water clinging to a tree. Writing in the wake of the 1986 student unrests, Zhao Yifan praised the "balanced" educational philosophy of Derek Bok, president of Harvard University, and blamed Americans such as Clark Kerr, president of the University of California, for what he considered America's ill-fated student activism of the 1960s. "Conservatism," Zhao wrote, "makes sense in its own way."[63]

For similar reasons, Zhao found the cases of Lionel Trilling and Daniel Bell interesting. With regard to Trilling, Zhao traced the transition of the leading New York intellectual from his early Marxist years to moderation in the 1960s, from his work as an alienated Jewish critic to his later role in America's "mainstream" culture. Zhao wrote:

> Traditional liberals revere reason and progress, and they try to draw a clear line between light and darkness, between order and chaos. We should remember, however, that when the will of man becomes absolute . . . its holistic impulse to explain everything and embrace the whole world can actually cause damage to human civilization.[64]

The solution, according to Zhao, was the fusion of diverse cultural tendencies, liberal as well as conservative.[65]

In Daniel Bell Zhao saw a nice mixture of economic socialism, political liberalism, and cultural conservatism. Zhao observed that Bell, in his *Cultural Contradictions of Capitalism*, correctly diagnoses the cultural problem of capitalism: the separation of acquisitiveness and religiosity. While the former is still going strong in today's capitalism, the latter has dwindled significantly. To cure this illness, Bell proposes the creation of what amounts to a new kind of religion. Zhao was not sure if Bell's suggested solution would work, but he certainly appreciated the fact that Bell highlighted the spiritual crisis of a capitalist society.[66]

Zhao Yifan was not the first critic in *Dushu* to identify religion as a key cultural underpinning of capitalism. In 1985, recognizing the importance of

Max Weber, *Dushu* had organized a forum devoted to the German sociologist's theory on the link between religion and economic development.[67] *Dushu* then followed up on the subject with the publication of excerpts from *The Protestant Ethic and the Spirit of Capitalism*.[68] In so doing *Dushu* helped focus Chinese intellectuals' attention on the cultural and the religious aspects of capitalist development, at a time when many Chinese wondered what could make China's economic reform not only materially beneficial but also culturally worthy and morally noble.

Following the guidance of Max Weber, Chinese critics used Protestant Christianity to explain how individualism does not necessarily equal selfishness. Zhou Guoping, for instance, took up the case of Ralph Waldo Emerson. Upon examining the experience of the American Transcendentalist, he declared that "Every Man Can Be a Universe by Himself."[69] Xu Haixin, for his part, reviewed *The Puritans in America*, an anthology edited by Alan Heimert and Andrew Delbanco. Xu expressed his admiration for people such as Roger Williams and Anne Hutchinson, marveling at their steadfast devotion to a higher being, even when such dedication cost them the good will of their community. Puritanism, Xu wrote, emphasized man's inadequacy as well as his independence; it demanded the submission of man not to traditional state power but to a social and political order created by individuals committed to a higher moral principle. The Puritans were thus "constantly challenging themselves, challenging evil, and challenging their own community," and "in their uncompromising position on these issues there lies the inspiration and hope for man and his society."[70]

Other *Dushu* critics also contemplated the relationship between Christian religion and the social and political life of the United States. In an article published in January 1989, at a time when political protests once again started to make waves in China, Mo Mo ("The Silent One") commended American theologian Reinhold Niebuhr for his Christian activism. Sermons and prayers alone do not eliminate social injustice, Mo Mo acknowledged, but history has shown repeatedly that political actions can only relieve the pains of society temporarily; in fact, too often, political movements go terribly awry, leading to horrendous destruction. Divorced from faith, Mo Mo observed, politics cannot secure lasting peace and justice—hence the great importance of people like Niebuhr.[71]

Mo Mo's article on Niebuhr was entitled "No Illusion, Nor Despair." Yet, compared to the can-do spirit of *Dushu* in the earlier years, Mo Mo's article revealed a somber mood. This sentiment also permeated other writings by Mo Mo that appeared in *Dushu* about this time—"The Love and Fear of Our Generation," "Truth Crucified," and "Facing God, Should We Be Silent?"[72]

Events of 1989 soon made it clear that there were good reasons for Chinese intellectuals to feel anxious and disconsolate. Ten years of intense reform, all its accomplishments notwithstanding, had ended in a great political disaster. Even more ominous for Chinese intellectuals, their search for ways to modernize China seemed to have come to a dead end. With particular regard to their reflections on America, after a long intellectual journey, they came upon Protestant Christianity, which was said to be of critical importance to the process of modernization. For a country such as China with a drastically different cultural background, what did this mean? The search for common ground between China and America, it seemed, only spotlighted a glaring difference between the two.

Still, all was not in vain. In the 1980s, as part of their reaction to the challenges of their times, Chinese intellectuals actively explored the national experience of the United States. When they first set out on their expedition, China was just emerging out of the shadow of the Great Cultural Revolution. In the years that followed, driven by changing conditions in their country, Chinese intellectuals successively worked through the historical forces that shaped the United States in the past and were shaping China in contemporary times—science and technology, economics, politics, and values of people. True, situations in America and in China do not always coincide and Chinese interpretations often deviated from American originals. True, too, at the end of their intellectual journey, the Chinese explorers were still in want of solutions to many of their problems. Already, however, in ten short years, the Chinese intellectuals creatively absorbed American experiences that had evolved over a far longer period, and, in doing so, they confronted a whole range of issues that all modernizing nations have to face. In this sense, the Chinese intellectuals' discourse on America in the 1980s was highly valuable and rewarding.

7

Popular and Not-So-Popular America

The Chinese Masses and the U.S.A. in the 1980s

In the 1980s, the average Chinese, like officials and intellectuals of China, viewed the United States in a milieu shaped by the major developments of the decade. First, an ongoing market-oriented reform helped legitimize the socioeconomic system that America epitomized. Secondly, as China's economy grew, contacts and exchanges with the United States expanded, dramatically increasing Chinese people's exposure to America. Thirdly, significant social changes took place in China, including a revolution in mass communications, which made the average Chinese better informed on events in China, in the U.S., and in Sino-American relations.

Under these general circumstances, the United States came to affect the life of Chinese people to an unprecedented extent. America was no longer an issue that the Chinese state or China's intelligentsia could simply monopolize and arbitrarily manipulate. Now, China's general populace knew more about America, in which they also possessed some vested interest, be it the American movies their kids watched in theaters or the local offices of U.S. companies where they hoped to find employment. At times, it appeared that the Chinese masses genuinely enjoyed the expanded American presence in their life. At other times, however, they seemed to be wary about, even disgusted by, what they encountered. In a decade of rapid liberal changes, China's general populace, by observing the United States, developed a sense of what the future might hold for them, to which they reacted with both excitement and trepidation.

I

At the time of Mao's death in 1976, the average Chinese knew precious little about life in the United States. The Nixon visit in 1972 surprised the general populace and caused some excitement among them, but, given that the Sino-American relations thus reopened were confined strictly to strategic cooperation between the two countries, the high dealings of Beijing and Washington had little direct effect on the ordinary Chinese. The Cultural Revolution would go on for four more years, which kept China in extended isolation from the outside world.

When Mao passed away in September 1976, the moderate and the radical factions in the Communist Party fought each other over succession. In the end, with the support of the Chinese military, Hua Guofeng, a previously little-known offocial, was established as the new leader of the country, and Mao's widow Jiang Qing and her radical associates, who together were known as the Gang of Four, were sent to prison. For a short while, however, the moderate leaders could not agree among themselves on what should happen next. Hua Guofeng, a gentle but indecisive leader, wanted to keep alive Mao's socialist legacy and was willing to make only the mildest changes. Some other officials, led by the veteran leader Deng Xiaoping, wanted to implement comprehensive reforms to liberalize China's economic system and modernize their country more quickly. For about three years, it was not certain in which direction the nation would move.

As this high-level power struggle went on, some young Chinese took advantage of the temporary easing of state control and came forward to voice their opinions on what course China should take. Ecstatic over the downfall of the Gang of Four, riding high on hopes engendered by proposed reforms, these Chinese youth thought that China's democratic era had dawned. Eager to have their voices heard, they initiated open public debates on the future of their country. Working feverishly, the activists formed associations among themselves, brought out primitive publications, including mimeographed pamphlets and the so-called *dazibao*—big-character posters pasted on walls in public places. Most of these Chinese were in their twenties; many of them had only high school education, since Chinese colleges were shut down for a few years during the Cultural Revolution. Some of them, however, had tilled land in countryside, worked at factories, or served in the People's Liberation Army; they had thus had opportunities to observe real life in China at close range. A leading figure in the movement, Wei Jingsheng, was a veteran of the People's Liberation Army who worked as a factory electrician in Beijing. What the young activists lacked in intellectual or political sophistication, they made up with youthful vigor and idealism. It was these young Chinese who ushered in what came to be known as the Beijing Spring.

Having lived through the Great Cultural Revolution and observed conditions in various quarters of Chinese society up close, the young participants of the Beijing Spring brought to their free speech movement an attitude of skepticism. In particular, they questioned what their government told them about the outside world. At this time, the insulation of China instituted during the Great Cultural Revolution was still in place; information on real conditions of the world beyond China's borders was scarce. The young activists of the Beijing Spring could not help suspecting that truth had been withheld from the Chinese people. One of them, writing in *Zhongguo renquan* (*Human Rights in China*), which was one of the "underground publications" at the time, commented on the lack of communication between China and the world. He noted that China's media sneered at the fact that many Americans could not tell the difference between the Republic of China based in Taiwan and the People's Republic of China located on the mainland. Are we, the writer asked, actually any better than these Americans? How much do we know about the United States? Just a few years ago, "to many of us, the U.S. was nothing more than American Imperialism, a hideous monster, with green eyes and red hair. Such is the consequence of isolation and deception."[1]

In *Renmin zhisheng* (*People's Voice*), another underground publication, someone with the penname Xiaoming ("Light at dawn") wrote to protest a particular practice in China then, namely, the showing of what were known as "inner-circle movies." Although, as a matter of official policy, foreign films were still largely prohibited in China at this time, some of them, including Hollywood productions such as *Gone with the Wind* and *Star Wars*, were often screened for privileged Chinese—government officials and their relatives, for example. Such practices, the writer pointed out, smacked of "feudalism" and showed strong distrust of the people. If something is good enough for "public servants," it should be good enough for the people themselves.[2]

Hungry for information about the outside world, especially on a taboo subject such as America, activists in the Beijing Spring tried to scrape together whatever tidbits they could lay their hands on—for example, magazines left behind by foreign visitors or "inner-circle reference readings" intended for Party officials. With information thus acquired, the young Chinese attempted to punch holes in the government's official line and to ascertain the true comparison between China and foreign countries. The December 1979 issue of *People's Voice*, for instance, reported on the unemployment in the United States. Unlike official newspapers, which would highlight the problem as evidence for the decline of the American capitalist system, the dissident publication chose to tell its readers about programs of public assistance to jobless Americans, which, according to the *People's Voice*, was "considerable."[3] This was at a time when millions of former Red Guards had just returned to urban areas from countryside—where they had been dispatched during the Great Cultural Revolution—and many of them now had no jobs.

For its part, *Qunzhong cankao xiaoxi* (*The Masses' Reference News*), covered "agricultural mechanization in the world's leading capitalist countries," another subject that fascinated the Chinese at the time. "Not only do the 2.8 million farmers in the United States produce enough to feed the 220 million

Americans in their own country, they have also made the U.S. the world's largest grain exporter." The story also listed some other statistics to highlight the gap in development between China and leading industrialized countries. "GNP: Japan, $6,052; China, $254; U.S., $8,715." "TV sets per 100 people: Japan, 23.6; China, 0.04; US, 55.6." "Automobiles per 1,000 people: Japan 247; China: 1; US, 623."[4]

These were shocking figures to the Chinese who, for a long time now, had heard about all the wonderful accomplishments of China and the continuing decay of the West. Driven by the desire to catch up with the advanced countries in the world, activists of the Beijing Spring tried to identify reasons for the Western success. One underground journal, *Qiushi Bao* (*Quest for Truth*), reprinted Karl Marx's remarks on Abraham Lincoln, in which the communist forefather praised the U.S. economic and political system for allowing a commoner such as Lincoln to rise to greatness.[5] Over at *Renmin zhilu* (*People's Path*) editors published an introduction to American politics and government, which was based on a piece from the Voice of America, the U.S.-government sponsored radio broadcast, at a time when listening to such programs was still illegal.[6] In the *Masses' Reference News*, there appeared some translated materials under the title "Science and Policies in the United States," which were about how U.S. academics advised their government in decision making.[7]

Not everyone, however, held such positive views of the U.S. Toward the end of 1978, as Deng Xiaoping prepared for his historic visit to the United States, the debate on the virtues and failings of America intensified in China. On what was known as the Democracy Wall in central Beijing there appeared challenges to the government's new policy of Sino-American reconciliation. One particular "big-character poster" raised a pointed question, "Is the United States a Paradise of Democracy?" The author of the poster answered his own question with an unmistakable "No!" "I feel I must speak out, having read so much on the Democracy Wall about how the United States is an enlightened society where common workers and monopoly capitalists enjoy equal, democratic rights." Look at the record of America, the indignant writer urged. In international affairs, the United States has associated itself with "the most reactionary, the darkest regimes" around the world. Domestically, racial discrimination, the assassination of President Kennedy, the Watergate scandal, the Jonestown mass suicides—all this points to a lack of justice and democracy. "How can any individual with any sense of responsibility . . . ," demanded the poster writer, "try to whitewash an imperialist political system like this?"[8]

Angry replies soon appeared on the Democracy Wall. One respondent, Xie Jun, entitled his rejoinder "The United States Is a Paradise of Democracy." Xie faulted the anti-American poster writer with "building an image of the U.S. with old newspaper materials that date back to the 1950s and 1960s."[9] He wrote:

Our country and the United States have been isolated from each other for almost thirty years now, and we do not understand each other. . . . What was our perception of the United States? Slums, traffic accidents, robberies, murders, blacks' uprisings, workers' strikes. . . . From all this we derived our impression of an America at the sunset time, an America lying in deathbed gasping for air, an America destined to the historical dustbin. This is really a distorted image.[10]

Xie continued:

How can anyone with a head above his shoulders, who is capable of the most rudimentary independent thinking, fail to wonder: Does American people's modern life come exclusively from the magic power of science and technology? Does it not have anything to do with their social system? . . . Facts are facts. You can make up one hundred theories to fool people. You can simply dismiss everything as "sham" or "humbug" for the thousandth time. You can disparage for another twenty years. You can stifle millions of political prisoners who dare to utter something positive about America. You cannot, however, change the fact that the United States is more democratic than we are.[11]

At this time, participants in the Beijing Spring were evidently supportive of Deng Xiaoping, who promised to overcome conservative resistance to move China forward with his economic reform and his policy to open China up to the world. So, when it was reported that while Deng was visiting in the United States some American leftists heckled him for betraying Mao's revolution, activists of the Beijing Spring came to Deng's defense and sneered at the American radicals. One of them wrote in *Wusi luntan* (*May Fourth Forum*): "It is a funny thing that the specters of the Gang of Four popped up in Washington. What an awful show they put on!"[12]

It was not funny at all that Deng, upon his return from his successful visit of the United States, decided to put an end to China's spontaneous pro-democracy movement. By this time, Deng and reformist associates had essentially won the power struggle against the more conservative leaders in the Chinese Communist Party. Now that they were at the helm of the party, they did not want to see any political agitation that might threaten the political stability of the country. Deng banned all the underground publications, closed down the Democracy Wall in Beijing, and generally ordered the participants of the free speech movement to discontinue all their activities. When some of the activists refused to cooperate, he sent them to jail. One underground journal, *People's Road* based in Guangzhou, survived into the fall of 1979 and, in its September issue, published a piece of old news about a fight between student protestors at Cornell University and police, an event that had taken place back in 1973.[13] The veiled attack on the Chinese government hardly made a dent. The Beijing Spring was over.

II

Deng Xiaoping, a veteran politician, was quite astute in recognizing the danger of open challenges to the authority of the Communist Party. He did not worry as much about the gradual social changes that his economic reform generated, even though in the long run the more subtle social transformation had significant political consequences too. As Deng's free market reform moved forward, it changed the life of the average Chinese, creating a new setting in which Chinese people looked upon their own life as well as affairs abroad.

One notable change for the average Chinese in the 1980s was a revolution in mass communications. After the Communist victory in 1949, Chinese media came under strict state control. During the Great Cultural Revolution from 1966 to 1976, after a period of chaos, ideological puritanism led to further contraction of the Chinese media as the radicals banned books, movies, and plays they considered "poisonous" and shut down newspapers and journals for alleged "bourgeois tendencies." In the last few years of the Great Cultural Revolution, for entertainment Chinese people had virtually nothing but a few plays and movies that Jiang Qing, Mao's wife, personally approved and promoted (these were the so-called Eight Model Plays). In one case, Jiang Qing banned the release of a feature film that actually glorified the growth of China's oil industry. The makers of the particular film had done their best to make their production politically acceptable. The movie, for instance, opens with a scene in which an American businessman, being evacuated out of China at the time of the Communist victory, shouts to approaching revolutionaries: "Standard Oil! Standard Oil! Without Standard Oil, there will be nothing but darkness in China!"[14] From this opening scene, the movie goes on to show Chinese workers laboring heroically to build up China's own oil industry with no foreign assistance. Still, Jiang Qing found the movie lacking in revolutionary spirit. Ultimately, Mao himself intervened on behalf of the moviemakers, feeling that, in this case, Jiang Qing had gone too far.[15]

With Mao's intervention, moderate leaders in the Chinese government tried to breathe some life into China's cultural scene, but they accomplished very little. In many fields of arts and scholarship, only one or two official publications subsisted, with predictable titles such as *People's Literature* or *People's Music*. The hunger for information and amusement drove many Chinese, especially the young, to so-called underground literature, which often took the form of secretly written and hand-copied novels and poems. Mostly amateurish and poorly crafted, such creations proved to be better than nothing for young Chinese hungry for any kind of entertainment and the illicitness of these works only made them even more tempting and popular. One of the best-known works of this nature was the novel *The Second Handshake*, a story of love and patriotism that has the United States as an exotic backdrop. When this work of fiction was formally published after the Great Cultural Revolution, a million copies were printed.[16]

With Mao's death in 1976 and the onset of Deng's reforms three years later, the mass media of China expanded dramatically. In 1978, China had 186 newspapers. Eight years later, the number had risen to 1,574, an eight-fold increase. During the same period, the number of published magazines jumped from 930 to 5,248, with total circulation rising from 760 million to 2,409 million.[17] In 1976, the year Mao died, just 2 or 3 percent of the Chinese population had access to television. Three years later, in 1979, China's television audience was six times larger, with more than 120 million Chinese now watching television. In the ten-year period beginning in 1978, China's TV-watching population expanded drastically, on average adding tens of millions of people every year. In 1987, 590 million Chinese, or 55 percent of China's total population, were watching television. By that time, 93 percent of city dwellers and 38 percent of rural residents had access to television.[18]

The dramatic expansion of the media in China gave the Chinese people unprecedented exposure to the outside world, which fascinated the Chinese who had lived through the isolation of the Mao Era. Polls consistently showed that the most popular program on China Central Television (CCTV) was the half-hour-long evening news, and, of this particular program, the most popular segment was the ten minutes of world news.[19] Not incidentally, at this time CCTV largely derived its international news from satellite-transmitted footage provided by foreign agencies such as UPINT in the U.S. and VIS-NEWS of Great Britain.[20] "I love 'World News'!" one excited viewer wrote in. "Every evening I spend the brief ten minutes in front of my TV, with my rice bowl in my hand."[21] "I watch your news program every evening," another viewer reported, "and I especially appreciate 'World News.' " This particular viewer also hoped that CCTV would expand its world news segment. If that was not feasible, said the viewer, the TV station should repeat its program "World Today" a few more times, so that people like him could catch this other popular offering.[22] In fact, some government officials came to feel that the world news carried by CCTV was too popular—the events covered in the particular newscast threatened to upstage activities of China's own leaders. After the 1980 U.S. presidential election, Chen Hanyuan, Director of CCTV, admitted morosely that during the campaign, "Carter, Reagan, along with some other Americans, were the leading stars on our television screen."[23]

In print media, world news was similarly popular. A 1982 survey conducted in Beijing and surrounding areas revealed that world news topped all other subjects as the newspaper readers' favorite: the largest percentage (42 percent) of those polled listed international news as "the most interesting," followed by reports on China's own political leaders (38.9 percent), and coverage of sports (23 percent).[24]

In book publishing, the number of literary works published increased notably, as did the percentage of those works that came from the West, which proved to be big draws for publishing houses. In 1978, Chinese publishers released 14,987 literary titles; in 1986, the number rose to 51,789.[25] In the thirty years prior to 1979, including the years in which China experienced difficulties in her relationship with the Soviet Union, 63.7 percent of all literary translations were of Russian origin; only 18.4 percent came from the United States, Great Britain, France, and Japan combined. This trend was reversed in the new era: from 1979 to 1986, 58.9 percent of translated literary works came from the West.[26]

Most notable was the increase in the number of American works brought to the Chinese readers. In 1976, not counting books in science and technology, China published just one translated American work—*John Brown* by W. E. B. Du Bois, which was originally published in the U.S. in 1909.[27] The following year saw a similar situation; this time the lone translated American book was *Ancient Society*, authored by the nineteenth-century anthropologist L. H. Morgan.[28] Evidently, the Chinese chose this particular work because Friedrich Engels, Karl Marx's close friend and comrade, extensively cited Morgan in his own writings. Then the scene began to change. In 1978 about a dozen American works outside the field of natural sciences and technology made their appearance.[29] In 1979, this number rose to about forty.[30] In 1982, Chinese publishers brought out approximately two hundred American works in the humanities and social sciences.[31]

Not only did many more American works become available, but there was also a greater variety of them for Chinese readers. After *John Brown* in 1976 and *Ancient Society* in 1977, there came, in 1978, among the dozen or so American works published in China, Richard Nixon's memoirs, Leslie R. Groves's story about the first atomic bomb entitled *Now It Can Be Told*, and an abridged biography of Lincoln.[32] The following year, Chinese readers found in their bookstores memoirs of Henry Kissinger and H. R. Haldeman, C. L. Sulzberger's *Seven Continents and Forty Years*, Paul Samuelson's *Economics*, Alex Haley's *Roots*, Isaac Singer's *Magician of Lublin*, William Hoffman's *Paul Mellon: Portrait of an Oil Baron*, William Manchester's *Glory and Dream*, and *The Greek Coffin Mystery*, the first of the detective genre to appear in China in a long time.[33] The influx of American works would continue, and some of them did very well commercially. When Herman Wouk's hefty *Winds of War* came out in 1981, the first printing numbered 280,000.[34]

Those Chinese who did not want to read big books could turn to periodicals, which mushroomed all across the country. Between 1976 and 1986 about twenty journals and magazines devoted exclusively to Western literature sprang up.[35] The most popular of these periodicals was *Yilin* (*Forest of Translations*), which often carried the full text of foreign bestsellers. After just one year in existence, the monthly magazine's circulation reached three hundred thousand.[36] Some other Chinese periodicals had larger circulations than *Yilin*, but these were mostly official publications with mandatory subscriptions. *Yilin*, in contrast, supported itself by selling foreign tales.

These foreign tales were predominantly American. In 1982, of the eight full-length novels and movie scripts published in *Yilin*, six were by American authors, including, among others, *Rage of Angels* by Sidney Sheldon, *Sphinx* by Robin Cook, and *Love Story* by Erich Segal.[37] *Love Story* having been a success, *Yilin* quickly followed up with its sequel, *Oliver's Story*.[38] In the same issue in which *Oliver's Story* appeared, there was Danielle Steel's *Promise*.[39] One satisfied customer, after reading Segal's story about a married couple whose peaceful life is shattered by the unexpected arrival of the husband's illegitimate son, wrote to thank *Yilin* editors for a great story that helped him to see "what life is like in America"; he wanted the magazine to keep up the good work.[40]

Meanwhile, more lively scenes of America started to show up in China's movie theaters. After decades of absence, Hollywood returned to entertain the millions of Chinese who watched movies in theaters on any given day.[41] But even Hollywood would not claim that in the 1980s it sent to China the best it had to offer. In fact, many of these productions were low-budget "B movies" or oldies. Two main factors were responsible for this fact. First, because motion pictures was a more popular medium, the Chinese government maintained tighter control over films than they did over books. The authorities tended to choose productions that were ideologically safe; films that depict the dark side of American life—crime movies, for example—would entertain Chinese audience without creating too much of a political problem. Secondly, since at the time China had very limited foreign currency reserves, the country imported mostly inexpensive Hollywood productions. In the early 1980s, among American movies shown in China were *Illegal*, *The Legend of the Lone Ranger*, *Shane*, *End of the Game*, *Undercurrent*, *Wait until Dark*, *The Bat*, *Villa*, *Francis*, *Future World*, *Nightmare*, and *Convoy*.[42] The last on this list, *Convoy*, was once described by an American film critic as a mere "excuse for a series of chases and crashes."[43] *Nightmare*, for its part, tells the ordeal of two female college students—one white and the other black—who, while driving through a small town in the South, are bullied and persecuted by the town's vicious sheriff. The bad cop rapes one of the girls and sends both of them to a labor farm, where scantily clad female prisoners suffer further humiliation at the hands of sadistic wardresses.

Given their past grooming in Marxist literary realism, there was a tendency for Chinese readers and viewers to take what they found in books or movies as faithful presentation of, or serious comment on, real life. In any event, since at this time most Chinese had extremely limited knowledge on the United States, they were in no position to contextualize what they encountered on paper or screen. In Guanzhou, when an American journalist asked a local resident whether he had seen *Nightmare*, the movie mentioned above, the young man responded: "*Nightmare?* Oh, yes, it's a film about capitalism."[44] In one of his short stories, novelist Gao Min tells how one peasant living in a remote hamlet bragged about his connections to the outside world. A railway nearby was recently completed, and an international express train now regularly roared by, but never stopped at, the small village. This somehow stirred up the imaginative power of the poor villager, who told everyone that he had a rich relative who lived in America. The relative had asked him to travel to the U.S., but he had repeatedly declined the invitations. He did not want to go, said the peasant, because he worried that he would lose his way in the big cities, not to mention that he was scared of the free and aggressive American women, about whom he had heard so much.[45]

It was not just Chinese peasants who had foggy ideas about life in America. In the spring of 1983, American playwright Arthur Miller cooperated with the People's Artistic Theater in Beijing, one of China's best players' troupes, to stage his *Death of a Salesman*. Miller soon found out that, just a few years after the end of the Great Cultural Revolution, even the worldliest Chinese had little knowledge on what it was like to live in the United States. The playwright did not have much difficulty with the lead actor in the play, Ying Ruocheng, who was a pre-1949 graduate of Yenching University, the American missionary school in Beijing. Most other Chinese players, however, grew up or came of age in Mao's China; Miller strained to make them understand the American life that was so alien to them all. The Chinese actress who played Linda, the salesman Willy's wife, instinctively set out to portray her character as a model Chinese family woman, *xian qi liang mu*, "virtuous wife, loving mother," who is constantly in tears worrying about her husband and son. Miller's direction about the toughness of American women could not get through to her. Another Chinese woman, who was cast for a role in a bar scene, asked Miller whether her character is a prostitute. Miller explained that the girl is not a prostitute but a "pick-up." The Chinese woman was puzzled and could not figure out the concept; she knew good woman, she even knew prostitute, but she had no idea what a "pick-up" was.

In particular, the young man chosen to play Willy's son had a difficult time in getting his role right. Formerly a solider in the People's Liberation Army, the Chinese actor had no clue how to act an irreverent American playboy. Miller had to let him go in the end. As the director, Miller also thought that the Chinese should focus on the substance of his play and he asked the Chinese players to get rid of the wigs and heavy makeup they put on to make them look Caucasian. The Chinese balked at the suggestion; they were certain that, without such visual aids, Chinese audience would never believe that they were watching an American play and would only get all confused. Miller had to relent on this particular point and go along with the Chinese. At the end of his stay in Beijing, Miller thought that overall his experiment was a success. The audience at the first preview night mostly consisted of Chinese peasants from villages outside Beijing, who, as suppliers of produce for the Beijing People's Artistic Theater, received their tickets as gifts. Miller was glad to see that the audience stayed long enough after the show "to clap their hands and risk losing the last bus."[46] Still, the American playwright could not help wondering whether the Chinese had really understood why "Willy is desperate." After all, Miller ruminated, Willy "owns a refrigerator, a car, his own house, and is willing to 'settle' for sixty dollars a *week*!"[47] That was decades ago in America. In China of the early 1980s, an average urban worker made about $15 a month; for peasants, it was much less.

Miller had good reason to ponder if the Chinese truly comprehended America or if they understood what America meant to them in real life. To most Chinese, whose exposure to the United States was almost exclusively though a few movies and TV shows, America was still largely exotic and crazily eccentric. As the initial feeling of wonder and excitement started to wear off, and as Deng's economic reform in China generated widespread social changes, not all of which were pleasant or reassuring, some Chinese came to realize that the American way of life was not just a fairy tale but something that they themselves would have to face before long. A sense of discomfort and even alarm set in.

III

In the early 1980s, when Deng Xiaoping's economic reform began in China, one resounding slogan, promoted by the Chinese government itself, was "To get rich is glorious!" Previously, under Mao, the Chinese people had sacrificed their own interests for the ever-elusive Communist Revolution. Now, Deng's new policies gave them the opportunity to work hard to improve their material well-being and to get ahead of their neighbors. In both rural and urban areas, increased productivity brought personal rewards; all across the country, ambitious entrepreneurs were setting up their own businesses to take advantage of the new economic freedom.

Still, there was a widespread uneasiness, resulting largely from a sense of insecurity and from the social dislocation caused by Deng's reform. Some of the new events in their life—the collapse of the People's Communes, the emerging gap between the well-to-do and the poor, the hitherto unheard of competition for jobs, the sheer acquisitiveness that one encountered everywhere—were all disconcerting to the Chinese, who were accustomed to the stability and egalitarianism of the Mao Era, poverty-ridden as it was. When, in 1980, one young Chinese woman openly voiced her misgivings about the new situation in China, she set off a major public debate. In her letter to the national magazine *Zhongguo qingnian* (*Chinese Youth*), Pan Xiao, twenty-three years old, complained that all of her youthful idealism came to naught in the current time when people only cared about money. "Why does the road of life become evermore narrow?" asked the despondent young Chinese. Pan's disenchantment with what was happening in China struck a responsive chord in many Chinese, who similarly experienced disillusion and gloom as the revolutionary Mao Era gave way to Deng's materialist reform age.[48] After all, individualism had never been a particularly inspiring high ideal for Chinese society as a whole, either under Mao or in the country's more remote Confucian past.

Liberal-minded Chinese tried to defend the new trend in the country. One participant in the dialogue started by Pan Xiao was a young Chinese-American woman, Yang Xiaoyan, whose life had followed an unusual course: upon her graduation from Harvard University, she relocated to Beijing and started working there. Writing in *Chinese Youth*, Yang explained how Americans might look at the issue raised by Pan. Many young Americans also care about living a meaningful life, Yang wrote, except that Americans do not necessarily see an inescapable conflict between individual interests and public good. Americans, Yang told her readers, tend to believe that individual interests can be identical to those of the larger society. In the U.S., if a waiter "wants to make more money, he will try to provide good service; his appreciative customers may then decide to reward him by leaving more in tips. For the waiter, this is to work for himself and for other people at the same time."[49] From an American point of view, therefore, Chinese people put too much emphasis on the desirable end, namely public good, but not enough on the necessary means, which is individual effort. Her Chinese friends, Yang noted, mostly agree with her on the need to balance idealism and realism.[50]

Still, coping with a difficult issue in real life is much more challenging than achieving a theoretical understanding of it. Having lived under socialism for decades, many Chinese found it hard to accept the drastic changes that were taking place all around them. Some of the problems they encountered were rather difficult ones, which they could not simply ignore or explain away. There was, for instance, the disturbing issue of a rising crime rate. In the Mao Era, while political persecution was widespread and frequent, criminal activities such as robbery, rape, and murder were relatively rare. According to official statistics, during the ten years from 1956 to 1965, crime rate in China was 30 per 100,000 people.[51] Partly, this was owing to the egalitarianism in Mao's China—most people were about equally poor back then. Additionally, a comprehensive system of social control was in place, with peasants organized into communes, urban residents tied to their work units, and neighborhood committees keeping a close watch on their own districts.

In the 1980s, as a free market economy evolved, Chinese society grew ever more open and Chinese people came to enjoy greater freedom in their life. At the same time, liberalization led to serious social dislocation, especially for the urban workers who lost their jobs due to privatization and for the millions of Chinese peasants who now roamed around China seeking opportunities to make a little extra money. As this happened, criminal activities became more prevalent. According to official figures, the crime rate in 1981 reached 89 per 100,000 people, which was three times as high as that for the period from 1956 to 1965.[52] To fight against the crime wave, the Chinese government carried out several major nationwide crackdowns over the course of the 1980s, but these efforts only produced temporary effects and failed to stop the overall trend. In 1991, the crime rate in China reached a high of 210 per 100,000, which marks an increase of 236 percent over the figure ten years before.[53] Of particular concern was the young age of many lawbreakers. In 1986, authorities in Beijing identified thirty thousand delinquent youths in the city, with one-fifth of them in the age group from thirteen to seventeen.

In addition to crime, the weakening of marriage and the family also caused concerns. In the past, divorces were rare occurrences. Starting in the late 1970s, as Chinese society became more liberalized, an increasing number of marriages failed. In 1978, just over 170,000 Chinese couples ended their marriages in courts. Three years later, the number more than doubled to reach 389,000. In 1984 the number rose again to 445,000—a rise of 262 percent in seven years.[54] The trend would continue: in 1992, 850,000 divorces were recorded; in 1995, more than one million marriages ended in divorce.[55]

At least partially, many Chinese attributed the weakening of their social fiber to wicked Western influence. In 1984, a survey conducted in the city of Tianjin showed that people considered "bourgeois influence from abroad" as one of the major causes of the rise in criminal activities.[56] Commenting on the survey result, Li Ruihuan, who headed the Communist Party in the city and who later would become China's culture czar in charge of ideology, called for more vigorous scrutiny of foreign films and TV programs shown in China, "which are known to have very large followings."[57] In Beijing, concerns over the undesirable Western influence ran so high that specific instructions were given to hotels to ensure the proper handling of materials such as *Playboy* left behind by foreign guests so that they would not find their way into the society at large.[58]

In the early 1980s, very few Chinese had actually been to the United States. For most Chinese, therefore, contact with America was indirect. Those Chinese who did have the rare opportunities to tour the U.S. often returned with rather negative impressions. Often poorly prepared for their visits, these travelers spent just a few days or at most one or two weeks in the U.S, and they almost always went to destinations such as New York, Los Angeles, and Washington, D.C., which were "must see" for the Chinese. Accustomed to the much slower pace of life in China, the Chinese visitors often found the frenzy in the major cities of the U.S. shocking and terrifying. After his tour of the United States as a member of an official writers' group, Jiang Zilong, a well-known author, reported his experience in rather bleak and depressing terms. He was surprised to find that the subway system of New York was dark and dirty, full of confusion and chaos:

> On the platform there hovered some strange characters, with rather haughty and brutish looks. They didn't get on trains, nor would they leave the station. They loitered about, like ghosts. If you have weak nerves, you do not have to be actually robbed to feel the shaking of your knees.[59]

Eerie too was the scene on Broadway at 42nd Street:

> Adding a sense of terror to the surreal atmosphere created by the numerous, crazily flashing neon lights were some male and female figures in the streets, who walked about dreamily, either drunk or drugged. Some of them, with cigarettes sticking out of the corners of their mouths, stared and glared as people went by.
>
> Policemen patrolled the streets, up and down, their walkie-talkies blaring, their guns ready to go. On some parts of the streets, there was one of them every several yards, all looking alert and deadly, as if swarms of enemies would descend upon the place at any moment.
>
> By now, our two female companions had had enough sightseeing. Taking tight hold of our arms, they urged us to return to our hotel.
>
> This is the night scene of New York. What can I tell you? Pornography, greed, violence, lunacy . . . What else?[60]

With images like this in their mind, confronted with mounting social problems around them, many Chinese could not help feeling threatened by the American pop culture that was quickly spreading in China. In 1981, for instance, there broke out a public outcry against a particular U.S. television series broadcast by China's CCTV, *Garrison's Gorillas*. Produced by ABC, the World War II adventure series features a group of American commandoes recruited from federal penitentiaries who operate behind enemy lines. The show—the first of its kind to appear in China after the Great Cultural Revolution—achieved great popularity among young Chinese. Before long, however, the program ran into troubles. The concept of former cons acting heroically was controversial. There came reports that teenagers in some parts of the country started imitating characters in the show. Gathering into their own Garrison gangs, these youngsters terrorized their neighborhoods and boasted their exploits. As protests poured in, CCTV had to pull the series off the air halfway through its first season.[61]

In 1986, the American movie *First Blood* stirred up a similar controversy. Again, the American movie, which features Sylvester Stallone as a Vietnam War veteran driven to revenge against his persecutors, became extremely popular among young Chinese. "Within ten days of its opening in Beijing," reported a Western journalist, "a million people went to theaters to watch it, and black market tickets were sold at seven times the official price."[62] However, the extreme violence and the exaltation of one individual's war against society troubled many Chinese. One Chinese, writing in *Dazhong dianying* (*Popular Cinema*), thus expressed his dismay:

> It is thrilling, it is awesome, but it is not beautiful. It is violence, it is the search for death, it is the thirst for blood. In the end, the worship of the so-called noble savage is nothing more than the glorification of bandits, murderers, and arsonists, the glorification of blood and corpses.

All this, the commentator wrote, goes against "our national sentiment, our national aesthetics, our social system, and our political beliefs."[63]

In book publishing, the proliferation of American popular fiction gave rise to similar concerns. A few years into the 1980s, Chinese publishers had come a long way from the days when reprinting an old translation of *Gone with the Wind* was a daring act. By this time, Chinese publishing houses had gone beyond novelists such as Herman Wouk or Arthur Hailey and moved on to more spicy and thrilling tales. In 1988, about 45 percent of all translated foreign fictional works published in China fell in the category of Popular Literature.[64] One observer of China's publishing scene noted:

> Back in 1986, most translations were adventures, mysteries, and classic popular works. Among the well-received authors back then were Irwin Shaw, Herman Wouk, Somerset Maugham, and Sidney Sheldon. There were few works with heavy sex. A major change

took place in 1987, when Irwin Wallace, Danielle Steel, and Jackie Collins surfaced as leading authors, which began a trend that led to the publication of many virtually pornographic books.[65]

In 1988, three Chinese publishing houses, independent of one another, brought out their translations of Vladimir Nabokov's *Lolita*. On the market were also four different versions of *Hollywood's Wives* by Jackie Collins.[66] A reporter interviewed a particularly enterprising college student who, seeing an opportunity to make money, set up a little book rental operation in his dorm room. Authors such as Jackie Collins and Irwin Wallace, the young entrepreneur reported, were very well liked, and they were not just for guys either—they were "rather popular among female students too."[67]

Thus, by the end of the 1980s, in spite of all the uneasiness and protests, many Chinese, especially the young, had become far more open about many social and cultural issues. This created tension between them and surviving traditionalists, who frowned upon what was happening in their society and tried hard to contain the impact of American culture in China. The conservatives, however, were fighting an uphill battle because something more fundamental was taking place in their society. Rambo and Jackie Collins were certainly thrilling and popular, but increasingly many Chinese turned to some other aspects of American culture, which were not all about consumption and entertainment but focused on independence and hard work. These Chinese wanted to get ahead in a competitive society, and in this endeavor of theirs they derived inspiration from the American Way.

IV

Halfway into the 1980s, as Deng's economic reforms steamed ahead, the overall outlook on life in China changed considerably. After initial shock and dismay, many Chinese came to accept and then embrace an economic system in which individual efforts could significantly alter one's own life. This inevitably transformed Chinese attitudes toward concepts such as freedom. Liberalism, in its classical sense, started to gain some ground in Chinese society.

Indicative of the trend was a new entrepreneurial spirit in the country. American rags-to-riches stories became immensely popular, firing up the desire to take advantage of the fresh economic opportunities in China. Many successful American businessmen, like the pop stars before them, achieved celebrity status. There was, for instance, Armand Hammer, the legendary capitalist who made his millions by trading with the Soviet Union in the 1920s;[68] or Ken Olsen who founded Digital Equipment with just $70,000;[69] or Peter Ueberroth, the organizer of the 1984 Los Angeles Olympics. The L.A.

Olympics were the first Olympic Games in which China participated after a long absence during the Cold War. Chinese media, especially the newly established television, covered both the preparation for the event and the event itself extensively and minutely, widely publicizing figures such as Ueberroth. The national journal *Chinese Youth*, which just four years before had hosted the somber discussion on "Why does the road of life become evermore narrow?" now profiled Ueberroth as a wonderfully successful businessman and a public-minded model citizen. According to the report, even when Ueberroth was just a little boy, he was remarkably independent and industrious. Having lost his mother at the age of four, Ueberroth started working at the age of sixteen, getting through college by selling women's shoes and helping out at a chicken farm. Success soon followed and Ueberroth became a millionaire. The newly found wealth did not corrupt the good American, who chose to work for the L.A. Olympic Games as an unpaid volunteer.[70]

Such tales were evidently well received. In 1986, when *Chinese Youth* introduced to its readers yet another celebrated American businessman, Lee Iacocca, then the CEO of Chrysler Corporation, the magazine noted that "this American business legend" was still little known in China.[71] Later, when the Chinese edition of Iacocca's autobiography was published in the book form, it quickly became a best-seller. Even in the relatively remote province of Sichuan, Iacocca made popular reading, as observed by an American scholar who traveled there.[72]

In the Chinese magazine *Zhongguo qiyiejia* (*Entrepreneurs of China*), biographies of successful American businessmen constituted a major attraction. One such tale begins with a scene at the harbor of New York in 1848:

> Among the immigrants newly arrived from Great Britain there was a thirteen-year-old boy, who, in fifty years' time, would turn his great American dream into reality. From a penniless immigrant he rose to be the world's richest man, the Steel King. He was Andrew Carnegie.[73]

Then there was the story of George Eastman, founder of Eastman Kodak: "Born in a remote little town in the state of New York, he lost his father at the age of eight, and his family lived in poverty." "He worked as a mail-boy for three dollars a week and began to fill his mother's small kitchen with little bottles full of chemicals." The innovative and hardworking young man founded his own company, and, numerous setbacks later, "fate finally smiled upon this industrial perfectionist of Rochester."[74]

Of course, the appeal of such stories was to be found not only in the tales themselves, but also in the fact that their Chinese readers lived in a time of great business expansion, which rendered the American experience all the more relevant and fascinating. In fact, during the 1980s, an increasing number of American businesses, ranging from Ford Motor Company to obscure operations such as California Noodle King, arrived in China, bringing with them American business culture. In 1986, the first Kentucky Fried Chicken restaurant opened its door in China, which was located just a stone's throw from Mao's Mausoleum in Tiananmen Square. Inside the restaurant itself, exchanges of ideas took place. The Chinese manager at the restaurant was a Communist official in his sixties; upon seeing that unsold food was simply discarded at the end of the day, he suggested that restaurant employees be allowed to take the food home as they left work. The American manager rejected the idea, citing the importance of maintaining workplace discipline. The Chinese manager yielded and was apologetic about it—he had looked at the issue in the old Chinese mindset and was not up to date with the ways of modern management.[75]

While the idea that fast food restaurants such as Kentucky Fried Chicken brought modern managerial science to China sounds curious, in the 1980s it was not all that far-fetched—at least in terms of people's perceptions. In 1986, a new Sheraton Hotel in Shanghai advertised vacant positions on its staff; several hundred young men and women with college and postgraduate degrees sent in their applications, making it a competition of eight for one. This took place at a time when college education, not to mention postgraduate education, was still a privilege for the smartest Chinese; some Chinese found the rush to take up positions on a hotel staff a disgrace. Why would these elite Chinese want to work as virtual servants? There was the talk about the need to "re-educate" the young Chinese to make them to see their error. The applicants, however, thought quite differently. When asked why they wanted to work at the hotel, many of the job seekers said that they believed that an American business was more likely to reward hard work and would thus give them better opportunities for career advancement.[76]

Thus, as contacts with the United States in the real world expanded, Chinese popular images of America, previously largely derived from novels and movies, began to change. Perceptions of America as the land of overflowing riches, wild adventures, and inexplicable craziness never fully disappeared, but now information obtained from other channels mitigated such views. In the nation's capital, at Beijing Jeep, which was one of the largest Sino-American joint ventures set up in the 1980s, American personnel impressed their Chinese colleagues with qualities not often seen in the American movies that Chinese watched. R. G. Chatterton, the president of the company was perceived to be calm, responsible, and amicable. Having served in the military and studied engineering and management, he generally appeared to be a respectable and highly efficient business leader.[77]

Figure 7.1

Actor Gregory Peck with college students in Beijing, 1987. *Roman Holiday* is one of the most popular American films in China, especially among the young.

Ji Zhongliang, a schoolteacher from Beijing, had an opportunity to take an up-close look at the infamous American teenagers when, in 1986, he helped host a large group of American high school students who had come to China through an educational exchange program. Having heard much about spoiled American brats, Ji and his colleagues were surprised to find that his charge were no troubles at all. Ji noticed that the American youngsters had their simple ways: casually dressed, "they would just sit on the concrete floor" when there were not enough chairs for them. One particular concern for Ji and his colleagues had been how to get a large group of American youngsters, supposedly all highly individualistic, to move around together in a timely fashion, especially since the Americans did not seem to have the equivalent of Chinese "class cadre"—teachers' little helpers—to serve as functionaries. Yet, when it came to it, chauffeuring the students did not pose too much of a challenge. When buses arrived, everyone showed up and was ready to go. A young American may have a mind of his own, Ji reflected, but that does not necessarily mean that he is irresponsible. In fact, exactly because the young fellow feels that he is his own man, he has to answer for all his actions.[78]

Just as more Americans came to China in the late 1980s, an increasing number of Chinese traveled to the United States. Compared to those Chinese who toured the United States earlier in the decade, the Chinese who visited America a few years later were better informed and better prepared for their journeys, and they also had greater freedom to explore America. When novelist Jiang Zilong and his writers' group went to the United States in 1982, their knowledge of the country was very limited, as was their exposure to the American society while on the trip. In contrast, Wu Jisong, a science administrator, had a very different experience. He traveled extensively abroad, including two trips to New York. Whereas chaos and terror dominated Jiang's impression of New York, Wu had a broader view of the Big Apple. When Wu visited New York for the first time in 1981, he took a walk in Harlem; on his second trip in 1985, Wu lived on Park Avenue. While in the city, Wu noticed the difference between the western and the eastern sections of forty-second street, partitioned by the Avenue of the Americas. On the one side, Wu observed, there were "seedy bars, sex shops, nightclubs, X-rated movie theaters, dirty and chaotic, swarmed with hooligans, thieves, drug dealers . . ." On the other side, it was "sparkling windows of fancy shops, casually dressed people ambling along with ease, and suited up corporate employees bustling about, carrying on their business."[79] Wu confessed to mixed feelings about New York, a city of both abundant opportunities and serious decay, "a sweet big apple with bad spots."[80]

Other Chinese visitors ventured off the beaten path for Chinese sojourners in America and visited the flyover land of the U.S. Zhao Jianjun, a farm worker from the remote Xinjiang Autonomous Region in northwestern China, came to the United States in 1986 through an agricultural exchange program and found himself in rural Massachusetts, where he worked for a year. Zhao left the United States with a rather positive view. He found his American friends conscientious and diligent. "The United States is a country of both high consumption and intense competition," Zhao observed, "and if you do not work hard, you cannot stand up on your own." Zhao fondly remembered a young fellow by the name of Bob, who plugged away so that he could save enough money to ride his bicycle around the world—"a typical American youth," Zhao said.[81] The Chinese farmer was also quite moved by a local restaurant worker who took care of a large wounded bird, nursing it back to health before releasing it.[82]

Contributing to the creation of a more rounded image of America were also some Chinese who had decided to stay in the U.S. for longer terms, who, as they toiled to support themselves and cope with life in general, experienced hardships that often eluded short-term visitors. One struggling Chinese student reported his daily routine. He would get up at 4:30 in the morning and report to work at the office of a local Chinese newspaper at 6:00. At 12:00 he would leave to attend classes in the afternoon. While traveling on a subway train he would have a sandwich for lunch and do his reading. In the evening, he would take care of homework for school and watch TV news to gather materials for his newspaper work the next day. Still, the student sounded upbeat and optimistic, believing that all his effort would pay off in the end. The United States, said the student, "is a nation of immigrants, of people with diverse cultural backgrounds. These people have one common prospect—only those who make good use of their time and opportunities will succeed."[83]

Idiosyncratic and incidental as they are, such experiences, as they accumulated, built up toward some larger conclusions. A Communist official, a veteran who had joined the party during World War II, went to Washington to attend a conference. Speaking no English and trying to get around the city, he received gracious help from two strangers, an African American couple. The official later commented to a companion: "Maybe the Americans are not the way we used to describe them after all."[84] His younger associate, Zhang Mingshu, was more straightforward in his assessment. For a long time now, Zhang wrote, we have arbitrarily divided "civility" into the socialist and capitalist kind, with the idea that the former is far superior to the latter.

> But, having had learned a few things about the world of capitalist civility and that of socialist civility, I, and others with similar experiences, feel that such a differentiation is not warranted. . . . Truth be told, the difference between the two kinds of civility is negligible. The real difference lies between civility and the simple lack of it.[85]

Zhang then recalled a church service he witnessed in a small town in the U.S., noting that piety and virtues still constitute a very important part of American life. He urged fellow Chinese to remember such examples and redouble their efforts to promote civility "among our own people."[86]

There were good reasons for Chinese people to think about civility at this particular time. It was early 1989, when a great political storm was gathering in China. Before long, large-scale protests would break out all across China as Chinese citizens rose up to voice their unhappiness with conditions in their country. While the unfolding struggle was largely political by nature, it was also driven by the accumulated effects of the economic, social, and cultural changes that took place in the 1980s. For better or worse, America, with all its inspiring power and contradictions, played a notable role in the overall transformation of the Chinese society during the period, which sent China down a path to an uncertain future.

8

Shall the Twain Ever Meet?

Old Themes and New Trends in the Last Decade of the Century

During the 1990s, China experienced a notable transition from the political idealism typical of the preceding decade to a much less exciting but far more comforting economic pragmatism. The tragic failure of the 1989 protest movement destroyed the hope, held by many Chinese, for rapid democratic changes in China. The watershed event shifted the attention of the nation from politics to the improvement of Chinese people's material well-being. In this latter enterprise, China proved to be rather successful. Economic growth soon resumed, on a far larger scale, spreading wealth across the country, although by no means evenly.

China's newly found prosperity significantly altered the dynamic process that shaped Chinese attitudes toward the United States of America. Not only continued economic growth substantially broadened China's contact with the U.S., but the liberalization of the Chinese society that occurred along with economic growth also created an environment more tolerant of American culture and lifestyle. As the exchanges across the Pacific expanded and the situation in China continued to evolve, America lost much of its exoticness and became more familiar, even likeable, to Chinese people.

Meanwhile, China's economic success greatly boosted the Chinese nation's self-confidence and gave rise to a heightened sense of national pride. After struggling for over a hundred years, China seemed to have finally found a path forward and started to compete with the world's great powers on an equal footing. The accomplishment was real enough, and the national pride derived from the accomplishment was quite palpable. Against this background, many Chinese found disputes between China and the U.S., of which there were plenty, increasingly irritating and insufferable. Some of these quarrels had long historical roots, such as the continued U.S. support for Taiwan; others were more recent in origin, such as trade frictions or the U.S. Congress' effort to prevent Beijing from hosting the Olympic Games.

In these disputes with the United States many Chinese perceived inherent American hostility to China.

For much of the 1990s, therefore, two opposing and paradoxical forces converged to shape Chinese perspectives on the United States of America. On the one hand, the development of a free market economy and the related liberalization of the Chinese society led to an increasingly positive reception of American ideas and the American way of life. On the other hand, emboldened by their recent national success, many Chinese increasingly resented what they viewed as American arrogance and selfishness in Sino-American relations and in world politics. These two trends, antithetical as they were, came out of the same larger events in China and in Sino-American relations in the 1990s, which affected the behavior of the Chinese state, intelligentsia, and masses as a whole. Compared to the situation in the preceding decade, the Chinese government, intellectuals, and general populace now shared a broader common ground and greater consensus in their attitude toward the U.S.A.—nationalism appealed to them all, albeit to different extents. At the same time, given the fact that the new Chinese nationalism was largely based on China's economic success, which in turn had resulted from liberal economic reforms, national pride did not simply translate into the rejection of American culture. In the 1990s, therefore, Chinese resentment toward the United States as a world power and Chinese acceptance of American lifestyle, which were manifestations of the antithetical nationalist and liberal tendencies unified at their roots, balanced each other out and prevented a movement to either extreme. One may characterize the end result as either indecisiveness or maturation of views. In any event, the phenomenon reflects what the Chinese, based on their own life experience, made of the United States of America at the end of the twentieth century.

|

The Chinese government entered the last decade of the twentieth century in a precarious state. By brutally suppressing the 1989 pro-democracy movement, the Communist Party survived a severe crisis and maintained its hold on power, but the violent crackdown also delivered heavy blows to its prestige and claim to political legitimacy. It is quite understandable that in the wake of the June 1989 upheavals, leaders in Beijing felt deeply insecure and were highly defensive about their policies. Therefore, immediately after the Tiananmen Square crackdown, officials in Beijing instinctively tightened ideological control to fend off criticism and further challenges. A nationwide campaign of thought rectification was launched because hardline Chinese leaders felt that behind the 1989 upheavals was ideological confusion in the minds of the Chinese people, partly caused by undesirable Western influence.

The events leading up to the Tiananmen Square crackdown had caused the downfall of Zhao Ziyang, General Secretary of the Chinese Communist Party, who was blamed for the failure to head off the crisis. Replacing the disgraced Zhao was Jiang Zemin, who had headed the party organization in Shanghai. The old guard in the party chose Jiang because they felt they could trust the younger man. The adoptive son of a revolutionary martyr, Jiang had received his training as an engineer in the Soviet Union and had loyally and ably served the party for many years. Not a hardliner himself, Jiang, like many Chinese at the time, recognized the need to continue the reform in China. Still, having come to the top office in China shortly after a bloody crackdown, Jiang was cautious; he certainly did not want to alienate the party elders who had just installed him, nor did he want to do anything rash to further destabilize an already precarious situation. After his arrival in Beijing, therefore, Jiang dutifully pushed the ideological rectification campaign designed to make the Chinese people see that Western democracy was the wrong idea for China and that the Western countries encouraged chaos in China out of their selfish desire to keep China weak.

In particular, the Chinese audience was reminded how, in 1949, as Chinese revolutionaries took control of China, American imperialists were already plotting the overthrow of the People's Republic. The enemy's strategy, as outlined by U.S. Secretary of State Dean Acheson, was to achieve the so-called peaceful transformation. Having failed in their military support for Chiang Kai-shek's Nationalist forces, Americans such as Acheson pinned their hope on the Chinese they termed as "democratic individualists," who, in due time, would successfully reshape China from the inside to the satisfaction of American capitalists.[1] The traitorous, pro-American "democratic individualists" made a run on power in May and June 1989, an evil attempt that the Chinese Communist Party rightfully thwarted, saving China from total chaos. The Chinese people "should not forget, even for one second, the aggressive nature of imperialism. They should stay alert always!"[2]

In its general thrust, the drive for ideological rectification after the Tiananmen Square crisis resembled some earlier political movements—the short-lived campaign against "Bourgeois Liberalization" in the mid-1980s, for instance. But the latest effort also exhibited some new characteristics. Most notably, acknowledging the widespread skepticism in the country, the Chinese government tried to be as realistic as possible in their efforts to "educate" Chinese people. So, in addition to reiterating some standard official rhetoric—as illustrated by the talk about the Acheson plot—the government tried to discuss issues of substance in a down-to-earth manner.

In the *People's Daily*, the Communist Party's official newspaper, there appeared a series of articles under the overall title "Why Only under Socialism Can China Develop?" Published over the course of several months, the writings addressed various aspects of developments in China and the West.

Detailed contrasts between China and the United States, in terms of natural resources, historical experience, and so on, were drawn to demonstrate that certain objective factors determined that China must follow a course different from that of America. It was pointed out that a simple comparison between the current levels of development in China and the United States was unfair and misguided. Before reaching its current stage of development, the U.S. had enjoyed more than two hundred years of mostly peaceful growth; during the same period, China had struggled with the scarcity of natural resources, domestic unrest, and most important of all, endless foreign invasions. To compare China and America meaningfully, one ought to adopt a historical viewpoint. The modern development of China had started rather late, but once it got under way in a generally stable environment after 1949, it sped ahead rather impressively, the detrimental effects of the Great Cultural Revolution notwithstanding. "During the period from 1953 to 1980, the industrial growth rates for the United States and Britain averaged just 3.7 percent and 2.2 percent respectively; for China, it was 11.1 percent." "In the five years from 1981 to 1986, annual GDP growth rates for the U.S., Japan, Britain and France were 3 percent, 3.7 percent, 2 percent and 1 percent; for China, it was 9.8 percent." So, during the post-1949 years, China's economic growth outpaced that of the West, including the United States, by a large margin, a feat of which Chinese people should be proud.[3]

The post-1989 effort of thought rectification revealed willingness on the part of the Chinese state to discuss specifics rather than simply feed the people with dry party jargon. This new trait partly reflected how seriously the 1989 crisis affected Chinese leaders—they recognized the gravity and direness of the situation and wanted to be as pragmatic as possible to avoid a total collapse. Partly, the new realist approach indicated a self-confidence that arose out of the economic success in the 1980s—the government was willing to invite the Chinese people to examine its recent record on promoting economic development in China. In fact, on a broader basis, many Chinese leaders believed that necessary as they were immediately after the Tiananmen Square incident, defensive measures such as the tightening of ideological control and the denunciation of the ill-intentioned West were not enough to save the rule of the Chinese Communist Party in the long run. One such party leader, who happened to be the one that truly mattered, was Deng Xiaoping. Deng, China's paramount leader at the time, was ultimately responsible for sending in armed troops to clear demonstrators from the streets of Beijing in June 1989, but he was also the mastermind behind the post-Mao reform. While believing the Tiananmen Square crackdown to be absolute necessary, Deng also recognized the peril and futility of trying to dam up the deluge of changes altogether, a lesson that was clearly borne out by the implosion of the Soviet Union in 1991. As soon as the political crisis caused by the Tiananmen Square Incident subsided, Deng decided to resurrect his economic reform.

To overcome the hardliners' resistance to the return of the reform, at the beginning of 1992, Deng, now at the advanced age of eighty-seven, took a lengthy inspection tour of South China, where he boldly advocated the continued liberalization of China's economic system. Scolding conservative leaders for their timidity, Deng encouraged officials to experiment with ideas and policies that would further economic growth. At the time, for instance, some Chinese were debating whether China should set up stock exchanges to facilitate the flow of capital that China's emerging free market economy much needed. Deng told officials not to worry too much about the ideological implications of the matter. "Stocks and stock markets—are they really too dangerous to touch? Are they exclusively capitalist? Can't they serve socialism as well? People may argue over such issues, but let's go ahead and try the measures out."[4]

Deng's bold advocacy for the resumption of liberal economic reform brought many similarly minded Chinese leaders out of the long shadow cast by conservative communist ideologues. Among those emboldened officials was the Communist Party's new general secretary Jiang Zemin. Shortly after Deng's South China tour, China's official media began to shift its focus from ideological purification back to reform and openness. The first sign of change appeared on February 23, 1992, when the People's Daily published an editorial entitled "On Open Door Policy and Capitalizing on Capitalism," which emphasized that there was still a great deal for China to learn from the West.[5] In another prominent commentary, the People's Daily expounded on the concept of "internationally accepted conventions." China now operated in a global environment; for China to do well, economically and otherwise, Chinese people must learn about, and conform to, standards observed by the international community as a whole.[6] A message such as this, of course, differed significantly from the condemnation of the malicious West that was a major part of the post-1989 ideological rectification.

At a critical CCP Politburo meeting in March 1992, General Secretary Jiang Zemin declared that the Chinese Communist Party had made a solemn commitment to a fundamental policy with economic development as its top priority. The party, Jiang proclaimed, would not waver on this commitment "for at least one hundred years."[7] Ideological purity was no longer as important a consideration as it used to be.

The party's decision to re-launch liberal economic reform released tremendous energy among the Chinese people. Disillusioned by the failure of the 1989 pro-democracy movement, many Chinese were now willing and eager to focus their attention on money making. Rapid economic growth soon resumed. In 1993, the year immediately following Deng's South Tour and the Communist Party's decision to continue economic reform, China's Gross National Product expanded by a whopping 13.5 percent.[8] The cumulative effects of the growth in the 1980s and new stimulations in the 1990s combined to create an economic dynamic that quickly took on a life of its own. The surging forward was unstoppable now. Old taboos were smashed one after another; economic liberalization spread from sectors such as services to manufacturing and then to key areas such as real estate, energy, and finance. In the new decade, China's economy grew at an average rate of over 9 percent a year. As part of the overall development, trade with the United States expanded considerably. In 1989, Chinese imports from the U.S. were valued at $5.76 billion while Chinese exports to the U.S. totaled $11.99 billion. Ten years later, in 1999, China's imports from the U.S. reached $13.11 billion while exports to the U.S. exploded to $81.79 billion.[9]

The economic boom in the 1990s significantly improved the living standard in China, even though the distribution of the new wealth was by no means even. Back in the 1980s, with envy and admiration Chinese used the term *wan yuan hu*— "a ¥10,000 household"—to refer to extraordinary financial successes. In the 1990s, that income level became just about average in many parts of China. Now, one had to be a millionaire or better to make news. A sizable middle class was in the making, with proud ownership of purchased apartments and automobiles. Along with this there emerged a bourgeois mindset, which understandably supported official policies designed to maintain economic growth and political stability at the same time.

The new economy of China thus brought the Chinese people and their government closer to each other, at least on issues such as China's foreign relations. Now the Chinese government's success or failure in dealing with the outside world would directly affect the Chinese workers' pocketbooks. This was welcomed by leaders in Beijing, who, just a few years before, had worried about a total political collapse in the face of combined pressure from inside China and abroad. The state did not have to try very hard to push some trite conspiracy theories about how the evil West always wanted to undermine China; there were now plenty real disputes between China and the West on which Chinese leaders could count on the support of the Chinese people. All of a sudden, the government found it much easier now to get a sympathetic hearing from Chinese citizens on the official presentation of the West, especially the all-important United States.

Of course, the phenomenon did not come about all by itself; the Chinese government certainly did its part to effect the transition. A case in point is the Chinese government's initiative for Beijing to host the 2000 Olympic Games. Launched in 1991, just two years after the bloody Tiananmen Square crackdown, the bid to stage one of the world's most prestigious international events in China's capital was a fail-proof political endeavor for the Chinese government. Regardless of their differences with the government, most Chinese were proud of their country. If China won the bid to host the Olympic Games, the victory would do much to rehabilitate China from the shame associated with the 1989 Tiananmen Square crackdown. If the Chinese bid was rejected, it would surely arouse patriotic sentiments in China and strong displeasure with the outside world. Once declared, the Beijing Olympic initiative quickly gained momentum and popularity among Chinese people. As expected, the United States came out strongly to oppose Beijing's bid. In July 1993, as the International Olympic Committee evaluated applications of the candidate cities, the U.S. House of Representatives passed a resolution formally objecting to staging the Olympic Games in Beijing.[10] In August, sixty U.S. Senators took the unusual action of addressing a letter to the IOC, urging the members of the committee to vote against the Chinese effort.[11] A month later, when the IOC made its selection, Beijing lost narrowly to Sydney, Australia, by a margin of just two votes, 43 to 45.[12]

Given the great fanfare that surrounded Beijing's bid for the 2000 Olympic Games, the rather vocal intervention by the U.S. to rebuff China infuriated many Chinese. The Chinese government lost no time in expressing outrage over the spiteful American actions. Li Peng, the premier of China, denounced the U.S. Congress for "blatantly trampling over the Olympic spirit." Defiant and solemn, Li declared: "China is a sovereign nation. The Chinese people, who are no longer on their knees but standing firmly on their feet, will not bow their heads to pressure or intimidation."[13] Vice Premier Li Lanqing observed that the U.S. government's interference with the IOC decision "understandably aroused strong resentment within the IOC itself and definitely among Chinese people."[14] State Councilor Li Tieying, who headed the Chinese delegation to the IOC selection, stated that the loss of Beijing's bid "in no way indicates China's lack of capability or qualification." China's temporary loss, Li said, would "only inspire all of our people to unite in their common endeavor to build a stronger China."[15] The *People's Daily*, for its part, published an emotional front page editorial in the wake of China's loss: "We are fully confident that someday the Olympic flag will fly high and proud over this eastern land, 9.6 million square kilometers in area, populated by one-fifth of the whole mankind, home of a 5,000-year-old civilization. That day will come soon."[16] It was eight years later, in 2001, that Beijing won the right to host the 2008 Olympic Games.

There were many other disputes in Sino-American relations on which the Chinese government deftly presented itself as a determined advocate of China's national interests and the United States as a bully inherently hostile toward China. In July 1993, as China and the U.S. wrestled over the right to host the 2000 Olympic Games, what is known as the *Yinhe* Incident flared up, which received prominent media coverage in China. At that time, the U.S. government charged that a Chinese cargo ship, the *Yinghe*, then on the high seas en route to Iran, was carrying contraband materials that could be used to produce biochemical weapons; Washington demanded immediate inspection.

The Chinese government squarely rejected the accusation and resisted U.S. requests for boarding and searching.[17] As the two sides debated the matter, U.S. warships and airplanes placed the Chinese vessel under close surveillance. To break the standoff, Beijing assented to a joint inspection. From August 28 to September 4, officials from the U.S., Saudi Arabia, and China searched the *Yinhe* but found no suspected substances on board.

The forced boarding of the *Yinghe* was a serious loss of face for China and the Chinese government reacted strongly. The foreign ministry issued a stern statement, carried on the front page of the *People's Daily*. "On what legal basis did the United States act? If such behavior by a self-appointed 'world cop' go unchecked, where on earth do we find justice? Or equality among sovereign states? Or normal international relations?"[18] The ministry demanded an apology from the U.S. government, which was not forthcoming. On September 25—two days after the loss of Beijing's bid to host the 2000 Olympic Games—the *Yinhe* returned to her home port Tianjin. A major welcome ceremony was held, led by China's Vice Premier Zou Jiahua. In his speech at the rally, Zou denounced "U.S. hegemonism." "In recent years, the United States has behaved like a world cop. This policeman is quick at making something out of nothing, relentless in its efforts to chase wind and catch shadows."[19]

Whereas disputes over matters such as Olympic Games and the boarding of the *Yinghe* took place only once in a while, some other Sino-American frictions were more routine in nature, constantly reminding the Chinese people of the problems between China and the United States. One such issue was trade. As noted above, Sino-American economic exchanges expanded considerably in the 1990s, leading to a sizable surplus on the Chinese side. The U.S. accused China of unfair trade practices, an accusation the Chinese government vehemently denied. In the early 1990s, for example, the two nations engaged in a lengthy struggle over the protection of intellectual property rights. Toward the end of 1994, U.S. officials broke off an ongoing trade negotiation and departed for home, leaving behind the warning that, unless China met the U.S. conditions, Washington would impose heavy tariffs on a wide range of Chinese exports. Beijing's reaction was highly public and intense, to the effect that the U.S. was acting arrogantly and making unreasonable demands—the worst of which, according to Chinese officials, encroached upon China's judicial rights and sovereignty.[20] Beijing declared that, if necessary, China would retaliate with her own tariff sanctions on American goods so as to "defend our national autonomy and dignity."[21] On February 25, 1995, two days before the declared U.S. sanctions were to go into effect, the two sides reached an agreement. These dramatic events, covered extensively by Chinese media, were rather emotionally charged to Chinese citizens who had only recently entered the age of globalized economic competition and who were inclined to view such disputes as matters of right and wrong rather than simply practical bargaining and compromises.

Similarly, China's effort to obtain membership in the World Trade Organization (WTO), in the face of strong American resistance, also appeared like a showdown between the aspiring Chinese nation and the innately hostile United States. It was in the 1980s that China launched its drive to join the forerunner of the WTO, the General Agreement on Tariffs and Trade (GATT). In 1994, as the GATT prepared to reorganize itself as the WTO, Beijing made a major push to complete negotiations with various countries so that China could be a founding member of the WTO. The U.S., claiming that China was not a market economy yet, insisted that China must open further before the country could join the WTO. As China and the U.S. battled over complicated trade issues, Chinese officials who spearheaded the Chinese efforts emerged as national heroes, the most famous of them being the sharp-tongued Long Yongtu, China's top negotiator, and Wu Yi, the female Minister of Foreign Trade and Economic Cooperation. Wu, in particular, made quite a name for herself in her contentions with the Americans, and came to be known as China's Iron Lady. Wu was later promoted to be a state councilor and for a while was the only female member in the CCP Politburo.[22]

As the end of 1994 approached and with no WTO deal with the U.S. in sight, the *People's Daily* published a long and unusual "open memorandum," in which the government explained to the Chinese people how the U.S. had acted unjustly to deny China the membership in the world's top trade organization:

> In round after round of strenuous and often repetitive negotiations, the Chinese side answered numerous questions and clarified thousands of issues for certain concerned parties with regard to the GATT. The length of time taken so far to review China's membership and the scope of the related investigation are simply unprecedented. . . . Yet, as we approach the end of the negotiations, the resistance against our entry has only further intensified.[23]

The resistance, the Chinese government noted, had no merits in itself; it came largely from U.S. hostility—"the lack of political will on the other side of the Pacific."[24] In the open letter, the *People's Daily* declared that China would not yield to pressure and would never "sacrifice China's social and economic stability" to please the United States.[25] Shortly thereafter, negotiations with the U.S. did collapse. The *People's Daily* published the news on its front page under the headline "Due to Certain Party's Lack of Good Faith and Deliberate Obstruction, No Agreement on Our Country's Entry of the GATT."[26] It was five years later, in 1999, that China finally concluded negotiations with the U.S. on China's membership in the WTO.

Events such as the boarding of the *Yinghe* or trade friction with the U.S. angered many Chinese, but some other matters in Sino-American relations irked them even more, among them U.S. policies on Hong Kong, Tibet, and Taiwan. As many Chinese saw it, the United States devilishly encouraged separatism in these Chinese territories, aiming to weaken China and prevent the rise of the Chinese nation. The Chinese government could very well count on popular support on issues such as this. The strong positions the government took on such matters brought the Chinese state and general populace closer to each other and placed the United States on the opposing side of the rising national consciousness in China.

This was the situation in 1995–96, when a visit to the United States by a Taiwanese leader touched off a crisis over Taiwan, which Beijing considered a renegade province of the People's Republic of China. In that year, in a departure from a long-standing tradition, Washington issued a visa to Mr. Lee Teng-hui, the President of the Republic of China based in Taiwan, and thus allowed the top Taiwanese leader to visit the U.S. This trip was booked as private in nature, during which Lee was to speak at Cornell University, where decades before he had studied. This hardly mollified the Chinese, who viewed the event as a dangerous precedent that violated what was known as the "One China Policy," which they believed to be the most critical element in Sino-American relations. The Chinese found the issue particularly sensitive because Lee, who, unlike his predecessors Chiang Kai-shek and Chiang Ching-kuo, was a Taiwanese native with a clear separatist inclination.

Finding their protests against Lee's visit falling on deaf ears, the infuriated Chinese government reacted strongly. In the middle of 1996, the Chinese People's Liberation Army staged large-scale military exercises on the coast of China and test-fired advanced missiles off the shores of Taiwan. Later the same year, the Chinese military fired more test missiles to further demonstrate its determination to stop the separation of Taiwan from China. As a countermeasure, the U.S. deployed two nuclear-armed aircraft carrier battle groups to the region, a move that, in the eyes of Chinese, made clearer Washington's intention to keep Taiwan apart from Motherland China. In terms of domestic politics, at least, the Chinese government had little to lose and a great deal to gain from such contentions with the United States.

The same pattern can also been seen in Sino-American clashes over the issue of human rights in China. In the 1980s, many liberal-minded Chinese had appreciated and welcomed American criticism of the lack of freedom and democracy in China, a fact that was crystallized in a replica of the Statue of Liberty erected at Tiananmen Square at the height of the 1989 pro-democracy movement. In the overall international and domestic contexts of the 1990s, however, it became easier for the Chinese government to portray American criticism as malicious demonization of China, designed to ruin China's reputation and create political troubles to slow down China's development. It did not help that, in this ongoing struggle, many Americans often acted carelessly or arbitrarily, paying relatively little attention to the changed circumstances in China and to the distinction between badgering the Chinese government and humiliating the Chinese people. For example, in attacking China's human rights record, the United States tended to focus on issues related to personal liberties—free speech, etc.—while overlooking subjects such as the economic well-being of the Chinese, which mattered even more in a developing country such as China. This created openings for the Chinese government's countercharges that, at best, the Americans were out of touch with reality in China, where "the people's right to survive and develop" was of the utmost importance, and where political stability was a necessary condition for economic growth.[27]

In addition to the substance of disputes over China's human rights record, some of the ways in which Washington pursued the issue were also counterproductive, arousing strong resentment in China with little actual accomplishment to show. In 1990, in the wake of the Tiananmen Square crackdown, the United States sponsored resolutions at the United Nations Human Rights Commission to condemn China. The U.S. was unable to push the resolutions through the commission, and, as time passed, the likelihood that the commission would adopt the resolution diminished significantly. The U.S., however, doggedly persisted in the effort, even after close allies such as the European Union had stopped taking part in the initiative. In nine out of the twelve years from 1990 to 2001, the U.S. sponsored or otherwise led endeavors at the U.N. Human Rights Commission to condemn China, but none of the resolutions ever passed. Thus, at a certain time in a given year, China's official media would report on how the U.S. was once again trying to publicly humiliate China, and how, once again, China was able to rally international support to thwart the vicious American attack. This almost became an annual ritual, a race between China and the United States, in which one side must win over the other. Quite conveniently and successfully, the Chinese government presented itself as a defender of China's national dignity and the United States as a mean bully bent on tormenting China.

Thus, in the 1990s, the overall changes in China and in the state of Sino-American relations created a context in which the Chinese government could easily portray the United States as an arrogant world power determined to harass and assail China whenever possible. The Chinese government and the Chinese populace gravitated toward each other, and, as a stronger sense of nationhood emerged, the political fortunes of the Chinese government, insofar as the United States was concerned, improved significantly. With China's economy continuing to boom and Chinese disdain toward the United States as a world power on the rise, the Chinese government experienced less and less political pressure resultant from American influence in China.

While the Chinese government reaped considerable benefits from the new nationalist trend in China, the Chinese leaders, for the most part, were careful not to push their luck too far and too hard in this particular undertaking. After all, the newly acquired national pride of the Chinese people came largely from China's economic success in the 1980s and 1990s, which, in turn, arose out of the liberal reforms that had been carried out during the period. Because of this, the Chinese government could not turn its back on the West altogether, nor did it want to do so. For the Chinese Communist Party to keep the trust and the confidence of Chinese people, it had to continue to improve the people's living standard, which meant it had to continue the liberal reformist policies of the past two decades. If nothing else, given how heavily the Chinese economy had become export-dependent, a breakdown in relations with the West, especially with the United States, would be devastating to China.

Given this liberal and cosmopolitan imperative, the Chinese government, even as it struggled with the United States on a wide range of issues, maintained a sense of moderation, endeavoring not to push Sino-American relations to the breaking point or to represent America in such negative terms that cooperation with the Americans became logically or morally questionable. This was the case after the U.S.-China face-off over Taiwan in 1996. By then, both Beijing and Washington recognized the grave nature of the issues on hand and demonstrated willingness to ease tension. A series of diplomatic maneuvers led to agreements on an exchange of visits by President Bill Clinton and President Jiang Zemin. As the Chinese-American relationship gradually warmed up again, especially as the planned state visits drew near, the Chinese government worked diligently to prepare China's public opinion to create a favorable environment for its policies. The importance of Sino-American cooperation was emphasized, U.S.-China friendship eulogized, and certain aspects of American culture celebrated.

It was against this backdrop that, in March 1998, Jiang Zemin, the CCP general secretary and president of the People's Republic, made the highly public comments about the moral worthiness of Hollywood, praising movies such as *Titanic*, which was about to be shown in China. Jiang went so far as to say that he had urged his colleagues in the Politburo to watch the film so that they could see how moral education was done in the United States.[28]

President Jiang visited the United States in late 1997. President Clinton made his trip to China in mid-1998. The exchange of the presidential visits appeared to be a great success; at least that was the way they were presented to the Chinese public. Sino-American relations appeared to be back on track again. But, before the Chinese leaders could take a breath of relief, some terrible events took place, which tremendously embarrassed those who had spoken favorably of the United States. On May 8, 1999, U.S. warplanes taking part in the NATO bombing campaign in Yugoslavia attacked and destroyed the Chinese embassy in Belgrade, killing three and wounding twenty Chinese diplomats and journalists. Two years later, on April 1, 2001, a U.S. spy plane flying off the Chinese coast bumped into a Chinese jet fighter that was tailing it, leading to the crash of the Chinese plane and the loss of the Chinese pilot. The damaged U.S. aircraft made an emergency landing on Chinese territory.

These events, taking place in the context of numerous other Sino-American disputes in the 1990s, aroused strong anti-American feelings in China. In spite of the American explanations that the embassy attack was an error and that plane collision resulted from the aggressive maneuvering on the part of the Chinese airman, many Chinese viewed the U.S. actions deliberate provocations, designed to humiliate China and test Chinese resolve. Large crowds of Chinese students gathered outside the U.S. embassy in Beijing to protest the American atrocity. These activities made a stark contrast to events in 1989, when Chinese students protesting against their own government erected a replica of the Statue of Liberty in Tiananmen Square.

Facing the rising anti-American sentiment in China, the Chinese state was not so much concerned with fanning the fire against the United States. On the contrary, leaders in Beijing now worried that the Chinese people would fault them for being soft and cowardly in dealing with the Americans. They tried to control a volatile situation to avoid severe damage to Sino-American relations and forestall domestic disturbances. Within an hour of the U.S. attack on the Chinese embassy in Belgrade, General Secretary Jiang Zemin conferred with his top advisers to manage the crisis. According to Wang Guangya, a deputy foreign minister at the time, at the emergency meeting that Jiang convened, "we all recognized right away that our major challenge was not how to deal with the Americans—that was the easy part—but what to do with our own citizens, particularly our students, how to prevent inappropriate behavior, how to persuade them not to overreact."[29] On this occasion, it was decided that Hu Jintao, then vice president of China, should deliver a speech, televised to the whole country, to make clear the Chinese government's position. The speech, according to Wang Guangya, served two purposes—"to express the grave concern with which the Chinese government viewed the incident, and to urge our citizens to exercise restraint in their reaction."[30]

Overall, during the 1990s, imperatives for China's official presentation of the United States changed notably. Immediately after the bloody crackdown of the 1989 pro-democracy movement, in an instinctive reflex, Chinese leaders revived some old official rhetoric of the Mao era and portrayed the United States as an imperialist power bent on the destruction of socialist China. By doing so, the Chinese government tried to dissuade the Chinese people from American influence and stabilize the political situation in China. Then, as the crisis generated by the 1989 protests subsided and after economic liberalization in China resumed, Chinese leaders grew more comfortable in the triangular relationships among the United States, the Chinese people, and the Chinese government itself. China's economic boom and the expansion of her international profile created plenty of opportunities for the government to play the role of an advocate of national interests, who heroically fights the domineering United States. This was both an act and reality, because many issues in Sino-American relations that the government tackled were quite real. In this way, as nationalism grew stronger, the political position of the Chinese government in the domestic scene, in its relation to the United States, improved notably. More self-confident than it used to be, the Chinese government had less reason to artificially demonize the U.S. In fact, by the end of the 1990s, as anti-U.S. sentiments intensified in China, the Chinese government felt the need to keep the rage under control and called for moderation. In doing so, the Chinese state acted out of the recognition that, in the 1990s, it was largely the dual forces of nationalism and economic liberalism that shaped the affairs in China and the country's relationship with the United States.

II

The larger events of the 1990s that affected the behavior of the Chinese government also helped shape Chinese intellectuals' attitudes toward the United States of America. As we have seen, in the 1980s, the Chinese intelligentsia derived much of its inspiration from America, which, to a great extent, accounts for the liberal tinge of China's intellectual life during the first decade of China's Reform Era. After the 1989 political debacle and amid the subsequent economic expansion, Chinese intellectuals' passion and admiration for the West cooled off considerably and sinocentric thinking gained strength, gradually creating a new outlook on the United States of America.

The transition started with the Chinese government's campaign for ideological rectification in the wake of the 1989 Tiananmen Square crisis. Given the background and the repressive nature of this official drive, most Chinese intellectuals, careful to protect their own reputation, stayed away from it. There was one notable exception—a young scholar by the name of He Xin, who came forward unabashedly to propose a largely nationalist line of thinking, which differed from both the liberalism of the 1980s and the socialist ideology that a panicky Communist Party tried hard to revive.

A self-educated man with no college education, He Xin made his name as a scholar in the 1980s for his studies on Chinese antiquity. With interest that extended far beyond his specialized field, He Xin, who was based in the Chinese Academy of Social Sciences, had also written on a wide range of other subjects, including the issue of China's changing national identity. After the Tiananmen crisis, with his characteristic eccentricity, He Xin threw himself into the ideological rectification campaign pushed by the Chinese government at the time. In December 1990, in a very unusual move, the Communist Party's official publication, the *People's Daily*, devoted two full pages out of its daily eight to a long piece penned by He Xin, in which the young author defended various policies of the Chinese government and attacked Western liberalism as a wrong idea for China. As He Xin saw it, the so-called liberal world order, to which so many Chinese intellectuals paid tribute in the 1980s, was a device by which the developed West deceived and exploited the poorer countries in the world. Under the system of the global free market economy, He Xin suggested, affluent countries such as the United States and Japan had grown richer while the less fortunate nations had been further impoverished.[31] "A decade ago," He Xin wrote, "I bought into the myth about the superiority of free market economy, thanks to P. A. Samuelson. After ten years of study and hard thinking, after comparing reform practices of China, Eastern Europe and the Soviet Union, I am now strongly convinced that, in general, in terms of inner vitality, socialism is definitely better than capitalism."[32]

Only through socialism, He Xin asserted, can developing countries achieve true prosperity. He ridiculed those who declared the death of socialism simply because the Soviet Union had collapsed. He singled out Francis Fukuyama, the U.S. State Department analyst who declared that the failure of the Soviet Union marked the "end of history" and that the Western socioeconomic and political system would inevitably spread all over the world. He Xin sneered: "This is the most pompous and superficial notion that I have ever known."[33]

Responding to those who would point to the national success of the United States as evidence for the strength of classical liberalism, He Xin stressed that in its historical development the United States enjoyed special advantages rarely found elsewhere in the world—abundant natural resources, for instance. Even with such singular blessings, the Americans had overplayed their hand, and "the decadent American way of life" would soon prove unable to sustain itself, He Xin wrote.[34] China, with her limited resources and huge population, should not attempt to model herself after America. The Chinese people should not, for instance, pin their hope on a swift realization of popular democracy in China. The Americans, who applauded and encouraged revolts such as the 1989 Tiananmen protests, did so either because they had no true understanding of China or because they wished China ill.[35] The "impatience and zealousness" of the young protesters in 1989, He Xin wrote, indicated a lack of confidence in their own country. Now that the great upheaval had passed, Chinese people should carefully assess their situation and recognize that "China is well and strong, with infinite potential," and that the Chinese nation can follow a path of her own to reach great success.[36]

Presented at the height of the post-1989 ideological rectification campaign, He Xin's ideas were scorned by Chinese intellectuals who were still mourning the failure of the Tiananmen protests, and He Xin appeared very much a political opportunist who chose to defend a brutal authoritarian government at a very bad time. In retrospect, however, He Xin, in his own oddball fashion, anticipated the rise of Chinese nationalist thinking in the coming years, which would have a strong effect on China's cultural life and on Chinese intellectuals' attitude toward the United States of America.

The changes, initially subtle and eventually unmistakable, can be first detected in a new tone acquired by *Dushu*, the book review journal that had served as the flagship of Chinese liberal thought in the 1980s. Take, for example, the American authors that the journal chose to introduce to its readers. As we have seen, in the 1980s, featuring prominently in the pages of *Dushu* were American authors such as Alvin Toffler, Thomas Kuhn, Milton Friedman, Richard Hofstadter, and Ralph Waldo Emerson, whose works were enthusiastically represented to promote the liberal cause in China. Entering the 1990s, as circumstances in China and the dynamic of Chinese intellectual life changed, the once-new ideas of the 1980s now looked somewhat old, and *Dushu* shifted its focus. In the early years of the 1990s, for instance, the two American authors who generated the greatest interest in *Dushu* were Edward Said and Samuel Huntington.

The first notable piece on Said appeared in *Dushu* in September 1993—a review of *Orientalism*. In this article, entitled "The 'Other' in the Eyes of the West," the reviewer, Zhang Kuan, expresses his appreciation of Said's portrayal of "despicable Western bias" against the non-Western world. Many Chinese have long admired the West as the land of liberty, democracy, and justice, Zhang wrote, and they have never or rarely considered the many defects of the Western civilization—not least of which is its prejudice and cruel treatment of non-Western people. In their adoration of the West, these Chinese have been "impetuous, blind, and irrational," not so different from the way in which the West has viewed the East. This, according to Zhang, was largely how Chinese intellectuals of the 1980s viewed the West.[37] It is high time, Zhang wrote, that the Chinese recognize the folly and correct the error. "If for the time being the West and the East are still unable to engage each other in meaningful exchanges . . . they should at least be allowed to lead their own lives as they each deem fit." In any event, there is no reason why Chinese should join the Western "chorus" that derogates and belittles the non-Western world.[38]

Voices like this were a far cry from what one would expect to find in *Dushu* just a few years before. *Dushu* was clearly aware of some important changes that were taking place in Chinese life. In an editor's note that accompanied the above-cited article, the journal observed that many years ago some Westerners asked themselves the question, "Are we civilized?" "So far they have not been able to answer that question with absolute confidence. In fact, in many areas there is now less of a reason to answer the question positively." It is still admirable, however, that in the West "one is allowed to point out this unsatisfactory state of affairs. This is definitely one good thing that we can say about European and American society. It is in the same spirit that here we are launching a discussion on Orientalism."[39]

Others joined the deliberation. Some endorsed Said and concurred with Zhang Kuan in his assessment that some Chinese had gone overboard in their veneration of the West, which, in a way, amounted to self-contempt. Why is it, one critic asked, that only Chinese movies such as *Raise the Red Lantern* have been successful in the West? The answer: movies like this exhibit the dark side of Chinese society and culture—poverty, polygamy, foot-binding, and whatnot. This is what the West expects China to look like, and some spineless and clueless Chinese readily met the expectation.[40]

Other critics disagreed and cautioned against overreactions to perceived Western bigotry. Like it or not, one critic wrote, the fact remains that "the Western dominance in today's world is based on modern science and technology":

> Call it military or cultural colonialism if you want to, but the West succeeded because the West entered the modern age first. Since the West first established the standard, subsequent differences between the West and the East came to be viewed as the distinction between the modern and the antiquated, between the new and the old, and between the progressive and the reactionary.[41]

The Chinese should keep this in mind and understand that, given how history has unfolded, to reject the West is to reject modernity. In spite of all the progress China has made in recent years, "modernization remains China's top priority." "It is dangerously reactionary to make too much out of matters such as Orientalism or post-colonial criticism."[42]

Were the Chinese overreacting to Western prejudices? Would calling the West out on its prejudices endanger reform in China? Some did not think so. Zhang Kuan, who had started the Said debate, returned to *Dushu* in September 1994 to defend his position:

> To examine Said and to combat colonialism is not to halt reform in China, nor is it to isolate and protect ourselves from the real world out there. It is to think about how we can strengthen China's

own cultural identity and enhance China's national cohesiveness, so as to prepare ourselves for the "clash of civilizations" that is being instigated. This is a serious issue that all responsible Chinese intellectuals must consider.[43]

The "clash of civilizations" here had its particular reference, of course—some recent works by American political scientist Samuel P. Huntington. To readers of *Dushu*, Huntington was a familiar name. In the late 1980s, when Chinese critics heatedly debated the need for political reform in their country, a number of Huntington's works, including *Political Order in Changing Societies*, generated considerable interest. These works partly contributed to the increasing popularity of the so-called elite politics, which suggests that gradual and prudent political reforms finely managed by the enlightened few, in contrast to popular democracy, can better serve the interests of third world countries. After the 1989 Tiananmen crisis, as the drive for political reform in China lost steam, Huntington briefly slipped off China's intellectual radar. When Huntington made his comeback in *Dushu* in the early nineties, he appeared in a very different incarnation. This time around, the American author drew Chinese attention not with his teachings on democratic changes but with his shocking prediction on the upcoming "clash of civilizations," in which China seemed to have been cast an inglorious role.

In fact, even prior to the appearance of Huntington's famed article in *Foreign Affairs* and the publication of his book *The Clash of Civilizations and the Remaking of World Order*,[44] his views on Confucianism had already been taken to task in China. Writing in the May 1992 issue of *Dushu*, Yitao challenged Huntington's assessment of Confucianism as presented in his *Third Wave: Democratization in the Late Twentieth Century*. Yitao disputes Huntington's assertion that as a political philosophy Confucianism constitutes one of the last obstacles to worldwide democratic changes. Confucianism certainly has its flaws when examined in the modern context, not least because the ancient value system has yet "to develop an effective mechanism to not only ensure long-term political stability but also allow legitimate political opposition," Yitao acknowledges.[45] Still, Confucianism is by no means inherently antimodern and antidemocratic. Yitao wrote:

> Of the world's existing cultures today, Confucianism remains the most flexible and inclusive. In this regard Confucianism is unique, its survival not dependent upon the rejection of other cultures. So we Chinese need not be so insecure as to cry "Cultural aggression!" every time we hear some derogatory words thrown at us by people like Huntington; there is just no reason why we should retreat and hide behind some kind of unhealthy cultural nationalism. On

the other hand, it is equally clear that we shouldn't slavishly eat up every bit of the so-called "new ideas" from the West, even if they seem to be rather fashionable at the time. It is no fun to be swung around like a dog's tail.[46]

That Huntington, in *The Clash of Civilizations and the Remaking of World Order*, identified Confucian culture as a rival and enemy of the West irked his Chinese readers. Western hostility toward China seen in works by authors such as Huntington poured cold water on Chinese intellectuals with a cosmopolitan outlook. The clear divide drawn between the West and the East threw these Chinese intellectuals off balance, who had believed that the difference between China and the West was merely a matter of historical stages and that sooner or later China would assimilate to the modern ways epitomized by the West. On the other hand, Chinese critics who had warned against Western chauvinism felt vindicated. Western prejudices were so deeply entrenched that no matter how much progress China made, the West would never accept her as an equal. The difference between the two sides was not simply developmental but cultural and national.[47]

In their respective ways, therefore, Said and Huntington compelled the Chinese to reconsider China's national identity, thus heightening Chinese intellectuals' national consciousness. Needless to say, Said and Huntington did not do all the work; an overall transition had been long in coming, which simply grew more noticeable in the 1990s. Back in the 1980s, when *Dushu* introduced various American authors to its readers, included were American scholars whose works shed light on the role of Confucianism in modern times; Wei-ming Tu, professor of philosophy at Harvard University, was among those scholars. In the 1990s, as China's economy continued to grow, the rise of East Asia as a whole—besides China, there were Japan, South Korea, Taiwan, Hong Kong, as well as Singapore—further stimulated Chinese interest in Western perspectives on the connection between Confucianism and modernization. Among American works reviewed in the *Dushu* magazine were *Modernity and the Confucian Tradition* by Wei-ming Tu, *Confucian China and Its Modern Fate* by Joseph Levenson, and *Thinking Through Confucius* by David L. Hall and Roger T. Ames.[48] Whereas in the eighties *Dushu* organized "forums" dealing with Toffler's *Third Wave* and Kuhn's *The Structure of Scientific Revolutions*, in the nineties similar efforts were devoted to issues such as Chinese archeology, conditions of rural China, and folk music.[49]

Beyond *Dushu*, a similar trend emerged on a broader basis, characterized by a shift of focus from Western culture to China's own tradition. In 1994, a high-profile international conference was held to celebrate the 2,545th birthday of Confucius. In 1996, a large group of prominent Chinese scholars and journalists gathered to launch an initiative aimed to promote "the Chinese culture of harmony."[50] At Beijing University, *guoxue* (national studies), became a subject popular among students and a School of National Studies was founded to foster learning and scholarship in the field.[51] Addressing a large gathering of students, Ji Xianlin, a distinguished professor of comparative philosophy and religion educated in the West, now in his eighties, expounded the importance of Chinese tradition in the modern age, not only to China herself, but to the West too. Ji's speech was later published under the title "Dusk in the West, Dawn in the East."[52]

In many ways, Chinese intellectuals' return to their roots was inevitable. Since the beginning of Deng's reform at the end of the 1970s, within a very short period of time, China experienced dramatic changes that the modern world had rarely seen. By the middle of the 1990s, Chinese life had become so different from just fifteen years before, the Chinese had to exert themselves to make sense of their new experience, to digest, and to rationalize. To accomplish such a daunting task, mere invocation of the Western experience, helpful as it was, would not suffice. Chinese intellectuals could no longer simply critique Chinese life from the Western perspective; now they had to live the Chinese life. The introduction of Western culture in the eighties served a good historical purpose; in the nineties, Chinese intellectuals had to creatively utilize the borrowed ideas to sort out the complex and rapidly evolving Chinese experience itself. In this context, the shift of focus from cosmopolitanism to nationalism in China's cultural and intellectual life was unsurprising and necessary—it was part of a process in which Chinese people redefined their national identity and its relationship to the world.

Naturally, Chinese intellectuals' reflection on China and the West in the 1990s did not just take place in the ivory tower of academia but also in the messy larger world. Both China and the United States have their own national interests; the numerous disputes between the two countries in the 1990s—described earlier—had their impact on Chinese intellectuals. The effects of these events were the most notable on the newly emerged petit-bourgeois intelligentsia of China. Traditional Chinese intellectuals mostly worked at China's universities or state-sponsored research institutions; they formed the intellectual establishment in the country. In contrast, the mass communications revolution in China during the eighties and nineties brought into being men of ideas and letters who were closely associated with the mushrooming periodicals, books, TV talk shows, radio call-in programs, public relations firms, as well as the ubiquitous Internet. Sharp, dynamic, irreverent, these young men and women differed significantly from their mandarin intellectual superiors. Struggling on a lower strung of the social ladder in China, the new petit bourgeois intellectuals were less influenced by the liberal tradition of the 1980s and they were more willing to speak out against what they viewed as inherent American hostility toward China.

A case in point is a little book entitled *China Can Say No*. Authored by five young men and published in 1995, *China Can Say No* was a scathing condemnation of the United States that became widely popular. More than a million copies of the book were sold, which was remarkable given the nature of the book and the fact that it was not an official undertaking. What appealed to readers was not so much the research or analysis found in the book, which is actually rather thin; instead, it was the uninhibited anti-American furor characteristic of the writing that animated many Chinese who had not seen anything like this since the beginning of the 1980s.

In their book, the authors of *China Can Say No* provide a long list of U.S. offenses against China, ranging from the American attempt to block China's entry of the World Trade Organization, to U.S. support for secessionist Taiwanese and Tibetans, to Washington's encouragement of Japan's rearmament. According to the Chinese writers, the Americans had a long-standing policy to harass China and keep the country weak so that the United States could continue to dominate the world. Given this, disputes between China and the U.S. were inevitable; sooner or later, there would be a confrontation. Having learned nothing from its failure in Vietnam, the U.S. would push China all the way to war. In that event, China would take a stand, fight, and win. In Washington, D.C., there would be another wall of remembrance, only much larger, which, "we strongly believe, will be the tombstone for the American soul."[53]

The five authors of *China Can Say No* were all young, in their twenties or thirties (the lead author, Zhang Zangzang, was thirty-two years old). They had gone to college and come of age in the Reform Era; they worked as teachers, journalists, and small businessmen and had no close ties to China's political or academic establishment.[54] None of them had ever been in the United States, and their English was rudimentary. (Later, responding to those who pointed out their lack of firsthand experience with America, the authors retorted: "Bob Dole, Pat Buchanan and their likes have never been in China. This has not stopped them from freely commenting on Chinese affairs."[55])

The ferocious anti-American feelings harbored by the young Chinese authors were not limited to issues in Sino-American relations but extended to the American way of life itself. In their view, the American civilization was decadent and in decline, as indicated by the closing of the American mind:

> Lively and serious political thinking has ceased to exist in the United States. Pursuit of cheap thrills and amusement is now applauded as endeavors for progress. Simply put, America no longer knows the joy of independent thinking, and gone are all its benefits. The great flowering of American literature and philosophy is now a thing of the past.[56]

Partly for this reason, the authors of *China Can Say No* loathed how Americans flaunted their power and wealth ("Apparently, a nation's might and riches are not always proportionate to the people's wisdom."[57]). They certainly resented the rapidly expanding American presence in China. With insuppressible disgust and contempt, they wrote about the Chinese who "blindly" admired America, who worked for multinational corporations with so much pride, who answered phone calls with English greetings, who spoke dreamily of the "clear blue sky of North America."[58]

> I cannot breathe. I am suffocating.
> That kind of Chinese! That kind of slaves to their foreign
>   masters! That kind of ugly, shameless faces and behavior!
> I must clear my throat. *Ah, pei!*[59]

Evidently, the great anger expressed in works such as *China Can Say No* had as much to do with America as with conditions in China. After about twenty years of liberalization and Westernization, some Chinese started to resent the relentless oppressive power of the free market, feeling that the United States, the world's largest free market, had pushed China on a perilous road. Antimodernism and anti-Americanism were thus interconnected. Viewed in this light, *China Can Say No*, the seemingly simplistic diatribe against the United States, was full of undertones and subplots.

Probably because of this, the popularity of *China Can Say No* unnerved some liberal Chinese intellectuals, who stepped forward to curtail what they viewed as excessive anti-Americanism. Jia Qingguo, professor of international relations at Beijing University, brought out *China Doesn't Just Say No*, in which he presents a more complex picture of Sino-American relations than that shown in *China Can Say No*.[60] Shen Jiru at the Chinese Academy of Social Sciences published *China Is Not Mr. No*, in which he argues that the United States is not China's enemy. The overall trend in the world after the Cold War was a movement toward convergence and integration, Shen wrote; neither old-stock communism nor Western capitalism could claim unqualified victory; most likely, the two conflicting forces would coalesce and consolidate into a hybrid political and socioeconomic system.[61] Given this larger trend, there was no reason why China and the United States could not cooperate and coexist with each other.

Shen's *China Is Not Mr. No* was published as a volume in a series, *Issues China Faces Today*. The editorial advisor for the series was Liu Ji, a vice president of the Chinese Academy of Social Sciences, who was believed to be close to China's top leader Jiang Zemin. On a trip to the United States in May 1997, Liu Ji spoke at Harvard University and put forward his views on Sino-American relations. Given the vast differences between China and the United States, it was very likely that in the coming years both the Chinese and the Americans would make mistakes in their dealings with each other, Liu said. The Chinese may make bad decisions due to lingering Marxist ideological influence, emotional reactions to provocations as well as overconfidence in China's recent economic success.[62]

The Americans, for their part, may blunder in their relationship with China if they fail to control their haughtiness born out of the U.S victory over the Soviet Union in the Cold War. The Americans must also deal with the possibility, suggested by many analysts, that the United States needed the challenge of an external enemy in order to thrive and do well. Additionally, the increasing ideological rigidity in American society, as exemplified by the rise of right-wing extremism and the American public's lack of knowledge about the outside world, might also adversely affect the United States' handling of her relationship with China.[63]

As serious as the mistakes likely to be made on both sides might be, they are not unavoidable, Liu thought. "The Chinese people are eager to learn from other nations. This is particularly true in modern times when China experimented with virtually all major schools of thought from around the world."[64] At the same time, Chinese people must work with the indigenous conditions of their country and find solutions to their own particular problems. America, with a long tradition of "cultural and ideological diversity," surely could find it within herself to understand the need for the Chinese people to solve their problems in their own way.[65]

If Americans wanted to lead the world, Liu emphasized, the best way to accomplish the goal was to lead by example, by setting affairs at home in good order. Liu gently observed:

> American society is not perfect, not yet mankind's dream come true. Wouldn't it be best if the U.S. concentrates on its own effort for self-improvement? If America convincingly demonstrates its own merits, surely we shall all heed the truth, and we Chinese will definitely try, out of our own free will, to emulate the good example.[66]

On the other hand, if, instead of working to improve itself, the United States simply tried to impose its own convictions on China, "then the Chinese will naturally ask: 'Is this all there is to the American claim of human rights and democracy?' Then there will be nothing but trouble."[67] Liu pleaded: "Let's pledge to work together to make the coming century one of friendship, cooperation, prosperity, and progress for China and the United States of America."[68]

Overall, Liu represented an attitude of moderation and realism. He attributed many problems in Sino-American relations to the arrogance and narrow-mindedness of the United States. In this, Liu shared views held by Chinese such as the young authors of *China Can Say No*. At the same time,

Liu refrained from totally rejecting America. He recognized that the Chinese nation's recent success had come from liberal economic reforms, which tied China closely to the U.S. both philosophically and in material terms. Given this, Chinese such as Liu Ji found it irrational and inadvisable for China to condemn America indiscriminately. The liberal tradition of the 1980s survived to keep rising nationalism in balance, insisting on more measured consideration of America.

III

The larger events of the 1990s that shaped China's official and intellectual outlooks on the United States also left their marks on China's general populace. Taken as a whole, the effect was mixed. On the one hand, liberal changes in the nineties narrowed the gap between China and the United States, giving the Chinese far more opportunities to experience and observe America. The U.S. now appeared less exotic and more familiar; it no longer shocked or impressed the Chinese as much. On the other hand, as the Chinese economy boomed and globalized, the average Chinese became more conscious of China's national image and interests; they increasingly resented perceived U.S. hostility and came to hold a dim view of the U.S. role in world politics. Here, even more than in the cases of the Chinese state and intelligentsia, Chinese differentiated between America as a way of life and the United States as a nation-state—on the former the Chinese became more permissive or tolerant while with the latter they grew notably sterner.

For many Chinese, the economic growth that began in the late 1970s came to fruition in the 1990s, resulting in significant improvement of the people's living standards. While twenty years before a hundred Chinese dollars was a decent monthly salary, in the nineties it had to be at least one thousand. Back in the early seventies, watches and bicycles were signs of wealth; now, young Chinese were thinking about buying apartments or automobiles. In the early 1980s, veteran communist leader Chen Yun lashed out at officials who allegedly lost their faith in communism after "taking just a few glimpses of the freeways and skyscrapers" while traveling abroad. Now freeways were built all across China. At amazing speeds five beltways were constructed around the national capital Beijing, but they were not enough to keep up with the increasing automobile traffic in the city. Also in Beijing, when in 1992 a fancy Lufthansa department store opened for business, many people wondered who would be crazy enough to shop at such an exorbitantly expensive place. Actually the store did extremely well.[69] Before long, many similar shopping centers appeared in Beijing and in other Chinese cities too as a new consumer culture flourished across the country.

The economic modernization of China continued to drive the revolution in mass communications, which greatly facilitated the flow of information and exposed Chinese people to an ever-larger world. In 1979, a total of 980 periodicals were published in China; by 1991, the number had reached 6,500, with hundreds of millions of copies of them printed and sold every year.[70] As for books, in 1997 a total of 120,106 titles were published in Mainland China, compared to 14,000 in Taiwan.[71] In the same year, China imported from the United States publications in the value of $30 million; about half of these books were on subjects other than science and technology.[72]

By this time television had become a household necessity, which brought Chinese families news and entertainment. Research conducted in 1996 showed that a youngster in Shanghai spent 3.77 hours per day watching TV. Kids of preschool age watched even more—5.8 hours.[73] Foreign-made programs for children continued to dominate China's airwaves, as they did in the 1980s. One critic lamented how traditional Chinese characters, such as Sun Wukong the magic monkey, were being pushed aside by cartoon figures such as the Ninja Turtles and the Lion King."[74] When asked to name their favorite cartoon characters, 95 percent of the polled kids reported Donald Duck and the like.[75] In another study, two hundred teenagers were asked to indicate their top preference for movies and TV programs made in China and abroad. Of the polled youngsters, 44 percent chose American productions, 34 percent favored programs from Taiwan/Hong Kong, and only 10 percent chose shows made in Mainland China as their top favorites.[76]

One panel of comic strips carried in the newspaper *China Daily* illustrated what was happening in many Chinese homes. Grandpa and his grandson fight for the remote control for TV; Grandpa wants to watch a revolutionary feature movie, *The Last Battle*, but his willful grandson insists on *The Lion King*. The boy's elder brother intervenes: "Come on, let Grandpa have his educational program!"[77]

On big screens in movie theaters, American productions were also making successful runs. Prior to the mid-1990s, foreign movies shown in China tended to be old and low-budget fare, partly due to strict state censorship on contents and partly because of China's inability to pay for big hits. In the late 1990s, control over the importation of Western movies loosened up, as China's movie theaters, now facing stiff competition from TV and other kinds of entertainment, fought for profitability and survival. The so-called "big movies" soon arrived, among them *Jurassic Park*, *Speed*, *Titanic*, and *Saving Private Ryan*, which premiered almost simultaneously in China and abroad. One reporter described the Chinese cinematic scene thus:

> Harrison Ford, the celebrated fugitive, takes our breath away as he leaps through his adventures. Charlie Chan kicks the butt of

China's own movie industry. *True Lies* challenges Chinese audience to tell the real from the phony; a mushroom cloud rises above the American horizon, and a tacky used-car salesman passes himself off as a spymaster and seduces a secret agent's wife. Back when we debated whether we should import the Big Hits, those who were concerned with the fate of China's own movie industry were accused of screaming "Wolf!" No wolf showed up, but there did come the Lion King! . . . The lion's roar so dear to our ears, his story so touching and full of humanity. Our viewers, young and adult alike, are all so very well pleased; they happily pay the twenty-eight-buck additional charge for a tiny little picture-book featuring that illustrious furry animal.[78]

Even more ubiquitous was the Internet, which came into wide use in China recently. The new technology opened a new window on America for many curious and inquisitive Chinese. After a slow start, the market mechanism kicked into gear in the late nineties, and Internet usage in China spread like wildfire. At the end of 1997, just 1.4 million Chinese could get online; two and a half years later, China's Internet population expanded to 16.9 million.[79] By the middle of 2002, more than 56 million Chinese had Internet connections at home, making it the world's second largest Internet population, next only to that of the United States.[80]

The Chinese government tried to control the use of the Internet.[81] But its major concerns were politically sensitive issues, such as those related to the banned Buddhist cult Falungong or the Tibetan independence movement. For average net surfers with no particular interest in such topics, censorship was not much of a problem. For those Chinese with some English proficiency, U.S. Web sites such as *USA Today,* MSNBC, Time-Warner, Amazon, and whitehouse.gov, were all just a couple of clicks away. This was quite a change from the 1980s when magazines like *Newsweek* or *Playboy* that Western guests left behind in their hotel rooms were carefully collected and disposed of.

In addition to exposure through mass media, exchanges with the U.S. in the real world also expanded dramatically. More and more Chinese and Americans traveled across the Pacific for diverse purposes. A 1997 survey of residents in Beijing, Shanghai, and Guangzhou shows that over 45.5 percent of the Chinese had a personal encounter with at least one American, compared to 20.2 percent, 5.1 percent, 4.3 percent and 3.2 percent with regard to Japanese, French, Germans, and Britons.[82] By the middle of the nineties, more than three hundred of the world's top five hundred corporations had set up operations in China. According to a 1994 study, of the 162 best-known brand names of consumer goods in China, fifty-two were of foreign origin. Leading off the list were "Coca-Cola, Pepsi Cola, IBM, Hewlett Packard, Microsoft, Intel, Compaq, Motorola, Kodak, Budweiser, Nestle, Gillette, Levis, and Nike."[83]

The big corporations, with their deep pockets and promotional skills, sold their goods and also built quite an aura of prestige around themselves. Now they were the most desirable employers in China. The Chinese working for these companies, known as *waiqi guyuan*, "foreign corporation employees," were considered a lucky bunch. Young, smart, English-speaking, earning salaries that were often ten times that of an average Chinese worker, these employees were the envy of their peers.[84]

It was not just American corporations in hi-tech areas such as IBM or Pfizer that did well in China; low-tech companies—including fast food chains like McDonald's, Kentucky Fried Chicken, Pizza Hut, and Popeye's—fared splendidly too. In the six months that followed the opening of China's first McDonald's in Beijing in April 1992, more than a half-million people ate at the restaurant.[85] In 1998, there were fifty-seven McDonald's restaurants in Beijing alone.[86] Equally successful was Kentucky Fried Chicken: the average annual sales of its restaurants in China doubled the amount back home in the U.S.[87] In 1994, KFC announced an ambitious four-year plan to invest $200 million to open and operate two hundred restaurants in forty-eight Chinese cities.[88]

To a great extent, the success of the American fast food chains in a country known for its culinary art came from the nice atmosphere that the restaurants provided. Spacious, clean, with popular American music broadcast in the background, these establishments turned out to be fashionable places for young Chinese to eat and hang out. Little children loved to eat with their hands and loved the playgrounds and free toys even more, and, being China's "Little Emperors," they took their parents and grandparents where they wanted to go.

Conscious of the reasons for their success, establishments such as McDonald's and KFC did much to build their image and cultivate the good will of customers. A common scene outside a McDonald's or KFC was a couple of young employees teaching groups of little kids some cute dance moves, as the children's parents looked on approvingly. In a commentary entitled "What McDonald's Community Services Suggest to Us," the august *People's Daily* noted how, twice a week, employees from a McDonald's restaurant in Beijing would take it upon themselves to sweep and clean the streets in the neighborhood. "Businesses naturally want to make profits, but they should look beyond money. . . . Let's hope that China's own businessmen will learn something from this example of McDonald's."[89]

It is not clear whether Chinese businessmen learned the particular lesson suggested by the *People's Daily*, but evidently quite a few Chinese entrepreneurs recognized the value of respected business names, even those that simply sound foreign. In Beijing, records at the city's Business Registration Agency reveal a trend—new businesses tended to choose foreign-looking names. "Before 1992, very few native companies carried names with overseas implications. In 1994, however, 10 percent of all the newly registered businesses bear names that made them appear foreign." "In the first three months of 1995, the percent-age of such businesses had risen to 13 percent."[90] In Shanghai, an observant visitor to a local kindergarten noticed that about 15 percent of the children there were named "Nina, Lisa, Louisa, Jenny, and so on."[91] According to a survey of residents in Beijing, Shanghai, and Guangzhou, America was the top destination where Chinese parents would like to send their children to study, leading other countries by a large margin: 32 percent of those polled chose the United States as their first choice, compared to 9.7 percent for Singapore, 8.6 percent for Australia, and 7.8 percent for Japan.[92]

Whereas Chinese viewing America as a land of opportunity was noth-ing new, in the nineties the notion had grown more tangible and realistic to many Chinese than back in the 1980s. Previously, Chinese views of the U.S. tended to be polarized between a frightful America full of debauchery and a fantastic America where money comes easily and people lead dreamy lives. In the new decade, with the market economy in their own country as refer-ence, the Chinese could better figure out life in the U.S., and their view of America started to focus in the middle to create the impression that America was neither hell nor wonderland. One best-selling Chinese book in the early nineties was *A Chinese Lady in Manhattan*. Crudely written with relatively little literary value, the autobiographical novel appeals to its readers with a "realistic" story about one Chinese woman who arrived in the U.S. penniless and struck it rich in just a few years.[93]

An even bigger hit, an artistically more satisfying one, was a long-running TV drama series called *A Beijing Man in New York*. In this story, a young musician from Beijing arrived in New York with great aspirations. The young man's dream soon crashed against harsh reality—with no money to live by, the hero struggled for bare survival, washing dishes endlessly at local Chi-nese restaurants. His life collapsed under the pressure as his wife left him for an American boyfriend. Wildly popular and widely discussed, *A Beijing Man in New York* became the most viewed TV program in China, making famous the byword: "If you love someone, send him to New York, because New York is Heaven. If you hate someone, send him to New York, because New York is Hell."[94]

Thus, as the direct and indirect contacts between China and the United States expanded, Chinese understanding of America grew more complex and sophisticated. Furthermore, changes in China also made Chinese people less judgmental on life in America. As China went through the second decade of their liberal reforms, numerous social issues inherent in a free market economy became ever more prevalent and severe, including the widening gap between the rich and poor, crimes, divorces, prostitution, and a general sense of insecurity and uncertainty. As they reaped the benefits of capitalism and suffered from its deficiencies, the Chinese could now more easily understand problems in American society, which they had thought would never occur in China. The Chinese were now suffering from the kind of troubles that had ailed America, which, insofar as China pursued a free market economy, could not be easily eliminated. For better or for worse, the Chinese were no longer as self-righteous or dismissive in their views of America as they had been before.

Take the issue of economic disparity for example. For many years, one major Chinese criticism of American society had been the inequality between the affluent and the impoverished. Now, as the free market reform expanded, the socialist system that dated from the Mao Era, including policies such as guaranteed employment, which had been the Chinese people's "Giant Iron Rice Bowl," went to pieces. Now, the official policy was "to let some Chinese get rich first" and Chinese life quickly came to resemble the situation in America. In Beijing, in 1975, the year before Mao's death, the one-fifth of families with the lowest income and the one-fifth of families with the highest income account for 9.52 percent and 37.68 percent of the total pay in the city. Twenty years later, in 1994, the gap in earnings had widened to be one of 4.43 versus 62.83 percent, a change of ratio from 1:4 to 1:14.[95] Nationwide, in 1993, the top 3 percent of the Chinese families held 40 percent of China's total bank deposits.[96] The trend would continue, and economic inequality in China would soon rival and surpass that of the United States.[97]

A similar situation emerged with regard to issues such as violent crimes, prostitution as well as narcotic usage and traffic. As the Chinese society liberalized after the 1970s, criminal activities in China—theft, burglary, rape, and homicide—took place far more frequently. To counter the trend, the government carried out periodic crackdowns, with only limited success. The crime rate continued to climb and crimes committed grew more violent. In 1997, nationwide, 522 policemen were killed and 8,142 wounded in the line of duty.[98] At the same time, offences related to illegal drugs, which were virtually unknown in China in the Mao era, also became ever more prevalent. In the two years from 1988 to 1989, Chinese police uncovered just 4,485 narcotics-related crimes; a few years later, in 1996, drug-related cases rose to 87,000, which led to 110,000 arrests. In 1989, officially identified narcotic addicts in China numbered about 70,000; in 1995, there were 520,000 of them. In the southern province of Guangdong, where the narcotic problem was particularly acute, a township with a population of 70,000 counted 500 verified addicts and 1,000 suspected offenders. By 1997, more than six hundred rehabilitation centers had been set up across China as the country struggled to deal with the crisis.[99] As for prostitution, which, too, had been virtually wiped out in the Mao Era, the situation had come to the point where the authorities would rather look the other way so that they could deal with more serious crimes. Consequently, massage parlors and karaoke houses that provided sex services became virtually legitimate businesses.

Confronted with issues such as these, many Chinese had to admit that their country was not immune to the kind of social ills that plagued American society. Some of them continued to view Western influence as a major cause of the social decay in China, but few of them would hold the West solely or even mainly responsible. In a poll conducted in the northern city Harbin, residents were asked to give their explanations for the rise of prostitution. For "Primary Contributing Factor," 43.2 percent of the surveyed pointed to "pornographic culture," 35.6 percent referred to "openness and liberalization," and 8 percent blamed "Western lifestyle." For the "Secondary Contributing Factor," 24.6 percent chose "Western lifestyle," 19.2 percent blamed "pornographic culture," and 14.8 percent pointed to "unemployment."[100]

Thus, over the course of the 1990s, the social life in China came to bear increasing resemblance to that in the United States. The Chinese had to face the fact that, as China liberalized, social ills that they had viewed as typically American were now widely present in their own country too. Still, given that most people had benefited from the positive changes brought about by the economic reform and the liberalization of their society, the attitude toward the social problems that accompanied the overall development was one of resignation and nonchalance. Now that they led a similar life, what happened in the U.S. no longer simply suggested to them that America was just off the hinges. There seemed to be a reluctant concession that, like it or not, human nature was the same everywhere—weak, ignoble, and pleasure-seeking. There was, therefore, greater willingness to accept American lifestyle, especially among younger Chinese. In 1995, a poll was conducted in Beijing, Shanghai, Shandong, Jiangsu, Anhui, and Sichuan in which residents aged thirty-five or under were asked about their opinion of the United States. More than 89 percent considered the U.S "a strong power"; 87 percent agreed that the U.S. is "prosperous"; over 75 percent believed that American society is efficient and productive. At the same time, 66.2 percent polled recognized that American society is one of intense competition; 86.7 percent acknowledged that there was "a wide gap" between the rich and poor in America; 91.6 percent felt that illegal drugs made a serious problem for the U.S.; and 82.6 percent agreed with the suggestion that Americans are somewhat promiscuous in sexual relationships. Interestingly enough, while 47.8 percent of the young Chinese thought that the Americans were "spiritually hollow," 32.3 percent held the contrary opinion, believing that American life is "spiritually dynamic."[101]

The last point mentioned above is notable because whereas the Chinese people had always readily acknowledged American superiority on matters such as technological advancement or economic prosperity, they had always held strong reservations on the morals of the American society. Now the situation seemed to be changing, with as much as one-third of young Chinese expressing their appreciation of American virtues and spirituality. For better or worse, what happened in the eighties and nineties clearly affected the way the Chinese saw life in China and life in the United States. The new development may have arisen out of better knowledge about American life, and it may simply reflect on the worsening of social problems in China, that is, in comparison, situation in the U.S. does not look so bad after all. Regardless of the causes, the Chinese had become more tolerant of, and more receptive to American culture and American way of life.

A distinction, however, must be made between the more tolerant Chinese view of American lifestyle on the one hand and their attitude toward the United States as a world power on the other. Just as the Chinese became more comfortable with the liberal way of life that America epitomized, they grew angrier and more impatient with U.S. policies toward China. As noted earlier, China's economic success in the 1990s nurtured strong national pride in the mind of many Chinese, who longed to see respect for their country in the international community. Against this background, continued friction and disputes between China and the United States aroused strong anti-U.S. sentiments among the Chinese. The U.S. opposition to Beijing's bid to host the 2000 Olympic Games, the forced boarding of the Chinese cargo ship *Yinhe*, the U.S. objection to China's membership in the World Trade Organization, the American support for Taiwanese and Tibetan separatist movements, Washington's persistent effort to condemn China at the U.N. Human Rights Commission, the U.S. bombing of the Chinese embassy in Belgrade in 1999—all these events drew broad public attention in China and fostered a strong resentment toward the United States. In a poll of Chinese residents in major Chinese cities, conducted in 1994, about 72 percent of those surveyed viewed the U.S. as the country "least friendly" to China."[102] In another study, conducted by *China Youth Daily* in 1995, shortly after Taiwanese leader Li Teng-hui made his controversial visit to the U.S., more than 87 percent of the polled Chinese saw the U.S. as the "the least friendly" nation to China, with 57.2 percent of the surveyed holding a "negative view" of the United States.[103] The above-cited 1995 survey of young Chinese in Beijing, Shanghai, and four provinces, yielded similar results—over 90 percent of those sampled believed that the United States behaved "imperiously" on Taiwan.[104]

This attitude toward the U.S. did fluctuate along with conditions of Sino-American relations. Following the Taiwan crisis in the mid-nineties, Beijing and Washington took actions to reduce tension between the two sides. To warm up their relationship, the two governments arranged an exchange of presidential visits. As this happened, Chinese views of the United States slightly improved. When surveyed in September 1997—two weeks before President Jiang Zemin's scheduled visit of the U.S.—58 percent of the residents in Beijing, Shanghai, and Guangzhou reported that they had "positive feelings" about the United States. In another survey conducted about the same time, when asked their first thoughts upon hearing mention of the United States, 40.4 percent of the respondents chose "strong and affluent power" while a smaller percentage of the polled instinctively conjured up images of crimes, narcotics, etc.[105]

President Jiang's official visit to the U.S. took place in October 1997, which Chinese media reported extensively and positively. President Clinton prepared for his visit in return. A study conducted at this time showed that a large segment of the Chinese public—75.9 percent—was aware of Clinton's upcoming trip. Additionally, the survey indicated that many Chinese knew about major historical events in Sino-American relations: the Korean War (98.7 percent); Jiang Zenmin's recent trip to the U.S. (75.9 percent); Nixon's historic journey to Beijing (74.0 percent); Deng's visit to the U.S. in 1979 (65.0 percent); American pilots' involvement in China's war effort against Japan during World War II (57.9 percent); the U.S.-China Communiqué of 1972 (57.7 percent); the normalization of the diplomatic relationship between China and the U.S. in 1979 (53.5 percent); and the "Ping Pong Diplomacy" (50.6 percent).[106]

As for basic facts about the United States, 48.3 percent of the Chinese knew that July Fourth is the U.S. National Day; 46.3 percent gave the correct number of the U.S. states. Over 35 percent could provide an educated guess on the size of the U.S. population. About 28 percent could do the same with the size of the U.S. territory.[107]

U.S. Presidents who left "strong impressions" on the Chinese came out in the following order: Nixon (22.7 percent), Clinton (17.1 percent), Reagan (11.9 percent), Roosevelt (9.6 percent), Kennedy (6.4 percent), Eisenhower (5.0 percent), George H. W. Bush (4.2 percent), Truman (3.5 percent), Johnson (1.3 percent), Carter (1.0 percent), and Ford (0.3 percent).[108] American celebrities other than politicians were known to a large number of Chinese: Charlie Chaplin (80.7 percent), Michael Jordan (69.3 percent), Einstein (67.7 percent), Mark Twain (60.6 percent), Bill Gates (42.6 percent), Dr. Martin Luther King (27.2 percent), Marlon Brando (18.9 percent), Paul A. Samuelson (14.1 percent), and Warren Buffett (10.8 percent).[109]

When asked about Clinton's upcoming visit, 67 percent of Chinese said that they expected "positive effects" while 18 percent thought there would be "very positive effects." Looking forward, 52 percent of the Chinese saw a "very good" or "fairly good" relationship with the U.S. in the twenty-first century while 36 percent felt that the relationship would be "so-so."[110] In contrast, two years before, in the wake of the 1995–96 Sino-American disputes over Taiwan, as high as 80 percent of Chinese polled believed that the U.S. was seeking world domination and was hostile toward China.[111] Now, in between Jiang's visit to the United States and Clinton's trip to China, just 38.2 percent of Chinese held the view that the United States was bent on establishing her "hegemony" over the world.[112]

Figure 8.1

MacDonald's, Starbucks, and *China Can Say No*. Economic success and overall improvement in conditions of China during the 1990s gave many Chinese a new sense of national pride. The rising nationalist sentiment made popular works such as *China Can Say No*, which condemned U.S. policies toward China as unfair, arrogant, and hypocritical. At the same time, in a converse movement, American culture spread steadily in China, rendering American lifestyle more familiar and acceptable to the Chinese.

Whatever positive effects produced by the presidential visits of Jiang and Clinton (the latter took place in mid-1998) were virtually wiped out by what happened shortly afterward, in May 1999. On the eighth of that month, U.S. warplanes taking part in the then ongoing NATO air-raid campaign in Yugoslavia dropped bombs on the Chinese embassy in Belgrade, killing three and wounding twenty Chinese diplomats and journalists, totally destroying the building. The event shattered the fragile and recently rebuilt Sino-American relations and caused a great furor among Chinese people. Few Chinese accepted Washington's explanation that the bombing was due to "faulty information." In a survey conducted in Guangzhou two days after the embassy attack, more than 90 percent of the surveyed rejected the idea that the attack was accidental, and almost all of the polled believed that anti-American protests were justified and deserved support.[113]

Large-scale popular protests did take place across China, with tens of thousands of demonstrators besieging the U.S. embassy and consulates in Beijing, Shanghai, Chengdu, Shengyang, Guangzhou, and Hong Kong. These were the largest popular protests China had seen in a decade. The last time something like this happened in China was back in 1989, when pro-democracy Chinese rallied against the government, an event that culminated with the erection of a replica of the Statue of Liberty at Tiananmen Square. Ten years later, outraged Chinese protesters could barely control their hatred of the United States, calling for their government to take strong actions against the bully that had terribly hurt and humiliated China. The recent improvement in Sino-American relations, so carefully orchestrated by the Clinton administration and the Chinese government, quickly evaporated. Now, a majority of Chinese—70 percent, according to a survey conducted by Horizon Research—viewed the United States as the country most hostile toward China.[114]

Again, it should be noted that the strong Chinese dislike of the United States as a world power did not simply translate into a rejection of the American lifestyle, which continued to enthrall the Chinese. This differed significantly from the situation back in the Mao Era when culture and politics coalesced to generate strong anti-Americanism. For better or worse, by the end of the 1990s, there had emerged a notable divergence between Chinese resentment toward the United States as a world power and their tolerance of American values and culture. Evidently, what happened in China during the preceding twenty years had created a state of affairs where liberal social life and nationalist politics coexisted. In the 1999 Horizon Research survey cited above, whereas over 70 percent of Chinese considered the United States the country most unfriendly toward China, a large number of the polled also expressed their partiality for American culture. Later studies confirmed the pattern. When in 2004 Horizon Research once again investigated Chinese views on the subject in question, the percentage of the Chinese who considered the U.S. the country most unfriendly toward China rose to 74.4 percent; at the same time, almost as many Chinese—74.1 percent—stated that they liked America fairly well or very much. In this study, too, America remained the favored destination for study abroad, followed by Australia, Britain, France, Japan, and Germany.[115]

The Chinese differentiation of the United States as a nation-state and America as a lifestyle reflected the dual influence of nationalism and liberalism in the 1990s. China's economic success in the Reform Age greatly boosted the national consciousness and the national pride of the Chinese people, who became increasingly aware of the emerging Sino-American rivalry and resented U.S. hostility toward China. At the same time, because China's recent economic success came largely from the liberalization of the Chinese society and the openness to the outside world, cosmopolitanism also grew over the years, moderating the surging nationalist trend referred to above. Thus, whereas the dual forces of nationalism and liberalism in China in the nineties were antithetical to each other, the two were also closely connected. The overall effect was one of balancing-off and constraint—national consciousness kept the Chinese from embracing America indiscriminately while the general liberal outlook prevented the abhorrence of the U.S. the haughty world power from bursting out of control. To a greater extent than before, China was coming together as a nation that was at once keenly aware of her own interests and mindful of the need to be on good terms with the Western world, the United States in particular.

But tension was always there, with a tendency to heighten quickly whenever Sino-American relations and conditions in China took a turn for the worse, threatening to destroy the delicate equilibrium between Chinese nationalism and liberalism. Frequent disputes with the United States reinforced the Chinese belief that the U.S. was inherently hostile toward China while side effects of the liberal reform in their country such as the widening disparity between the rich and the poor stirred up in the minds of many Chinese misgivings about the rightness and adequacy of the American Way. As the twentieth century came to its end and the twenty-first century began, the Chinese, gazing across the Pacific Ocean, viewed the United States of America with hope, suspicion, and uncertainty.

Conclusion

The creation of Chinese images and interpretations of the United States is a continuous historical process, featuring active interplay of multiple factors. Foremost among these are the cultural differences between China and the United States; the particular circumstances under which China attempted modernization; the distinct preoccupations and propensities of various sociopolitical groups such as the Chinese state, intelligentsia, and masses; the interactions between China's domestic affairs and Sino-American relations. These factors, along with many others, converged to shape and reshape Chinese views of the United States of America in the twentieth century. Specific conceptions and attitudes varied considerably over time and across the sociopolitical spectrum, but the same larger forces were at work constantly, maintaining a general pattern in a complex and dynamic process.

To be sure, the Chinese nation was not the first in history that, pressed by circumstances, had to reassess and reinvent its culture and institutions. Of the better-known examples one may cite Peter the Great, who moved boldly to reform Russia in the image of Western Europe; or the Japanese, who had actively borrowed from the Chinese civilization before they shifted to a new source of inspiration in more recent times and modernized their country at an astonishing speed. Even Western Europe, which led the world in marching into the modern age, used to have self-doubts and looked outward for ideas. The *philosophes* of the Enlightenment earnestly sought information about China, which they thought provided a good model of enlightened government. In the nineteenth century, a new experiment in social and political organization—the United States of America—drew the attention of thoughtful Europeans such as the young French nobleman Alexis de Tocqueville. In seeking fresh ideas for national rejuvenation from foreign lands, China of the twentieth century indeed carried on a long-standing human tradition.

Still, a number of factors made the Chinese experience more complex and intense than many others. First, in some ways traditional Chinese civilization stands as the virtual antithesis of modern American culture. Whereas old

227

China was a predominantly agrarian society with strong emphasis on harmony and stability, modern America has thrived on innovation and individual initiative. There exist, therefore, fundamental differences between Chinese and American ideas regarding what constitutes a good society and by what means a good society can be built. In the Chinese Confucian context, virtues are defined largely in terms of proper relationships among men. In that context, individualism and self-reliance—high ideals so eloquently expounded by Americans such as Ralph Emerson and Henry Thoreau—hardly make sense and are indistinguishable from mere selfishness. To comprehend America, the Chinese must take a wild leap of imagination outside the influence of their traditional culture. This proved to be a daunting, even impossible task for many Chinese.

Adding to the difficulty of the matter are the rather unfavorable conditions under which the Chinese had to attempt the modernization of their country. It was only after numerous devastating and humiliating defeats at the hands of Western powers that the Chinese came to recognize that, in order for China to survive as a nation, they must bid farewell to their traditional way of life and seek a new one in the modern world. To the Chinese, the West was at once a model to emulate and a mortal enemy. Should the Chinese adore or should they hate? Should they imitate or should they resist? As some Chinese asked: What do you do with a mentor who is bent on the destruction of his disciple? In that the West seemed to be seeking the annihilation of the Chinese nation, it was a dangerous predator that China must fend off; in that the West stood for a more advanced way of life, it was a model that China should respect and follow. The Chinese thus found themselves in a quandary, plagued by emotional complications that they could not easily rationalize.

This paradox can be seen clearly in China's relationship with the United States, which is marked by some wild swings between acts of heart-warming goodwill and outbursts of deadly hostility. From the mid-nineteenth century to the mid-twentieth century, for the most part, the United States came across to the Chinese as a friendly nation, which, unlike the other Western powers, did not seek territorial expansion in China. During World War II, when China and the U.S. fought as allies against imperialist Japan, Sino-American friendship reached an all-time high. Shortly afterward, however, the relationship between the two countries took a drastic turn for the worse. The United States supported Chinese Nationalists in a civil war where the Chinese Communists eventually triumphed. The talk about a special relationship, a natural affinity between China and America, abruptly ended, and mutual disdain and hostility became the norm.

During the twenty-odd years that followed, China and the U.S. engaged in direct confrontations and numerous other endeavors to weaken and undermine each other, fighting a fierce battle that was both geopolitical and ideological by nature. In the early 1970s, changes in circumstances led to the Mao-Nixon reconciliation, which ended overt hostility between Beijing and Washington. Once again the two countries were on relatively good terms, with great hopes for peaceful cooperation. As the Chinese pursued a policy of liberal reform and openness to the world, U.S.-China relations improved notably. Trade grew, cultural exchanges expanded, and the Chinese became more and more familiar with America. In the 1990s, however, China's rapid rise led to further changes in the trans-Pacific relationship. Increasingly there was the talk on the American side about the need to contain China, backed with corresponding policies. The Chinese felt that the U.S. had acted unjustly and resented what they viewed as endless bullying and harassment. Inside China, the liberal reform had come to the point where singled-minded fervor was giving way to second thoughts and reflection, prompting a reassessment of American culture and values and thus carrying on the century-long search for a new national identity for China in the modern times.

In terms of the general circumstances under which China had to modernize, there is also an element that may be termed as a "lagging effect"—that is, how China trailed behind the West in modern development. While modernization had begun in the West three or four hundred years before, it was only in the twentieth century that the process made much headway in China. As result, by the time the Chinese finally recognized that they must modernize and consequently turned to the West for guidance, what they encountered was no longer the West of Voltaire, Adam Smith, or John Stuart Mill. It was now the West of Karl Marx, Sigmund Freud, Franklin Roosevelt, and Allen Ginsberg. Thus, when it came to capitalist development, there was no "age of innocence" for the Chinese; the model presented to them was old and proven to be flawed, a fact that made the Chinese think about the need for remedial measures. At a time when many respectable Western critics openly decried failings of their own society, it was difficult for the Chinese to assume that all was well with free capitalism. Such postmodern skepticism fortified China's premodern reluctance to change, creating serious confusion in Chinese assessment of the West generally and of the United States in particular.

Domestically, various sociopolitical groups in Chinese society often disagreed among themselves over what to make of the United States. China's political leaders, preoccupied with unity and stability, were typically wary of American influence, which tended to encourage individualism and dissent, much to the concern of Chinese leaders. Chinese intellectuals, keen on the idea of progress, generally considered American ideas to be valuable stimulation for changes and improvement in China. As for the average Chinese, at times the United States tempted them with prosperity and freedom, but at other times it frightened them with elements such as aggressiveness or the lack of security that appeared to be inherent of American life. Given all these distinct predispositions, the Chinese state, intelligentsia, and masses often found themselves at odds with one another over what to make of the United States. After all, the debate on the proper interpretation and assessment of America was in reality the debate on China's future. Given their respective concerns, aspirations, and preoccupations, it is no wonder that China's political leaders, intellectuals, and general populace frequently engaged in heated arguments over the U.S.A.

Historically, the multiple factors that fashioned Chinese views of the United States exerted their influence in diverse ways during different periods of the twentieth century. In the decades from 1900 to 1949, when China experienced continuous war and revolution, the chaos in the country actually allowed extensive contact with the United States. As such, competing interpretations and assessments of America flourished. Already, however, certain patterns were emerging. China's political leaders, such as the reformed Confucianist Liang Qichao, the republicans and nationalists Sun Yat-sen and Chiang Kai-shek, and the communist Mao Zedong, all initially expressed their admiration for the liberal ideal embodied by the United States. But eventually they reversed their positions, to varying extents. They were bowing to a political reality—the need to rally popular support in a collectivist struggle for China's national survival and for effective sociopolitical reorganization.

During the same period, Chinese intellectuals engaged in relatively free debate on what lessons China might learn from America. Even in their case, however, the "idealist" intellectuals who appreciated America most were losing to the "realist" intellectuals who moved toward political activism. In the case of the Chinese masses, the period from 1900 to 1949 began with a violent antiforeign and antimodern peasant uprising—the Boxers' Rebellion—and ended with emotional anti-American protests in the late 1940s. With relatively little knowledge of the outside world, the Chinese masses intuitively reacted to issues that affected their daily life. To them, the collectivist social and political programs advocated by the Chinese Communists were easier to comprehend than the individualistic culture that America embodied, especially when the Communists acted so skillfully as grassroots organizers and propagandists.

The 1950s in China saw the establishment of official control over the appraisal of the United States. In the decade's early years the Chinese government, eager to consolidate its position in the country and mobilize the masses to support the Korean War, effectively combined efforts of comprehensive social and political reorganization with stringent rectification of Chinese views of the United States. Socialist reforms and anti-American instruction naturally aided each other, since the advocacy of socialist life amounted to the rejection of American individualism and vice versa. In 1957, Chinese intellectuals, concerned with the increasing rigidity that was stifling Chinese society, spoke out against many Communist policies—including the strict control over China's America issue. This challenge to the authority of the

Communist Party failed, and this unexpected outbreak of dissent only further hardened the government's determination to restrain what could and could not be voiced about the United States.

Against this general background, throughout the 1960s and especially during the early years of the Great Cultural Revolution, America virtually became a synonym for decadence and evil. Ironically, this severe verdict on America became a great liability for Chinese leaders in the early 1970s, when Mao reopened the relationship with the United States. The Communist Party did all it could to explain and justify changes in its policies, but some irreparable damage was done, which seriously undermined the Chinese government's ideological integrity and political credibility.

Entering the 1980s, as China went through a liberal reform and built a free-market economy, the reputation of the United States was rehabilitated to a certain extent. The Chinese state, now with the dual goals of stability and development on its mind, struggled to maintain a balance between the need to allow openness to the U.S. and the desire to prevent American influence from getting out of control. This delicate task was made more difficult by the fact that the Chinese intellectuals were actively advocating the introduction of Western culture into Chinese life, and the fact that the Chinese masses wavered frequently between their longing for a better life and the fear of unpredictable changes. Overall, the atmosphere in the 1980s was one of eager exploration and hopefulness.

In the last decade of the twentieth century, there emerged some new patterns in how the Chinese viewed the United States. The reform that had begun in the late 1970s significantly liberalized Chinese society, reducing the differences in the lifestyles of China and America. In this sense, general conditions in China made it easier for the Chinese to comprehend the American way of life, and the exoticism associated with the United States diminished. In the meantime, however, China's economic success had given rise to a strong nationalist sentiment. Increasingly, many Chinese grew impatient with the arrogance and hostility they saw in U.S. policies toward China. A new paradox came into play and it remains to be seen how the contradiction will work itself out in the time to come.

In the final analysis, the Chinese people's endeavor to make sense of the United States of America constitutes an integral part of a nation's search for an ideal way of life, productive, balanced, and just. Substantial differences still exist between China and the United States, but this is not just something to frown upon. The very existence of these differences provides both the Chinese and the Americans with a valuable opportunity to reexamine their own lives and seek further improvements. It is hoped that the two nations will take full advantage of the opportunity, carry on a meaningful dialogue, learn from each other's mistakes and achievements, and together build a better world for all.

Historiographical Note

Until recently, research on Chinese views of the United States has been relatively limited. When, in 1991, David Shambaugh published his *Beautiful Imperialism: China Perceives America, 1972–1990*, Gilbert Rozman of Princeton University noted: "A vast literature is concerned with American images of China and the Soviet Union and Soviet images of America, but this is the first substantial study of Chinese images of America."[1] The paucity of study on an evidently important subject seems to be largely due to the lack of contact between China and the United States during the Mao Era from 1949 to the mid-1970s. During the period, the West had virtually no direct access to China while conditions in China made it impossible for scholars there to tackle the subject. Furthermore, the plain hostility between China and the U.S. at the time seemed to have rendered how Chinese viewed America a moot issue.

Even then, however, some scholars recognized the significance of the subject. Many general works on Chinese history and Sino-American relations produced during the Mao Era created the necessary context and framework for future specialized studies. There were, for instance, *The United States and China*, a classic by John King Fairbank; *The Chinese World Order*, a collection of historical essays edited by Fairbank (1968); *Across the Pacific: An Inner History of American–East Asian Relations* by Akira Iriye (1967); *Nations in Darkness: China, Russia, and America* by John Stoessinger (1971); and *Discovering History in China* by Paul Cohen (1984).[2]

With the onset of the Reform Age in China at the end of the 1970s, exchanges between China and the U.S. expanded quickly and scholarly interest in the history of Chinese attitudes toward the United States increased greatly. Michael Hunt, in *The Making of a Special Relationship: The United States and China to 1914*, published in 1983, confronts the notion that the Chinese and Americans possessed a natural fondness for each other. Examining Sino-American relations before World War I, Hunt concludes that, if indeed a special relationship existed between China and the United States, it was largely that "two distinctly different and widely separated peoples became locked in conflict, the victims in some measure of their own misperceptions and myths."[3] Other scholars, working in the tradition of diplomatic and political history, focused on Chinese Communist leaders' assessment of the U.S. and its effect on policymaking. In *Yenan and the Great Powers: The Origins of Chinese Communist Foreign Policy, 1944-1946*, published in 1981, James Reardon-Anderson examines how, during a period of critical importance, Mao and the Chinese Communist Party struggled to ascertain Washington's intention in China as they readied themselves for a showdown with the U.S.-backed Chinese Nationalists.[4] Zhang Shuguang and Chen Jian, in their respective works *Deterrence and Strategic Culture: Chinese-American Confrontations, 1949-1958* and *China's Road to the Korean War: The Making of Sino-American Confrontation*, probe into the worldview and strategic considerations that shaped Communist China's U.S. policies in the 1950s.[5] Michael Sheng, in *Battling Western Imperialism: Mao, Stalin, and the United States*, investigates the impact of a revolutionary ideology on the Chinese Communist outlook on international politics.[6] Over in China, scholars such as Tao Wenzhao, Niu Jun, and Zhang Baijia made use of recently available sources and produced important scholarship that further illuminated Chinese Communist leaders' attitudes and policies toward the United States.[7]

Thomas J. Christensen also investigated China's U.S. policies in the 1940s and 1950s, but he did so from a different angle. In his *Useful Adversaries: Grand Strategy, Domestic Mobilization, and Sino-American Conflict, 1947-1958*, Christensen examines the connection between domestic conditions and foreign affairs both in China and the U.S. and suggests that the two states' antagonistic rhetoric and policies should be considered as manifestations of some larger goals. During the period examined, Christensen points out, the U.S. government sought to "reverse the very popular postwar trend of demobilization" so as to maintain and increase America's military strength; Mao, for his part, tried to mobilize the Chinese nation to achieve rapid socialist reform and industrialization by constantly reminding his people of an external menace.[8] In this connection, Jianwei Wang, in his *Limited Adversaries: Post–Cold War Sino-American Mutual Images*, surveys the cognitive structures and substance in Chinese and American elites' views in the 1990s and uses the concept "limited adversaries" to characterize the mutual strategic assessment of China and the U.S during the period examined.[9] In *Zhongguo ren de Meiguo guan: yige lishi de kaocha* (Chinese views of the United States: A historical investigation), Chinese scholar Yang Yusheng produces a straightforward, if somewhat matter-of-fact, general narrative of changing Chinese attitudes toward the United States from the middle of the nineteenth century onward.[10]

In 1991, political scientist David Shambaugh brought out *Beautiful Imperialist: China Perceives America, 1972-1990*. In this work, the author closely inspects the writings of China's "America Watchers"—Chinese scholars specializing in the study of the United States—and systematically presents how these Chinese specialists depicted the U.S. during the years covered in the study. Whereas it remains difficult to establish a concrete connection between the images presented and actual policymaking, Shambaugh's work proves to be a significant contribution to the study of Chinese views on the Untied States.[11]

Whereas the scholars identified above examined Chinese perceptions of the United States mostly in the tradition of political science or diplomatic history, others approached Chinese views of America more broadly as a social and cultural phenomenon. Professor Wei-ming Tu, in an essay published in 1978, emphasizes that Chinese attitudes toward the United States can only be understood with reference to the cultural differences of China and America.[12] Chen Chang-fang, in his doctoral dissertation, "Barbarian Paradise: Chinese Views of the United States, 1784–1911," surveys a wide range of Chinese writings on American society in the early era of Sino-American contacts.[13] Of great value is also *Land without Ghosts: Chinese Impressions of America from the Mid-Nineteenth Century to the Present*. In this collection of carefully chosen and well-translated Chinese writings on America, editors David R. Arkush and Leo O. Lee identify several stages in the development of Chinese perceptions of the United States, each with a predominant theme, including "Exotic America," "Menacing America," "Model America," "Flawed America," and "Familiar America."[14]

In the meantime, studies focused on particular historical periods made their appearance. Guo Xixiao, in her doctoral thesis "The Climax of Sino-American Relations: 1944–1947," looks into how China's civil war in the late 1940s transformed Chinese attitudes toward the United States.[15] In four essays collected in *Image, Perception, and the Making of U.S.-China Relations*, Hongshan Li, Michael Sheng, Yawei Liu, and Guangqiu Xu respectively examine the experience of Chinese students in the United States in the early twentieth century, the effects of Mao's ideology and personality on Chinese Communist foreign policies, Mao's misperceptions of the United States in the 1960s, and Chinese anti-American nationalism in the 1990s.[16]

Two other interesting studies that appeared in recent years, done in the tradition of cultural studies, are *Occidentalism: A Theory of Counter-Discourse in Post-Mao China*, by Xiaomei Chen, and *Significant Other: Staging the American in China*, by Claire Conceison. In the former, the author demonstrates how, after the Mao Era, China appropriated the West to advance certain political and cultural agendas.[17] In the latter, Conceison analyses a half dozen Chinese plays that contain American characters, suggesting that "the range of inter-polations of the American Other that occur in these plays . . . reflects the variety of manifestations of such images in Chinese society in general . . . and their synthesis of both positive and negative essentializations of the foreigner emerging from China's long history and contemporary proliferation of cross-cultural contacts."[18]

The complex relationship between the subjective and the objective is also an important theme in sociologist Richard Madsen's *China and the American Dream: A Moral Inquiry.* In this work, Madsen raises some larger issues concerning the ways in which the Chinese envision not only American society, but also their own future. Madsen argues that, over time, America created a "liberal myth about China" and that this "master narrative" strongly influenced the way Chinese society looked at America and viewed itself. The Chinese have internalized a vague but powerful "American Dream," Madsen suggests, "a dream about individualistic independence in a land of opportunity, a dream of not being constrained by the past or bound to community by rigid ties of convention." It is observed that the illusive promises of the unrealistic dream may very well demoralize the Chinese and that, ultimately, the Chinese have to find a dream of their own.[19]

Notes

Introduction

1. Wu Xiaoli, *Zu yin* (*Echoes of footsteps*) (Beijing: Huayi Chubanshe, 1998), 247.

2. Ibid.

3. Song Qiang, Zhang Zangzang, and Qiao Bian, *Zhongguo keyi shuo bu* (China can say no) (Beijing: Zhonghua Gongshang Lianhe Chubanshe, 1996).

4. "Spy Plane Collision Enrages Chinese Public," Associated Press, 2 April 2001.

5. Yang Miao, " 'Chengjiu dabing Ruien' yinqi de sikao: jingti baquan zhuyi wenhua de shentou" (Thoughts on *Saving Private Ryan*: be alert against the influence of hegemonist culture), Jiefang ribao (Liberation daily), 8 June 1999; reprinted in Baokan wenzhai (Digest of periodicals), 14 June 1999, 3.

6. For a discussion on the difficulties surrounding the Enlightenment in China, see Vera Schwarcz, *The Chinese Enlightenment: Intellectuals and the Legacy of the May Fourth Movement of 1919* (Berkeley: University of California Press, 1990).

7. Jacques Barzun, "Cultural History: A Synthesis," in *The Varieties of History*, ed. Fritz Stern (New York: Meridian Books, 1956), 393.

8. Ibid.

Chapter 1. Statesmen, Scholars, and Men in the Street 1900–1949

1. Liang Qichao, *Liang Qichao shiwen xuan* (Selected essays and poems of Liang Qichao), ed. Fang Zhiqin and Liu Sifen (Guangzhou, Guangdong: Guangdong Renmin Chubanshe, 1983), 522.

2. Ibid., 521.

3. For Chinese reactions to anti-Chinese incidents in the United States, see Chang-fang Chen, "Barbarian Paradise: Chinese Views of the United States, 1784–1911" (PhD dissertation, Indiana University, 1985), 139–49, 218–43, and 266–318. For more general discussions on early Sino-American contacts and Chinese views of the United States, see Kenneth S. Latourette, *The History of Early Relations between the United States and China, 1784–1844* (1917; reprint, New York: Kraus Reprint Corporation, 1964); George H. Danton, *The Culture Contacts of the United States and China: The Earliest Sino-American Culture Contacts, 1784–1844* (New York: Octagon Books, 1974); and Earl

Swisher, *China's Management of the American Barbarians: A Study of Sino-American Relations, 1841–1861, with Documents* (New Haven: Yale University Press, 1953).

4. Michael H. Hunt, *The Making of a Special Relationship: The United States and China to 1914* (New York: Columbia University Press, 1983); Paul Varg, *The Making of a Myth: The United States and China, 1897–1912* (East Lansing: Michigan State University Press, 1968); David L. Anderson, *Imperialism and Idealism: American Diplomats in China, 1961–1898* (Bloomington: Indiana University Press, 1985).

5. For a further discussion of this issue, see Chang-fang Chen, 31–82.

6. Liang Qichao, *Xindalu youji* (Notes on a tour of the New Continent) (N.p.: Xinmin Congbao, n.d.), 52.

7. Liang Qichao, *Xindalu youji* (Notes on a tour of the New Continent), ed. He Shouzhen (Changsha, Hunan: Hunan Renmin Chubanshe, 1981), 49-50.

8. Liang Qichao, *Xindalu youji* (Notes on a tour of the New Continent) (Xinmin Congbao), 1.

9. Ibid, 192.

10. Liang Qichao, *Xindalu youji* (Notes on a tour of the New Continent) (Hunan Renmin Chubanshe), 151.

11. Liang Qichao, "Meiquo zhengzhi lüeping" (On American politics), in *Xinhai Geming qian shi nian jian shilun xuanji* (Selected commentaries on contemporary affairs from the decade preceding the Revolution of 1911), ed. Zhang Dan and Wang Renzhi (Beijing: Sanlian Shudian, 1960), 1:2,799.

12. Ibid., 800.

13. Ibid., 801.

14. Liang Qichao, *Xindalu youji* (Notes on a tour of the New Continent) (Hunan Renmin Chubanshe), 74–75.

15. Liang Qichao, "Meiguo zhengzhi lüeping" (On American politics), in Zhang Dan and Wang Renzhi, eds., 792.

16. Ibid., 794.

17. Liang Qichao, *Xindalu youji* (Notes on a tour of the New Continent) (Hunan Renmin Chubanshe), 78–79.

18. Ibid., 45.

19. Ibid., 35.

20. Ibid., 45.

21. Ibid., 48.

22. Ibid.

23. Ibid., 148.

24. Liang Qichao, "Jinggao liuxuesheng zhujun" (Advice for students studying abroad), in *Zhongguo wenti lunji* (Collected papers on the China problem), ed. *Zhangwang* Editorial Board (Hong Kong: Zilian Chubanshe, 1966), 33.

25. Sun Yat-sen, "Zhongguo wenti de zhen jiejue" (The true solution to China's problems), in *Zhongguo wenti lunji* (Collected papers on the China problem), ed. *Zhangwang* Editorial Board (Hong Kong: Zilian Chubanshe, 1966), 63.

26. Ibid., 323.

27. Ibid.

28. Sun Yat-sen, *Sun Zhongshan quanji* (Complete works of Sun Yat-sen), ed. Guangdong Shekeyuan Lishi Suo, Zhongguo Shekeyuan Jindaishi Suo, and Zhongshan Daxue Sun Zhongshan Yanjiu Shi, vol. 8 (Beijing: Zhonghua Shuju, 1986), 477.

29. Ibid., vol. 5 (1985), 491; vol. 8 (1986), 477.

30. Ibid., vol. 8, 476–77.

31. Ibid., 320.

32. Sun Yat-sen, *Guofu quanji* (Complete works of the Founding Father), ed. Guomindang Dangshi Weiyuanhui (Taibei: Guomindang Dangshi Weiyuanhui, 1973), Vol. 1, 86–87.

33. Sun Yat-sen, *Sun Zhongshan quanji* (Complete works of Sun Zhongshan), vol. 5 (1985), 475.

34. Ibid. 2:520.

35. Ibid., 333.

36. Ibid., 369–74, 506–24.

37. Ibid. 8:521–22.

38. Chiang Kai-shek, *Jiang zongtong ji* (Works of President Chiang), ed. Guofang Yanjiu Yuan (Taibei: Guofang Yanjiu Yuan, 1960), vol. 1, 612.

39. Chiang Kai-shek, *Zongtong Jiang Gong sixiang yanlun zongji* (A complete collection of speeches and works of President Chiang) (Taibei: n.d.), *Yanjiang* (Speeches), 10.

40. Ibid.

41. Chiang Kai-shek, *Jiang Zongtong ji* (Works of President Chiang), vol. 1, 150.

42. Ibid., vol. 1, 135.

43. Chen Duxiu, *Chen Duxiu wenzhang xuanbian* (Collected works of Chen Duxiu), ed. Sanlian Shudian, vol. 1 (Beijing: Sanlian Shudian, 1984), 73–78.

44. *Xin qingnian* (New youth), 1915, no. 1.

45. Ibid.

46. *Xin Qingnian* (New youth), 1915, no. 2.

47. Ibid., 1916, no. 5; ibid., no. 6.

48. Chne Duxiu, *Chen Duxiu wenzhang xuanbian* (Collected works of Chen Duxiu), vol. 2 (1984), 241–42.

49. Ibid., 372, 483.

50. Ibid., 520.

51. Ibid., 556.

52. "You Meiguo ji lai de yifeng xin" (A letter from America), *Minguo ribao*, 20 February 1923.

53. Zhang Wentian, *Lütu* (The journey) (Shanghai: Shangwu Yinshuguan, 1925).

54. Zhang Wentian, *Zhang wentian zaonian wenxue zuopin xuan* (Selected works of Zhang Wentian from his early years), ed. Cheng Zhongyuan (Beijing: Renmin Chubanshe, 1983), 356.

55. Ibid.

56. Mao Zedong, *Mao Zedong ji bujuan* (Supplementary volume to the collected works of Mao Zedong), ed. Takeuchi Minoru, vol. 2 (Tokyo: Sōsōsha, 1984), 21.

57. Ibid., 33–35.

58. Ibid. 1:223.

59. Mao Zedong, *Mao Zedong ji* (Collected works of Mao Zedong), ed. Takeuchi Minoru, vol. 2 (Tokyo: Sōsōsha, 1983), 54.

60. Mao Zedong, *Mao Zedong ji bujuan* (Supplementary volume to the collected works of Mao Zedong), vol. 1 (1983), 51.

61. Ibid. 9:181–87.

62. Mao Zedong, *Selected Works of Mao Tse-tung*, vol. 2 (London: Lawrence and Wishart, 1954), 75.

63. David M. Lampton, Joyce A. Madancy, and Kristen M. Williams, *A Relationship Restored: Trends in U.S.-China Educational Exchanges, 1978–1984* (Washington, DC: National Academy Press, 1986), 18.

64. Ibid. For further information on related topics, see Peter Buck, *American Science and Modern China, 1876–1936* (Cambridge: Cambridge University Press, 1980); Ning Qian, *Chinese Students Encounter America*, trans. T. K. Chu (Seattle: University of Washington Press, 2003); and Ting Ni, "The Cultural Experiences of Chinese Students Who Studied in the United States During the 1930s-1940s" (Chinese Studies, Vol. 22.) (Lewiston, NY: Edwin Mellen Press, 2002).

65. Wei Zichu, *Meidi zai Hua jingji qinlüe* (Imperialist America's economic invasion of China) (Beijing: Renmin Chubanshe, 1951), 31.

66. Ibid., 30.

67. *Zhongguo xiandai shi renwu zhuan* (Characters in modern Chinese history) (Chengdu, Sichuan: Sichuan Renmin Chubanshe, 1986), 595–96.

68. Hu Shi, *Hu Shi yanlun ji* (Collected speeches of Hu Shi), vol. 2 (Taibei: Huaguo Chubanshe, 1953), 28.

69. Hu Shi, *Hu Shi wencun* (Collected works of Hu Shi), vol. 3, no. 1 (Taibei: Yuandong Tushu Gongsi, 1953), 31–32.

70. Ibid., vol. 4, no. 4, 617.

71. Hu Shi, *Hu Shi liuxue riji* (Hu Shi's diary: studying abroad) (Taibei: Taiwan Shangwu Yinshuguan, 1959), 1053–54.

72. Ibid., 268–69.

73. Ibid., 1051.

74. Ibid., 149.

75. Having been criticized for the idea, Hu Shi later used a substitute which he believed to express his idea better: *chongfen shijiehua* ("full internationalization").

76. Hu Shi, "Shiping suowei de 'Zhongguo benwei de wenhua jianshe' " (On the so-called 'Sinocentric cultural construction'), *Duli pinglun* (Independent criticism) no. 145: 4–7.

77. Hu Shi, *Hu Shi wencun* (Collected works of Hu Shi), 3:1, 10–12.

78. Ibid., 28.

79. Hou Wailu, "Jielu Mei Diguozhuyi nucai Hu Shi de fandong mianmao" (Uncover the true face of Hu Shi, a slave of American imperialism), in *Hu Shi sixiang pipan* (Criticism of Hu Shi thought), vol. 3 (Beijing: Sanlian Shudian, 1955), 60.

80. Hu Shi, *Hu Shi yanlun ji* (Collected speeches of Hu Shi), vol. 2 (1953), 35.

81. Ibid.

82. Ibid., 29.

83. Li Rui, *Yaodong zashu* (Notes from caves) (Changsha: Hunan Renmin Chubanshe, 1981), 293.

84. Shen Weiwei, "Hu Shi hunyin lüelun" (On Hu Shi's marriage), *Minguo dangan* (Archives of the Republic of China) (1991), 1:88.

85. Gao Yihan, "Mantan Hu Shi" (On Hu Shi), *Wenhua shiliao* (Materials of cultural history) no. 5 (1983): 191.

86. *Zhongguo xiandai shi renwu zhuan* (Characters in modern Chinese history), 696; Xu Youchun, ed., *Minguo renwu da cidian* (Biographical dictionary for the Republican period) (Shijiazhuang: Hebei Renmin Chubanshe, 1991), 1080.

87. Tao Xingzhi, *Tao Xingzhi quanji* (Complete works of Tao Xingzhi), ed. Huazhong Shifan Xueyuan Jiaoyu Kexue Yanjiu Suo, vol. 1 (Changsha, Hunan: Hunan Jiaoyu Chubanshe, 1983), 62.

88. Li Xin, *Minguo renwu zhuan* (Biographies of Republican China), vol. 1 (Beijing: Zhonghua Shuju, 1978), 343.

89. Tao Xingzhi, *Tao Xingzhi quanji* (Complete works of Tao Xingzhi), vol. 2 (1984), 700.

90. Ibid., 24.

91. Ibid. 5:188–91.

92. Ibid. 2:701.

93. Li Xin, *Minguo renwu zhuan* (Biographies of Republican China), vol. 1 (1978), 344.

94. Tao Xingzhi, *Tao Xingzhi quanji* (Complete works of Tao Xingzhi), vol. 2 (1984), 180–184.

95. Ibid., 756.

96. Ibid., 757.

97. Ibid., 182.

98. Zhou Yi, *Tao Xingzhi huanxing shijie lu* (Tao Xingzhi's journey around the globe) (Nanjing, Jiangsu: Jiangsu Renmin Chubanshe, 1987), 98–101.

99. Tao Xingzhi, *Tao Xingzhi quanji* (Complete works of Tao Xingzhi), vol. 3 (1985), 567.

100. Ibid., 5:930–34. For a focused study on the experience of American-educated Chinese students, see Stacey Bieler, *"Patriots" or "Traitors"?: A History of American-Educated Chinese Students* (Armonk, NY: M. E. Sharpe, 2003).

101. *Zhongguo xiandai renwu zhuan* (Characters in modern Chinese history), 511; Zou Taofen, *Taofen wenji* (Collected works of Taofen), vol. 1 (Hong Kong: Sanlian Shudian, 1957), 5.

102. Ibid., 10.

103. Zou Taofen, *Taofen wenji* (Collected works of Taofen), vol. 3 (Hong Kong: Sanlian Shudian, 1957), 490.

104. Taofen, *Pingzong yiyu* (Travel recollections) (Shanghai: Shenghuo Shudian, 1937), 1–12.

105. Taofen, *Pingzong yiyu* (Travel recollections), 250–300.

106. Zou Taofen, *Taofen wenji* (Collected works of Taofen), 3:646.

107. Zou Taofen, *Pingzong yiyu* (Travel recollections), 9–16.

108. Ibid., 48–55.

109. Ibid., 9–16, 32–39.

110. Ibid., 509–10.

111. Ibid., 145–52.

112. Ibid., 153–60.

113. Zou Taofen, *Taofen wenji* (Collected works of Taofen), 3:681.

114. Ibid., 595, 550.

115. Ibid., 540.

116. Ibid., 512.

117. Ibid., 688–89.

118. Yang Ming, *Taofen de liuwang shenghuo* (Taofen in exile) (N.p.: Sanlian Shudian, 1951), 84–85.

119. Song, *Dadao Lieqiang* (Down with the Powers).

120. Hanfu (Zhang Hanfu), *Zhongguo yu Meiguo* (China and the United States) (N.p.: Yinqing Chubanshe, 1937), 123.

121. Ibid.

122. Shi Xiangrong, "Heping meigui chuan youyi" (Rose is for peace and friendship), *Zongheng* no. 1 (1984): 95–98.

123. Wang Tingyue, *Yingjiu Meiguo bing: Zhongguo dihou kang Ri junmin jiuyuan Meiguo feixingyuan jishi* (Rescue U.S. airmen: Chinese anti-Japanese troops and civilians save U.S. pilots) (Beijing: Zhonggong Dangshi Chubanshe, 2005), 29.

124. Chen Duxiu, "Wo de genben yijian" (My final opinion), in *Zhanwang* Bianjibu, ed., *Zhongguo wenti lunji* (Essays on the China problem), 143.

125. David D. Barrett, manuscript on the Dixie Mission, Box 1, Accession No. 48005-9.14, Hoover Institution on War, Revolution and Peace, 71.

126. Bai Laode, "Meiquo minzhu zhenxian de xingqi" (The emergence of America's democratic front), *Qunzhong zhoukan* (The masses weekly) 2, no. 3 (25 June 1938): 473–74.

127. Editorial, "Aidao Luo Sifu Zongtong" (A eulogy on President Roosevelt), *Qunzhong* (The masses) 10, no. 7–8 (combined issue) (3 April 1945): 216.

128. Mao Zedong, *Mao Zedong ji bujuan* (Supplementary to collected works of Mao Zedong), 7:205.

129. Ibid., 223.

130. Editorial, "Aidao Luo Sifu Zongtong" (A eulogy on President Roosevelt), *Qunzhong* (The Masses): 216.

131. Mao Zedong, *Mao Zedong ji bujuan* (Supplementary to collected works of Mao Zedong), 7:255; "Minzhu juren Luo Sifu" (Democratic giant Roosevelt), *Qunzhong* (The masses) 10, no. 7–8 (combined issue): 220.

132. Mao Zedong, *Mao Zedong ji bujuan* (Supplementary to collected works of Mao Zedong), 7:281.

133. David D. Barrett, manuscript on the Dixie Mission, Box 1, Accession No. 48005-9.14, Hoover Institution on War, Revolution and Peace, 59–60; Ross Terrill, *Mao: A Biography* (Stanford: Stanford University Press, 1999), 206.

134. Mao Zedong, *Mao Zedong ji bujuan* (Supplementary to collected works of Mao Zedong), 7:226.

135. Mao Zedong, *Mao Zedong xinwen gongzuo wenxuan* (Selected writings and speeches on journalism by Mao Zedong) (Beijing: Xinhua Chubanshe, 1982), 130.

136. Tuan Zhongyang Qingyun Shi Yanjiushi and Zhongyang Dangan Guan, eds., *Zhonggong Zhongyang qingnian yundong wenjian xuanbian* (Selected documents of the Chinese Communist Party on youth movement) (Beijing: Zhongguo Qingnian Chubanshe, 1988), 631–32.

137. In *Qunzhong* 11, no. 10 (30 June 1946): 7–8.

138. Editorial, "Lun Hualaishi shijian" (On the Wallace incident), *Jiefang ribao* (Liberation daily), in *Zhengbao xunkan* no. 8 (October 1946): 5.

139. Zhiren, "Cong Boensi dao Hualaishi" (From Byrnes to Wallace), *Qunzhong* 12, no. 9: 81.

140. *Qunzhong,* 12:10; *Zhengbao xunkan* no. 9 (October 1946), 26–27.

141. Wei Zichu, *Meidi zai Hua jingji qinlüe* (Imperialist America's economic invasion of China), 32 and 27–29.

142. Wang Shenyin, "Jiefang qian Jidujiao zai Shandong suo ban zhong xiao xue gaikuang" (An overview of Christian missionary primary and middle schools in Shandong before 1949), *Wenshi ziliao xuanji* (Selected historical materials) (Shangdong) no. 19 (1986): 176–77.

143. Ibid., 157–58.

144. Ibid., 163.

145. Wei Zichu, *Meiguo zai Hua jingji qinlüe* (Imperialist America's economic invasion of China), 32.

146. Ibid.

147. Edgar Snow, Red Star over China: The Classic Account of the Birth of Chinese Communism (New York: Grove Press, 1994), 344–45.

148. Ibid; Liu Kang, Wei Jian, and Qiu Qingrong, "Kangzhan shengli hou Meiquo dianying zai Guangzhou de fanlan" (American movies flooded Guangzhou after the Resistance War), *Guangzhou wenshi ziliao (xuanji)* (Guangzhou historical materials [selected]) no. 20 (1980), 174.

149. Wei Zichu, ibid., 29.

150. Liu Kang et al., ibid., 192.

151. Sutton Christian, "Chinese Cry 'Kan-pei' to OWI," the Sutton Christian collection, Accession no. 78038-8M.07, Hoover Institution on War, Revolution and Peace.

152. Ibid.

153. *Meijun zhu Hua shiqi de xuezhai* (Crimes committed by American troops during their occupation of China) (Beijing: Renmin Chubanshe, 1950), 2–3.

154. Ibid., 14–15.

155. Ibid., 17.

156. *Dagongbao,* 31 January 1947, 10.

157. David D. Barrett, manuscript on the Dixie Mission, 103.

158. Claire Chennault to W. K. Lin, 12 December 1941; Claire Chennault to Peter S. T. Shih, 23 February 1942. The Claire Chennault collection, Box 1, Accession no. 67002-8M.39, Hoover Institution on War, Revolution and Peace. Catherine Forslund, *Anna Chennault: Informal Diplomacy and Asian Relations* (Wilmington, DE: Scholarly Resources, Inc., 2002), 23.

159. Sutton Christian, "Report on Sian," March 1945, the Sutton Christian collection, Accession no. 78038-8M.07, Hoover Institution on War, Revolution and Peace, 18.

160. Circular, "Relations between American Troops abroad and the Nationals of Friendly Foreign Countries," 27 April 1945, Department of State Decimal File, 1945–1949, 811.22/4-2745, National Archives, Washington, DC.

161. Department of State Decimal File, 811.22/7-1345.

162. Ibid., 811.22/7-245.

163. Ibid., 811.22/7-2345.

164. *Qunzhong* 14, no. 1 (1 January 1947); 14, no. 2 (13 January 1947).

165. Tuan Zhongyang Qingyun Shi Yanjiu Shi and Zhongyang Dangan Guan, *Zhonggong Zhongyang qingnian yundong wenjian xuanbian* (Selected Chinese Communist Party's documents on youth movement), 636–37.

166. Ibid., 541–42.

167. Ibid., 644.

168. Mao Zedong, *Selected Works*, vol. 4 (Beijing: Foreign Language Press, 1969), 135.

169. Ibid., 119.

Chapter 2. "Farewell, Leighton Stuart!"

1. For further information on the episode, see Pei Jianzhang et al., *Xin Zhongguo waijiao fengyun* (Turbulences in New China's Diplomacy) (Beijing: Shijie zhishi Chubanshe, 1990), 22–32.

2. *Foreign Relations of the United States*, U.S. Department of State, 1948, vol. 7, 826.

3. Hu Qiaomu, *Hu Qiaomu huiyi Mao Zedong* (Hu Qiaomu's Memories on Mao Zedong) (Beijing: Renmin Chubenshe, 1994), 537.

4. Mao Tse-tung [Mao Zedong], *Selected Works of Mao Tse-tung*, vol. 4 (Beijing: Foreign Languages Press, 1969), 371.

5. Ibid.

6. Ke Bainian et al., *Meiguo shouce* (The United States Handbook) (Beijing: Zhongwai Chubanshe, 1950), Preface.

7. Ibid., 1.

8. Ibid., 2.

9. Ibid., 3.

10. Ibid.

11. Ibid., 30.

12. Ibid., 29.

13. Ibid., 54–55.

14. Ibid., 294.

15. Ibid.

16. Ibid., 291.

17. Ibid., 288.

18. Ibid., 295.

19. Ibid., 378.

20. Ibid., 379.

21. Ibid., 380.

22. Ibid., 381.

23. Ibid., 384.

24. Ibid.

25. Ibid., 382.

26. Ibid., Preface.

27. Mao, *Selected Works*, 415.

28. The U.S. Department of State, *The China White Paper* (Stanford: Stanford University Press, 1967), XVI.

29. Mao, *Selected Works*, 427.

30. Ibid.

31. Ibid., 447.

32. Ibid., 437.

33. Ibid.

34. Ibid., 443.

35. Ibid., 444.

36. Ibid., 445.

37. Ibid., 451.

38. Zhonggong Tianjin Shiwei Zong Xuexi Hui, *Fan Baipishu xuexi ziliao* (Study Materials on the Anti-White Paper Campaign) (Tianjin: Zhonggong Tianjin Shiwei Zong Xuexi Hui, 1949), 81.

39. Mao, *Selected Works*, 438.

40. For further information on the event, see Pei Jianzhang et al., *Xin Zhongguo waijiao fengyun*, 22–32.

41. Xie Guoming, "Shilun Yang Gang xinwen huodong de fengge" (On Yang Gang as a Journalist), *Xinwen yanjiu ziliao* (Materials of journalist studies) 18 (March 1983): 53.

42. Ibid., 60–61.

43. Ibid., 64.

44. Ibid., 62.

45. Yang Gang, *Meiquo Zhaji* (Notes on America) (Beijing: Shijie Zhishi Chubanshe, 1951), 2.

46. Ibid., 6.

47. Ibid., 1.

48. Cao Juren, *Xinshi shilun* (On ten new things) (Hong Kong: Chuangken Chubanshe, n.d.), 79.

49. Xu Zhucheng, *Xu Zhucheng huiyilu* (Xu Zhucheng's memoirs) (Beijing: Sanlian shudian, 1998), 210.

50. Zhou Peiyuan, "Pipan wo de zichan jieji de fuxiu sixiang" (Denounce my decadent bourgeois views), in *Pipan wo de zichan jieji sixiang* (Denounce my decadent bourgeois views), ed. Wushi Niandai Chubanshe (Beijing: Wushi Niandai Chubanshe, 1952), 126.

51. Ibid., 125.

52. Ibid.

53. Ibid., 128–29.

54. Ibid., 133.

55. Zhou Jinhuang, "Chedi chanchu congbai Meidiquozhuyi de sixiang" (Uproot the worship of American imperialism), in *Piban wo de zichan jieji sixiang* (Criticism of my own bourgeois ideas), ed. Wushi Niandai Chubanshe (Beijing: Wushi Niandai Chubanshe, 1952), 172–73.

56. Ibid., 173.

57. Ibid.

58. Ibid.

59. Zheng Junli, "Wo bixu tongqie de gaizao ziji" (I must truly renew myself), in *Piban wo de zichan jieji cixiang* (Criticism of my own bourgeois ideas), ed. Wushi Niandai Chubanshe (Beijing: Wushi Niandai Chubanshe, 1952), 209.

60. Chen Jieying, "Kongsu zicha jieji cixiang dui wo de fushi he duhai" (The wicked effects of bourgeois ideas in my case), in *Piban wo de zichan jieji sixiang* (Criticism of my own bourgeois ideas), ed. Wushi Niandai Chubanshe (Beijing: Wushi Niandai Chubanshe, 1952),1–2.

61. Ibid., 3.

62. Ibid., 7.

63. Shi Qili, *Liu Mei xuesheng gui guo ji* (Notes by an America-returned student) (Hong Kong: Ziyou Chubanshe, 1952), 23–29.

64. Ibid., 18.

65. Ibid., 185.

66. For attacks on Hu Shi, see Sanlian Shudian, ed., *Hu Shi sixiang pipan* (Criticism of Hu Shi thought), vols. 1–7 (Beijing: Sanlian Shudian, 1955).

67. "Zhenyang renshi Meiquo" (How to view the United States), *Shishi shouce* (Handbook on contemporary affairs), 2 (5 November 1950), reprinted in Guofang Bu Qingbao Ju, ed., *Gongfei de fan Mei yundong* (Communist bandits' anti-American movement) (Taibei: Guofang Bu Qingbao Ju, 1961), 205.

68. Ibid., 205.

69. Fu Zhensheng, *Dongbei qu jianli xuanchuan wang de jingyan* (The experience of the Northeast in establishing a propaganda network) (Shenyang, Liaonning: n.p, 1951), 13.

70. "Zhonggong Zhongyang guanyu zai quan dang jianli dui renmin qunzhong de xuanchuan wang de jueding" (The CCP Central Committee's decision on the establishment of a countrywide people-oriented propaganda network), *Xuanchuan Shouche* (Propaganda handbook) 1 (16 January 1951): 2–6.

71. Ibid., 7.

72. "Zhonggong Zhongyang Huadong Ju guanyu zhixing Zhongyang zai quan dang jianli dui renmin qunzhong de xuanchuan wang de jueding de zhishi (The East China Party Committee's directive on the execution of the Central Committee's decision on the establishment of a countrywide people-oriented propaganda network), ibid. 2 (1 February 1951): 1–4.

73. Fu Zhensheng, 20.

74. Ibid., 13.

75. Ibid., 39.

76. Ibid., 38.

77. Guofang Bu Qingbao Ju, 64–65.

78. Ibid., 62.

79. Qian Huanan Nüzi Wenli Xueyuan Xuesheng Hui, "Nanhua Nüzi Wenli Xueyuan de duibian" (Changes at Huanan Women's College of Art and Sciences), *Xiandai funü* (Modern women), no. 5 (January 1951): 26.

80. Tao Qi, "Huiwen Zhongxue shisheng jianjue suqing chong Mei sixiang" (Teachers and students at Huiwen School thoroughly cleanse America worship), *Jiaoshi yuebao* (Teachers' monthly) 3 (May 1951): 13.

81. Ibid., 14.

82. Data based on Zhongyang Renmin Zhengfu Chuban Zongshu Bianyi Ju, ed., *Quanguo fanyi tushu mulu: 1950* (A national bibliography of translated books, 1950) (Beijing: Zhongyang Renmin Zhengfu Chuban Zongshu Bianyi Ju, 1951). Author's own tally.

83. Ibid.

84. Zhongyang Renmin Zhengfu Chuban Zongshu Tushu Guan, ed., *1951 nian di yi ji quan guo xinshumu* (New Books Nationwide: First quarter 1951) (Beijing: Zhongyang Renmin Zhengfu Chuban Zongshu Tushu Guan, 1951).

85. *Meiquo shenghuo fangshi* (The American way of life) (Beijing: Renmin Huabao She, 1951).

86. *Meiquo wenming zhenxiang* (The true face of American civilization), Supplementary no. 10 (15 January 1951).

87. Ding Ziming et al., "Transformation" (Change), *Xiandai funü* (Modern women) 2, no. 2 (1 February 1951): 25–28.

88. Cao Yu, "Minglong de tian" (Bright sky), *Renmin wenxue* (People's literature), nos. 1–2 (1954).

89. Hong Shen, *Zhe jiu shi Meiguo de shenghuo fangshi* (This is the American way of life) (Beijing: Zhongguo Tushu Faxing Gongsi, 1951).

90. *Dazhong dianying* (Popular cinema) (November 1950): 1.

91. Ibid. (July 1950): 10.

92. Ibid. (November 1950): 1.

93. Ibid. (January1950); (April 1950): 10–11; (November 1950): 26.

94. Ibid. (September 1950): 25.

95. Ibid. (October 1953): 30; (November 1953): 27–29; (August 1955): 16–25; (August 1960): 21.

96. Xing Shiqing, "Yi ben you hai de *Dili jiaoxue shouce*" (Geography Instruction Handbook: A harmful work), *Xin jiaoyu* (New education) 4, no. 3 (15 November 1951): 30.

97. Zhang Haisheng, "Wo suo jiandao de yuwen jiaoxue zhong de ji zhong pianxiang" (A few problems in the teaching of Chinese that I've observed), *Xiaoxue jiaoshi* (Elementary school teacher) (July 1953): 17–18.

Chapter 3. Challenging a Taboo

1. The earliest book-length coverage of the Hundred Flowers Campaign is *The Hundred Flowers Campaign and the Chinese Intellectuals*, by Roderick MacFarquhar. The work combines background information, analysis, and translated Chinese texts. For Mao's views on domestic and international issues in the late 1950s, see *The Secret Speeches of Chairman Mao: From the Hundred Flowers to the Great Leap Forward*, edited by Roderick MacFarquhar, Timothy Cheek, and Eugene Wu (Cambridge: Council on East Asian Studies / Harvard University, 1989). For a general study of the Anti-Rightist Movement that followed the Hundred Flowers Campaign, see Naranarayan Das, *China's Hundred Weeds: A Study of the Anti-Rightist Campaign in China, 1957–58*. A related work is Theodore H. E. Chen, *Thought Reform of the Chinese Intellectuals* (Hong Kong:

University Press, 1960). On literary works and literary politics during the period, see Nie Hualing, *Literature of the Hundred Flowers* (New York: Columbia University Press, 1981); Merle Goldman, "The Party and the Intellectuals," in *The Cambridge History of China*, vol. 14 (Cambridge: Cambridge University Press, 1987), and, by the same author, *China's Intellectuals: Advise and Dissent* (Cambridge: Harvard University Press, 1988).

2. See Bo Yibo, " 'Shida guanxi' xingcheng qianhou de diaocha he tansuo" (The investigation and study before and after the writing of "On Ten Cardinal Relationships"), *Qiushi* (Quest for truth), no. 12 (16 June 1991): 23.

3. Ibid.

4. Mao Zedong, *Mao Zedong ji bujuan* (Supplementary volume to the works of Mao Zedong), ed. Takeuchi Minoru, vol. 2 (Tokyo: Sōsōsha, 1984), 1:223.

5. David M. Lampton, Joyce A. Madancy, and Kristen M. Williams, *A Relationship Restored: Trends in U.S.-China Educational Exchanges, 1978-1984* (Washington, DC: National Academy Press, 1986), 18.

6. Ibid.

7. Wei Zichu, *Meidi zai hua jingji qinlüe* (Imperialist America's economic invasion of China) (Beijing: Renmin Chubanshe, 1951), 31.

8. Ibid., 30.

9. Zhongguo Shiyan Gejuyuan Tongxunzu, "Guanyu Zhang Quan" (About Zhang Quan), *Wenyi bao* (Literature and arts), no. 21 (1957), reprinted in *Xinhua banyuekan*, no. 18 (1957), 110–12.

10. Tie Zhuwei, "Wo xinzhong de Zhou Enlai" (Zhou Enlai as I know) *Wenhui yuekan* (Wenhui monthly), no. 1 (1990): 20–22.

11. Luo Longji, "Wo zai Tianjin Yishi bao shiqi de fengfeng yuyu" (My days with Yishi Daily in Tianjin), *Wenhua shiliao* (Sources of cultural history) (Beijing), no. 8 (1984): 82–93.

12. "Luo Longji zai zhengfeng hui shang de jiaodai" (Luo Longji's confessions at the rectification meeting), *Renmin ribao* (People's daily), August 13, 1957, reprinted in *Xinhua banyuekan* (Xinhua bimonthly), no. 17 (1957): 152.

13. Ye Duyi, "Jielu Luo Longji de benlai mianmu, bing jiantao wo ziji de cuowu" (Uncover the true face of Luo Longji and confess my own errors), ibid., 33.

14. "Minmeng Zhongyang zuotanhui jiefa youpai fengzi Luo Longji de yinmu huodong" (The Central Committee of the Democratic Alliance uncovers the conspiracy and activities of the Rightist Luo Longji), *Renmin ribao* (People's daily), 8 July 1957, reprinted in *Xinhua banyuekan*, no. 15 (1957): 167.

15. Ibid.

16. Ibid., 197.

17. Luo Longji, "Wo de chubu jiaodai" (My preliminary confession), *Xinhua banyuekan*, no. 18 (1957), 96.

18. "Minmeng Zhongyang zuotanhui jiefa youpai fengzi Luo Longji de yinmu huodong" (The Central Committee of the Democratic Alliance uncovers the conspiracy and activities of the Rightist Luo Longji), *Renmin ribao* (People's daily), 8 July 1957, reprinted in *Xinhua banyuekan*, no. 14 (1957): 72.

19. Editorial, "Wenhui bao de zichanjieji fangxiang yingdang pipan" (The bourgeois tendency of Wenhui daily must be criticized), *Renmin ribao* (People's daily), 1 July 1957, 1.

20. Wu Han, "Wo fenhen, wo kongsu" (Enraged, I Expose), *Xinhua banyuekan*, no. 15 (1957): 101.

21. "Zeng Zhaolun shi Zhang Luo lianmeng de jixianfeng" (Zeng Zhaolun is a champion of the Zhang-Luo Alliance), *Xinwen ribao* (News daily), 16 July 1957, 2. Also, *Jiefang ribao* (Liberation daily), 6 July 1957, 2.

22. *Jiefang ribao*, 6 July 1957, 2.

23. "Zai 'fan jiaotiao' qizhi de yanhu xia fanmai zibenzhuyi sihuo, Qian Weichang shi Zhang Luo lianmeng zai kexuejie de qianke" (In the name of anti-dogmatism, Qian Weichang, an agent of the Zhang-Luo Alliance in the scientific field, promotes capitalist ideas), *Renmin ribao*, July 6, 1957, reprinted in *Xinhua banyuekan*, no. 14 (1957): 183.

24. Ibid.

25. "Qian Weichang yu zhong xin chang tan maodun" (Qian Weichang discusses contradictions), *Renmin ribao*, 17 May 1957, 3.

26. "Zai 'fan jiaotiao' qizhi de yanhu xia fanmai zibenzhuyi sihuo, Qian Weichang shi Zhang Luo lianmeng zai kexuejie de qianke" (In the name of anti-dogmatism, Qian Weichang, an agent of the Zhang-Luo alliance in the scientific field, promotes capitalist ideas), *Renmin ribao*, July 6, 1957, reprinted in *Xinhua banyuekan*, no. 14, 1957, 183.

27. Ibid.

28. Wanli, "Huacong xiaoyu" (Thoughts in bushes and flowers), *Shoudu gaodeng xuexiao fan youpan douzheng de juda shengli* (A great victory in the anti-rightist movement in colleges and universities in Beijing) (Beijing: Beijing Chupanshe, 1957), 293–94.

29. Mu Linsen, "Jiuqu Huanghe wanli sha" (Sands of the ten-thousand li yellow river), *Minzhu Zhongguo* (Democratic China) (Princeton, New Jersey), November 1993, 13–16.

30. Mary Brown Bullock, *An American Transplant: The Rockefeller Foundation and Peking Union Medical College* (Berkeley: University of California Press, 1980), 35.

31. John Z. Bowers, *Western Medicine in a Chinese Palace: Peking Union Medical College, 1917–1951* (n.p., The Hosiah Macy, Jr. Foundation, 1972), 224; *Renmin ribao*, 20 August 1957, 4.

32. *Beijing ribao* (Beijing daily), 11 October 1957, 2.

33. Ibid., 6 October 1957, 3.

34. "Beida shisheng yuan gong tongchi youpai fenzi Long Yinghua niulun" (Students and faculty at Beijing University denounce Rightist Long Yinhua), in *Shoudu gaodeng yuanxiao fan youpan douzheng de juda shengli*, Vol. 2, 193.

35. Ibid., 22 August 1957, 4.

36. Pan Dakui, "Wo chengren cuowu" (I admit my mistakes), *Xinhua banyuekan*, no. 18, 1957, 111.

37. *Beijing ribao*, 24 July 1957, 4.

38. *Gansu ribao* (Gansu daily), 14 July 1957, 3.

39. *Jiefang ribao*, 7 August 1957, 3; "Shanghai youpai jituan yinmu da baolu" (Expose the rightists' conspiracy in Shanghai), *Renmin ribao*, 24 June 1957 and 30 June 1957, reprinted in *Xinhua banyuekan*, no. 14 (1957): 93; *Jiefang ribao*, 6 July 1957, 2.

40. See Xiaonong, "Wang Zaoshi mengyuan shimo" (How Wang Zaoshi was wronged), *Shiji* (Century), no. 3, 2000.

41. *Guangming ribao* (Bright light daily), 14 August 1957, 2.

42. For events in Sino-American relations from 1949 to 1950, see Jian Chen, *China's Road to the Korean War: The Making of the Sino-American Confrontation* (New York: Columbia University Press, 1994).

43. "Kan Zhang Luo jituan de neimu" (An inside look at the Zhang-Luo clique), *Renmin ribao*, 8 August 1957, reprinted in *Xinhua banyuekan*, no. 18 (1957): 148.

44. Pan Dakui, "Wo chengren cuowu" (I admit my mistakes), *Xinhua banyuekan*, no. 18 (1957): 109.

45. Ibid.; *Xinhua banyuekan*, no. 16 (1957): 159.

46. *Xinhua banyuekan*, no. 18 (1957): 64.

47. Wang Yunsheng, "Bixu kefu xiaai de minzu zhuyi" (We must overcome narrow-minded nationalism), *Renmin ribao*, 23 August 1957, 2. Tan Tiwu, "Wo wei shenme fan liao yanzhong de cuowu" (Why I committed serious errors), *Xinhua banyuekan*, no. 18 (1957): 105. *Jiefang ribao*, 3 August 1957, 3.

48. Mao Zedong, "Zai Chengdu huiyi shang de jianghua" (Speech at the Chengdu conference), in *Zhonggong jimi wenjian huibian* (Secret documents of the Chinese Communist Party) (Taibei: Guoli Zhengzhi Daxue Guoji Guanxi Yanjiu Zhongxin, 1978), 77.

49. Yang Xiufeng, "Jianchi xuexi Sulian de fangzhen" (Insist on the policy of learning from the Soviet Union), *Renmin ribao*, 6 November 1957, 3.

50. Ibid.

51. *Guangming ribao*, 6 April 1957, 3.

52. Ibid., 20 April 1957, 2.

53. Ibid., 19 May 1957, 3.

54. Ibid.

55. *Renmin ribao*, 30 April 1957, 2.

56. Yu Cifei, "Eryu xuesheng xiang Guowuyuan qingyuan" (Students of the Russian language petition the State Council), in *Mingfang huiyi* (Recollections of the blooming and contending) (n.p.: Zilian Chubanshe, 1966), 70–77.

57. *Guangming ribao*, 6 May 1957, 2.

58. See Bo Yibo, " 'Shida guanxi' xingcheng qianhou de diaocha he tansuo."

59. Qian Junrui, "Chedi fensui youpai de jingong" (Smash the Rightist offensive), *Xinhua banyuekan*, no. 18 (1957): 125.

60. Ibid.

61. Xiang Chong, "Zichan jieji shehuixue zai jiu Zhongguo sanbu le shenme dusu?" (The poison that bourgeois sociology released in old China), *Jiaoxue yu yanjiu* (Teaching and research), combined issues 8–9, 1957, 39.

62. For a focused study on the growth and demise of Western-influenced sociology in China, see Ambrose Yeo-Chi King and Tse-Sang Wang, "The Development and Death of Chinese Academic Sociology: A Chapter in the Sociology of Sociology," *Modern Asian Studies* 12, no. 1. (1978): 37–58; Li Hanlin et al., "Chinese Sociology, 1898–1986," *Social Forces* 65, no. 3. (Mar. 1987): 612–40. Relatedly, on the development of anthropology in China, see Shinji Yamashita, Joseph Bosco, and Jeremy Seymour Eades, ed., *The Making of Anthropology in East and Southeast Asia* (New York and Oxford: Berghahn Books, 2004).

63. Tung-li Yuan, *Guide to Doctoral Dissertations by Chinese Students in America, 1905–1960* (Washington, DC: Sino-American Cultural Society, Inc., 1961).

64. R. David Arkush, *Fei Xiaotong and Sociology in Revolutionary China* (Cambridge: Harvard University Press, 1981), 106.

65. Xiang Chong, ibid.

66. Zhao Chengxin, "Wo dui yuanxi tiaozheng de tihui" (My understanding of the higher education reorganization), *Xihua banyuekan*, no. 13 (1957): 162–63; *Renmin ribao*, 16 May 1957, 7.

67. Fei Xiaotong, "Zhishi fenzi de zao chun tianqi" (Intellectuals' early spring), *Renmin ribao*, 24 March 1957, 3.

68. *Renmin ribao*, 30 August 1957, reprinted in *Xinhua banyuekan*, no. 18 (1957): 173–75.

69. Ibid.

70. Ibid.

71. Ruo Su, "Jielu Li Jinghan huifu zichan jieji shehui xue de yinmu jiqi she-hui diaocha de fandong benzhi" (Expose Li Jinghan's conspiracy to restore bourgeois sociology and the reactionary nature of his social investigation), *Jiaoxue yu yanjiu*, combined issues 8–9 (1957): 104.

72. Chen Da, "Shanghai gongren de shenghuo fei, 1929–1948" (Shanghai workers' living costs, 1929–1948), ibid., no. 5 (1957): 40–45.

73. *Xinhua banyuekan*, no. 18 (1957): 173–77.

74. Ibid.

75. Ibid.

76. *Guangming ribao*, 4 September, 1957, 2.

77. Chen Zhenhan et al., "Women duiyu dangqian jingji kexue gongzuo de yixie yijian" (Our opinions on the current state of economic studies), *Jingji yanjiu* (Economic work), no. 5 (1957): 130.

78. Ibid., 133.

79. Ibid.

80. *Renmin ribao*, 22 April 1957, 3.

81. For two examples of the articles on Keynesian economics published at the time, see Liu Tianyi, "Kaiensi jingji sixiang pipan" (Criticism of Keynesian economic ideas), *Jingji yanjiu*, no. 6 (1956): 39–59; Xu Yidan, "Kaiensi shi ziben zhuyi de baowei zhe" (Keynes is a defender of capitalism), ibid., no 1, 81–104, and no. 2 (1957): 25–35. On courses offered at universities, see *Renmin ribao*, 16 April 1957, 4; ibid., 1 May 1957, 4; and *Guangming ribao*, 6 April 1957, 3. On books published on the subject, see *Guangming ribao*, ibid.

82. Chen Zhenhan et al., ibid., 128.

83. *Guangming ribao*, 12 June 1957, 3.

84. *Renmin ribao*, 3 May 1957, 7.

85. *Renmin ribao*, 27 April 1957, 7; Qian Jiaju, "Guangyu zhubian Zhengming yuekan suo fan de cuowu de jiancha" (My self-criticism concerning errors committeed while editing Zhengming monthly), *Zhengming*, no. 8 (1958): 28.

86. Qian Jiaju, ibid.

87. Ibid.

88. For an example, see Ji Long, "Meiguo jingji qingkuang" (Economic conditions of the United States), *Renmin ribao*, 11 March 1957, reprinted in *Xinhua banyuekan*, no. 7 (1957): 169–73.

89. Wu Dakun, "Guangyu dangqian Meiguo jingji de yanjiu" (On the state of studies on the U.S. economy), *Guangming ribao,* 20 May 1957, 4.

90. *Guangming ribao* 12 June 1957, 3.

91. Chen Zhenhan, ibid., 128.

92. "Guangyu wuchan jieji pinkunhua de lunzhan" (On the debate over the poverty of the proletariat), *Dushu yuebao* (Reader's monthly), no. 6 (1957): 26.

93. Wang Weizhong, "Bochi youpai fenzi dui wuchan jieji pinkunhua lilun de wumie" (Refute Rightists' attack on the theory of proletarian poverty), *Xueshu yuekan* (Scholarship monthly), no. 12 (1957): 17.

94. Wu Chengxi, *Ziben zhuyi zong weiji* (Total crisis in the capitalist world) (Shanghai: Xin Zhishi Chubanshe, 1956), 23.

95. Zhang Youren, "Youpai fenzi Chen Zhenhan de zhengzhi yinmu" (The political conspiracy of the Rightist Chen Zhenhan), *Jingji yanjiu* (Economic studies), no. 5 (1957): 28.

96. Editor's Note, *Jingji yanjiu,* no. 5 (1957): 26; *Renmin ribao,* 4 September 1957, 2.

97. Chen Zhenhan et al., "Opinions," 125.

98. Zhao Gongmin, "Zhongguo de Moergen" (The Morgan of China), *Renwu* (Historical figures), no. 1 (1989): 6–13.

99. Li Peishan et al., *Baijia zhengming, fazhan kexue de bi you zhi lu* (Contention of hundred schools—the only way of scientific development) (Beijing: Shangwu Yinshuguan, 1985), 2. Also, an article on the Qingdao Conference on Genetic Studies, based on the book cited above and authored by Li Peishan, "Genetics in China: The Qingdao Symposium of 1956," appears in *Isis* 79, no. 2. (June 1988): 227–36.

100. Li Peishan et al., *Baijia zhengming,* 3.

101. Ibid., 4.

102. Zhao Gongmin, ibid., 15.

103. Ibid., 16.

104. Li Peishan et al., *Baijia zhengming,* 6–7.

105. Chen Qingquan and Song Guangwei, *Lu Dingyi zhuan* (Lu Dingyi: a biography) (Beijing: Zhonggong Dangshi Chubenshe, 1999), 415.

106. Li Peishan et al., *Baijia zhengming,* Table of Contents, 1–3; Tung-li Yuan, *Guide to Doctoral Dissertations by Chinese Students in America, 1905–1960.* Approximate number; my own tally.

107. Li Peishan et al., *Baijia zhengming,* 408–409.

108. Ibid., 301–11.

109. Ibid.

110. Li Ruqi, "Fazhan kexue de biyou zhi lu" (The only way of scientific development), *Renmin ribao,* 1 May 1957, 7.

111. *Guangming ribao,* 28 May 1957, 2.

112. *Guangming ribao,* 20 April 1957, 2.

113. *Guangming ribao,* 6 May 1957, 2.

114. Li Ruqi, "Yichuanxue jiben yuanli" (Basics of genetics), *Shengwu xue tong bao* (Biological gazette), no. 2 (1957); no 3 (1958).

115. Hu Xiansu was not formally labeled a Rightist. Probably due to the gaffe in 1955 when the Communist Party's Central Department of Propaganda hastily denounced

Hu to defend the soon-to-fall Lysenko, party officials were relatively lenient with Hu in the Anti-Rightist Movement. Lu Dingyi, who headed the Central Department of Propaganda, declared that Hu was "a Rightist who does not have to 'wear a Rightist cap.'" Hu did suffer during the Cultural Revolution a decade later. See Hu Zonggang, "Bugai yiwang de Hu Xiansu" (Hu Xiansu should be remembered), *Shengming shijie* (World of Life), no. 8 (2006).

Chapter 4. Communist Crusade and Capitalist Stronghold

1. For a comprehensive study of political events in China in the 1950s and 1960s, see Roderick MacFarquhar's trilogy, *The Origins of the Great Cultural Revolution.* Vol. 1, *Contradictions among the People: 1956–1957* (New York: Columbia University Press, 1974); vol. 2, *The Great Leap Forward, 1958–1960* (New York: Columbia University Press, 1983); vol. 3, *The Coming of the Cataclysm: 1961–1966* (Oxford: Oxford University Press, 1997.

2. *Guangming ribao*, 28 May 1957, 4; 30 May 1957, 4.

3. *Jiefang ribao*, 1 June 1957, 1.

4. *Guangming ribao*, 27 May 1957, 4.

5. Ibid., 13 September 1957, 6.

6. Ibid., 3 September 1957, 6.

7. Ibid., 22 June 1957, 5.

8. See *Guangming ribao*, 11 June-5 July 5 1957, 4.

9. *Changjiang ribao* (Yangzi River Daily), 8 June 1957, 3.

10. Ibid., 18 June 1957, 4.

11. Ibid., 24 June 1957, 3; 25 June 1957, 4.

12. Ibid., 22 June 1957, 4.

13. Ibid., 21 June 1957, 4.

14. Ibid., 13 June 1957, 3.

15. Ibid., 11 June 1957, 4.

16. *Shijie zhishi* (Knowledge on the world), no. 9 (1957): 30.

17. Chu Yukun, "Meiguo jingji yi chuxian shuaitui xianxiang" (The US economy has already shown signs of a recession), *Shijie zhishi*, no. 14 (1957): 11–13.

18. Zhang Wentian, "Guanyu Meiguo jingji weiji" (On the economic crisis in the United States), *Hongqi* (Red flag), no. 1 (1958): 19.

19. Ibid., 20.

20. Ibid., 27.

21. Wu Dakun, "Cong Makesi de jingji weiji lilun kan jinri Meiguo de jingji weiji" (A Marxist analysis of the economic crisis in the United States today), *Xinjianshe* (New construction), no. 5 (1958): 7.

22. Zhongguo Renmin Daxue Jingji Xi Meiguo Jingji Weiji Yanjiu Xiaozu, "Lun dangqian Meiguo jingji weiji xia de huobi xinyong weiji" (On the credit crisis amid the economic crisis in the United States), ibid., no 12 (1957): 45–51.

23. Ding Gu, "Kaiensi 'chengshu lun' de pipan" (Criticism of the Keynesian "multiplier effect"), *Jingji Yanjiu* (Economic studies), no. 2 (1958): 66.

24. Ibid., 73.

25. Meng Yongqian, "Duiyu Meiguo jingji weiji de jidian kanfa" (A few thoughts on the economic crisis in the United States), *Hongqi*, no. 7 (1959): 18.

26. *Renmin ribao*, 7 October 1957, 1.

27. For examples, see *Beijing ribao*, 24 October 1957, 4; 30 October 1957, 4; 31 October 1957, 6.

28. *Beijing ribao*, 24 October 1957, 4.

29. *Renmin ribao*, 23 October 1957, 4; 5 November 1957, 4.

30. Ibid., 6 November 1957, 6.

31. *Guangming ribao*, 8 December 1957, 4.

32. Editorial, "Wei Sulian de weida kexue chengjiu huanhu" (Applaud the great scientific achievements of the Soviet Union), *Renmin ribao*, 7 October 1957, 1.

33. *Renmin ribao*, 7 November 1957, 2.

34. Mao Zedong, "Zai Chengdu huiyi shang de jianghua" (Speech at the Chengdu conference), in *Zhonggong jimi wenjian huibian* (A collection of secret documents of the Chinese Communist Party), ed. Guoli Zhengzhi Daxue Guoji Guangxi Yanjiu Zhongxin (Taibei: Guoli Zhengzhi Daxue Guoji Guangxi Yanjiu Zhongxin, 1978), 77.

35. *Renmin ribao*, 23 July 1958, 1 and 6.

36. Meng Yongqian, "Wo guo xiaomai zong chanliang yadao Meiguo" (Our wheat output surpasses that of the United States), *Hongqi*, no. 4 (1958), reprinted in *Xinhua banyuekan*, no. 15 (1958).

37. *Mao Zedong sixiang wansui* (Long live Mao Zedong thought) (no publication information), 268.

38. Liu Yalou, "Renzhen xuexi Mao Zedong sixiang" (Carefully study Mao Zedong thought), *Jiefangjun bao* (The Liberation Army Daily), 23 May 1958, reprinted in *Xinhua banyuekan*, no. 12 (1958): 25.

39. Commentary, *Hongqi*, no. 10 (1958): 2–3.

40. "Mao Zedong sixiang wansui" (Long live Mao Zedong thought), 254.

41. Chen Yi, "Zai quanguo huaju, geju, ertongju chuangzuo zuotanhui shang de jianghua" (Talk at the symposium on the creation of plays, operas, and juvenile shows), in Zhonggong Zhongyang Shujichu Yanjiushi Wenhuazu, eds., *Dang he guojia lingdaoren tan wenyi* (Party and state leaders on arts and literature) (Beijing: Wenhua Yishu Chubanshe, 1982), 121–22.

42. Mao Zedong, "Sulian zhengzhi jingji xue dushu biji" (Notes on Soviet Political Economics), in *Zonggong jimi wenjian huibian*, ed. Guoli Zhengzhi Daxue Guoji Guanxi Yanjiu Zhongxin, 327.

43. Ibid., 329.

44. *Mao Zedong sixiang wansui* (Long live Mao Zedong thought), 197.

45. Kang Sheng, "Nansilafu de xiuzheng zhuyi qiaqia shihe Meidiguozhuyizhe de xuyao" (Yugoslavian revisionism meets the needs of American Imperialists), *Renmin ribao*, 14 June 1958, reprinted in *Xinhua banxuekan*, no. 12 (1958): 140.

46. Ibid.

47. Chen Boda, "Meidiguozhuyi zai Nansilafu de duzhu" (American Imperialists' gamble in Yugoslavia), *Hongqi*, no. 2 (1958): 17.

48. *Renmin ribao* Bianji Bu and *Hongqi* Zazhi Bianji Bu, "Nansilafu shi shehui zhuyi guojia ma?" (Is Yugoslavia a socialist country?), *Hongqi*, no. 19 (1963): 16–17.

49. Ibid., 17.

50. Mu Hui, "Nansilafu you zhe zhenyang de 'chuangzuo ziyou'?" (What kind of 'creative freedom' is there in Yugoslavia?), *Hongqi*, no. 5 (1964): 40–41.

51. *Renmin ribao* Bianjibu and *Hongqi* Zazhi Bianjibu, *Zai zhanzheng yu heping wenti shang de liang tiao luxian* (Two different views on the issue of war and peace) (Beijing: Renmin Chubanshe, 1963), 8.

52. Ibid., 43.

53. Ibid., 8–9.

54. Ibid., 10.

55. Guo Jizhou, "Kennidi qi neng niuzhuan lishi chao liu" (Kennedy cannot reverse the historic trend), *Hongqi*, combined issue no. 15/16 (1961): 53–57.

56. Chen Yuan, "Meiguo shi de 'ziyou' " (Freedom, American style), *Hongqi*, combined issue no. 3/4 (1962): 41.

57. Gu Jizhou, "Yuehanxun zhengfu shi ge shenme huose" (The nature of the Johnson administration), *Hongqi*, combined issue 23/24 (1964): 50.

58. Hua Xuesi, "Yuehanxun de 'Minquan Ziwen' shi qi shi huo zhong de da pianju" (Johnson's civil-rights policy-statement is intended to deceive the people and the world), *Zhengfa yanjiu* (Political and legal studies), no. 2 (1965): 33.

59. Ibid.

60. Mei Zupei, "Cong Bominghan dao Saierma: Meiguo heiren douzheng de xin fazhan" (From Birmingham to Selma: New development in American blacks' struggle), *Guoji wenti yanjiu* (Studies of international affairs), no. 3 (1965): 16. For another example of Chinese reports on the Civil Rights Movement in the U.S., see Si Mu, "Meiguo renmin de geming xinhao" (Signals for the American people's revolution), *Zhongguo qingnian* (Chinese youth), no. 23 (1965): 6–7.

61. Mao Zedong, "Huyu shijie renmin lianhe qilai, fandui Meiguo Diguo Zhuyi de zhongzu qishi, zhichi Meiguo heiren fandui zhongzu qishi de douzheng" (A call for the people of the world to unite to oppose American imperialists' racial descrimination and to support American blacks' struggle against racial discrimination), *Hongqi*, no. 16 (1963): 2.

62. "Zhongguo Gongchan Dang Zhongyang Weiyuanhui Zhuxi Mao Zedong tongzhi zhichi Meiguo heiren kangbao douzheng de shengming" (Comrade Mao Zedong, Chairman of the Central Committee of the Chinese Communist Party, issues a statement in support American blacks' struggle against persecution), *Hongqi*, no. 1 (1968): 4.

63. Mao Tse-tung [Mao Zedong], *People of the World, Unite and Defeat the U.S Aggressors and All Their Lackeys: Statements Supporting the American Negroes and the Peoples of Southern Vietnam, Panama, Japan, the Congo and the Dominican Republic in Their Just Struggle Against US Imperialism* (Beijing: Foreign Languages Press, 1966).

64. Zhang Xianliang, *Lühuashu* (Trees are green) (Tianjin: Baihua Chubanshe, 1986), 244–45.

65. Liang Liang, "Yi ge Hongweibing faqiren de zishu" (Recollections of a founding member of the Red Guards), in *Renmin gongheguo chunqiu shilu* (Records of the People's Republic), ed. Lin Yunhui, Liu Yong, and Shi Bonian (Beijing: Zhongguo Renmin Daxue Chubanshe, 1992), 730–34.

66. Ibid., 732.

67. Gao Gao and Yan Jiaqi, *"Wenhua Da Geming" shi nian shi* (A history of ten years of the "Great Cultural Revolution") (Tianjin: Tiajin Renmin Chubanshe, 1986), 39.

68. Yanfan, *Da Chuanlian* (Great propaganda travels) (Beijing: Jingguan Jiaoyu Chubanshe, 1993), 69–71.

69. Gao Gao and Yan Jiaqi, ibid., 53.

70. Ibid., 52.

71. Ibid.

72. Ibid., 52–53.

73. Ibid., 54.

74. Chang Wangdong, "Liu Shaoqi wangtu zai Zhongguo fubi zibenzhuyi zhidu de zuizheng: er ping Liu Shaoqi 'Tianjin jianghua' " (The evidence of Liu Shaoqi's attempt to restore capitalist system in China: the second commentary on Liu Shaoqi's 'Tianjin speech' "), 7, in pamphlet, "Dadao Liushaoqi" (Down with Liu Shaoqi), printed by Tianjin Shi Geming Shi Yanjiu Suo Geming Zaofan Weiyuanhui Hong Paoshou Bianjibu, 4 April 1967.

75. Ibid., 4–6.

76. Ibid., 7.

77. Li Yong, ed., *"Wenhua da geming" zhong de mingren zhi yu* (Promient Chinese jailed during the "Great Cultural Revolution") (Beijing: Zhongyang Minzu Xueyuan Chubanshe, 1993), 265.

78. Duan Tiean, "Li Tiemei yi jia rujin nali qu le?" (Where is Li Tiemei and her family now?), http://www.sinotimes.com/102/ltm.htm (accessed 14 March 1999).

79. Huang Zongjiang, "Wo de tanbai shu" (My confessions), *Dazhong dianying* (Popular cinema), no. 2 (1998): 28–29.

80. Pamphlet, "Ye Fu Zhuxi jianghua" (Vice Chairman Ye's speech), printed by Mao Zedong Sixiang Zhexue Shehui Kexue Bu Hongweibing Lian Dui, 1 Dec. 1966, 1–2.

81. Pamphlet, "Chen Fu Zhuxi jianghua" (Vice Chairman Chen's speech), printed by Mao Zedong Sixiang Zhexue Shehui Kexue Bu Hongweibing Lian Dui, 1 Dec. 1966, 1.

82. Gao Gao and Yan Jiaqi, ibid., 249; Jin Chunming, Huang Yuchong, and Chang Huimin, eds., *"Wenge" shiqi guaishi guaiyu* (Strange events and strange language in the "Cultural Revolution") (Beijing: Qiushi Chubanshe, 1989), 85–86.

83. Yanfan, ibid., 292.

84. Ibid., 388–89.

85. Yang Jian, "Wenhua Da Geming zhong de dixia wenxue" (The underground literature of the Great Cultural Revolution), http://www.tonghua.com.cn/bookbar/jhjs_dx2.htm (accessed 14 March, 1999).

86. Ibid.

87. Ibid.

88. Mao Zedong, "Quan shijie renmin tuanjie qilai, dabai Meiguo qinlüezhe jiqi yiqie zougou!" (All people in the world unite and defeat American aggressors and all their lackeys!), *Hongqi*, no. 6 (1970): 4.

89. Zhongguo Dalu Wenti Yanjiu Suo, *Jinnian lai Gongfei dui wai guanxi biaojie* (Chronology of recent events in the foreign relations of the Communist bandits) (Taibei: Zhongguo Dalu Wenti Yanjiu Suo, 1972), 234.

90. *Renmin ribao*, 27 April 1971, reprinted in *Guoji wenti pinglun xuan* (Selected commentaries on international affairs) (Beijing: Beijing Renmin Chubanshe, 1971), 104.

91. Zhou Enlai, "Guanyu guoji xingshi de liangpian baogao" (Two speeches on international affairs), in *Zhonggong jimi wenjie huibian* (Secret documents of the Chinese Communist Party), ed. Guoli Zhengzhi Daxue Guoji Guanxi Yanjiu Zhongxin (Taibei: Guoli Zhengzhi Daxue Guoji Guanxi Yanjiu Zhongxin, 1978), 352.

92. Ibid.

93. Ibid.

94. Ibid.

95. Ibid., 359.

96. Henry Kissinger, *Years of Upheaval* (Boston: Little, Brown, 1982), 67.

97. Zhonggong Kunming Junqu, "Xingshi jiaoyu cankao ziliao" (Educational sources on current affairs) (Kunming: Kunming Junqu, 1972), 361–63.

98. Ibid., 373.

99. Ibid., 374.

100. Shi Jun, "Xue yi dian shijie shi" (Let's study world history), *Hongqi*, no. 5 (1972): 24.

101. Shi Jun, "Du yi dian youguan diguo zhuyi de lishi" (Let's study the history of imperialism), *Hongqi*, no. 6 (1972): 38.

102. Ibid., 39.

103. Ibid., 39–40.

104. Gao Gao and Yan Jiaqi, ibid., 498–99.

105. Jiang Qing, "Dui Zhonggong lingshi yi shang waijiao ganbu de jianghua" (Speech delivered to Chinese communist diplomats of the consular rank and above), 390.

106. Ibid., 391.

107. Ibid.

108. Ibid.

Chapter 5. A Balancing Act

1. *Renmin ribao* (People's daily), 20 May 1978, 1 and 4. Unless otherwise noted, citations in this chapter are from the same newspaper.

2. 23 September 1978, 2.

3. 4 October 1978, 6.

4. 19 October 1978, 6.

5. 18 October 1978, 6.

6. 18 December 1978, 6.

7. 29 January 1979, 3.

8. 2 February 1979, 5.

9. 31 January 1979, 4.

10. 1 February 1979, 4.

11. 4 February 1979, 4.

12. Ibid.

13. 7 February 1979, 5.

14. Ibid.

15. 23 September 1978, 2.

16. 28 February 1979, 6.

17. 17 June 1980, 7.

18. 16 January 1980, 7.

19. 6 May 1979, 6.

20. 13 March 1980, 7.

21. 14 March 1980, 7.

22. 18 March 1980, 7.

23. 30 April 1981, 7.

24. 2 May 1981, 7.

25. 7 May 1981, 7.

26. 8 July 1981, 5.

27. 27 May 1980, 7; 2 April 1981, 6; 18 April 1981, 6; 18 July 1981, 7.

28. See Zhonggong Zhongyang (The Central Committee of the Chinese Communist Party), "Zhonggong zhongyang guanyu dangqian baokan xinwen guangbo xuanchuan fangzhen de jueding" (The resolution by the Central Committee of the Chinese Communist Party on propaganda work), in *Jianchi sixiang jiben yuanze, fandui zichanjieji ziyouhua* (Insist on Four Cardinal Principles and oppose bourgeois liberalization), ed. Zhonggong Zhongyang Shujichu Yanjiushi and Zhonggong Zhongyang Wenxian Yanjiushi (Beijing: People's Press, 1987).

29. 18 November 1981, 1.

30. 2 January 1983, 4.

31. Hu Qiaomu, "Guanyu zichanjieji ziyouhua ji qita" (On bourgeois liberalization and other matters), *Hongqi* (Red flag), no. 8 (1982): 11–24.

32. Ibid., 12.

33. To retaliate, the government announced that it would boycott sports events in the United States and cancel programs of cultural exchanges with the United States for the year. 8 April 1983, 1 and 6.

34. Hu Yaobang, "Makesi zhuyi weida zhenli de guangmang zhaoyao women qianjin" (March on under the guidance of Marxist truth), 14 March 1983, 1 and 2.

35. Chen Yun, "Zai dang de shier jie erzhongquanhui shang de fayan" (Speech at the second plenary meeting of the Central Committee of the Chinese Communist Party), in *Jianchi sixiang jiben yuanze, fandui zichanjieji ziyouhua* (Insist on the Four Cardinal Principles and oppose bourgeois liberalization), ed. Zhonggong Zhongyang Shujichu Yanjiushi and Zhonggong Zhongyang Wenxian Yanjiushi (Beijing: People's Press, 1987), 277.

36. Deng Xiaoping, "The Party's Urgent Tasks on the Organizational and Ideological Fronts," in *Fundamental Issues in Present-day China*, ed. And trans. Bureau for the Compilation and Translation of Works of Marx, Engels, Lenin and Stalin under the Central Committee of the Communist Party of China (Beijing: Foreign Languages Press, 1987), 23.

37. Ibid., 24–40. Speaking at a conference of the National Academic Degrees Committee on 24 September, Deng Liqun brought forward the idea of combating "Spiritual Pollution." The Central Department of Propaganda, meanwhile, sent instructions to party organizations in the country, urging them to take action. 25 September 1983, 1.

38. 11 January 1982, 4.

39. 6 December 1981, 7.
40. 21 November 1981, 7.
41. 2 May 1983, 7. Also 14 April 1983, 7, and 1 June 1983, 7.
42. 8 February 1983, 7.
43. 1 March 1983, 7.
44. 5 August 1983, 7.
45. 25 April 1982, 7.
46. 11 January 1984, 5.
47. 15 August 1980, 5.
48. 11 January 1984, 1.
49. Ibid.
50. 11 January 1984, 6.
51. Ibid.
52. Ibid.
53. Ibid.
54. 15 January 1984, 1.
55. 14 January 1984, 6.
56. 18 January 1984, 6.
57. 15 January 1984, 6.
58. See Deng Xiaoping, "On Special Economic Zones and Opening More Cities to the Outside World," in *Fundamental Issues in Present-Day China*, ed. and trans. Bureau for the Compilation and Translation of Works of Marx, Engels, Lenin and Stalin under the Central Committed of the Communist Party of China (Beijing: Foreign Language Press, 1987), 43–45.
59. Hu Yaobang, the CCP General Secretary, reaffirmed this policy at a party meeting in February 1985. Several conservative leaders challenged him by interrupting his speech. See Hu Yaobang, "Guanyu dang de xinwen gongzuo" (On the Party's propaganda work), *Xinwen zhanxian* (Journalist front), May 1985, 2–10.
60. 28 April 1984, 4.
61. 1 May 1984, 3.
62. 30 April 1984, 6.
63. 7 September 1984, 5.
64. 18 May 1984, 5.
65. 4 March 1984, 7.
66. 18 May 1984, 7.
67. 24 June 1985, 6.
68. 11 May 1984, 7.
69. 9 September 1984, 7.
70. 20 March 1985, 8.
71. Ibid.
72. 30 July 1985, 8.
73. 24 September 1985, 2.
74. 27 November 1986, 4.
75. 15 January 1987, 5.
76. 26 August 1986, 7.
77. 15 November 1986, 1.

78. 27 December 1986, 1.
79. 3 January 1987, 1.
80. 23 January 1987, 4.
81. 31 December 1986, 6.
82. 30 December 1986, 4.
83. 12 January 1987, 5.
84. 2 March 1987, 5.
85. 3 March 1987, 5; 24 March 1987, 5.
86. 4 November 1987, 1 and 4.
87. 21 October 1987, 7; 22 October 1987, 7; 23 October 1987, 7; 28 October 1987, 7; 29 October 1987, 7.
88. 11 January 1987, 5.
89. 15 November 1987, 7; 21 June 1987, 7.
90. 19 February 1989, 7.

Chapter 6. Chinese Review America

1. Li Honglin, "Dushu wu jinqu" (There should be no prohibition in reading), *Dushu* (Reading), no. 1 (April 1979): 7. Unless otherwise noted, citations in this chapter are from *Dushu*. With the exception for the year of 1979, month and year are used to indicate the issue of the journal referenced.

2. Zhang Shoubai, "Dushu buneng wu 'jinqu' " (It won't do to have no "prohibition" in reading), no. 6 (September 1979): 7.

3. Duzhe laixin (Letters to the editor), ibid.: 6.

4. Ziqi, "Ziben zhuyi you shenme ke xianmu de?" (What is there of capitalism that is worth our envy?), no. 3 (June 1979): 9.

5. Xiao Mu, "Meiguo Nanbei Zhanzheng yu *Piao* de renshi jiazhi" (The U.S. Civil War and the educational value of *Gone with the Wind*) (March 1981): 54.

6. Huang Songkang, "Cong lishi de jiaodu kan *Piao* he *Huanle de jieri*" (A historical view of *Gone with the Wind* and *Jubilee*) (March 1981): 55.

7. Huang Shaoxiang, "Ping Xierderliesi de *Bainu*" (On Hildreth's *White Slave*) (April 1980): 49.

8. Deng Shusheng, "Huang Shaoxiang zhu *Meiguo tongshi jianbian*" (On Huang Shaoxiang's *Outline History of the United States*) (June 1980): 28.

9. Ibid.

10. Deng Shusheng, "Linken zhe ge ren" (Lincoln the Man), no. 1 (January 1979): 60.

11. Ibid.

12. Huangwu, "Mantan Weiteman" (On Whitman), no. 6 (June 1979): 35.

13. Qiu Xiaolong, "Cong 'Xiangei Aimili De Meigui' zhong de lütoujin xiangdao de" (Reflections on the green scarf in "A Rose for Emily") (September 1980).

14. Shi Xianrong, "Mantan Meiquo xin chaoxianshi zhuyi shige" (On American neo-surrealist poetry) (February 1982): 128.

15. Chen Bukui, "Cong Situokesi de xinzuo kan Meiquo shi de qingxiang" (A trend in American poetry: the case of Stokes) (July 1982): 115–20.

16. Yu Jianzhang, "Dayang bian" (The other side of the ocean) (December 1982): 68.

17. Zhu Shida, "Cong shiben shu kan Meiguoren de jingshen shijie" (America's spiritual world as revealed in ten books) (May 1982): 116.

18. Ibid.

19. Li Ping "Kexue meiyou guojie" (Science has no national boundaries) (October 1981): 13–18.

20. "Bianhou shuyu" (Endnote) (February 1984): 155.

21. November 1981, 146–57; December 1981, 146–57.

22. "Shuxue, ziran kexue yu zhexue, shehui kexue de xianghu jiehe" (The integration of mathematics and natural sciences with philosophy and social sciences) (November 1981): 2–19.

23. Yao Zong, "Dai qushi" (Megatrends) (October 1983): 97–110.

24. Yang Mu, "Yige zhide zhuyi de xinxi" (A noteworthy signal) (February 1984): 18.

25. Xia Yan, "Guanyu dushu wenti de duitan" (A dialogue on reading) (April 1984): 27–33.

26. "Bianhou shuyu" (Endnote) (January 1984): 155.

27. "Bianhou shuyu" (Endnote) (March 1984): 155.

28. See March 1982, July 1982, December 1983, September 1984, and October 1984.

29. Yang Yang, "Kexue geming de jiegou yu xueshu sichao de bianqian" (Scientific revolution and progress in scholarship) (October 1984): 40.

30. Ji Shuli, "Kexue lishi de banlan huamian" (Great scenes in the history of sciences) (March 1982): 118.

31. Li Xinhua, "Kuen he ta de *Kexue geming de jiegou* (Kuhn and his *Strcuture of Scientific Revolution*) (September 1984): 24.

32. Michael Ruse, *Sociobiology: Sense or Nonsense?* (Dordrecht: D. Reidel, 1979), 1.

33. Li Kunfeng, "Kexue de tongyi shi zhishi fazhan de da qushi" (The unification of sciences is the trend) (March 1985): 9.

34. Ibid., 12.

35. Ibid., 14.

36. "Bianhou shuyu" (Endnote) (August 1984): 155.

37. Wang Yizhou, "Cong ISM dao DIM" (From ISM to DIM) (May 1985): 3. Also see Egon Neuberger and William J. Duffy, *Comparative Economic Systems: a Decision-making Approach* (Boston: Allyn and Bacon, 1976), Preface.

38. Liang Xiaomin, "Dui 'Kaiensi geming' de zai renshi" (A re-evaluation of the "Keynesian revolution") (March 1985): 35.

39. Zhang Weiping and Wu Xiaoying, "Jingji ziyou sichao de duihua: chuangxin jizhi" (A dialogue on economic liberalism: the mechanism of innovation) (February 1987): 24.

40. Ibid., 30.

41. Nan Shizhong, "Xuanze bingbu ziyou" (Not so free to choose) (April 1984): 44, 49.

42. Ibid., 45–46.

43. Wu Xiaoying and Zhang Weiping, "Jingji ziyou zhuyi de duihua: xiaofeizhe zhuquan" (A dialogue on economic liberalism: consumer sovereignty) (November 1986): 57–58.

44. Ibid.

45. Wu Xiaoying and Zhang Weiping, "Jingji ziyou zhuyi sichao de duihua: gongping yu xiaolü" (A dialogue on economic liberalism: equality and efficiency) (April 1987): 73–82.

46. Wu Xiaoying and Zhang Weiping, "Jingji ziyou zhuyi sichao duihua: jingji ren" (A Dialogue on economic liberalism: economic man) (January 1987): 33.

47. Ibid., 35.

48. Su Shaozhi, "Zhengzhi tizhi gaige chuyi" (A preliminary discussion on political reform) (September 1986): 3–7.

49. Zhao Yifan, "Huofusitade yu Meiquo zhengzhi sixiang shi" (Hofstadter and the history of American political thought) (February 1987): 118–26.

50. "Bianhou shuyu" (Endnote) (October 1985): 158.

51. Chen Kuide and Chen Jiade, "Kuanrong zhi dao" (The way of tolerance) (June 1986): 12.

52. "Bianhou shuyu" (Endnote) (June 1986): 160.

53. Ibid., 159.

54. Zhao Yifan, "Xiandaihua lilun yu Huo shi gaige shi guan" (Modernization theories and Hofstadter's view on the history of reforms) (March 1987): 122–26.

55. Ibid., 120–22.

56. "Bianhou shuyu" (Endnote) (April 1987): 160.

57. Zhao Yifan, "Qiandele yu guanli geming lilun" (Chandler and the theory of management revolution) (October 1987): 130–40; same author, "Bailing, quanli jingying, xing jieji" (White collar, power elite, and new class) (December 1987): 115–25.

58. Yan Bofei, "Paoqi wutuobang" (Abandon utopia) (February 1989): 5–12.

59. Shen Zhongmei, "Hantingdun yu ta de qiangda zhengfu lun" (Huntington and his theory on powerful government) (May 1989): 73–76.

60. Dingxin Zhao, The Power of Tiananmen: State-Society Relations and the 1989 Beijing Student Movement (Chicago: University of Chicago Press, 2004), 203–204.

61. Gu Xi, "Minzhu yu quanwei" (Democracy and authority) (June 1989): 29.

62. Cheng Bukui, "Cong Situokesi de xinzuo kan Meiquo shi de qingxian" (The trend in American poetry: the case of Terry Stokes) (July 1982): 118.

63. Zhao Yifan, "Hafo jiaoyu sixiang kaocha" (An examination of Harvard's educational philosophy) (January 1987): 127.

64. Zhao Yifan, "Quruilin yu Niuyue wenren shidai" (Trilling and the era of New York intellectuals) (August 1987): 132.

65. Ibid.

66. Zhao Yifan, "Dannier Beier yu dangdai ziben zhuyi wenhua piping" (Daniel Bell and the cultural criticism of modern capitalism) (December 1986): 108–15.

67. Wang Yan, ed., "Maikesi Weibo: yiwei sixiangjia de xiaoxiang" (Max Weber: a portrait of a thinker) (December 1985): 34–42.

68. "Xinjiao lunli yu ziben zhuyi jingshen" (Protestant ethics and the spirit of capitalism) (January 1986): 135–45.

69. Zhou Guoping, "Meige ren dou shi yige yuzou" (Every man is a universe by himself) (September 1987): 33.

70. Xu Haixin, "Meiquo de Qingjiaotu—jiangjiexing xuanji" (The Puritans in America: a Narrative Anthology) (October 1986): 136–37.

71. Mo Mo, "Bu bao huanxiang, ye bu juewan" (No illusion, nor despair) (January 1989): 114.

72. Mo Mo, "Women zhe yidai de pa he ai" (The Love and fear of our generation) (June 1988); "Bei ding si zai shizijia shang de zhenli" (Truth crucified) (December 1988); "Dui shangdi bixu baochi chenmo ma?" (Facing God, should we be silent?), supplementary issue no. 1 (1989).

Chapter 7. Popular and Not-So-Popular America

1. "Qipian de meili" (The power of deception), *Zhongguo renquan* (Human rights in China) 1 (1979), in *Dalu dixia kanwu huibian* (Mainland China's underground publications), vol. 2, compl. by Zhonggong Yanjiu Zazhishe (Taibei: Zhonggong Yanjiu Zazhishe, 1980), 195.

2. Xiaoming, " 'Neibu dianying' he shi liao?" (When will we see the end of "inner-circle movies"?), *Renmin zhisheng* (People's voice) 9 (1979), in ibid., vol. 16, 114–15.

3. "Meiquo shiye zhuangkuang diandi" (Glimpses of unemployment in the United States), *Renmin zhisheng* 12–13 (December 1979), in ibid., vol. 16, 198.

4. "Shijie zhuyao ziben zhuyi guojia nongye jixiehua sudu" (The pace of agricultural mechanization in the world's leading capitalist countries), *Qunzhong cankaoxiaoxi* (The Masses' reference news) 1 (December 1978), in ibid., vol. 2, 161.

5. *Qiushi bao* (Quest for truth) 15 (October 1979), in ibid., vol. 6, 65.

6. "Meiguo zhengzhi yu zhengfu" (U.S. politics and government), *Renmin zhilu* (People's path) 1 (September 1979), in ibid., vol. 17, 281–83.

7. "Lüelun Meiguo kexue zhengce" (On the science policies of the United States), *Renmin zhilu* 5 (February 1979), in ibid., vol. 3, 206–207.

8. "Meiguo shi minzhu de leyuan ma?" (Is the U.S. a paradise of democracy?), in *Kexue, minzhu, fazhi: minzhu qiang shiwenxuan* (Science, democracy, the rule of law: A collection of essays and poems from the democracy wall), ed. Gong Nianzhou (Beijing: 1979), in ibid., vol. 8, 307.

9. Xie Jun, "Meiguo shi minzhu de leyuan" (The U.S. is a paradise of democracy), in ibid., vol. 14, 21.

10. Ibid., 22.

11. Ibid., 24.

12. Gesheng, " 'Si ren bang' zai Meiquo de liudu" (The lingering influence of the 'Gang of Four' in America), *Wusi luntai* (May Fourth forum) (Beijing) 5 (February 1979), in ibid., vol. 2, 99.

13. "Meiguo xuesheng yundong de tedian" (Characteristics of the American students' movement), *Renming zhilu* 1 (September 1979), in ibid., vol. 17, 290–91.

14. Chuangye (Pioneers) (Changchun dianying zhipian chang, 1975). Motion picture.

15. Henry Yuhuai He, *Cycles of Repression and Relaxation : Politco-literary Events in China, 1976–1989* (Bochum: N. Brockmeyer, 1992), 25–27.

16. Zhang Yang, *Di er ci woshou* (The second handshake) (Beijing: Zhongguo Qingnian Chubanshe, 1979).

17. Editorial, "Dang de Sanzhong Quanhui yilai de chuban gongzuo" (The publishing industry since the Party's Third Plenary Meeting), *Chuban gongzuo* (Work in publishing) 12 (1987): 11.

18. Liang Xiaotao, "Zhongyang Dianshitai quanguo dianshi guanzhong chouyang diaocha fenxi baogao" (An analytical report on an audience survey conducted by the CCTV), *Zhongguo guangbo dianshi nianjian 1988* (The China yearbook on radio, broadcast, and television, 1998) (Beijing: Zhongguo Guangbo Dianshi Chubanshe, 1988), 401.

19. Zhongyang Dianshi Tai, "Zhongyang Dianshi Tai dianshi guanzhong shoushi qingkuang diaocha" (A survey of the CCTV audience), *Zhongguo guangbo dianshi nianjian 1986* (China's radio, broadcast, and television yearbook, 1986) (Beijing: Zhongguo Guangbo Dianshi Chubanshe, 1987), 573; *Zhongguo guangbo dianshi nianjian 1988* (The China yearbook on radio, broadcast, and television, 1998) (Beijing: Zhongguo Guanbo Dianshi Chubanshe, 1988), 414.

20. Chen Hanyuan, "Tantan tongguo weixing shoulu de guoji xinwen (shang)" (International news by satellite, part 1), *Xinwen zhangxian* (Journalist front) 5 (1981): 39.

21. Ibid., 38–40.

22. "Guanzhong dui Zhongyang Dianshi Tai jiemu de fanying" (Viewer responses to CCTV programs), *Zhongguo guangbo dianshi nianjian 1986* (Beijing: Zhongguo Guangbo Dianshi Chubanshe, 1987), 625.

23. Chen Hanyuan, "Tantan tongguo weixing shoulu de Guoji Xinwen (xia)" (International news by satellite, part 2), *Xinwen zhangxian* 6 (1981): 39–41.

24. Beijing Xinwen Xuehui Diaochazu, *Beijing duzhe, tingzhong, guanzhong diaocha* (A Survey of readers, listeners and viewers in Beijing) (Beijing: Gongren Chubanshe, 1985), 19.

25. "Dang de Sanzhong Quanhui yilai de chuban gongzuo," *Chuban gongzuo* 12 (1987): 11.

26. Li jingrui, "Fanyi chubanxue chutan" (On translation and publication), *Chuban gongzuo* 6 (1988): 97.

27. Chuban Shiye Guanli Ju Banben Tushu Guan, *Quanguo zong shumu: 1976* (Books published nationwide: 1976) (Beijing: Zhonghua Shuju, 1980), 799.

28. Ibid., volume for 1977 (Beijing: Zhonghua Shuju, 1981), 479.

29. Ibid., volume for 1978 (Beijing: Zhonghua Shuju, 1982), 595–96.

30. Ibid., volume for 1979 (Beijing: Zhonghua Shuju, 1983), 745–50.

31. Ibid., volume for 1982 (Beijing: Zhonghua Shuju, 1985), 1262–75.

32. Ibid., volume for 1978, 595–96.

33. Ibid., volume for 1979, 745–50.

34. Shi Xianrong, "Meiguo wenxue zai Zhongguo" (American literature in China), *Fanyi tongxun* (Translation bulletin) (December 1983): 13–17.

35. Jiang Chunfang, "Tuanjie qilai, kaichuang fanyi gongzuo xin jumian" (Unite and embrace a new era in translation), *Zhongguo fanyi* (Translation in China) 4 (1986): 8.

36. Zhongxuanbu Chuban Ju (Bureau of Publications, the CCP Department of Propaganda), "Dangqian tushu chuban de jige tuchu wenti" (Some notable problems in publishing), *Xuanchuan dongtai (Xuanbian) 1980* (Trends in Propaganda [collected essays], 1980) (Beijing: Zhongguo Shehui Kexue Chubanshe, 1981), 84.

37. *Yilin* (Translations) 1 (1983): 271–72.

38. Ibid. 2 (1983): 118–61.

39. Ibid. 2 (1983): 38–117.

40. Chen Fan, "Xiwang duo liaojie bianhua zhe de dangjin shijie" (We want to learn more about the changing world), *Yilin* 4 (1984): 262.

41. Editorial, *Dazhong dianying* (Popular cinema) (December 1983): 3.

42. John L. Scherer, ed., *China Figures & Facts Annual*, vol. 3 (1980) (Gulf Breeze, FL: Academic International Press, 1980), 218 and 221–22; John L. Scherer, ed., *China Figures & Facts Annual*, vol. 4 (1981) (Gulf Breeze, FL: Academic International Press, 1981), 301; John L. Scherer, ed., *China Figures & Facts Annual*, vol. 5 (1982) (Gulf Breeze, FL: Academic International Press, 1982), 230; John L. Scherer, ed., *China Figures & Facts Annual*, vol. 8 (1985) (Gulf Breeze, FL: Academic International Press, 1985), 321.

43. Jay Robert Nash and Stanley Ralph Ross, *The Motion Picture Guide*, vol. 2, (Chicago: Cinebooks, Inc., 1985), 483.

44. Pico Iyer, *Video Night in Kathamandu and Other Reports from the Not-So-Far East* (New York: Random House, 1988), 180.

45. Gao Min, "Zai guoji lieche tongguo de difang" (Where the international train passes by), *Xiaoshuolin* (Fiction) (June 1983): 38–41.

46. Arthur Miller, *Salesman in Beijing* (New York: The Viking Press, 1984), 232.

47. Ibid., 86.

48. Peng Bo, ed., *Pan Xiao Taolun: Yidai Zhongguo qingnian de sixiang chulian* (The Pan Xiao debate: The first love of a thoughtful generation of young Chinese) (Tianjin: Nankai Daxue Chubanshe, 2000).

49. Yang Yanzi and Wang Yaping, "Yige Meiguo qingnian he yige Zhongguo qingnian de duihua" (A dialogue between a young American and a young Chinese), *Zhongguo qingnian* (China youth) (November 1980): 8.

50. Ibid., 9.

51. Zheng Tianxiang, "Zuigao Renmin Fayuan gongzuo baogao" (Report on the work of the Supreme People's Court), *Zuigao renmin fayuan gongbao* (The Supreme People's Court bulletin) 2 (20 June 1987): 4.

52. Ibid., 4.

53. Kjeld Erik Brodsgaard and Susan Young, *State Capacity in East Asia: China, Taiwan, Vietnam, and Japan* (New York: Oxford University Press, 2000), 187.

54. Gao Jiansheng and Liu Ning, *Lihun wenti mianmian guan* (Facets of the divorce issue) (Zhengzhou, Henan: Henan Renmin Chubanshe), 95–96.

55. William C. Kirby, ed., *Realms of Freedom in Modern China* (Stanford: Stanford University Press, 2003), 363.

56. Xu Yamin, "Guanyu yi baiming shaonian fanzui de diaocha" (A investigative study of 100 cases of youth crime), *Tianjin fanzui wenti diaocha wenji* (Collected articles based on a survey of crimes in Tianjin) (Tianjin: Tianjin Renmin Chubanshe, 1985), 102–103.

57. Li Ruihuan, "Jiaqiang zonghe zhili, zhengqu shehui zhian de genben haozhuan" (Intensify integrated social control and and strive for a fundamental improvement in public security), in ibid., 11.

58. "Beijing Shiwei Xuanchuanbu diaocha chuli fei zhengchang liuru de waiguo shukan" (The Propaganda Department of the Party's Beijing Municipal Committee

investigates illegally imported foreign books and periodicals), *Xuanchuan dongtai (xuanbian) 1980* (Beijing: Zhongguo Shehui Kexue Chubanshe, 1981), 189–91.

59. Ibid., 183.

60. Ibid., 188.

61. Shao Daosheng, Zhongguo qingshaonian fanzui de shehuixue sikao (Sociological reflections on youth crimes in China) (Beijing: Shehui Kexue Wenxian Chubanshe, 1987), 149; Shen Ying, "Zhongshi shehui xinxi dui qingnian de yingxiang" (Pay attention to the effects of information on our youth), *Wenhui bao* (Wenhui daily), 24 March 1982, 3.

62. Iyer, 3.

63. Lu Hanwei, "Zhen shi nanxing mei ma?" (Is this masculine beauty?), *Dazhong dianying* (November 1986): 19.

64. Situ Shuzhang, "Xin de xingshi, xin de wenti" (New trends, new problems), *Chuban tongxun* (Publishing bulletin) (June 1989): 34–35.

65. Ibid., 35.

66. Ibid., 40.

67. Zhuang Yu, "Bianji xianhua, 19" (Editor's notes, 19), *Chuban gongzuo* 9 (1989): 29.

68. Xiaoying, "Qiyejia de qingnian shidai: Hamo" (The early years of entrepreneurs: Hammer), *Zhongqingnian jingji luntan* (Forum for young and middle-aged economists) (March 1985): 76–78.

69. *Zhongguo qiyejia* (China's entrepreneurs) (January 1987): 44–47; (February 1987): 42–46; (March 1987): 30–34.

70. Tian Xiaodong, "Meiguo ren cong ta shenshang faxian le shenme" (What do Americans see in him?), *Zhongguo qingnian* (April 1985): 40–43.

71. He Lifeng, trans. and ed., "Wo de Meiguo meng" (My American dream), *Zhongguo qingnian*, August 1986: 38–39.

72. Peter G. Beidler and Shi Jian, "Translating America: Books about the US Available in a Provincial Chinese City," *China Exchange News* 3, vol. 18 (September 1990): 22.

73. Si Yan, "Gangtie dawang Andelu Kaniji de chenggong" (Steel King Andrew Carnegie's success), *Zhongguo qiyejia* (June 1987): 47.

74. Liu Yibing, "Keda gongsi de chuangshiren: Qiaozhi Yishiman" (The Founder of Kodak: George Eastman), *Dangdai qiyejia* (Contemporary entrepreneurs) (March 1986): 63.

75. Zhao Xiuyun, "Xin jueqi de Meishi kuaican ting" (Rising American fast-food restaurants), *Zhongguo qiyejia* (May 1988): 17.

76. Zhang Yuan, "Xieerdun jiudian de zhaopin fengbo" (The controversy over Sheraton Hotel's hiring), *Zhongguo qingnian* (combined issues January and February 1987): 45–47.

77. Ai Tiesheng and Xie Qiang, "Yige Meiguo ren yan li de Zhongguo qingnian" (Chinese youth in the eyes of an American, *Zhongguo qingnian bao* (Chinese youth daily), 5 January 1985, 2.

78. Ji Zhongliang, "Taipingyang bi an chuilai de feng" (The wind from the other side of the Pacific), *Zhongguo qingnian* (combined issue January and February 1987): 28.

79. Wu Jisong, *Yige Zhongguo ren kan shijie* (The world through the eyes of a Chinese) (Beijing: Gongren Chubanshe, 1987), 318.

80. Ibid., 319.

81. Zhao Jianjun, "Meiquo qingnian zhi wojian" (American youth as I see it), *Qingnian* (Youth) (June 1988): 28.

82. Ibid.

83. Li Cheng, "Zai Meiquo, tan shijian" (Time in America), *Qingnian wenzhai* (Young readers' digest) (January 1987): 41.

84. Zhang Mingshu, "Meiguo 'jingshen wenming' yinxiang ji" (My impressions of the 'American spiritual civilization'), *Kaifang shidai* (The Era of the open door) (March 1989): 53.

85. Ibid., 53.

86. Ibid., 54.

Chapter 8. Shall the Twain Ever Meet?

1. Zhang Weiping, ed., *Liangzhong zhanlüe: "heping yianbian" yu "heping fangbian"* (Two conflicting strategies: Peaceful transformation and peaceful resistance) (Chongqing: Chongqing Press, 1991), 100–30; 145.

2. Ibid., 145.

3. Yang Qianli, "Cong hengxiang bijiao zhong kan Zhongguo de shehui zhuyi" (Evaluate Chinese socialism through horizontal comparisons), *Renmin ribao* (People's daily), 14 December 1990, 5.

4. "Dongfang feng lai manyuan chun—Deng Xiaoping zai Shenzhen jishi" (Breeze from the east brings spring: Reports on Deng Xiaoping's trip to Shenzhen), *Shenzhen Tequ Bao* (Shenzhen Special Zone daily), 26 March 1992.

5. Fangsheng, "Duiwai kaifang he liyong zibenzhuyi" (The open door policy and the use of capitalism), *Renmin ribao*, 23 February 1992, 4.

6. "Deng Xiaoping duiwai kaifang sixiang de weidai shijian—tantan Zhongguo jingji he shijie jingji de jiegui" (The great application of Deng Xiaoping's theory on open door policy: On the economic connectivity of China and the world), ibid, 28 February 1995, 9.

7. "Jiang Zemin zhuchi Zhonggong Zhongyang Zhengzhiju quanti huiyi taolun woguo gaige he fazhan ruogan zhongyan wenti" (Jiang Zemin chairs a plenary meeting of the CCP Politburo, discussing issues of reform and development), ibid., 12 March 1992, 1.

8. "Book of the Year (1993, 1994, 1995, 1996, 1997): World Affairs: CHINA," Britannica Online. <http://www.eb.com:180/cgi-bin/g?DocF=boy/94/H03045.html> <http://www.eb.com:180/cgi-bin/g?DocF=boy/95/I02985.html> <http://www.eb.com:180/cgi-bin/g?DocF=boy/96/J03820.html> <http://www.eb.com:180/cgi-bin/g?DocF=boy/97/K03925.html> <http://www.eb.com:180/cgi-bin/g?DocF=boy/98/L03925.html> (accessed November 27, 1998).

9. U.S. Census Bureau, Foreign Trade Division, Dissemination Branch, Washington, DC.

10. Xi Laiwang, *Zhong Mei jiaowang shilu* (Records on Sino-American relations) (Beijing: Jinghua Chubanshe, 1995), 232. "House Panel Opposes Beijing Olympics Bid," *Washington Post*, 22 July 1993, D02.

11. Xi Laiwang et al., *Dayang jifeng: liangge shijie daguo de boyi guize* (Seasonal winds: The rules of the game played by two world-class powers) (Beijing: Zhongguo Shehui Chubanshe, 1996), "Mulu" (Table of contents), 29–30.

12. Christine Brennan, "A Vote for Common Sense," *Washington Post*, 25 September 1993, G02.

13. *Renmin ribao*, 11 September 1993, 1.

14. "Li Lanqing zai Monte Carlo jizhe zhaodaihui shang shuo, women quanli yifu zhengqu shenban chenggong" (We'll try our best to ensure the ssuccess of our application, says Li Lanqi at a press conference in Monte Carlo), ibid., 23 September 1993, 1.

15. "Li Tieying dianwei Beijing shenban daibiaotuan" (Li Tieying sends telegram, praising the Beijing application team), ibid., 24 September 1993, 1.

16. "Jianding buyi de zouxiang shijie" (March on to the world with no doubts), ibid., 24 September 1993, 1.

17. "Mideast Allies Frustrate Ship Inspection by U.S., Prohihited Chemicals May Be Bound for Iran," *Washington Post*, 10 August, 1993, A06. " 'Yinhe Hao' shijian shime" (The Yinhe Incident), *Renmin ribao*, 6 September 1993, 7.

18. "Zhonghua Remin Gonghe Guo Waijiaobu Guanyu 'Yinhe Hao' Shijian de Shengming" (Statement on the Yinhe Incident by the Ministry of Foreign Affairs, People's Republic of China), ibid., 5 September 1993, 1.

19. "Yihe Hao huolun shengli fanhang" (Yinhe returns triumphantly), ibid., 26 September 1993, 1.

20. *Renmin ribao*, 1 January 1995, 2. Yingqian: "Manheng de xingwei" (Outrageous behavior), ibid., 2 January 1995, 7.

21. "Meiguo xuanbu duihua shishi maoyi baofu" (US declares trade retaliation against China), ibid., 5 Feburary 1995, 1.

22. "Wu Yi zai Yajiada tan wo fuguan wenti, Zhongguo bu fangqi genben liyi, Meiguo yaojia ying shike erzhi" (Wu Yi, in Jakarta, talks about our country's return to the GATT: China will not give up her essential interests, U.S. should limit her demands to reasonable bounds), ibid., October 7, 1994, 7; 19 March, 1998, 1.

23. Gong Wen, "Qianfan jinqu dai dongfeng--Zhongguo fuguan beiwanglu" (Memorandum on China's effort to join GATT), ibid., 20 December 1994, 2.

24. Ibid.

25. Ibid.

26. "Youyu shaoshu tiyuefang quefa chengyi xuyi zuonao, wo fuguan xieyi weineng dacheng" (Due to the obstruction by certain parties, no agreement on our country's membership in the GATT), ibid., 21 December, 1994, 1.

27. On 12 December 1995, the *People's Daily* published a three-page document, prepared by the Press Office of the State Council, entitled "Zhongguo renquan shiye de jinzhan" (The progress in Human Rights in China), 1, 2, and 3.

28. Wu Xiaoli, *Zu yin* (Echoes of footsteps) (Beijing: Huayi Chubanshe, 1998), 247.

29. Robert Lawrence Kuhn, *The Man Who Changed China: The Life and Legacy of Jiang Zemin* (New York: Crown, 2004), 5.

30. Ibid.

31. He Xin, "Shijie jingji xingshi yu Zhongguo jingji wenti—He Xin yu Riben jingjixue jiaoshou de tanhualu" (Conditions of the world economy and China's options: He Xin's dialogue with a Japanese professor of economics), *Remin ribao*, 11 December 1990, 2.

32. Ibid.

33. Ibid., 2.

34. Ibid., 3.

35. Ibid.

36. Ibid.

37. Zhang Kuan, "Ou Mei ren yan zhong de fei wo zu lei—cong 'dongfang zhuyi' dao 'xifang zhuyi' "(The other in the European and American eyes: From Orientalism to Occidentalism), *Dushu* (Reading) (September 1993): 8.

38. Ibid., 9.

39. "Bianhou shuyu (Endnote)," *Dushu* (September 1993).

40. Ibid., 149.

41. Wang Yichuan et al., "Bianyuan, zhongxin, dongfang, xifang" (Periphery, center, East, West), ibid. (January 1994): 147.

42. Ibid., 150–51.

43. Zhang Kuan, "Zai tan Said" (On Said, Part two), ibid. (September 1994): 14.

44. Samuel P. Huntington, "The Clash of Civilizations?" *Foreign Affairs* (Summer 1993); *The Clash of Civilizations and the Remaking of World Order* (New York: Simon and Schuster, 1993).

45. Yitao, "Rujia: minzhu de zuihou zhangai?" (Confucianism: The last obstacle to democratization?), *Dushu* (May 1992): 129.

46. Ibid.

47. For a collection of essays on the subject, see Wang Jisi, ed., *Wenming yu guoji zhengzhi: Zhongguo xuezhe ping Hantingdun de wenming chongtu lun* (Civilization and international politics: Chinese scholars on Huntington's theory on the clash of civilizations) (Shanghai: Shanghai Renmin Chubanshe, 1995).

48. Feng Keli, "Cong Rujia geti lun dao xin renyu shuo" (From the Confucian view of the individual to a new theory on human desires), *Dushu* (May 1992): 130–37; Liu Junning, "Singapore: Rujia ziyou zhuyi de tiaozhan" (Singapore: the challenge of Confucian liberalism), ibid. (February 1993): 9–15; David L. Hall and Roger T. Ames, "Kefao tongguo Kongzi er si?" (Thinking through Confucius), ibid. (May 1995): 51–56; Tu Wei-ming, "Wei Ruxue fazhan buxie chenci" (Speak out for the advancement of Confucian studies), ibid. (October 1995): 34–43; Chen Jianhua, "Zaitan Levenson yu Rujia Zhongguo de xiandai mingyun" (Another discussion of Liewenson and his *Confucian China and Its Modern Fate*), ibid. (December 1996): 60–64.

49. "Kaogu xue yu Zhongguo de lishi tujing" (Archeology and Chinese history), ibid. (September 1996): 3–25; "Xiangtu Zhongguo de dangdai tujing" (Rural China in modern times), ibid. (October 1996): 48–68; Chen Mingdao, "Zhongguo yinyue de 'xuerou wenben' " (The blood-flesh 'text' of Chinese music), ibid. (September 1996): 31–37.

50. Zhonghua Hehe Wenhua Hongyang Gongcheng Mishuchu, "Zhonghua hehe wenhua yanjiu gaishu" (A review of the current studies on the Chinese culture of harmony and peace), *Guangmin ribao*, 6 February 1997, 7.

51. " 'Guoxue, zai Yanyuan you qiaoran xingqi' yinqi fanxiang, duzhe toushu benbao biaoshi zanshang bing tichu reqie xiwang" ('The quiet rise of the national learning at Beijing University' receives enthusiastic response: Readers write in to express their appreciation and their support), *Renmin ribao*, 20 September 1993, 3.

52. Ji Xianlin, "Xifang bu liang dongfang liang: Ji Xianlin jiaoshou zai Beijing Waiguoyu Daxue Zhongwen Xueyuan·de yanjiang" (Dusk in the West, dawn in the East: Professor Ji Xianlin's speech at the School of Chinese Studies, the Beijing University for Foreign Studies), *Zhongguo wenhuan yanjiu* (Chinese cultural studies) (Winter 1995): 1–6, reprinted in *Renda baokan fuyin ziliao: wenhua yanjiu* (People's University photocopied periodical materials: cultural studies), no. 1, 1996, 46.

53. Ibid., 60.

54. Pan Jie, "Shui shi 'shuo bu' zhe?" (Who are those who said no?), originally published in *Beijing qingnian zhoukan* (Beijing youth weekly), appears in Jia Qingguo, *Zhongguo bu jinjin shuo bu* (China does not just say no) (Beijing: Zhonghua Gongshang Lianhe Chubanshe, 1996), 399.

55. Jia Qingguo, ibid., 316.

56. Ibid.

57. Ibid.

58. Ibid.

59. Ibid.

60. Ibid.

61. See Shen Jiru, *Zhongguo bu dang bu xiansheng* (China doesn't want to be Mr. No) (Beijing: Dangdai Zhongguo Chubanshe, 1998).

62. Liu Ji, "21 shiji Zhong Mei guanxi de xuanze" (Choices in Sino-American relations in the twenty-first century), *Xinhua wenzhai* (Xinhua digest), no. 1 (1998), 7. The article was originally published in *Zhanlüe yu guanli* (Strategy and management), no. 5 (1997).

63. Ibid., 10.

64. Ibid., 11.

65. Ibid., 10:

66. Ibid., 11.

67. Ibid.

68. Ibid.

69. "Huo baobao Yansha cheng" (Good business at Yansha Shopping City), *Renmin ribao*, 5 December 1992, 2.

70. "Qikan, dalu chuban 6500 zhong—Xinwen Chubanshu Qikan Si fuzeren fangtan lu" (6,500 periodicals published in Mainland China, according to an official at the Periodical Section, the Bureau of Journalism and Publishing), ibid., 11 January 1992, 3.

71. Sally Taylor, "Book Publishing in the People's Republic of China," *Publisher's Weekly* Online, http://www.bookwire.com/pw/country-reports.article$10101 (accessed January 11, 1999).

72. Ibid.

73. Li Jianjun, "Shilun wenhua shentou" (On cultural infiltration), *Renda baokan fuyin ziliao: wenhua yanjiu* (People's University photocopied periodical materials: cultural studies), no. 6, 1997, 22.

74. Ibid.

75. Haifei, "Shidai huhuan Zhongguo katong tushu" (New times call for China's own cartoon books), *Remin ribao*, 18 April 1995, 5.

76. Yang Lianyun, "Wenhua chanpin shangpinhua dui qingshaonian de weihai jiqi duice" (On the harm on younsters done by commercialized cultural products and the efforts to control the damage), *Renda baokan fuyin ziliao: wenhuan yanjiu* (People's University photocopied periodical materials: cultural studies), no. 4, 1997, 21–22.

77. S. Xiaochuan, "Life with the Liu Family," *China Daily*, 17 July 1998, 14.

78. Hao Jian, "Yihetuan bing de shenyin" (The murmurs of the Boxers), *Dushu* (March 1996): 3.

79. "China Poised to Lead Asia in Internet Users after Japan, Firm Says," Reuters News Service, 26 October 1998; Zhongguo Hulian Wangluo Xinxi Zhongxin, "Zhongguo hulian wangluo fazhan zhuangkuang tongji baogao, 2000 nian 7 yue" (Statistical report on the state of Internet development in China, July 2000), http://tech.sina.com.cn/internet/china/2000-07-27/31904.shtml (accessed September 29, 2000).

80. Statistics released by Nielsen/NetRatings. Xinhua News Agency, 22 April 2002.

81. "PRC Net Dreams: Is Control Possible? A Report from the U.S. Embassy, Beijing," the Voice of America, September 1997; "Chinese Restrictions on Internet," Editorial, ibid., 4 February 1998.

82. Yuan Yue and Fan Wen: "1997–1998 nian: Zhongguo chengshi shehui redian wenti diaocha" (Surveys of hot topics in China's urban areas: 1997–1998), in *Shehui lanpi shu: 1998 nian de Zhongguo shehui xingshi fenxi yu yuce* (Bluebook on social conditions in China: Trends, analyses, and predictions, 1998), ed. Ru Xin, Lu Xueyi, and Shan Tianlun (Beijing: Zhongguo Shehui Kexue Chubashe, 1998), 190–91.

83. Chou Xuezhong, "Renqing dashi, shenhua gaige, polang qianjin, zaichuang huihuang" (Accurately assess the current situation, steadily deepen reform, overcome obstacles, and create new glory), *Zhongguo guanggao* (Chinese advertising), no. 1 (1998): 14.

84. Yang Yiyong et al., "Zhongguo chu le ge furen ceng" (An affluent class emerges in China), *Changxiao shu zhai* (Bestseller excerpts), no. 1, 1998, 44. This is part of the same authors' *Gongping yu xiaolü* (Justice and efficiency) (Yinchuan, Gansu: Gansu Renmin Chubanshe, 1996).

85. Pi Shuyi, "Maidanglao lai le" (Here comes McDonald's), *Renmin ribao*, 13 June 1992, 3.

86. "Company Briefing: KFC," http://www.cns.com.jo/Company/KFC/brief.htm (accessed 12 December 1998).

87. Ian Hunter, "Big Mac in China: And the Cattle Grew Restless," Anomalies Project, Stockholm School of Economics & EIJS, 1997.

88. "Company Briefing: KFC."

89. Zhou Bin, "Maidanglao shequ fuwu de qishi" (The lesson of the community services of McDonald's), *Renmin ribao*, 17 December 1992, 1.

90. Ibid.

91. Sun Wu, "Jingti 'zhimin wenhua' chenzha fanqi—weirao 'zhimin wenhua' de yichang zhengyi" (Watch out for the return of the rotten "colonial culture": A debate), *Renda baokan fuyin ziliao: wenhua yanjiu* (People's University photocopied periodical materials: cultural studies), no. 3, 1996, 39.

92. Yuan Yue and Fan Wen: "1997–98 nian: Zhongguo chengshi shehui redian wenti diaocha" (Surveys of hot topics in China's urban areas: 1997–98), in *Shehui lanpi shu: 1998 nian de Zhongguo shehui xingshi fenxi yu yuce* (Bluebook on social conditions: Trends, analyses, and predictions, 1998), ed. Ru Xin, Lu Xueyi, and Shan Tianlun (Beijing: Zhongguo Shehui Kexue Chubashe, 1998), 190–91.

93. "Dui yi ben changxiao xiaoshuo de piping" (Reactions to a bestselling novel), *Dushu* (January 1993): 155–56.

94. "Shoudu wenyi tushu xiaoshou mingxian shangsheng" (Sales of books on arts and liberature in Beijing are on the rise), *Renmin ribao*, 4 January 1992, 3.

95. Li Qiang,"Zhengzhi fenceng yu jingji fenceng" (Political stratification and economic stratification), *Shehui xue yanjiu* (Sociological studies), no. 4 (1997); in *Renda baokan fuyin ziliao: shehui xue* (People's University photocopied periodical materials: sociology), no. 5, 1997, 89.

96. Yang Yiyong et al., op. cit.

97. Ibid.

98. "Baiwan shankuan fuxu gongan yinghun" (A million yuan donated to assist heroic policemen), *Beijing wanbao* (Beijing evening news), 10 November 1998, 2.

99. Zhang Panshi, "Lun shishi quanmin jindu jiaoyu jihua de jinpo xing" (On the urgent need for a whole-out effort on the education against narcotics), *Renda baokan fuyin baokan ziliao: shehui xue* (People's University photocopied periodical materials: sociology), no. 5, 1997, 152.

100. Zhang Yibing, "Dui ceqing fuwu de gongzhong yinxiang de diaocha yu fenxi" (A survey and analysis of the public's attitude toward sexual services), ibid., no. 4, 1997, 157–62.

101. Wu Luping, "Zhongguo qingnian yanzhong de Meiguo" (The United States in the eyes of Chinese youth), *Zhongguo qingnianbao* (Chinese youth daily), 11 May 1996, 4.

102. Zhongguo Qingshaonian Yanjiu Zhongxin, "Zhongguo qingnian fazhan zhuangkuang diaocha: chengshi" (A survey of the developmental state of Chinese youth today: cities), in *Zhongguoren yu waiguoren* (Chinese and foreigners), ed. Sun Zhenzhi (Beijing: Guoji Wenhua Chuban Gongsi, 1997), 444–45.

103. *Zhongguo qingnian bao*, 14 July 1995, 8.

104. Wu Luping, op. cit.

105. Yuan Yue and Fan Wen, op. cit.

106. Results of a poll by Horizon Research, reported in *Beijing qingnian zhoukan* (Beijing youth weekly), 8 June 1998, 10–11.

107. Ibid., 11.

108. Ibid.

109. Ibid.

110. Ibid.

111. Peng Qian et al., *Zhongguo wei shengme shuo bu? Lengzhan hou Meiguo dui Hua zhengci de wuqu* (Why does China say no? Errors in the U.S. policies toward China in the post-Cold War era) (Beijing: Xinshijie Chubanshe, 1996), 78.

112. Ibid.

113. *Nanfang ribao* (Southern daily), 12 May 1999. Other reports confirm the finding. See Yongnian Zheng, "Nationalism, Globalism, and Chna's International Rela-

tions," in *China's International Relations in the 21st Century*, ed. Weixing Hu, Gerald Chan, and Daojiong Zha (Lanham, MD: University Press of America, 2000), 107.

114. "Zhongguo ren xinmu zhong de shijie" (The world in Chinese eyes and mind), study by Horizon Research, 1999.

115. Ibid.

A Historiographical Note

1. The comment appears on the book jacket of David Shambaugh's *Beautiful Imperialists: China Perceives America, 1972–1990* (Princeton: Princeton University Press, 1991). In contrast to the lack of scholarship on Chinese understandings of the U.S., a vast body of literature exists on American images of China. Here are a few examples: Harold Isaacs, *Scratches on Our Minds: American Images of China and India* (New York: John Day, 1958); Robert McClellan, *The Heathen Chinese: A Study of American Attitude toward China, 1890–1905* (Columbus: Ohio State University Press, 1971); Warren I. Cohen, *America's Response to China; An Interpretative History of Sino-American Relations* (New York: John Wiley, 1971); John King Fairbank, *China Perceived: Images and Policies in Chinese-American Relations* (New York: Knopf, 1974); Benson Lee Grayson, ed., *The American Image of China* (New York: Frederick Ungar, 1979); Leonard A. Kusnitz, *Public Opinion and Foreign Policy: America's China Policy, 1949–1979* (Westport, CT: Greenwood Press, 1984); Steven W. Mosher, *China Misperceived: American Illusions and Chinese Reality* (New York: BasicBooks, 1990); Jonathan Goldstein, Jerry Israel, and Hilary Conroy, eds., *America Views China: American Images of China Then and Now* (Bethlehem, PA: Lehigh University Press, 1991).

2. John King Fairbank, *The United States and China* (Cambridge: Harvard University Press, 1976); John King Fairbank, ed., *The Chinese World Order: Traditional China's Foreign Relations* (Cambridge: Harvard University Press, 1968); Akira Iriye, *Across the Pacific: An Inner History of American–East Asian Relations* (New York: Harcourt, Brace and World, 1967); John G. Stoessinger, *Nations in Darkness: China, Russia, and America* (New York: Random House, 1971); Paul, A. Cohen, *Discovering History in China: American Historical Writing on the Recent Chinese Past* (New York: Columbia University Press, 1984).

3. Michael H. Hunt, *The Making of A Special Relationship: The United States and China to 1914* (New York: Columbia University Press, 1983), 300.

4. James Reardon-Anderson, *Yenan and the Great Powers: The Origins of Chinese Communist Foreign Policy, 1944–1946* (New York: Columbia University Press, 1980).

5. Zhang Shuguang, *Deterrence and Strategic Culture: Chinese-American Confrontations, 1949–1958* (Ithaca: Cornell University Press, 1993); Chen Jian, *China's Road to the Korean War: The Making of Sino-American Confrontation* (New York: Columbia University Press, 1994).

6. Michael M. Sheng, *Battling Western Imperialism: Mao, Stalin, and the United States* (Princeton: Princeton University Press, 1997).

7. For example, Tao Wenzhao, *Zhong Mei guanxi shi* (A history of Sino-American relations) (Shanghai: Shanghai Renmin Chubanshe, 2004), 3 vols.; Niu Jun, *From Yan'an to the World: The Origins and Development of Chinese Communist Foreign Policy,*

trans. Steven I. Levine (Norwalk : EastBridge, 2004); Michael Hunt and Niu Jun, *Toward a History of Chinese Communist Foreign Relations, 1920–1960: Personalities and Interpretive Approaches* (Washington, DC: Woodrow Wilson International Center for Scholars, [1995]); Zhang Baijia, "Zhou Enlai yu Maxieer shihua" (Zhou Enlai and the Marshall Mission to China), in *Jindaishi yanjiu* (Studies of modern history), no. 5 (September-October 1997); Yang Kuisong, "The Soviet Factor and the CCP's Policy toward the United States in the 1940s," in *Chinese Historians* 5, no. 1 (Spring 1992).

8. Thomas J. Christensen, *Useful Adversaries: Grand Strategy, Domestic Mobilization, and Sino-American Conflict, 1947–1958* (Princeton: Princeton University Press, 1996). The text quoted appears on page 242.

9. Jianwei Wang, *Limited Adversaries: Post–Cold War Sino-American Mutual Images* (New York: Oxford University Press, 2000).

10. Yang Yusheng, *Zhongguo ren de Meiguo guan: yige lishi de kaocha* (Chinese views of the United States: A historical investigation) (Shanghai: Fudan Daxue Chubanshe, 1996).

11. David Shambaugh, *Beautiful Imperialists: China Perceives America, 1972–1990* (Princeton: Princeton University Press, 1991).

12. Tu Wei-ming, "Chinese Perceptions of America," in *Dragon and Eagle: United States-China Relations : Past and Future*, ed. Michel Oksenberg and Robert B. Oxnam (New York: Basic Books, 1978).

13. Chang fang Chen, "Barbarian Paradise: Chinese Views of the United States, 1784–1911" (PhD diss., Indiana University, 1985).

14. David R. Arkush and Leo O. Lee, trans. and eds., *Land without Ghosts: Chinese Impressions of America from the Mid-nineteenth Century to the Present* (Berkeley: University of California Press, 1989).

15. Guo Xixiao, "The Climax of Sino-American Relations, 1944–1947" (PhD dissertation, University of Georgia, 1997).

16. Hongshan Li and Zhaohui Hong, eds., *Image, Perception, and the Making of U.S.-China Relations* (Lanham, MD: University Press of America, 1998).

17. Xiaomei Chen, *Occidentalism: A Theory of Counter-Discourse in Post-Mao China* (Lanham, MD: Rowman and Littlefield, 2003).

18. Claire Conceison, *Significant Other: Staging the American in China* (Honolulu: University of Hawaii Press, 2004).

19. Richard Madsen, *China and the American Dream: A Moral Inquiry* (Berkeley: University of California Press, 1995).

Bibliography

Sources in Chinese

Beijing ribao (Beijing daily). May-December 1957.

Beijing Xinwen Xuehui Diaochazu, ed. *Beijing duzhe, tingzhong, guanzhong diaocha* (A survey of readers, listeners, and viewers in Beijing). Beijing: Gongren Chubanshe, 1985.

Cao Juren. *Xinshi shilun* (On ten new phenomena). Hong Kong: Chuangken Chubanshe, n.d.

Cao Yu. *Minglang de tian* (Bright sky). Part 1 and 2, *Renmin wenxue* (People's literture), nos. 1 and 2, 1954.

Chang Huimin, Jin Chunming, and Huang Yuchong, eds. *"Wenge" shiqi guaishi guaiyu* (Strange events and strange language from the "Cultural Revolution"). Beijing: Qiushi Chubanshe, 1989.

Changxiao shu zhai (Best-seller excerpts), no. 1, 1998.

Chen Duxiu. *Chen Duxiu wenzhang xuanbian* (Collected works of Chen Duxiu). Edited by Sanlian Shudian. Vol. 1. Beijing: Sanlian Shudian, 1984.

Chiang Kai-shek. *Zongtong Jiang Gong sixiang yanlun zongji* (A complete collection of speeches and works of President Chiang). Taibei: n.d.

————. *Jiang zongtong ji* (Works of President Chiang). Edited by Guofang Yanjiu Yuan. Vol. 1. Taibei: Guofang Yanjiu Yuan, 1960.

Chuangye (Pioneers). Changchun, Jilin: Changchun Ddianying Zhipian Chang, 1975. Motion picture.

Chuban gongzuo (Work in publishing), no. 12, 1987; no. 6, 1988; no. 9, 1989.

Chuban Shiye Guanli Ju Banben Tushu Guan, ed. *Quanguo zong shumu* (Books published nationwide). For years 1976, 1977, 1978, 1979, 1980, 1981, and 1982. Beijing: Zhonghua Shuju, 1980–85.

Chuban tongxun (Publishing bulletin). June 1989.

Dalu dixia kanwu huibian (Mainland China's underground publications). Vols. 1–16. Taibei: Zhonggong Yanjiu Zazhishe, 1980.

Dangdai qiyejia (Contemporary entrpreneurs). March 1986.

Dazhong dianying (Popular cinema). January-November 1950, October 1953, August 1955, August 1960, December 1983, August 1981, and November 1986.

Ding Ziming et al. "Zhuanbian" (Transformation). No. Pub. info.

Ding Mingnan et al. *Zhong Mei quanxi shi lun wen ji* (Essays on the history of Sino-American relations). Vol. 2 of *Zhong Mei quanxi shi congshu* (Series on the history of Sino-American relations). Chongqing: Chongqing Chubanshe, 1988.
———. *Xin de shiye* (New vista). Vol. 3 of *Zhong Mei quanxi shi congshu* (Series on the history of Sino-American relations). Nanjing: Nanjing Daxue Chubanshe, 1991.
Dong Hengxun. *Meiguo xiandai xiaoshuo jian lun* (On modern American novelists). Beijing: Zhongguo Shehui Kexue Chubanshe, 1987.
Dushu (Reading). 1979–2000.
Dushu yuebao (Reader's monthly), no. 6, 1957.
Fan Baipishu xueshi ziliao (Study materials from the anti–White Paper campaign). Tianjin: Zhonggong Tianjin Shiwei Zong Xuexi Hui, 1949.
Fanyi tongxun (Translation bulletin), December 1983.
Fu Zhensheng. *Dongbei qu jianli xuanchuan wang de jingyan* (The ecxperience of the Northeastern Region in establishing a propaganda network). Shenyang, Liaonning: n.p.,1951.
Gansu ribao (Gansu daily), July 1957.
Gao Gao and Yan Jiaqi. *"Wenhua Da Geming" shi nian shi* (A history of the ten years of the "Great Cultural Revolution"). Tianjin: Tianjin Renmin Chubanshe, 1986.
Gao Jiansheng and Liu Ning. *Lihun wenti mianmian guan* (Facets of the divorce issue). Zhengzhou: Henan Renmin Chubanshe, 1989.
Gongfei de fan Mei yundong (The Communist bandits' anti-American movement). Taibei: Guofang Bu Qingbao Ju, 1961.
Gongren ribao, Sixiang Jiaoyu Bu, ed. *Aiqing, hunyin, daode* (Love, marriage, and morality). Beijing: Gongren Chubanshe, 1983.
Guangming ribao (Guangming daily), April-December 1957.
Guangzhou wenshi ziliao (xuanji) (Sources of the history of Guangzhou [collections]), no. 20, 1980.
Guoji shishi (Current international affairs), nos. 4, 6, and 7, 1972; nos. 3, 4, 5, 6, and 7, 1973.
Guoji wenti yanjiu (Studies in international affairs), no. 3, 1965.
Guoji wenti pinglun xuan (Selected commentaries on international affairs). Beijing: Beijing Renmin Chubanshe, 1971.
Hanfu. *Zhongguo yu Meiguo* (China and the United States of America). N.p.: Yinqing Chubanshe, 1937.
Hongqi (Red flag), nos. 1, 2, and 10, 1958; no. 7, 1959; nos. 15/16 and 18, 1961; no. 3/4, 1962; nos. 16 and 23/24, 1963; nos. 5 and 19, 1964; no. 1, 1968; no. 6, 1970; nos. 5 and 6, 1972; no. 8, 1982.
Hong Shen. *Zhe jiu shi Meiguo de shenghuo fangshi* (This is the American way of life). Beijing: Zhongguo Tushu Faxing Gongsi, 1951.
Hu Shi. *Hu Shi yanlun ji* (Collected speeches of Hu Shi). Vol. 2. Taibei: Huaguo Chubanshe, 1953.
———. *Hu Shi wencun* (Collected works of Hu Shi). No. 1, vol. 3. Taibei: Yuandong Tushu Gongci, 1953.
Hu Shi sixiang pipan (Criticism of Hu Shi's thought). Vols. 1–8. Beijing: Sanlian Shudian, 1955.

Hu Zonggang. "Bugai yiwang de Hu Xiansu" (Hu Xiansu should be remembered). *Shengming shijie* (World of Life), no. 8 (2006).

Huang Yuchong, Jin Chunming, and Chang Huimin, eds. *"Wenge" shiqi guaishi guaiyu* (Strange events and strange language from the "Cultural Revolution"). Beijing: Qiushi Chubanshe, 1989.

Jia Qingguo. *Zhongguo bu jinjin shuo bu* (China does not just say no). Beijing: Zhonghua Gongshang Lianhe Chubanshe, 1996.

Jiang Zilong. *Guohai riji* (Overseas diary). Beijing: Zhongguo Wenlian Chuban Gongsi, 1983.

Jiaoshi yuebao (Teachers' monthly), no. 3, 1951.

Jiaoxue yu yanjiu (Teaching and research), combined issue 8–9, 1957.

Jiefang ribao (Liberation daily), May-December 1957.

Jin Chunming, Huang Yuchong, and Chang Huimin, eds. *"Wenge" shiqi guaishi guaiyu* (Strange events and strange language from the "Cultural Revolution"). Beijing: Qiushi Chubanshe, 1989.

Jingji yanjiu (Economic studies), nos. 1, 2, 5, and 6, 1957.

Jinnian lai Gongfei dui wai guanxi biaojie (Chronology of recent events in the foreign relation of the Communist bandits). Taibei: Zhongguo Dalu Wenti Yanjiu Suo, 1972.

Kaifang shidai (The open door era), March 1989.

Ke Bainian et al. *Meiguo shouce* (The United States handbook). Beijing: Zhongwai Chubanshe, 1950.

Li Rui. *Yaodong zashu* (Notes from caves). Changsha, Hunan: Hunan Renmin Chubanshe, 1981.

Li Xin. *Minguo renwu zhuan* (Biographies of Republican China). Vol. 1. Beijing: Zhonghua Shuju, 1978.

Li Yong, ed. *Wenhua Da Geming zhong de mingren zhi yu* (Jail life of famous people in the Great Cultural Revolution). Beijing: Zhongyang Minzu Xueyuan Chubanshe, 1993.

Liang Biying and Tao Wenzhao, eds. *Meiquo yu xiandai Zhongguo* (The United States and modern China). *Zhonghua Meiquo xue congshu* (American studies in China series). Beijing: Zhongquo Shehui Kexue Chubanshe, 1996.

Liang Qichao. *Liang Qichao shiwen xuan* (Selected essays and poems: Prose and verse of Liang Qichao). Edited by Fang Zhiqin and Liu Sifen. Guangzhou: Guangdong Renmin Chubanshe, 1983.

———. *Xindalu youji* (Notes on a tour of the New Continent). Edited by He Shouzhen. Changsha, Hunan: Hunan Renmin Chubanshe, 1981.

———. *Xindalu youji* (Notes on a tour of the New Continent). N.p.: Xinmin Congbao, n.d.

Lin Yunhui et al., eds. *Renmin gongheguo chunqiu shilu* (Historical records of the People's Republic). Beijing: *Zhongguo Renmin Daxue Chubanshe*, 1992.

Ling Ya. *Shi ge lihun de nüren* (Ten divorced women). Chongqing: Chongqing Chubanshe, 1988.

Liu Ning and Gao Jiansheng. *Lihun wenti mianmian guan* (Various facets of the divorce issue). Zhengzhou, Henan: Henan Renmin Chubanshe, 1989.

Mao Zedong. *Mao Zedong ji* (Collected works of Mao Zedong). Edited by Takeuchi Minoru. Vol. 1. Tokyo, Sōsōsha, 1983.

———. *Mao Zedong ji bujuan* (Supplementary volume to the collected works of Mao Zedong). Edited by Takeuchi Minoru. Vol. 2. Tokyo, Sōsōsha, 1984.

Mao Zedong sixiang wansui (Long live Mao Zedong thought). No publication information.

Meiquo shenghuo fangshi (The American way of life). Beijing: Renmin Huabao She, 1951.

Meijun zhu Hua shiqi de xuezhai (Crimes committed by American troops during their occupation of China). Beijing: Renmin Chubanshe, 1950.

Mingfang huiyi (Recollections of the "blooming and contending"). N.p.: Zilian Chubanshe, 1966.

Minguo dangan (Archives of the Republic of China), no. 1, 1991.

Minzhu Zhongguo (Democratic China), November 1993.

Niu Jun, *Cong Yanan zou xiang shi jie: Zhongguo gong chan dang dui wai guan xi di qi yuan* (From Yanan to the world: Origins of Chinese Communist foreign relations). Fuzhou: Fujian Renmin Chubanshe, 1992.

Peng Qian, Yang Mingjie, and Xu Deren. *Zhongguo wei shengme shuo bu? Lengzhan hou Meiguo dui Hua zhengci de wuqu* (Why does China say no? Errors in the United States' China policies in the post–Cold War era). Beijing: Xinshijie Chubanshe, 1996.

Pipan wo de zichanjieji sixiang (Denounce my bourgeois ideas). Beijing: Wushi Niandai Chubanshe, 1952.

Qingnian (Youth), June 1988.

Qiushi (Search for truth), no. 12, 1991.

Qunzhong (The Masses), 1945–1949.

Renmin ribao (People's daily).

Renmin Ribao Bianjibu and *Hongqi* Zazhi Bianjibu. *Zai Zhanzheng yu heping wenti shang de liang tiao luxian* (Two different lines on the issue of war and peace). Beijing: Renmin Chubanshe, 1963.

Renwen kexue xuebao (Journal of the humanities and social sciences), no. 1, 1958.

Ru Xin, ed. *Shehui lanpi shu: 1998 nian de Zhongguo shehui xingshi fenxi yu yuce* (The bluebook on social conditions: Trends, analyses, and predictions, 1998). Beijing: Zhongguo Shehui Kexue Chubashe, 1998.

Sanlian Shudian, ed. *Hu Shi cixiang pipan* (Criticism of Hu Shi's thought). Vols. 1–8. Beijing: Sanlian Shudian, 1955.

Shao Daosheng. *Zhongguo qingshaonian fanzui de shehuixue sikao* (Sociological reflections on China's youth crimes). Beijing: Shehui Kexue Wenxian Chubanshe, 1987.

Shen Jiru. *Zhongguo bu dang bu xiansheng* (China is not Mr. No). Beijing: Dangdai Zhongguo Chubanshe, 1998.

Shi Qili. *Liu Mei xuesheng gui guo ji* (Recollections of an America-returned student). Hong Kong: Ziyou Chubanshe, 1952.

Shijie zhishi (Knowledge on the world), nos. 9, 11, and 14, 1957.

Shoudu gaodeng xuexiao fan youpai douzheng de juda shengli (A great victory in the anti-rightist movement at colleges and universities in Beijing). Beijing: Beijing Chubanshe, 1957.

Song Qiang et al. *Zhongguo keyi shuo bu* (China can say no). Beijing: Zhonghua Gongshang Lianhe Chubanshe, 1996.

Sun Yat-sen. *Sun Zhongshan quanji* (Complete works of Sun Yat-sen). Edited by Guangdong Shekeyuan Lishi Suo, Zhongguo Shekeyuan Jindaishi Suo, and Zhongshan Daxue Song Zhongshan Yanjiu Shi. Vols. 1–8. Beijing: Zhonghua Shuju, 1986.

———. *Guofu quanji* (Complete works of the Founding Father). Edited by Guomindang Dangshi Weiyuanhui. Taibei: Guomindang Dangshi Weiyuanhui, 1973.

Sun Zhenzhi. *Zhongguoren yu waiguoren* (The Chinese and foreigners). Beijing: Guojiwenhua Chuban Gongsi, 1997.

Taofen. *Pingzong yiyu* (Travel recollections). Shanghai: Shenghuo Shudian, 1937.

Tao Wenzhao. *Zhong Mei guanxi shi* (A history of Sino-American relations). Vols. 1–3. Shanghai: Shanghai Renmin Chubanshe, 2004.

Tao Wenzhao and Liang Biying, eds. *Meiquo yu jin xian dai Zhongquo* (The United States and modern China). *Zhonghua Meiquo xue congshu* (American studies in China series). Beijing: Zhongquo Shehui Kexue Chubanshe, 1996.

Tao Xingzhi. *Tao Xingzhi quanji* (Complete works of Tao Xingzhi). Edited by Huazhong Shifan Xueyuan Jiaoyu Kexue Yanjiu Suo. Vols. 1–8. Changsha, Hunan: Hunan Jiaoyu Chubanshe, 1978–1992.

Tianjin fanzui wenti diaocha wenji (Collected articles based on a survey on crimes in Tianjin). Tianjin: Tianjin Remin Chubanshe, 1985.

Tuan Zhongyang Qingyun Shi Yanjiushi and Zhongyang Dangan Guan, eds. *Zhonggong Zhongyang qingnian yundong wenjian xuanbian* (Selected documents of the Chinese Communist Party on youth movement). Beijing: Zhongguo Qingnian Chubanshe, 1988.

Wang Jisi, ed. *Wenming yu guoji zhengzhi: Zhongguo xuezhe ping Hantingdun de wenming chongtu lun* (Civilization and international politics: Chinese scholars on Huntington's theory on the clash of civilizations). Shanghai: Shanghai Renmin Chubanshe, 1995.

Wang Renzhi and Zhang Dan, eds. *Xinhai Geming qian shi nian jian shilun xuanji* (Selected commentaries on contemporary affairs from the decade preceding the Revolution of 1911). Vol. 1. Beijing: Sanlian Shudian, 1960.

Wang Tingyue. *Yingjiu Meiguo bing: Zhongguo dihou kang Ri junmin jiuyuan Meiguo feixingyuan jishi* (Rescue U.S. airmen: Chinese anti-Japanese troops and civilians save U.S. pilots). Beijing: Zhonggong Dangshi Chubanshe, 2005.

Wang Yongjun et al. *Zhongguo xiandai shi renwu zhuan* (Historical figures in modern China). Chengdu, Sichuan: Sichuan Renmin Chubanshe, 1986.

Wenhua shiliao (Materials of cultural history), no. 5, 1983; no. 8, 1984.

Wenhui yuekan (Wenhui monthly), no. 1, 1990.

Wenshi ziliao xuanji (Selected historical materials), no. 19, 1986.

Wei Zichu. *Meidi zai Hua jingji qinlüe* (Imperialist America's economic invasion of China). Beijing: Renmin Chubanshe, 1951.

Wu Jisong. *Yige Zhongguo ren kan shijie* (The world through the eyes of a Chinese). Beijing: Gongren Chubanshe, 1987.

Wu Xiaoli. *Zu yin* (Echoes of footsteps). Beijing: Huayi Chubanshe, 1998.

Xiandai funü (Modern women), nos. 2 and 5, 1951.

Xiaoshuolin (Fiction), no. 6, 1983.

Xiaoxue jiaoshi (Elementary school teacher), no. 7, 1953.

Xinhua wenzhai (Xinhua digest), no. 1, 1998.

Xinwen yanjiu ziliao (Materials of journalist studies in history), no. 18, 1983.

Xinwen zhanxian (Journalist front), nos. 5 and 6, 1981.

Xin jianshe (New construction), no. 12, 1957; no. 5, 1958.

Xin jiaoyu (New education), no. 3, 1951.

Xin qingnian (New youth), 1915.

Xinhua banyuekan (Xinhua biweekly), 1957–58.

Xuanchuan dongtai (xuanbian), 1980 (Trends in propaganda, 1980 collection). Beijing: Zhongguo Shehui Kexue Chubanshe, 1981.

Xuanchuan shouce (Propaganda handbook), no. 1, 1951.

Xu Youchun, ed. *Minguo renwu da cidian* (Biographical dictionary for the Republican period). Shijiazhuang, Hebei: Hebei Renmin Chubanshe, 1991.

Yan Jiaqi and Gao Gao. *Wenhua Da Geming shi nian shi* (A history of the ten years of the Great Cultural Revolution). Tianjin: Tianjin Renmin Chubanshe, 1986.

Yang Gang. *Meiquo zhaji* (Notes on America). Beijing, Shijie Zhishi Chubanshe, 1951.

Yang Ming. *Taofen de liuwang shenghuo* (Taofen in exile). N.p.: Sanlian Shudian, 1951.

Yang Yusheng. *Zhongquo ren de Meiquo guan—yige lishi de kaocha* (Chinese views of the United States: A historical investigation). Vol. 15 of Zhong Mei guanxi yanjiu congshu (The history of Sino-American relations series), ed. Wang Xi. Shanghai: Fudan Daxue Chubanshe, 1996.

Yilin (Translations), 1981–84.

Zhang Dan and Wang Renzhi, eds. *Xinhai Geming qian shi nian jian shilun xuanji* (Selected commentaries on contemporary affairs from the decade preceding the Revolution of 1911). Vol. 1. Beijing: Sanlian Shudian, 1960.

[Zhang] Hanfu. *Zhongguo yu Meiguo* (China and the United States). N.p.: Yinqing Chubanshe, 1937.

Zhang Yang. *Di erci woshou* (The second handshake). Beijing: Zhongguo Qingnian Chubanshe, 1979.

Zhang Weiping, ed. *Liangzhong zhanlüe: "heping yianbian" yu "heping fangbian"* (Two conflicting strategies: Peaceful transformation and peaceful resistance). Chongqing: Chongqing Chubanshe, 1991.

Zhang Wentian. *Lütu* (The journey). Shanghai: Shangwu Yinshuguan, 1925.

———. *Zhang wentian zaonian wenxue zuopin xuan* (Selected works of Zhang Wentian from his early years). Edited by Cheng Zhongyuan. Beijing: Renmin Chubanshe, 1983.

Zhang Xianliang. *Lühua shu* (Green trees are green). Tianjin:, Baihua Chubanshe, 1986.

Zhangwang Bianjibu, ed. *Zhongguo wenti lunji* (Collected papers on the China problem). Hong Kong: Zilian Chubanshe, 1966.

Zhengbao xunkan (Zhengbao magazine), no. 8, 1946.

Zhengfa yanjiu (Political and legal studies), no 2, 1965.

Zhonggong jimi wenjian huibian (A collection of the secret documents of the Chinese Communist Party). Taibei: Guoli Zhengji Daxue Guoji Guanxi Yanjiu Zhongxin, 1978.

Zhonggong Zhongyang Shujichu Yanjiushi and Zhonggong Zhongyang Wenxian Yanjiushi, eds. *Jianchi sixiang jiben yuanze, fandui zichajieji ziyouhua* (Uphold four cardinal principles and oppose bourgeois liberaliazation). Beijing: Renmin Chubanshe, 1987.

Zhonggong Zhongyang Shujichu Yanjiushi Wenhuazu, ed. *Dang he guojia lingdaoren tan wenyi* (Party and state leaders on arts and literature). Beijing: Wenhua Yishu Chubanshe, 1982.

Zhongguo fanyi (Translation in China), no. 4, 1986.

Zhongguo guangbo dianshi nianjian (The China yearbook on radio, broadcast, and television), 1986, 1987, and 1988. Beijing: Zhongguo Guangbo Dianshi Chubanshe, 1987–89.

Zhongguo guanggao (Chinese advertising), no. 1, 1998.

"Zhongguo ren xinmu zhong de shijie" (The world in Chinese eyes and mind). Beijing: Horizon Research, 1999.

Zhongguo qingnian (Chinese youth), no. 23, 1965; no. 11, 1980; no. 4, 1985; no. 8, 1986; combined issue 1/2, 1987.

Zhongguo qiyejia (China's entrepreneurs), nos. 1, 2, 3, and 6, 1987; no. 5, 1988.

Zhongguo xiandai shi renwu zhuan (Historical figures in modern China). Chengdu, Cichuan: Cichuan Renmin Chubanshe, 1986.

Zhongqingnian jingji luntan (Forum for young and middle-aged economists), no. 3, 1985.

Zhongyang Dangan Guan, ed. *Zhonggong Zhongyang wenjian xuanji* (Selected documents of the Central Committee of the Chinese Communist Party). Vol. 9. Beijing: Zhongyang Dangxiao, 1989.

Zhongyang Renmin Zhengfu Chuban Zongshu Bianyi Ju, ed. *Quanguo fanyi tushu mulu: 1950* (A national bibliography of translated books: 1950). Beijing: Zhongyang Renmin Zhengfu Chuban Zongshu Bianyi Ju, 1951.

Zhongyang Renmin Zhengfu Chuban Zongshu Tushu Guan, ed. *1951 nian di yi ji quan guo xinshumu* (New books nationwide: the first quarter, 1951). Beijing, Zhongyang Renmin Zhengfu Chuban Zongshu Tushu Guan, 1951.

Zhou Yi. *Tao Xingzhi huanxing shijie lu* (Tao Xingzhi's journey around the globe). Nanjing, Jiangsu: Jiangsu Renmin Chubanshe, 1987.

Zou Taofen. *Taofen wenji* (Collected works of Taofen). Hong Kong: Salian Shudian, 1957.

[Zou] Taofen. *Pingzong yiyu* (Travel recollections). Shanghai: Shenghuo Shudian, 1937.

Zuigao Renmin Fayuan gongbao (The Supreme People's Court bulletin), no. 2, 1987.

Sources in English

Aaron, Daniel. "American Studies and the Chinese State." *China Exchange News* 18, no. 3 (September 1990).

Ames, Roger T., and David Hall. *The Democracy of the Dead: Dewey, Confucius, and the Hope for Democracy in China.* Chicago and Lasalle: Open Court, 1999.

Anderson, David L. *Imperialism and Idealism: American Diplomats in China, 1861–1898.* Bloomington: Indiana University Press, 1985.

Arkush, R. David. *Fei Xiaotong and Sociology in Revolutionary China.* Cambridge: Harvard University Press, 1981.

————, and Leo O. Lee, trans. and eds. *Land without Ghosts: Chinese Impressions of America from the Mid-Nineteenth Century to the Present.* Berkeley: University of California Press, 1989.

Barnds, William, ed. *China and America: The Search for a New Relationship.* New York: New York University Press, 1977.

Barrett, David D. *Dixie Mission: The United States Army Observer Group in Yenan, 1944.* Berkeley: University of California Press, 1970.

————. Manuscript on the Dixie Mission, Box 1. Accession No. 48005-9.14, Hoover Institution on War, Revolution and Peace, 71.

Beidler, Peter G., and Shi Jian. "Translating America: Books about the US Available in a Provincial Chinese City." *China Exchange News* 18, no. 3 (September 1989).

Bieler, Stacey. *"Patriots" or "Traitors"?: A History of American-Educated Chinese Students.* Armonk, NY: M. E. Sharpe, 2003.

Bowers, John Z. *Western Medicine in a Chinese Palace: Peking Union Medical College, 1917–1951.* N.p.: The Hosiah Macy, Jr. Foundation, 1972.

Brodsgaard, Kjeld Erik, and Susan Young. *State Capacity in East Asia: China, Taiwan, Vietnam, and Japan.* New York: Oxford University Press, 2000.

Buck, Peter. *American Science and Modern China, 1876–1936.* Cambridge: Cambridge University Press, 1980.

Bullock, Mary Brown. *An American Transplant: The Rockefeller Foundation and Peking Union Medical College.* Berkeley: University of California Press, 1980.

Bureau for the Compilation and Translation of Works of Marx, Engels, Lenin, and Stalin under the Central Committee of the Communist Party of China, ed. and trans. l. *Fundamental Issues in Present-day China.* Beijing: Foreign Languages Press, 1987.

Chang, Man. *The People's Daily and the Red Flag Magazine during the Cultural Revolution.* Hong Kong: Union Research Institute, 1969.

Cheek, Timothy, Roderick MacFarquhar, and Eugene Wu, eds. *The Secret Speeches of Chairman Mao: From the Hundred Flowers to the Great Leap Forward.* Cambridge: Harvard University Press, 1989.

Cheek, Timothy, Merle Goldman, and Carole Lee Hamrin, eds. *China's Intellectuals and the State: In Search of a New Relationship.* Cambridge: Harvard University Press, 1987.

Chen, Chang-fang. "Barbarian Paradise: Chinese Views of the United States, 1784–1911," PhD dissertation. Indiana University, 1985.

Chen, Jian. *China's Road to the Korean War: The Making of the Sino-American Confrontation.* New York: Columbia University Press, 1994.

Chen, Theodore H. E. *Thought Reform of the Chinese Intellectuals.* Hong Kong: Hong Kong University Press, 1960.

Chen, Xiaomei. *Occidentalism: A Theory of Counter-Discourse in Post-Mao China.* Lanham, MD: Rowman and Littlefield, 2003.

Cheng, Chi-pao, ed. *Chinese American Cultural Relations.* New York: China Institute in America and the American Association of Teachers of Chinese Language and Culture, 1965.

Chennault, Claire. The Claire Chennault collection, accession no. 67002-8M.39, Hoover Institution on War, Revolution and Peace.

Chiu, Kun-shuan. "Chinese Policy toward the United States under Deng Xiaoping, 1979–1988." PhD dissertation. George Washington University, 1990.

Christensen, Thomas J. *Useful Adversaries: Grand Strategy, Domestic Mobilization, and Sino-American Conflict, 1947–1958*. Princeton: Princeton University Press, 1996.

Christian, Sutton. The Sutton collection, accession no. 78038-8M.07, Hoover Institution on War, Revolution, and Peace.

Chu, Godwin C., ed. *Popular Media in China: Shaping New Cultural Pattern*. Honolulu: University of Hawaii Press, 1978.

Chu, T. K., trans. *Chinese Students Encounter America*. Seattle: University of Washington Press, 2003.

Clark, Donald N. "Bitter Friendship: Understanding Anti-Americanism in South Korea." In *Korea Briefing, 1991*, ed. Donald N. Clark. Boulder: Westview Press, in association with the Asia Society, 1991.

Clough, Ralph N. *Chinese Elites: World View and Perceptions of the U.S.* Research Report R-15-82. Washington. D.C.: International Communication Agency, 1982.

Cohen, Paul A. *Discovering History in China: American Historical Writing on the Recent Chinese Past*. New York: Columbia University Press, 1984.

Cohen, Warren I. *America's Response to China: An Interpretative History of Sino-American Relations*. New York: John Wiley and Sons, 1971.

Colombo, Claudias Michael. "Chinese Communist Perceptions of the Foreign Policy of JFK, 1961–1963." PhD dissertation. New York University, 1982.

Conceison, Claire. *Significant Other: Staging the American in China*. Honolulu: University of Hawaii Press, 2004.

Conroy, Hilary, Jonathan Goldstein, and Jerry Israel, eds. *America Views China: American Images of China Then and Now*. Bethlehem, PA: Lehigh University Press, 1991.

Danton, George H. *The Culture Contacts of the United States: The Earliest Sino-American Cultural Contacts, 1784–1844*. New York: Octagon Books, 1974.

Das, Naranarayan. *China's Hundred Weeds: A Study of the Anti-rightist Campaign in China, 1957–58*. Calcutta: K. P. Bagchi, 1979.

Davis, Elizabeth Van Wie. *Chinese Perspectives on Sino-American Relations 1950–2000*. Lewiston, NY: Mellen Press, 2000.

Deeny, John. "American Studies and the Open Door." *China Exchange News* 18, no. 3 (September 1989).

Deng, Frank. "American Studies at Beijing Foreign Studies University: A Decade in Retrospect." *China Exchange News* 18, no. 3 (September 1989).

Department of State, The U.S. *The China White Paper*. Stanford: Stanford University Press, 1967.

———. Department of State Decimal File, 1945–1949, National Archives, Washington, DC.

Duffy, William, and Egon Neuberger. *Comparative Economic Systems: A Decision-making Approach*. Boston: Allyn and Bacon, 1976.

Fairbank, John K. *China Perceived: Images and Policies in Chinese-American Relations*. New York: Alfred A. Knopf, 1974.

———, ed. *The Chinese World Order: Traditional China's Foreign Relations*. Cambridge: Harvard University Press, 1968.

———. *The United States and China*, 3rd ed. Cambridge: Harvard University Press, 1971.

Fairbank, Wilma. *America's Cultural Experiment in China: 1942–1949.* Cultural Relations Programs of the U.S. Department of State, Historical Studies, Number 1, Department of State Publication 8839, International Information and Cultural series 108, released in June 1976.

Forslund, Catherine. *Anna Chennault: Informal Diplomacy and Asian Relations.* Wilmington, DE: Scholarly Resources, Inc., 2002.

Friesen, Oris, and Stephen R. MacKinnon. *China Reporting: An Oral History of American Journalism in the 1930s and 1940s.* Berkeley: University of California Press, 1990.

Gaenslen, Fritz. "Culture and Decision Making in China, Japan, Russia, and the United States." *World Politics* 39, no. 1 (October 1986).

Garson, Robert. *The United States and China since 1949: A Troubled Affair.* Madison, NJ: Fairleigh Dickinson University Press, 1994.

Gewurtz, Margo Speisman. *Between America and Russia: Chinese Student Radicalism and the Travel Books of Tsou T'ao-fen, 1933–1937.* Toronto: University of Toronto-York University Joint Center on Modern East Asia, 1975.

Goldman, Merle. *China's Intellectuals: Advise and Dissent.* Cambridge: Harvard University Press, 1988.

———, Timothy Cheek, and Carole Lee Hamrin, eds. *China's Intellectuals and the State: In Search of a New Relationship.* Cambridge: Harvard University Press, 1987.

Goldstein, Jonathan, Jerry Israel, and Hilary Conroy, eds. *America Views China: American Images of China Then and Now.* Bethlchem, PA: Lehigh University Press, 1991.

Grayson, Benson Lee, ed. *The American Image of China.* New York: Frederick Ungar, 1979.

Hall, David L., and Rodger T. Ames. *The Democracy of the Dead: Dewey, Confucius, and the Hope for Democracy in China.* Chicago and Lasalle: Open Court, 1999.

Hamrin, Carole Lee, Timothy Cheek, and Merle Goldman, eds. *China's Intellectuals and the State: In Search of a New Relationship.* Cambridge: Harvard University Press, 1987.

Harding, Harry. *A Fragile Relationship: The United States and China since 1972.* Washington, DC: The Brookings Institution, 1992.

Hawkins, John. *The Media in China.* London: Nord Media, 1980.

He, Di. "The Evolution of the Chinese Communist Party's Policy toward the United States, 1944–1949," in *Sino-American Relations, 1945–1955*, ed. Harry Harding and Yuan Ming. Wilmington, DE: SR Books, 1989.

Hiltz, Jackie, Philip West, and Steven I. Levine, eds. *America's Wars in Asia: A Cultural Approach to History and Memory.* Armonk, NY: M.E. Sharpe, 1998.

Hollander, Paul. *Anti-Americanism: Critiques at Home and Abroad, 1965–1990.* New York: Oxford University Press, 1992.

Hong, Zhaohui, and Li Hongshan, eds. *Image, Perception, and the Making of U.S.-China Relations.* Lanham, MD: University Press of America, 1998.

Hsiao, Hsin-huang Michael. "From Europe to North America: A Structural Analysis of the Core Paradigm Shift in the Peripheral Development of Sociology in Twentieth Century China." In *China and Europe in the Twentieth Century*, ed. Yu-ming Shaw. Taibei: National Chengchi University, 1986.

Hu, Daojiong, ed. *China's International Relations in the 21st Century.* Lanham, MD: University Press of America, 2000.

Hu, Weixing, Gerald Cha, and Daojiong Zha. *China's International Relations in the 21st Century: Dynamics and Paradigm Shifts.* Lanham, MD: University Press of America, 2000.

Hunt, Michael H. "Themes in Traditional and Modern Chinese Images of America." In *Mutual Images and US-China Relations*, Occasional Paper No. 32, the Asian Program, Woodrow Wilson International Center for Scholars, Washington, DC, June 1988.

———. *The Making of a Special Relationship: The United States and China to 1914.* New York: Columbia University Press, 1983.

———, and Niu Jun, eds. *Toward A History of Chinese Communist Foreign Relations, 1920s-1960s: Personalities and Interpretive Approaches.* Washington, DC: Woodrow Wilson International Center for Scholars, [1995].

Huntington, Samuel P. *The Clash of Civilizations and the Remaking of World Order.* New York: Simon and Schuster, 1993.

———. "The Clash of Civilizations?" *Foreign Affairs*, Summer 1993.

Iriye, Akira. *Mutual Images: Essays in American-Japanese Relations.* Cambridge: Harvard University Press, 1975.

Isaacs, Harold. *Scratches on Our Minds: American Images of China and India*, New York: The John Day Co., 1958.

Israel, Jerry, Jonathan Goldstein, and Hilary Conroy, eds. *America Views China: American Images of China Then and Now.* Bethlehem, PA: Lehigh University Press, 1991.

Iyer, Pico. *Video Night in Kathmandu: And Other Reports from the Not-So-Far East.* New York: Random House, 1989.

Kapur, Harish, ed. *As China Sees the World: Perceptions of Chinese Scholars.* London: Frances Pinter, 1987.

Kirby, William C., ed. *Realms of Freedom in Modern China.* Stanford: Stanford University Press, 2003.

King, Ambrose Yeo Chi, and Tse Sang Wang. "The Development and Death of Chinese Academic Sociology: A Chapter in the Sociology of Sociology." *Modern Asian Studies* 12, no. 1. (1978): 37–58.

Kissinger, Henry. *Years of Upheaval.* Boston: Little, Brown, 1982.

Kuhn, Robert Lawrence. *The Man Who Changed China: The Life and Legacy of Jiang Zemin.* New York: Crown, 2004.

Kusnitz, Leonard A. *Public Opinion and Foreign Policy: America's China Policy, 1949–1979.* Westport, CT: Greenwood Press, 1984.

Lampton, David M., with Joyce A. Madancy, and Kristen M. Williams, eds. *A Relationship Restored: Trends in U.S.-China Educational Exchanges, 1978–1984.* Washington, DC: National Academy Press, 1986.

Laotz, Terry E. "All That Glitters Is Not Gold." In *China Facts & Figures Annual*, vol. 4 (1981), ed. John C. Scherer. Gulf Breeze, FL: Academic International Press, 1981.

Latourette, Kenneth S. *The History of Early Relations between the United States and China, 1784-1844.* 1917. New York: Kraus Reprint Corporation, 1964.

Lee, Leo O., and R. David Arkush, trans. and eds. *Land without Ghosts: Chinese Impressions of America from the Mid-Nineteenth Century to the Present.* Berkeley: University of California Press, 1989.

Levine, Steven I. *Anvil of Victory: The Communist Revolution in Manchuria, 1945–1948.* New York: Columbia University Press, 1987.

———, Philip West, and Jackie Hiltz, eds. *America's Wars in Asia: A Cultural Approach to History and Memory.* Armonk, NY: M. E. Sharpe, 1998.

Li, Hanlin, et al. "Chinese Sociology, 1898–1986." *Social Forces* 65, no. 3. (Mar. 1987): 612–40.

Li, Hongshan, and Zhaohui Hong, eds. *Image, Perception, and the Making of U.S.-China Relations.* Lanham, MD: University Press of America, 1998.

Li, Moying. "Hu Shi and His Deweyan Reconstruction of Chinese History." PhD dissertation. Boston University, 1990.

Li, Peishan. "Genetics in China: The Qingdao Symposium of 1956." *Isis* 79, no. 2. (June 1988): 227–36.

Li, Tszesun. "A Comparative Study of Reciprocal Coverage of the People's Republic of China in the *Washington Post* and the United States in the *People's Daily* in 1986: A Case Study of Foreign News within the Context of the Debate of the New World Information Order." EdD dissertation. Oklahoma State University, 1988.

Liao, Kuang-sheng. *Antiforeignism and Modernziation in China, 1860–1980.* New York: St. Martin's Press, 1984.

Lieberthal, Kenneth. "Domestic Forces and Sino-American Relations." in *Living with China: U.S.-China Relations in the Twenty-First Century,* ed. Ezra F. Vogel. New York: W. W. Norton, 1997.

Link, Perry. *Evening Chats in Beijing: Probing China's Predicament.* New York: W. W. Norton, 1992.

———, Richard Madsen, and Paul G. Pickowicz, eds. *Unofficial China: Popular Culture and Thought in the People's Republic.* Boulder: Westview Press, 1989.

MacFarquhar, Roderick. *The Origins of the Cultural Revolution,* 3 vols. New York: Columbia University Press, 1991–97.

———, Timothy Cheek, and Eugene Wu, eds. *The Secret Speeches of Chairman Mao: From the Hundred Flowers to the Great Leap Forward.* Cambridge: Council on East Asian Studies / Harvard University, 1989.

MacKinnon, Janice R., and Stephen R. MacKinnon. *Agnes Smedley: The Life and Times of an American Radical.* Berkeley: University of California Press, 1988.

MacKinnon, Stephen R., and Oris Friesen. *China Reporting: An Oral History of American Journalism in the 1930s and 1940s.* Berkeley: University of California Press, 1990.

MacKinnon, Stephen R., and Janice R. MacKinnon. *Agnes Smedley: The Life and Times of an American Radical.* Berkeley: University of California Press, 1988.

Madancy, Joyce A., David M. Lampton, and Kristen M. Williams, eds. *A Relationship Restored: Trends in U.S.-China Educational Exchanges, 1978–1984.* Washington, DC: National Academy Press, 1986.

Madsen, Richard, *China and the American Dream: A Moral Inquiry.* Berkeley: University of California Press, 1995.

———, Perry Link, and Paul G. Pickowicz, eds. *Unofficial China: Popular Culture and Thought in the People's Republic.* Boulder: Westview Press, 1989.

Mao Tse-tung [Mao Zedong]. *People of the World, Unite and Defeat the U.S Aggressors and All Their Lackeys: Statements Supporting the American Negroes and the Peoples of Southern Vietnam, Panama, Japan, the Congo and the Domini-*

can Republic in Their Just Struggle Against U.S. Imperialism. Beijing: Foreign Languages Press, 1966.

———. Selected Works of Mao Tse-tung. Vol. 2. London: Lawrence and Wishart, 1954.

———. Selected Works. Vols. 2 and 4. Beijing: Foreign Language Press, 1969.

Martin, Dorothea A. L. The Making of a Sino-Marxist World View: Perceptions and Interpretations of World History in the People's Republic of China. Armonk, NY: M. E. Sharpe, 1990.

McClellan, Robert. The Heathen Chinese: A Study of American Attitude toward China, 1890–1905. Columbus: Ohio State University Press, 1971.

McGiffert, Carola, ed. Chinese Images of the United States. Washington, DC: Center for Strategic and International Studies, 2005.

McGough, James P., trans. Fei Hsiao-t'ung: The Dilemma of a Chinese Intellectual. White Plains: M. E. Sharpe, 1979.

Meisner, Maurice. Mao's China and After. New York: The Free Press, 1999.

Miller, Arthur. Salesman in Beijing. New York: The Viking Press, 1984.

Mosher, Steven W. China Misperceived: American Illusions and Chinese Reality. New York: Basic Books, 1990.

Nash, Jay Robert, and Stanley Ralph Ross. The Motion Picture Guide. Vol. 2. Chicago: Cinebooks, 1985.

Nathan, J. Andrew. Chinese Democracy. New York: Knopf, 1985.

———. "The Place of Values in Cross-Cultural Studies: The Example of Democracy in China." In Ideas Across Cultures: Essays on Chinese Thought in Honor of Benjamin I. Schwartz, ed. Paul A. Cohen and Merle Goldman. Cambridge: Harvard University Press, 1990.

Neuberger, Egon, and William J. Duffy. Comparative Economic Systems: A Decision-making Approach. Boston: Allyn and Bacon, 1976.

Nie, Hualing. Literature of the Hundred Flowers. New York: Columbia University Press, 1981.

Niu, Jun. From Yan'an to the World: The Origins and Development of Chinese Communist Foreign Policy. Translated by Steven I. Levine. Norwalk: EastBridge, 2004.

———, and Michael H. Hunt, eds. Toward A History of Chinese Communist Foreign Relations, 1920s-1960s: Personalities and Interpretive Approaches. Washington, DC: Woodrow Wilson International Center for Scholars, [1995].

Orleans, Leo A. Chinese Students in America: Policies, Issues, and Numbers. Washington, DC: National Academy Press, 1988.

Pan, Zhongdang, ed. To See Ourselves: Comparing Traditional Chinese and American Cultural Values. Boulder: Westview Press, 1994.

———, Perry Link, and Richard Madsen, eds. Unofficial China: Popular Culture and Thought in the People's Republic. Boulder: Westview Press, 1989.

Qian, Ning. Chinese Students Encounter America. Translated by T. K. Chu. Seattle: University of Washington Press, 2003.

Reardon-Anderson, James. Yenan and the Great Powers: The Origins of Chinese Communist Foreign Policy, 1944–1946. New York: Columbia University Press, 1980.

Ross, Robert S., ed. After the Cold War: Domestic Factors and U.S.-China Relations. Armonk: M. E. Sharpe, 1998.

Ross, Stanley Ralph, and Jay Robert Nash. *The Motion Picture Guide*. Vol. 2. Chicago: Cinebooks, 1985.

Rubinstein, Alvin Z., and Donald E. Smith, eds. *Anti-Americanism in the Third World: Implications for U.S. Foreign Policy*. New York: Praeger, 1985.

Rudolph, Jorg-Meinhard. *Cankao Xiaoxi: Foreign News in the Propaganda System of the People's Republic of China*. Occasional Papers/Reprint Series in Contemporary Asian Studies, no. 6 (1984). College Park: University of Maryland School of Law.

Ruse, Michael. *Sociobiology: Sense or Nonsense?* Dordrecht: Reidel, 1979.

Scherer, John L., ed. *China Figures and Facts Annual*. Vols. 3, 4, 5, 6 and 8. Gulf Breeze, FL: Academic International Press, 1981–87.

Schwarcz, Vera. *Chinese Enlightenment: Intellectuals and the Legacy of the May Fourth Movement of 1919*. Berkeley: University of California Press, 1990.

Shambaugh, David. "Anti-Americanism in China." *Annals of the American Academy of Political and Social Sciences*, May 1988.

———. *Beautiful Imperialism: China Perceives America, 1972–1990*. Princeton: Princeton University Press, 1991.

———. "Books about America in the People's Republic of China, 1977–1987." Washington, DC: U.S. Information Agency, 1988.

———. "China's America Watchers." *Problems of Communism* 37, May-August 1988.

———. "Conflicting Chinese Images of America in the People's Republic of China." In *Mutual Images and US-China Relations,* Occasional Paper No. 32 of the Asia Program, Woodrow Wilson International Center for Scholars. Washington, DC: Woodrow Wilson International Center for Scholars, 1988.

———. "Coverage of the United States in Key Chinese Periodicals during 1984." Washington, DC: U.S. Information Agency, 1984.

Sheng, Michael M. *Battling Western Imperialism: Mao, Stalin, and the United States*. Princeton: Princeton University Press, 1997.

Shi, Jian and Peter G. Beidler. "Translating America: Books about the US Available in a Provincial Chinese City." *China Exchange News* 18, no. 3 (September 1989).

Smith, Richard J. *China's Cultural Heritage: Tthe Ch'ing Dynasty, 1644–1912*. 2nd edition. Boulder: Westview Press, 1994.

Snow, Edgar. *Red Star Over China: The Classic Account of the Birth of Chinese Communism*. New York, Grove Press, 1994. First revised and enlarged edition.

Spence, Jonathan D. *The Search for Modern China*. New York: W. W. Norton, 1990.

———. Introduction. In Wu Tingfang, *America through the Spectacles of an Oriental Diplomat*. London: Anthem Press, 2007.

———. *To Change China: Western Advisers in China*. Boston: Little, Brown, 1969.

Stoessinger, John G. *Nations in Darkness: China, Russia, and America*. 5th edition. New York: McGraw-Hill, 1990.

Swisher, Earl. *China's Management of the American Barbarians: A Study of Sino-American Relations, 1841–1861, with Documents*. New Haven: Yale University Press, 1953.

Tao, Wenzhao. "Hurley's Mission to China and the Formation of U.S. Policy to Support Chiang Kai-shek against the Chinese Communist Party." In *Sino-American Relations, 1945–1955*, ed. Harry Harding and Yuan Ming. Wilmington, DE: SR Books, 1989.

Terrill, Ross. *Mao: A Biography*. Stanford: Stanford University Press, 1999.

Thornton, Thomas Perry. *Anti-Americanism: Origins and Context.* Newbury Park, CA: Sage Publications, 1988.

Tian, Xiansheng. "Patrick J. Hurley's Mission to China, 1944–1945." In *China and the United States: A New Cold War History*, ed. Xiaobing Li and Hongshan Li. Lanham, MD: University Press of America, 1998.

Tu, Weiming. "Chinese Perceptions of America." In *Dragon and Eagle: United States-China Relations, Past and Future*, ed. Robert B. Oxnam and Michel C. Oksenberg. New York: Basic Books, 1973.

Tucker, Nancy Bernkopf. *Patterns in the Dust: Chinese-American Relations and the Recognition Controversy, 1949–1950.* New York: Columbia University Press, 1983.

Varg, Paul A. *The Closing of the Door: Sino-American Relations, 1936–1946.* East Lansing: Michigan State University Press, 1973.

Wang, Jianwei. *Limited Adversaries: Post–Cold War Sino-American Mutual Images.* New York: Oxford University Press, 2000.

Warren, John William. "Chinese Television News: A Content Analysis." PhD dissertation. Tennessee University, 1986.

West, Philip, Steven I. Levine, and Jackie Hiltz, eds. *America's Wars in Asia: A Cultural Approach to History and Memory.* Armonk, NY: M. E. Sharpe, 1998.

Whiting, Allen Suess. *Chinese Domestic Politics and Foreign Policy in the 1970's.* Ann Arbor: Center for Chinese Studies, University of Michigan, 1979.

Williams, Kristen M., David M. Lampton, and Joyce A. Madancy, eds. *A Relationship Restored: Trends in U.S.-China Educational Exchanges, 1978–1984.* Washington, DC: National Academy Press, 1986.

Wong, Siu-lun. *Sociology and Socialism in Contemporary China.* London: Routledge and Kegan Paul, 1979.

Wu, Eugene, Timothy Cheek, and Roderick MacFarquhar, eds. *The Secret Speeches of Chairman Mao: From the Hundred Flowers to the Great Leap Forward.* Cambridge: Council on East Asian Studies / Harvard University Press, 1989.

Wu, Tingfang. *America through the Spectacles of an Oriental Diplomat*, with an introduction by Jonathan D. Spence. London: Anthem Press, 2007.

Yamashita, Shinji, Joseph Bosco, and Jeremy Seymour Eades, ed. *The Making of Anthropology in East and Southeast Asia.* New York and Oxford: Berghahn Books, 2004.

Yang, Kuisong. "The Soviet Factor and the CCP's Policy toward the United States in the 1940s." *Chinese Historians* 5, no. 1 (Spring 1992).

Ye, Huanian. "Literary Criticism and Culture: Comparison of American and Chinese Scholarly Criticism of American Literature." PhD dissertation. New York University, 1989.

Ye, Weili, *Seeking Modernity in China's Name: Chinese Students in the United States, 1900–1927.* Stanford: Stanford University Press, 2004.

Young, Susan, and Kjeld Erik Brodsgaard. *State Capacity in East Asia: China, Taiwan, Vietnam, and Japan.* New York: Oxford University Press, 2000.

Yu, Taifa. "A Neglected Dimension of the Sino-U.S. Cultural Relationship: Cultural Exchanges, Cultural Diplomacy, and Cultural Interaction." PhD dissertation. University of South Carolina, 1988.

Yuan, Tung-li. *A Guide to Doctoral Dissertations by Chinese Students in America, 1905–1960.* Washington, DC: The Sino-American Cultural Society, 1961.

Zha, Gerald, ed. *China's International Relations in the 21ˢᵗ Century*. Lanham, MD: University Press of America, 2000.

Zhai, Qiang. "Reassessing China's Role in the Vietnam War: Some Mysteries Explored." In *China and the United States: A New Cold War History*, ed. Xiaobing Li and Hongshan Li. Lanham, MD: University Press of America, 1998.

Zhang, Hong. *America Perceived: The Making of Urban Chinese Images of the United States, 1945–1953*. Westport, CT: Greenwood Press, 2002.

Zhang, Shu Guang. *Deterrence and Strategic Culture: Chinese American Confrontations, 1949–1958*. Ithaca: Cornell University Press, 1992.

Zhao, Dingxin. *The Power of Tiananmen: State-Society Relations and the 1989 Beijing Student Movement*. Chicago: University of Chicago Press, 2004.

Index

"absolute poverty," 85–86
Acheson, Dean, 56–57, 193
African Americans: in Atlanta, 129; children of murdered, 130; in Civil Rights Movement, 93–94; in Deep South, 38; in *Gone with the Wind*, 147–48; in *Jubilee*, 147–48; killing of, 67; King, 104, 222; LBJ's policy on, 104; publication of *John Brown*, 176; publication of *Roots*, 176; in Washington, D.C., 189
agriculture, 101, 127–28, 152
airmen, U.S., 41–42
American-educated Chinese, 23, 26, 29–36, 60–62, 73–90
American Imperialism, 59, 68–69, 103, 105, 109, 120
American missionary schools in China, 58, 73, 81–82, 178
American schools in China, 29, 36, 46, 53, 66, 81–82
American Spirit, 15–16
American Volunteer Group, 48
Ames, Roger T., 209
Ancient Society (Morgan), 176
Anti-American Violence Movement (1947), 49–50
Anti-Rightist Movement, 72–73, 76–77, 80–81, 85–86, 89–90
Arkush, David R., 235

"Barbarian Paradise: Chinese Views of the United States, 1784–1911" (Chen), 235

Barrett, David, 42, 48
Barzun, Jacques, 9, 142
Battling Western Imperialism (Sheng), 234
Beautiful Imperialism (Shambaugh), 233. 234–45
Beijing Jeep, 186
Beijing Man in New York (*Beijing ren zai niuyue*) (TV series), 218
Beijing ren zai niuyue. See *Beijing Man in New York*
Beijing Spring, 170–74
Beijing University, 35, 77–78, 83, 85–86, 89–90, 210
Bell, Daniel, 165
Bellamy, Edward, 21
big-character posters (*dazibao*), 77, 107, 170, 172
Bitter Love (film), 131
bombing of Chinese embassy in Belgrade, 4–5, 203, 221, 223–24
"Bourgeois Liberalization," 131, 133, 142–43, 152, 161
Boxer Indemnity Scholarship Program, 13, 29–30, 75
Boxer Rebellion, 18, 230
boycott of foreign goods, 13, 26
brand names, foreign, 216
Brief Survey of the Maritime Circuits, A (*Yinghuan zhilue*) (Xu), 14, 14 fig. 1.1
business management, 15, 128, 162, 184–86, 217

California Noodle King, 186

Caltech, 60, 74, 75, 87–88
Cao Juren, 59–60
"capitalist roaders," 92, 105, 107, 114
Carnegie, Andrew, 25, 185
CCP. See Chinese Communist Party
CCTV. See China Central Television
celebrities, American, 222
Central Propaganda Department (CCP), 88, 139
Chandler, Alfred, Jr., 162
chao Ying gan Mei. See "Overtake Britain and Catch up with the U.S."
Chatterton, R. G., 186
Chen, Anna (Chen Xiangmei), 48
Chen Boda, 102–3
Chen Chang-fang, 235
Chen Duxiu, 25–26, 42
Chen Jian, 234
Chen Jieying, 62
Chen Junsheng, 141
Chennault, Claire L., 48
Chen Shiwei, 77
Chen Yi, 57, 74, 101, 110
Chen Yuan, 104
Chen Yun, 132, 138–39, 214
Chen Xiangmei. See Chen, Anna
Chen Xiaomei, 235
Chen Zhenhan, 83–86, 90
Chiang Kai-shek: and China's Destiny, 24–25; on Confucian values, 24; Dai Jitao and, 24; purging Communists, 22, 40; rejecting Communists' proposal, 43; and Song family, 23; Tao Xisheng and, 24–25
Chiang Monlin. See Jiang Menglin
China and the American Dream (Madsen), 236
China Can Say No (Zhongguo keyi shuo bu) (Zhang et al.), 3, 211–13, 223 fig. 8.1
China Central Television, 175, 183
China Doesn't Just Say No (Zhongguo bu jinjin shuo bu) (Jia), 212
China Is Not Mr. No (Zhongguo bu dang bu xiansheng) (Shen), 212
China's Destiny (Zhongguo zhi mingyun) (Chiang), 24–25

China's national survival crisis, 6–7, 19, 19 fig. 1.2
China White Paper, 56–57
Chinese Academy of Sciences, 83, 88–90
Chinese Academy of Social Sciences, 133, 142, 159, 205, 212
Chinese Americans, 137, 140, 142
Chinese Communist Party (CCP): and anti-American movement during the Civil War, 43–45, 49–50; in anti-liberalization campaign, 138–39, 141–42, 160; Ninth National Congress of, 112; in power struggle to succeed Mao, 101, 107, 109, 114–21; and pro-democracy movement in 1989, 143; and "Spiritual Pollution," 131–35; after Tiananmen Square Incident, 192–93, 195; before and during WWII, 41–43, 44 fig. 1.4. See also Mao Zedong, Deng Xiaoping, Jiang Zemin
Chinese Lady in Manhattan, A (Manhadun de Zhongguo nüren) (Zhou), 218
Chinese resentment toward U.S., 7, 47, 192, 224
Christensen, Thomas J., 234
Christianity, 31, 46, 166–67
Christian missions in China, 29, 36, 45–46, 53, 66, 73
Chuangye. See Pioneers
Chu Yukun, 95
Civil Rights Movement, 93–94, 104, 129
Cixi (empress dowager), 12, 17, 20
Clash of Civilizations and the Remaking of World Order, The (Huntington), 208
"clean house first and invite guests over afterward," 53
"The Climax of Sino-American Relations" (Guo), 235
Clinton, Bill, 4, 222–23
Cohen, Paul A., 233
Cohen, Warren I., 273n1
colleges, 61–62, 66, 76, 79–80, 185–86, 211
Collins, Jackie, 184

collision of U.S. and Chinese airplanes, 4–5, 203
Columbia University, 30, 33, 35 fig. 1.3, 74, 81–82, 85, 87
Comparative Economic Systems (Neuberger and Duffy), 155–56
Conceison, Claire, 235
Confucian China and Its Modern Fate (Levenson), 209
Confucianism, 23–24, 59, 153 208–10, 228
Congress, U.S., 140, 191, 197
Conroy, Hilary, 273n1
conservatives, Chinese Communist, 130–32, 138–40, 143, 161, 164, 193–94
Cook, Robin, 177
corporations, 212, 216–17
corruption, 137–38, 157, 159
countryside, 24, 34, 62, 82, 113, 128, 170–71
crime, 134, 165, 180–81, 219
Cultural Contradictions of Capitalism, The (Bell), 165
Cultural Revolution. *See* Great Cultural Revolution

Dai Jitao, 24
Dai Songen, 89
dazibao. See big-character posters
Death of a Salesman (Miller), 178–79
Declaration of Independence, U.S., 45, 126, 135
Delbanco, Andrew, 166
democracy: Chen Duxiu's view of, 26, 46; in *China White Paper*, 56–57; criticized in the eighties and nineties, 162–4, 193, 205–6, 208–9; He Xin's criticism of, 205–6; Jacques Barzun's idea of, 142; lack of in U.S., 57, 63, 93–94, 139–40; Liang Qichao on, 16, 18; Liu Shaoqi's praise for, 109; Peng Zhen on, 138–39; Sun Yat-sen on, 20; Tao Xingzhi's view of, 36; in U.S. debated on Democracy Wall, 172; Zhou Enlai on, 42
Democracy Wall, 172–73

Democratic Alliance (*Min Meng*), 74–75, 84
democratic individualism, 56–57
Deng Shusheng, 148
Deng Xiaoping: Mao's relationship with, 101, 107, 112, 114–115, 119; reformist policies of, 120–21, 155; and "Spiritual Pollution," 130, 132–136, 138–141; on South Tour in 1992, 194–95; suppressing Tiananmen Square protests in 1989, 143, 164; visiting U.S. in 1979, 123–24, 126 fig. 5.1, 126–27, 173
Deng Yingchao, 124
Dewey, John, 27, 30, 33–34, 36
Dierci wuoshou. See Second Handshake
differences among Chinese state, intellectuals, and masses, 6, 8, 122, 169, 192, 200, 227, 231
Ding Gu, 96
Disney, 133, 215
divorce, 181, 218
Dixie Mission (U.S. Army Observers Group), 42, 48, 124
Domhoff, G. William, 140
drugs, illegal. *See* narcotics
Du Bois, W. E. B., 176
Duffy, William, 155–56
Dulles, John Foster, 100
Dushu (Reading): Alvin Toffler in, 152–53; American economists presented in, 155–58; on American history, 147–48; on American literature, 150–51; on Confucianism in modern times, 208–10; on Daniel Bell, 165; on Edward Said, 206–9; on freedom to read, 146; *Gone with the Wind* debated in, 147; Hendrik Willem van Loon in, 159–61; image of, 149 fig. 6.1; John Maynard Keynes in, 156; John Naisbitt in, 152–53; Joseph Schumpeter in, 157; Lionel Trilling in, 165; Max Weber in, 166; Milton Friedman in, 157–58; in the 1980s, 145–67; persona of, 145–46; political reform discussed in, 159–64; Richard Hofstadter in, 159, 162; Samuel

Dushu (Reading) (continued)
  Huntington in, 163–64, 206–9; on
  sciences and technology, 151–54;
  sociobiology discussed in, 154; on
  spirituality, 164–67; Thomas Kuhn in,
  153–54

Eastman, George, 185
economic disparity, 17, 21–22, 94, 219,
  225
economic man, 158
economic reform under Deng:
  beginning of, 121–22; debated in
  the 1980s, 134–39; Deng's approach
  to, 155; entrepreneurism in, 184–85,
  217–18; ill social effects of, 179–80,
  218–19; and political reform, 159;
  resumption of after crackdown of the
  1989 protests, 194–96
economics, 81–83, 85–86, 95–97,
  155–58
Economics (Samuelson), 176
economy of China: American
  economists and, 155–58; critiqued
  in 1957, 83–84; and "Go up the
  Mountains and down into the
  countryside," 113; Great Leap
  Forward, 98–99, 101; service sector
  of, 128; transformed through Deng's
  reform, 121–22, 138, 155, 195–96
economy of U.S., 72, 84–85, 95–97
Eight Model Plays, 174
Eisenhower, Dwight D., 79, 98, 104, 222
"elite politics," 162–64, 208
embassy bombing. *See* bombing of
  Chinese embassy in Belgrade
Emerson, Ralph Waldo, 166, 228
Engels, Friedrich, 176

Fairbank, John King, 233
family: in agricultural reform, 135; in
  America as reported by Yu Lihua,
  137; broken up in divorces, 181; in
  Death of a Salesman, 178–79; Hu
  Shi and, 32; traditional emphasis on
  15, 18; of the Songs, 23; in Zhang

Xianliang's short story, 105–6; Zou
  Taofen's view of, 38–39
Fang Lizhi, 140
fast food restaurants, 186, 217, 223 fig.
  8.1
Faulkner, William, 150
Fei Xiaotong, 82, 90
fiction, American. *See* novels, American;
  literature, American
films, American: *First Blood*, 183; Jiang
  Zemin on, 1, 202; *Nightmare*, 178; in
  the 1980s, 177–78; in the 1990s, 215–
  16; in the Republican era, 46–47, 68;
  Saving Private Ryan, 5; and thought-
  reform in the early fifties, 66
First Blood (film), 183
Flying Tigers. *See* American Volunteer
  Group; Chennault, Claire L.
Ford, Gerald R., 222
Ford, Harrison, 215
foreign trade, 3, 119, 196, 198–99, 215
Ford Motor Company, 157, 186
Founding Fathers, U.S., 20–21, 126, 148,
  159
four stages in the evolution of Chinese
  views of U.S., 8
Friedman, Milton, 149 fig. 6.1, 156–58
Fudan University, 77, 87–88, 136, 139
Fukuyama, Francis, 205
*Future of Intellectuals and the Rise of the
  New Class, The* (Gouldner), 162

Gang of Four, 170, 173
Garrison's Gorillas (TV series), 182–83
GATT. *See* General Agreement on
  Tariffs and Trade
GDP (Gross Domestic Product), 194,
  195
General Agreement on Tariffs and
  Trade (GATT), 199
genetic studies. *See* Morganist-
  Lysenkoist dispute
George, Henry, 21
Gilder, George, 158
GIs, U.S., 41–42, 47–49
Glory and Dream (Manchester), 176

Goldstein, Jonathan, 273n1
Gone with the Wind (Mitchell), 147
Gouldner, Alvin, 162
"Go up the Mountains and down into the Countryside," 113
Grayson, Benson Lee, 273n1
Great Cultural Revolution: American studies affected by, 148; anti-Americanism in, 105–12; art and literature in, 174–75; and CCP policies toward U.S., 118–20; censorship in, 146; overview of, 92; as portrayed in film *Kulian*, 131; and Sino-American reconciliation, 114–18
Great Depression, 37, 39, 84–85, 95–96, 156–57
Great Leap Forward, 91, 99–101, 103
Greek Coffin Mystery, The (Queen), 176
Guangming Daily, 84, 89, 93–94. 98
Guangming ribao. See *Guangming Daily*
Guangzhou conference on arts, 101
Guo Jizhou, 103–4
Guo Xixiao, 235
guoxue. See National Studies

Hailey, Arthur, 150
Haley, Alex, 176
Hall, David L., 209
Hammer, Armand, 184
Harvard University, 59, 82, 159, 165, 212
"a heap of loose sand," Chinese nation as, 18, 21, 100
Heimert, Alan, 166
He Xin, 204–6
Hildreth, Richard, 147–48
Hinton, Carma, 129
Hinton, William, 124–25, 127
Hoffman, William, 176
Hofstadter, Richard, 149 fig. 6.1, 159, 162
Hollywood, 60, 68, 129, 184. *See also* films, American
Hollywood's Wives (Collins), 184
Hongqi. See *Red Flag*
Hong Zhaohui, 235
Horizon Research, 224

Hua Guofeng, 170
Huang Hua, 52, 58
Huang Shaoxiang, 147–48
Huang Wanli, 75–76
Huang Wu, 149
Huang Zongjiang, 110
human rights, 171, 200–1, 221
Hu Na, 131
Hundred Flowers Movement, 71–90
Hunt, Michael, 233
Huntington, Samuel, 149 fig. 6.1, 163–64, 206–9
Hu Qiaomu, 131
Hurley, Patrick, 43–44, 44 fig. 1.4
Hu Shih. *See* Hu Shi
Hu Shi (Hu Shih): CCP campaign against, 63; critical of students' movement, 32; on "Dollar Worship," 34; educated in the U.S., 29, 35 fig. 1.3; family life of, 32; on "issues" and "ism," 31; on Oswald Spengler, 31; and Wholesale Westernization, 29–30
Hutchinson, Anne, 166
Hu Xiansu, 88, 90
Hu Yaobang, 130–31, 139

Image, Perception, and the Making of U.S.-China Relations (Li and Hong), 235
immigrants, 13, 37–38, 185, 189, 218
imperialist aggression against China, 6–7, 18, 22, 40, 228
individualism, 41, 56–57, 132, 166, 228
intellectuals: as democratic individualists, 56; in *Dushu* magazine, 146–67; in Hundred Flowers Movement, 71–90; in the 1990s, 2–3, 204–14; portrayed in film *Kulian*, 131; as sociopolitical group, 8, 229–31; in thought-reform in the 1950s, 58–63
International Olympic Committee (IOC), 197
Internet, 216
IOC. *See* International Olympic Committee

Iriye, Akira, 233
Irving, John, 151
Isaacs, Harold, 273n1
Israel, Jerry, 273n1

Jeep Girl (*Jipu nülang*), 47
Jefferson, Thomas, 16, 45, 53, 57, 148
Jiang Jieshi. *See* Chiang Kai-shek
Jiang Menglin (Chiang Monlin), 34, 35
  fig. 1.3
Jiang Qing (Madame Mao), 48, 62, 115,
  118–21, 170, 174
Jiang Zemin: after Deng's South Tour,
  195; reacting to U.S. bombing
  of Chinese embassy in Belgrade,
  203; rising to top office, 2; after
  Tiananmen Square crackdown in
  1989, 193; on *Titanic*, 1, 202; visiting
  U.S. in 1997, 4, 202, 222
Jiang Zilong, 182
Jia Qingguo, 212
jingying zhengzhi. See "elite politics"
Jinmen (Quemoy), bombardment of,
  100
Jipu nülang. See Jeep Girl
Ji Xianlin, 210
Ji Zhongliang, 187–88
John Brown (Du Bois), 176
Johnson, Lyndon B., 103–4, 222
Journey, The (*Lütu*) (Zhang), 26–27
Jubilee (Walker), 147

Kang Sheng, 102
Kennedy, John F., 103–4, 172, 222
Kentucky Fried Chicken (KFC), 186,
  217
Keynesian economics, 84, 86, 96,
  156–57
KFC. *See* Kentucky Fried Chicken
Khrushchev, Nikita S., 79, 88, 103
King, Martin Luther, Jr., 104, 222
Kissinger, Henry A., 114, 117, 120–21,
  176
Kodak, 185, 216
Korean War, 51, 58, 63–67, 100, 222
Kuhn, Thomas S., 149 fig. 6.1, 153–54

Kulian. See Bitter Love
Kusnitz, Leonard A., 273n1

"lagging effect," 229
Land without Ghosts (Arkush and Lee),
  235
"Learn from the Soviet Union"
  campaign, 79–82, 87–88, 97–98
Lee, Leo O., 235
Lee Teng-hui (Li Denghui), 2, 200
legitimate opposition, 159
Lei Haizong, 84
Lenin, Vladimir Ilyich, 41, 117, 126,
  152
Levenson, Joseph, 209
Liang Qichao: on American Spirit,
  15–16; as author of *Qingdai xueshu
  gailun*, 153; criticism of Chinese, 16;
  on economic disparity in U.S., 17; on
  first voyage to America, 11; "Great
  Men" hoped for by, 18; and J. P.
  Morgan, 15; on socialism, 17; on U.S.
  presidents, 16; visiting U.S. in 1903,
  14–18
liberalism: and Bourgeois Liberalization,
  131; Chiang Kai-shek and, 24–25;
  and *China White Paper*, 57; in *Dushu*,
  145–67; He Xin against, 204–6; Liang
  Qichao and, 17; Mao and, 28; and
  nationalism, 225–26; in the 1990s, 3
Li Denghui. *See* Lee Teng-hui
Li Honglin, 146
Li Hongshan, 235
Limited Adversaries (Wang), 234
Lin Biao, 112, 114, 137
Lincoln, Abraham, 16, 20–22, 36, 45,
  57, 148, 172, 176
Lion King, 215–16
Li Ruqi, 87, 89
literature, American, 80, 147–48,
  150–51, 176, 183–84
literature, underground in China,
  111–113, 174–75
"Little Teachers," 33–34
Liu Ji, 212–14
Liu Shaoqi, 101, 107, 109, 120

Liu Yalou, 100
Liu Yawei, 235
Liu Zuochang, 148
Lolita (Nabokov), 184
Los Angeles, 125, 129, 137, 182
Love Story (Segal), 177
Luce, Henry, 23, 54
Lu Dingyi, 88
Lufthansa department store, 214
Luo Longji, 74–77, 79
Lushan Conference (1959), 91
Lütu (Zhang). See *Journey, The*
Lu Yizhong, 140
Lysenkoism, 87–89, 90n115

Madame Mao. See Jiang Qing
Madsen, Richard, 236
Maltz, Albert, 94
Manchester, William, 176
Manhadun de Zhongguo nüren. See
     Chinese Lady in Manhattan, A
Mao Tse-tung. See Mao Zedong
Mao Zedong: on African Americans,
     104; anti-liberalism of, 28; capitalist
     world, evaluating, 102; on *China
     White Paper*, 56–57; and *Chuangye*,
     174; corresponding with Americans
     in WWII, 127; on Franklin Roosevelt,
     42; and Great Cultural Revolution,
     107, 109–10, 112–13; in Great Leap
     Forward, 91–93, 99–100; in Hundred
     Flowers Movement, 73, 88–89; and
     Jiang Qing, 48; on John Foster
     Dulles, 100; and "leaning to one
     side," 55, 78–79; on learning from
     the U.S., 71–72, 80; on "Monroe
     Doctrine for Hunan," 27; and Patrick
     Hurley, 43, 44 fig. 1.4; and *Scientific
     American*, 151–52; and Sino-
     American reconciliation, 114–16; on
     U.S. and Soviet Union at the end
     of WWII, 44–45; world revolution,
     calling for, 105, 116
marriage, 23, 32, 181
Marx, Karl, 126, 148, 172
Marxism, 31, 84–85, 98–99, 131–33, 154

masses, Chinese, 40, 46–50, 63–69,
     105–12, 169–90, 214–24
Matthiessen, F. O., 59
Maugham, Somerset, 183–84
McCarthyism, 59, 94
McClellan, Robert, 273n1
McDonald's restaurant, 217
media, 169, 174, 210, 215. *See also*
     periodicals, publishing, television
Megatrends (Naisbitt), 152–53
Meiguo shouce. See *United States
     Handbook*
Meng Yongqian, 96–97
Michener, James A, 150
Miller, Arthur, 178–79
Mills, C. Wright, 162
Min Meng. See Democratic Alliance
Mitchell, Margaret, 147
modernism in literature, 80
Modernity and the Confucian Tradition
     (Tu), 209
Mo Mo, 166
Morgan, J. P., 15
Morgan, Lewis H., 176
Morgan, Thomas H., 87–88
Morganist-Lysenkoist dispute, 86–90
Mosher, Steven W., 273n1
movies, American. *See* films, American
multiplier effect, 84, 86, 96

Nabokov, Vladimir, 184
Naisbitt, John, 152–53
narcotics, 219
nationalism, 11, 17–18, 191–92, 204,
     208–12, 224
Nationalists, 24–25, 40, 44, 52, 79, 100
National Studies (*guoxue*), 209–10
Neuberger, Egon, 155–56
new technological revolution, 136,
     152–53
New York, 15–17, 32, 38, 182, 188, 218
New York Review of Books, 145
New York Times, 54
New Youth (*Xin Qingnian*), 25–26, 30
Niebuhr, Reinhold, 166
Nightmare (film), 177–78

Niu Jun, 234
Nixon, Richard M., 114, 116–18, 169, 222
Notes on a Tour of the New Continent (*Xin dalu youjin*) (Liang), 15–18
novels, American, 150–51, 147–48, 176–77, 183–84

Oates, Joyce Carol, 150
Occidentalism (Chen), 235
Oliver's Story (Segal), 177
Olsen, Ken, 184
Olympic Games (Beijing), 3, 185, 191, 196–98, 221
Olympic Games (Los Angeles), 184–185
Orientalism, 206–8
"Overtake Britain and Catch up with the U.S.," 99–100
OWI. *See* U.S. Office of War Information

Pan Dakui, 77
Pan Xiao debate, 180
Paul Mellon (Hoffman), 176
peasants, Chinese, 3, 39–42, 91, 105–6, 178–79
Peck, Gregory, 187 fig. 7.1
Peking Union Medical College (PUMC), 46, 61, 76
Peng Zhen, 138–39
People's Daily (*Renmin Ribao*): and Anti-Rightist Movement, 94, 97–99; He Xin's article in, 205; and Hundred Flowers Movement, 82, 84–85, 87, 89; on McDonald's, 217; in the 1980s, 121–43; in the 1990s, 197–99; on Revisionism, 102; and Sino-American reconciliation, 116; in thought rectification after 1989, 193, 195
People's Liberation Army (PLA), 2, 55, 67, 110–11, 117–18, 200
People's Temple mass suicides and murders, 133
People's University (*Remin Daxue*), 96
periodicals in U.S., 54–55
periodic crisis in capitalism, 84–85, 95–97, 102

Peter the Great, 227
petit bourgeois intellectuals, Chinese, 210–11
philosophes, 227, 229
Pioneers (*Chuangye*) (film), 174
PLA. *See* People's Liberation Army
Politburo (Chinese Communist Party), 1, 195, 199, 202
Political Order in Changing Societies (Huntington), 163
political reform, 143, 151, 158–60, 164, 208
polls, 175–76, 181, 215–16, 218, 220–24
posters, anti-American, 106 fig. 4.1
presidents, U.S., 16, 103–4, 140, 222
Promise (Steel), 177
propaganda network (*xuanchuan wang*), 64–65
prostitution, 3, 60, 134, 178, 218–20
Protestant Ethic and the Spirit of Capitalism, The (Weber), 166
Protestantism, 166–67
publishing: of American novels, 177, 183–84; censorship in the Cultural Revolution, 146, 174–75; of *China Can Say No*, 212; after Mao era, 175–77, 215; in the 1950s, 67, 80
PUMC. *See* Peking Union Medical College
Puritans in America, The (Heimert and Delbanco), 166

Qian Jiaju, 84–85, 90
Qian Weichang, 75–76, 90
Qian Xuesen, 74
Qin Deqian, 140
Qing Dynasty, 12–13, 20, 153
Qinghua University, 29, 60–61, 75–77, 81–83, 107–8
Queen, Ellery, 176
Quemoy. *See* Jinmen

racism, 13, 37–38, 67, 130. *See also* African Americans, Civil Rights Movement
Rage of Angels (Sheldon), 177

Raise the Red Lantern (film), 207
rape of Chinese student by U.S. marine soldier (1946), 49
Reader's Digest, 54–55, 165
Reading. See *Dushu*
Reagan, Ronald W., 135–36, 175, 222
Reardon-Anderson, James, 234
Red Flag (*Hongqi*), 95–96, 99–100, 104, 118–19, 131
Red Guards, 92, 107–8, 110–13, 134, 171
Remin Daxue. See People's University
Renmin ribao. See *People's Daily*
Revisionism, 102–3
Revolution of 1911, 20, 25, 148
Roosevelt, Franklin D., 36, 42–43, 45, 51, 162, 222
Roosevelt, Theodore 15, 162
Roots (Haley), 176
Rosenberg, Julius and Ethel, case of, 94
"A Rose for Emily" (Faulkner), 150
Rozman, Gilbert, 233
rural revolution, 24, 28, 40–41, 78, 124
Russian language, 80
Ru Xin, 133–34, 142

Said, Edward, 149 fig. 6.1, 206–9
Samuelson, Paul, 176, 205
Schumpeter, Joseph, 157
Scientific American (New York), 151–52
scientific revolutions, 153–54, 209
scientists, 56, 61, 73, 75–76, 80, 87–89, 154
Secondhand Shake (*Dierci wuoshou*) (Zhang), 175
Segal, Erich, 177
service industry. See tertiary sector of economy
Seven Continents and Forty Years (Sulzberger), 176
Shambaugh, David, 233, 234–35
Shaw, Irwin, 150, 183
Sheldon, Sidney, 177, 183
Sheng, Michael, 234, 235
Shen Jiru, 212
Sheraton Hotel, 186

Shi Qili, 62
Significant Other (Conceison), 235
Silicon Valley, 136
Singer, Isaac Bashevis, 150, 176
Sino-American reconciliation, 114–20, 115 fig. 4.2, 172
"Snail Incident," 119
Snow, Edgar, 46, 58, 116
Sociobiology (Wilson), 154
sociology, 81–83
Song family, 23
Soong famiy. See Song family
Soviet Union: accomplishments of, 97–98; books from, 67, 80, 176; bureaucratism in, 74; China's national interests and, 79; China's treaty with, 65 fig. 2.1; Chinese educated in, 74, 89, 101, 193; collapse of, 194, 205; democracy in, 42; as factor in Sino-American reconciliation, 114, 116–17; and the Korean War, 65; "leaning to one side" and, 55–56, 78–79; "Learn from the Soviet Union" campaign, 78–80; Lin Biao's flight to, 114; Mao's reservations on the system of, 72, 99; Mao's visits of, 65 fig. 2.1, 98; Revisionism of, 92, 103; U.S. relations with, 44, 92; Zou Taofeng's visit of, 37
Sphinx (Cook), 177
spirituality, 15–16, 31, 151, 165, 180, 189, 125–26, 220
"Spiritual Pollution," 130, 134–36, 138, 140
Sputnik, 97–98
spy plane collision. See collision of U.S. and Chinese airplanes
Stallone, Sylvester, 183
Standard Oil, 174
Steel, Danielle, 177, 184
stock market, 122, 139, 142, 195
Stoessinger, John, 233
Stokes, Terry, 140
Structure of Scientific Revolutions, The (Kuhn), 153–54
Stuart, John Leighton, v, 12, 52, 56–57, 74

students, Chinese: Chen Duxiu's criticism of, 26; Chiang Kai-shek's criticism of, 24; educated at Xiaozhuang School, 33–34; experience of in U.S. examined, 235; in Great Cultural Revolution, 108, 110, 111–13; in Hundred Flowers Movement, 76–77, 80; Hu Shi's criticism of, 31–32; in Japan and U.S., 29; and National Studies, 210; and pop culture of the West, 184, 187 fig. 7.1; in protests against Chinese government, 32, 138–40, 143, 159, 163 fig. 6.2; in protests against U.S., 4, 49–50, 203; Ronald Reagan speaking to, 136; in though reform of the early fifties, 61, 62, 66

Suez Crisis, 79

Sulzberger, C. L., 176

Sun Dayu, 77

Sun Yat-sen: disappointed in U.S. policies, 22; and ideas of Edward Bellamy and Henry George, 21; and "Three-People Doctrine," 21; on Washington and Lincoln, 20; Tao Xingzhi on, 36

Sun Zhongshan. See Sun Yat-sen

Su Shaozhi, 159

surveys. See polls

Taft-Hartley Act, 54

Taiwan: Chiang Kai-shek's retreat to 52; Communists' desire to retake, 92, 100; in Sino-American disputes in the 1990s, 2, 200, 211, 221–22; in Sino-American reconciliation, 114; U.S. dominance of, 93

Tan Jiazhen, 87, 89

Tan Tiwu, 79

Tao Wenzhao, 234

Tao Xingzhi, 33–36, 35 fig. 1.3, 39

television, 175, 182–83, 215

Teng Teng, 139

tertiary sector of economy, 128

theater, 67–68, 98, 110–11, 174, 178–79

Thinking through Confucius (Hall and Ames), 209

think tanks, 129–30

Third Wave (Huntington), 208

Third Wave, The (Toffler), 152–53, 208

Thoreau, Henry, 228

thought rectification after 1989 Tiananmen Square protests, 192–94

"Three Big Mountains," 40

three sociopolitical groups of China, 8

Tiananmen Square demonstrations (1989), 2, 138, 163 fig. 6.2, 164, 192

Time magazine, 23, 128, 150–51, 154

Titanic (film), 1, 202, 215

Tito, Josip Broz, 102–103

Tocqueville, Alexis de, 142, 227

Toffler, Alvin, 152–53, 208

Tolerance (Hendrik Willem van Loon), 160

Trilling, Lionel, 165

Truman, Harry S., 45, 54, 56, 104, 222

Tsinghua University. See Qinghua University

Tu, Wei-ming, 209, 235

TV. See television

twofold challenge to China, 6–7

Ueberroth, Peter, 184–85

underground publications, 171–74

United States Handbook (Meiguo shouce), 53–55

United States Relations with China. See China White Paper

University of California, 165

University of Chicago, 81–82, 84

Updike, John, 151

U.S. Army Observers Group. See Dixie Mission

Useful Adversaries (Christensen), 234

"U.S. Forces Out of China," 45

U.S. hostility toward China, 3, 192, 209–11, 214, 221

U.S. military personnel and Chinese civilians, 47–49

U.S. Office of War Information, 46–47

Van Loon, Hendrik Willem, 159–61

Vietnam, 110–11, 117, 211

Visible Hand, The (Chandler), 162

visits of China, U.S. presidents', 4, 115
fig. 4.2, 115–17, 136, 222–23
visits of U.S., Chinese leaders': Deng's
visit, 123–24, 126 fig. 5.1, 126–27,
173; Jiang's visit, 4, 202, 222; Zhao's
visit, 135–36

Wagner Act, 54
Walker, Margaret, 147
Wallace, Henry, 45, 55
Wallace, Irwin, 184
Wang Guangmei, 109, 120
Wang Guangya, 203
Wang Jianwei, 234
Wang Ruoshui, 125–26
Wang Yunsheng, 79
Wang Zaoshi, 77–78
Wang Zizhi, 79
warlords, 22, 24
Washington, George, 14 fig. 1.1, 16, 18,
20, 22, 45, 53, 148
Wealth and Poverty (Gilder), 158
Weber, Max, 165–66
Western powers, 6–7, 11, 13, 22–23, 40,
228
White Collar (Mills), 162
White Slave (Hildreth), 147–48
Whitman, Walt, 80, 148–49
Wholesale Westernization, 32
Who Rules America? (Domhoff), 140
Williams, Roger, 166
Wilson, Edward O., 154
Winds of War (Wouk), 176
women, 32, 47–48, 66, 105–6, 177–78,
218
world news, 175–76
world revolution, 107, 111–12, 117, 120
World War Two, Sino-American
cooperation in, 41–43, 44 fig. 1.4,
124, 127, 222, 228
Wouk, Herman, 150, 176
WTO (World Trade Organization), 199
Wu Dakun, 85, 96
Wu Jisong, 188
Wu Xiaoying, 157–59

Xiaozhuang School, 33–34

Xia Yan, 153
Xin dalu youji. See Notes on a Tour of
the New Continent.
Xin Qingnian. See New Youth
xuanchuan wang. See propaganda
network
Xu Guangqiu, 235
Xu Haixin, 166
Xu Jiyu, 14, 14 fig. 1.1
Xu Zhucheng, 60

Yanan, 42–43, 44 fig. 1.4, 48, 124, 130
Yang, Chen-ning. See Yang Zhenning
Yang Bofei, 164
Yang Gang, 58–59
Yanjing University. See Yenching
University
Yang Mu, 151–53
Yang Xiaoyan, 180
Yang Yang, 153
Yang Yusheng, 234
Yang Zhenning (Chen-ning Yang),
151–52
Ye Jianying, 110, 124
Yenching University (Yanjing
University), 29, 58, 76–77, 82–83, 87,
178
Yilin (Translations) (Nanjing), 177
Yinghe incident, 197–98, 200
Yinghuan zhilue. See Brief Survey of the
Maritime Circuits
Yitao, 208–9
YMCA (Young Men's Christian
Association), 21, 26, 37, 46
youth, American, 37, 38–39, 129, 137,
187–88
youth, Chinese, 33–34, 107–8, 111–13,
129–40, 170, 180, 187 fig. 7.1
Yugoslavia, 4, 102–3, 203, 223
Yu Lihua, 137

Zeng Zhaolun, 75, 77
Zhang Baijia, 234
Zhang Kuan, 206–7
Zhang Mingshu, 189
Zhang Quan, 74–75
Zhang Shuguang, 234

Zhang Weiping, 157–59
Zhang Wentian, 26–27, 95–96
Zhang Xianliang, 105–6
Zhang Zangzang, 211–12
Zhao Fusan, 141–42
Zhao Jianjun, 188–89
Zhao Yifan, 159, 162–63, 165
Zhao Ziyang, 134–35, 141–43, 161, 164
Zhejiang University, 87
Zheng Junli, 61–62
Zhongguo bu dang bu xiansheng. See
    China Is Not Mr. No
Zhongguo bu jinjin shuo bu. See *China
    Doesn't Just Say No*
Zhongguo keyi shuo bu. See *China Can
    Say No*
Zhongguo zhi mingyun. See *China's Destiny*

Zhou Enlai: on democracy in U.S. and
    Soviet Union, 42; Deng Yingchao,
    wife of, 124; explaining Sino-
    American reconciliation, 116–17; and
    Gao Yuqian, 109–10; and Hurley,
    43, 44 fig. 1.4; as moderate leader,
    115; and Nixon, 115 fig. 4.2; and
    Qian Xuesen, 74; on U.S. election,
    27
Zhou Gucheng, 139
Zhou Li, 218
Zhou Peiyuan, 60–61
Zhou Jinhuang, 61
Zhu Houze, 160–61
Zhu Kezhen, 87
Zou Jiahua, 198
Zou Taofen, 36–39, 145